冨 樫 義 博

Giraffes.

Yoshihiro Togashi

Yoshihiro Togashi's manga career began in 1986 at the age of 20, when he won the coveted Osamu Tezuka Award for new manga artists. He debuted in the Japanese **Weekly Shonen Jump** magazine in 1989 with the romantic comedy **Tende Shôwaru Cupid**. From 1990 to 1994 he wrote and drew the hit manga **YuYu Hakusho**, which was followed by the dark comedy science-fiction series **Level E**, and finally this adventure series, **Hunter x Hunter**, available from VIZ Media's SHONEN JUMP Advanced imprint. In 1999 he married the manga artist Naoko Takeuchi.

HUNTER X HUNTER Volume 16
SHONEN JUMP ADVANCED Manga Edition

STORY AND ART BY
YOSHIHIRO TOGASHI

English Adaptation & Translation/Lillian Olsen
Touch-up Art & Lettering/Mark Griffin
Graphic Design/Matt Hinrichs
Editor/Urian Brown

Printed in the U.S.A.

Published by VIZ Media, LLC
P.O. Box 77010
San Francisco, CA 94107

10 9 8 7 6 5 4 3 2
First printing, September 2007
Second printing, May 2016

www.viz.com

www.shonenjump.com

SHONEN JUMP ADVANCED MANGA

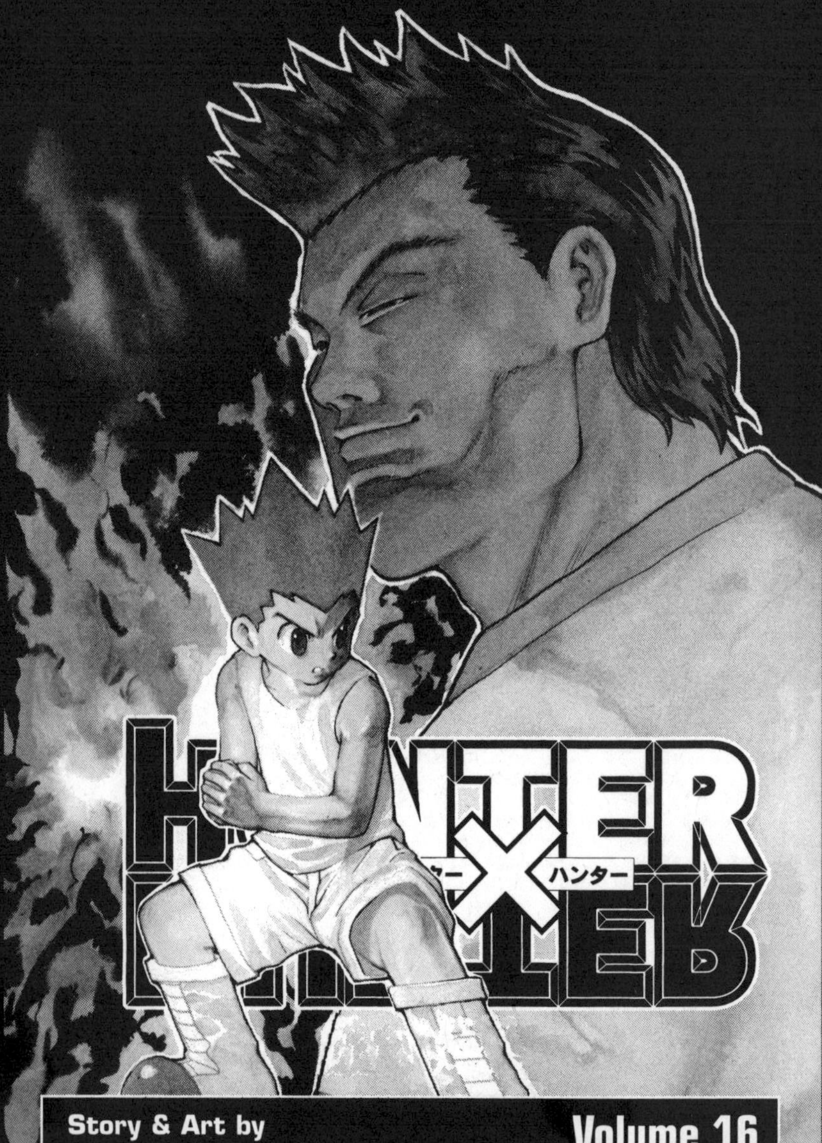
ハンター

Story & Art by
Yoshihiro Togashi

Volume 16

CHARACTERS

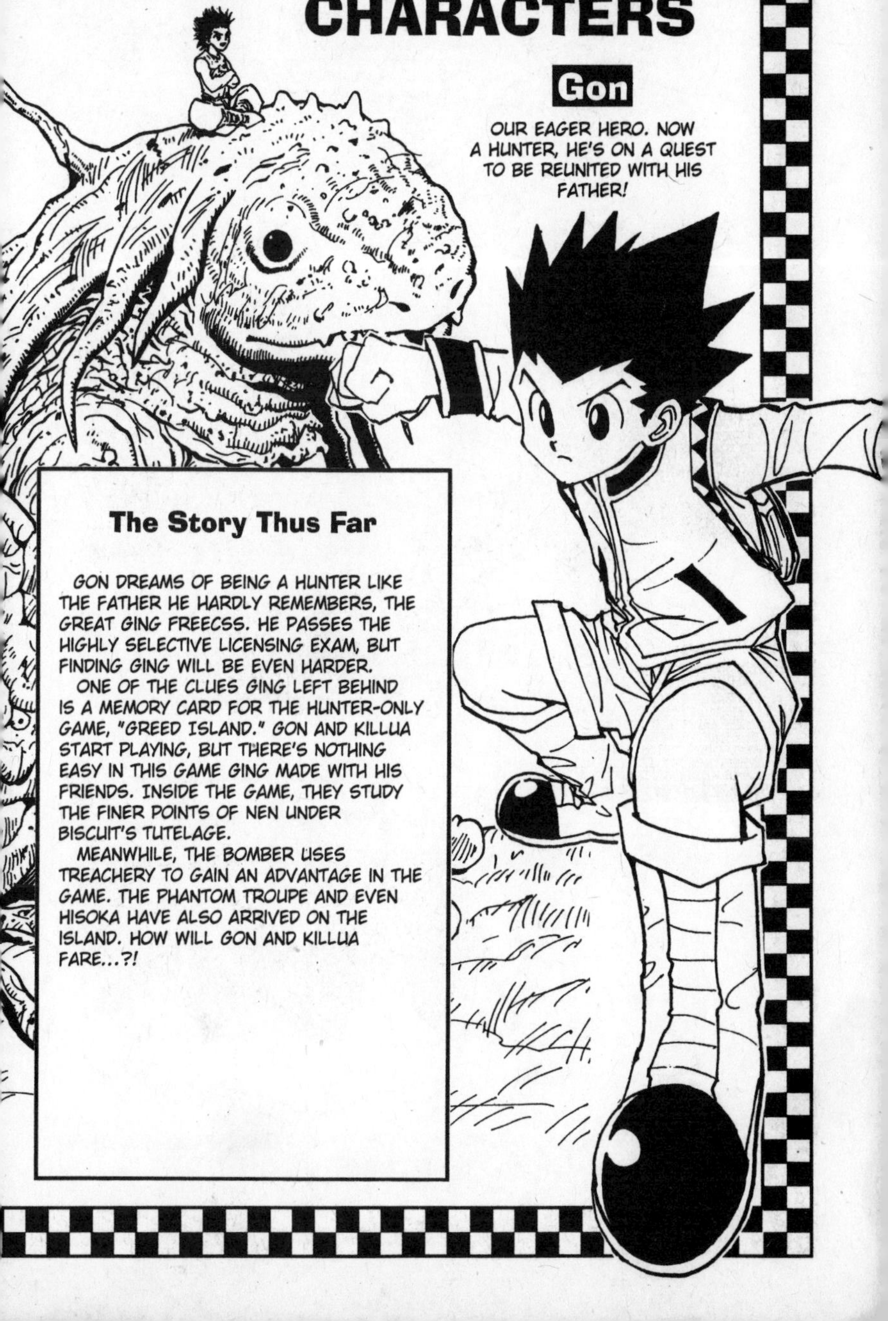

Gon

OUR EAGER HERO. NOW A HUNTER, HE'S ON A QUEST TO BE REUNITED WITH HIS FATHER!

The Story Thus Far

GON DREAMS OF BEING A HUNTER LIKE THE FATHER HE HARDLY REMEMBERS, THE GREAT GING FREECSS. HE PASSES THE HIGHLY SELECTIVE LICENSING EXAM, BUT FINDING GING WILL BE EVEN HARDER.

ONE OF THE CLUES GING LEFT BEHIND IS A MEMORY CARD FOR THE HUNTER-ONLY GAME, "GREED ISLAND." GON AND KILLUA START PLAYING, BUT THERE'S NOTHING EASY IN THIS GAME GING MADE WITH HIS FRIENDS. INSIDE THE GAME, THEY STUDY THE FINER POINTS OF NEN UNDER BISCUIT'S TUTELAGE.

MEANWHILE, THE BOMBER USES TREACHERY TO GAIN AN ADVANTAGE IN THE GAME. THE PHANTOM TROUPE AND EVEN HISOKA HAVE ALSO ARRIVED ON THE ISLAND. HOW WILL GON AND KILLUA FARE...?!

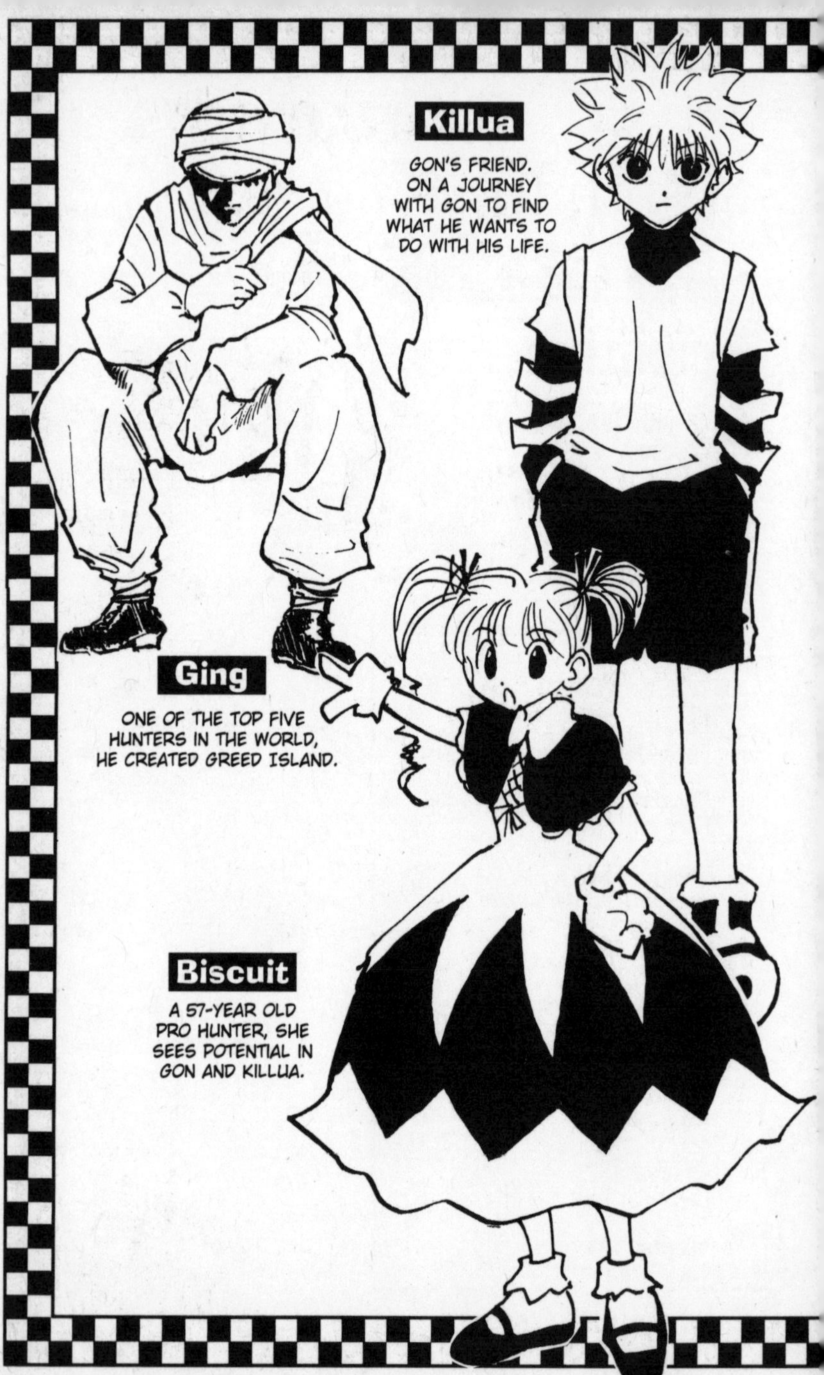
Killua
GON'S FRIEND. ON A JOURNEY WITH GON TO FIND WHAT HE WANTS TO DO WITH HIS LIFE.
Ging
ONE OF THE TOP FIVE HUNTERS IN THE WORLD, HE CREATED GREED ISLAND.
Biscuit
A 57-YEAR OLD PRO HUNTER, SHE SEES POTENTIAL IN GON AND KILLUA.

HUNTER × HUNTER

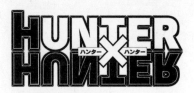

Volume 16

CONTENTS

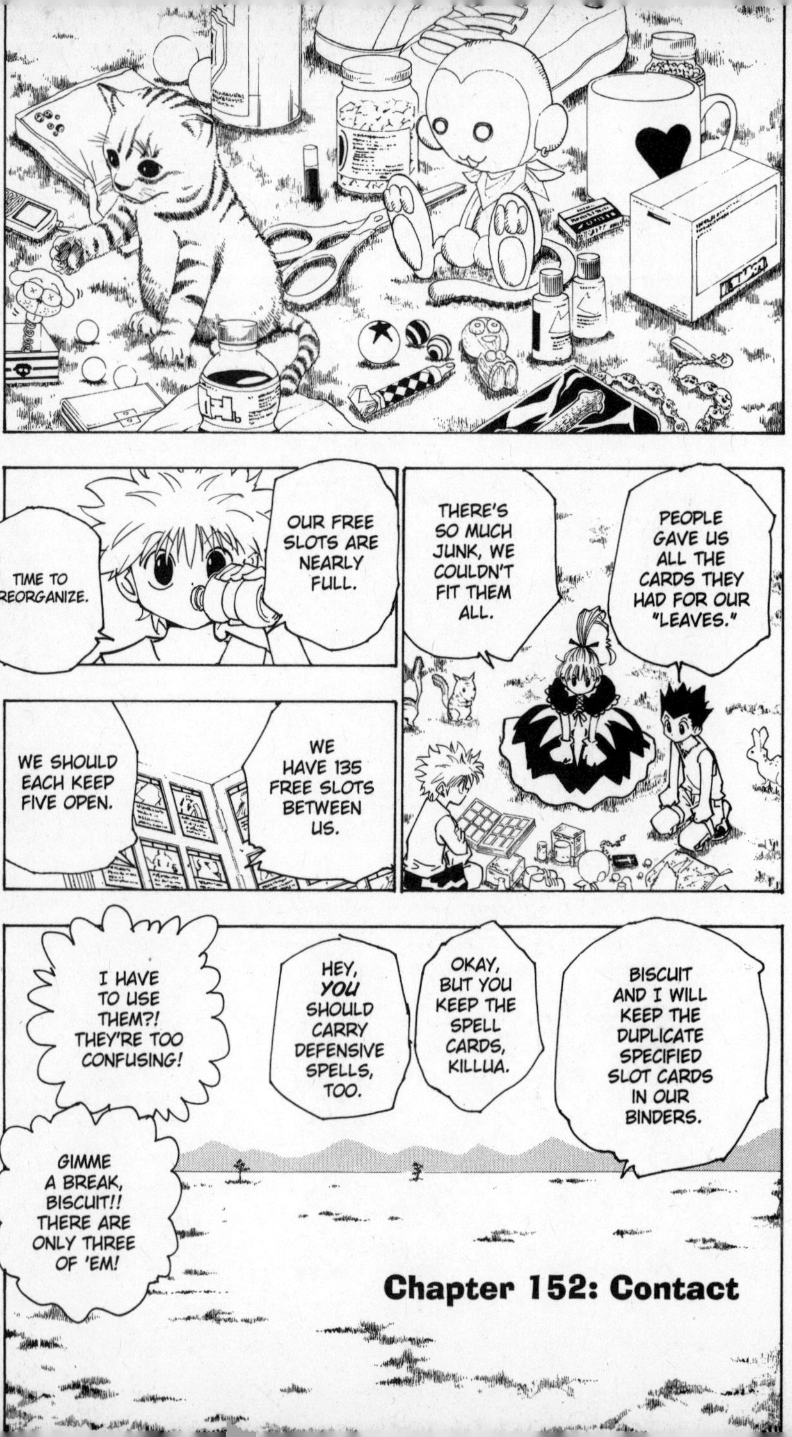
PEOPLE GAVE US ALL THE CARDS THEY HAD FOR OUR "LEAVES."
THERE'S SO MUCH JUNK, WE COULDN'T FIT THEM ALL.
OUR FREE SLOTS ARE NEARLY FULL.
TIME TO REORGANIZE.
WE HAVE 135 FREE SLOTS BETWEEN US.
WE SHOULD EACH KEEP FIVE OPEN.
BISCUIT AND I WILL KEEP THE DUPLICATE SPECIFIED SLOT CARDS IN OUR BINDERS.
OKAY, BUT YOU KEEP THE SPELL CARDS, KILLUA.
HEY, *YOU* SHOULD CARRY DEFENSIVE SPELLS, TOO.
I HAVE TO USE THEM?! THEY'RE TOO CONFUSING!
GIMME A BREAK, BISCUIT!! THERE ARE ONLY THREE OF 'EM!

Chapter 152: Contact

CURRENT SPECIFIED SLOT CARDS

NO. 3 PITCHER OF ETERNAL WATER
NO. 10 GOLDEN GUIDEBOOK X2
NO. 11 GOLDEN SCALES
NO. 19 POLTERGEIST PILLOW
NO. 20 MOOD CLOCK
NO. 21 X-RAY GOGGLES
NO. 23 TOME OF A THOUSAND TALES
NO. 24 HYPOTHETICAL T.V.
NO. 25 RISKY DICE
NO. 26 NIGHT SHIFT DWARVES
NO. 27 BOOK OF V.I.P. PASSES
NO. 37 FLEDGLING ATHLETE
NO. 38 FLEDGLING ARTIST
NO. 40 FLEDGLING MUSICIAN
NO. 41 FLEDGLING PILOT
NO. 43 FLEDGLING GAMBLER
NO. 44 FLEDGLING ACTOR
NO. 45 FLEDGLING CEO
NO. 46 GOLD DUST GIRL
NO. 47 SLEEPING GIRL
NO. 48 AROMATHERAPY GIRL
NO. 49 MINIATURE MERMAID
NO. 50 MINIATURE DINO
NO. 52 PEARL LOCUSTS X2
NO. 53 KING WHITE STAG BEETLE X3
NO. 54 MILLENNIUM BUTTERFLY
NO. 55 REVENGE SHOP
NO. 56 PERFECT MEMORY STUDIO
NO. 57 HIDEOUT REALTOR
NO. 58 SECRETS VIDEO RENTAL
NO. 59 INSTANT FOREIGN LANGUAGE SCHOOL
NO. 60 LONG LOST DELIVERY
NO. 61 VENDING CHECK-UP
NO. 62 CLUB "YOU RULE"
NO. 63 VIRTUAL RESTAURANT

NO. 64 WITCH'S LOVE POTION X2
NO. 66 WITCH'S DIET PILLS
NO. 67 DOYEN'S GROWTH PILLS X2
NO. 68 DOYEN'S VIRILITY PILLS
NO. 69 DOYEN'S HAIR RESTORER X2
NO. 70 MAD SCIENTIST'S STEROIDS
NO. 71 MAD SCIENTIST'S PHEROMONES
NO. 72 MAD SCIENTIST'S PLASTIC SURGERY
NO. 74 SAGE'S AQUAMARINE
NO. 76 WANDERING RUBY
NO. 79 RAINBOW DIAMOND
NO. 82 STAFF OF JUDGMENT
NO. 84 PALADIN'S NECKLACE
NO. 86 QUIVER OF FRUSTRATION
NO. 88 ETERNAL HAMMER
NO. 90 MEMORY HELMET

51 CARDS -- 61 INCLUDING DUPLICATES

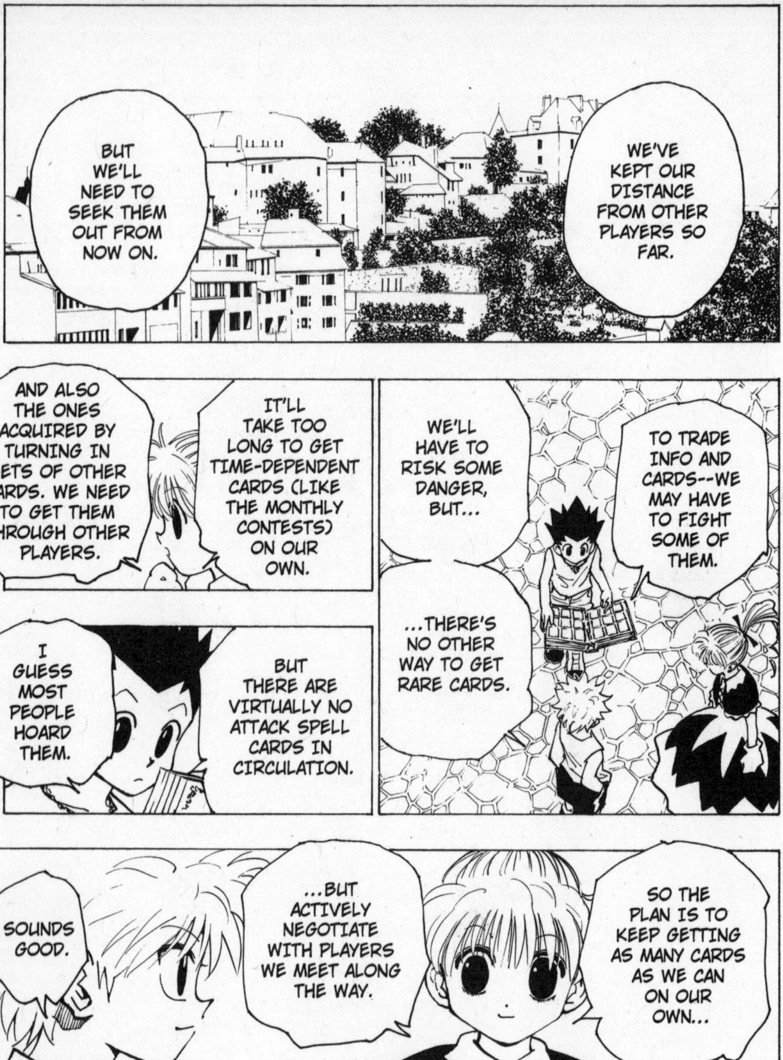
WE'VE KEPT OUR DISTANCE FROM OTHER PLAYERS SO FAR.
BUT WE'LL NEED TO SEEK THEM OUT FROM NOW ON.
TO TRADE INFO AND CARDS--WE MAY HAVE TO FIGHT SOME OF THEM.
WE'LL HAVE TO RISK SOME DANGER, BUT...
...THERE'S NO OTHER WAY TO GET RARE CARDS.
IT'LL TAKE TOO LONG TO GET TIME-DEPENDENT CARDS (LIKE THE MONTHLY CONTESTS) ON OUR OWN.
AND ALSO THE ONES ACQUIRED BY TURNING IN SETS OF OTHER CARDS. WE NEED TO GET THEM THROUGH OTHER PLAYERS.
BUT THERE ARE VIRTUALLY NO ATTACK SPELL CARDS IN CIRCULATION.
I GUESS MOST PEOPLE HOARD THEM.
SO THE PLAN IS TO KEEP GETTING AS MANY CARDS AS WE CAN ON OUR OWN...
...BUT ACTIVELY NEGOTIATE WITH PLAYERS WE MEET ALONG THE WAY.
SOUNDS GOOD.
SHALL WE MOVE ON TO ANOTHER CITY?
YEAH!

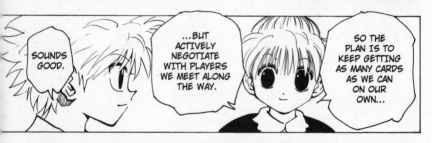

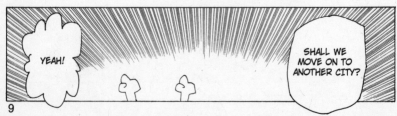

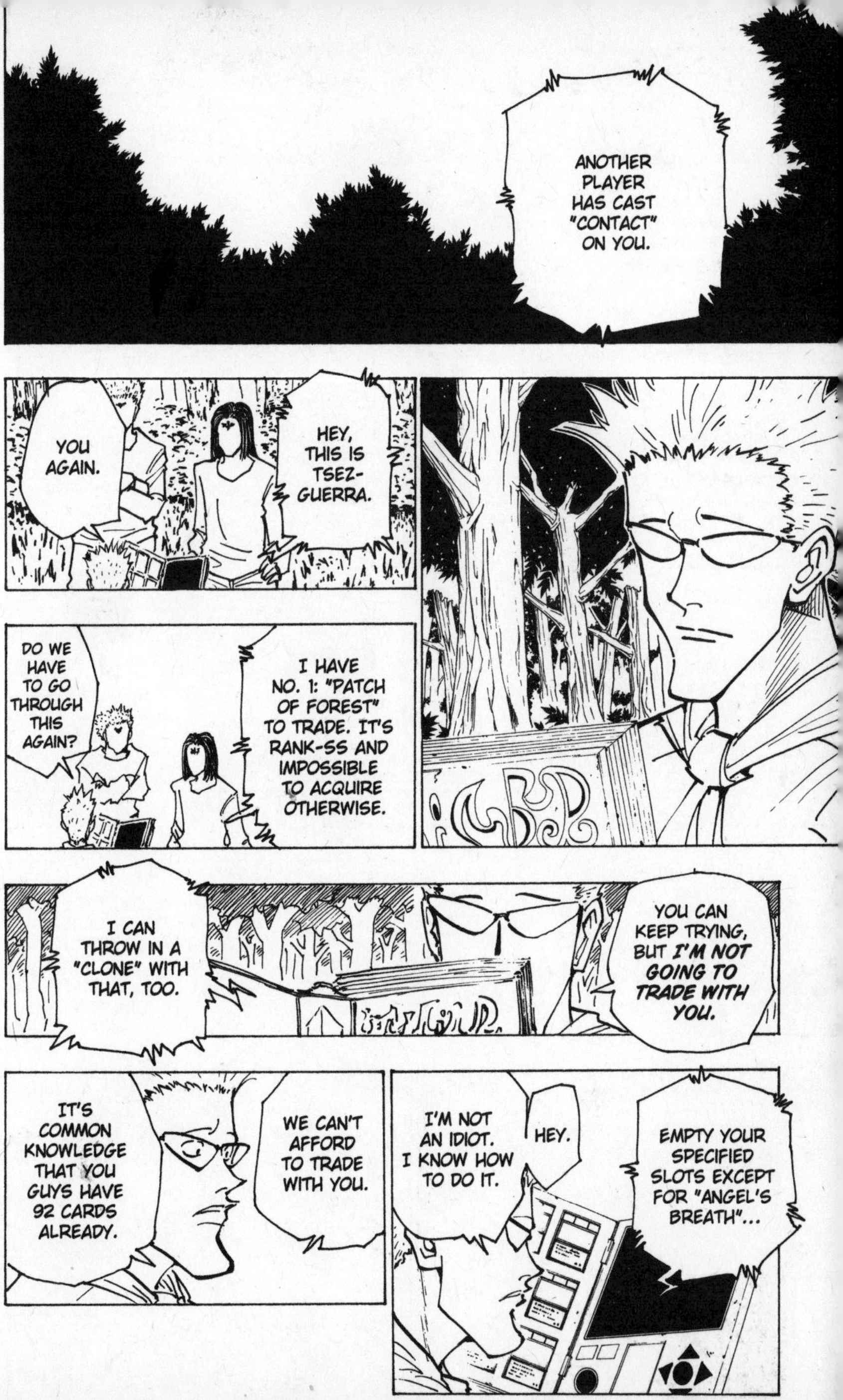

ANOTHER PLAYER HAS CAST "CONTACT" ON YOU.
HEY, THIS IS TSEZ-GUERRA.
YOU AGAIN.
I HAVE NO. 1: "PATCH OF FOREST" TO TRADE. IT'S RANK-SS AND IMPOSSIBLE TO ACQUIRE OTHERWISE.
DO WE HAVE TO GO THROUGH THIS AGAIN?
YOU CAN KEEP TRYING, BUT *I'M NOT GOING TO TRADE WITH YOU.*
I CAN THROW IN A "CLONE" WITH THAT, TOO.
EMPTY YOUR SPECIFIED SLOTS EXCEPT FOR "ANGEL'S BREATH"...
HEY.
I'M NOT AN IDIOT. I KNOW HOW TO DO IT.
WE CAN'T AFFORD TO TRADE WITH YOU.
IT'S COMMON KNOWLEDGE THAT YOU GUYS HAVE 92 CARDS ALREADY.

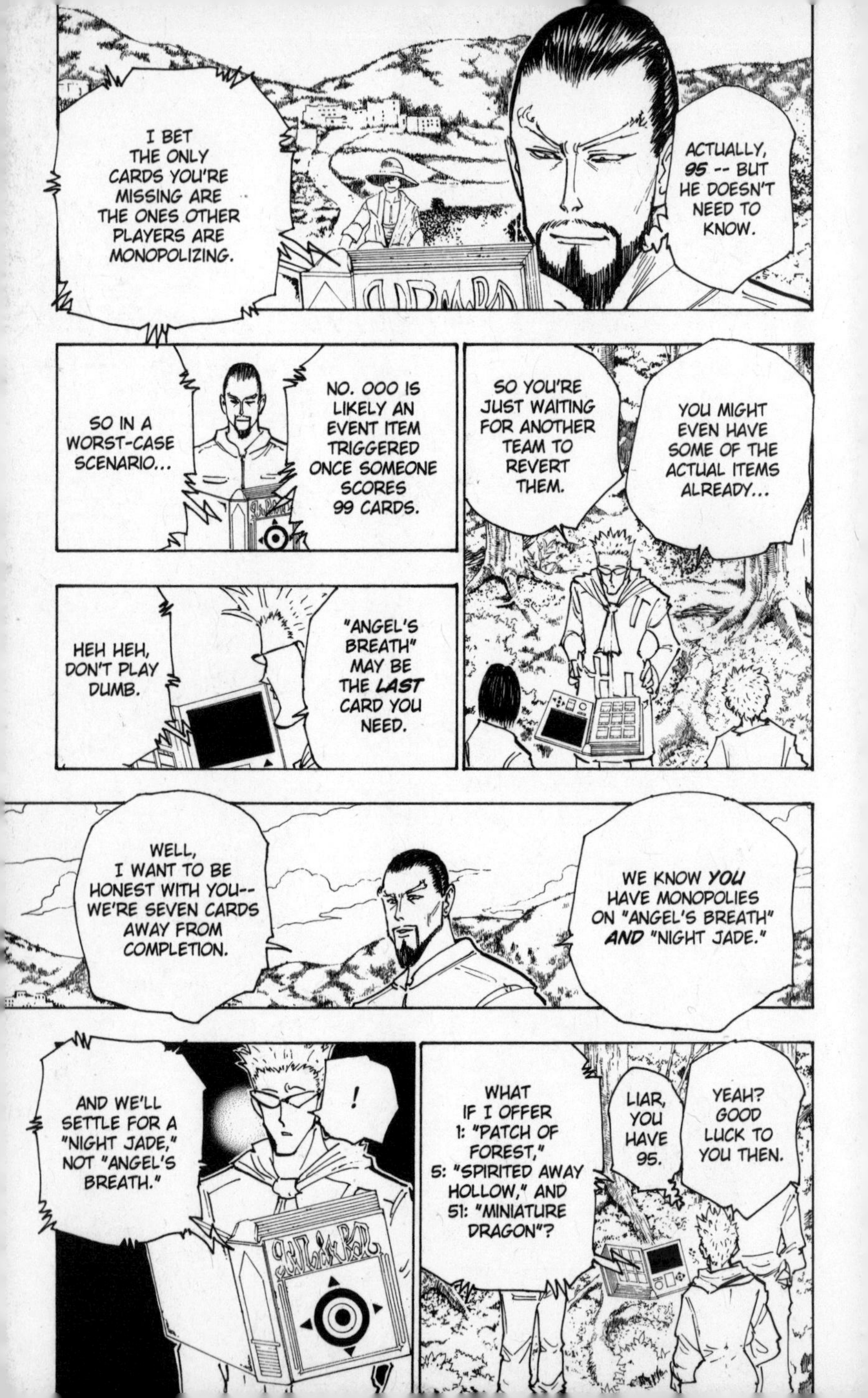
ACTUALLY, 95 -- BUT HE DOESN'T NEED TO KNOW.
I BET THE ONLY CARDS YOU'RE MISSING ARE THE ONES OTHER PLAYERS ARE MONOPOLIZING.
YOU MIGHT EVEN HAVE SOME OF THE ACTUAL ITEMS ALREADY...
SO YOU'RE JUST WAITING FOR ANOTHER TEAM TO REVERT THEM.
NO. 000 IS LIKELY AN EVENT ITEM TRIGGERED ONCE SOMEONE SCORES 99 CARDS.
SO IN A WORST-CASE SCENARIO...
"ANGEL'S BREATH" MAY BE THE LAST CARD YOU NEED.
HEH HEH, DON'T PLAY DUMB.
WE KNOW YOU HAVE MONOPOLIES ON "ANGEL'S BREATH" AND "NIGHT JADE."
WELL, I WANT TO BE HONEST WITH YOU-- WE'RE SEVEN CARDS AWAY FROM COMPLETION.
YEAH? GOOD LUCK TO YOU THEN.
LIAR, YOU HAVE 95.
WHAT IF I OFFER 1: "PATCH OF FOREST," 5: "SPIRITED AWAY HOLLOW," AND 51: "MINIATURE DRAGON"?
!
AND WE'LL SETTLE FOR A "NIGHT JADE," NOT "ANGEL'S BREATH."

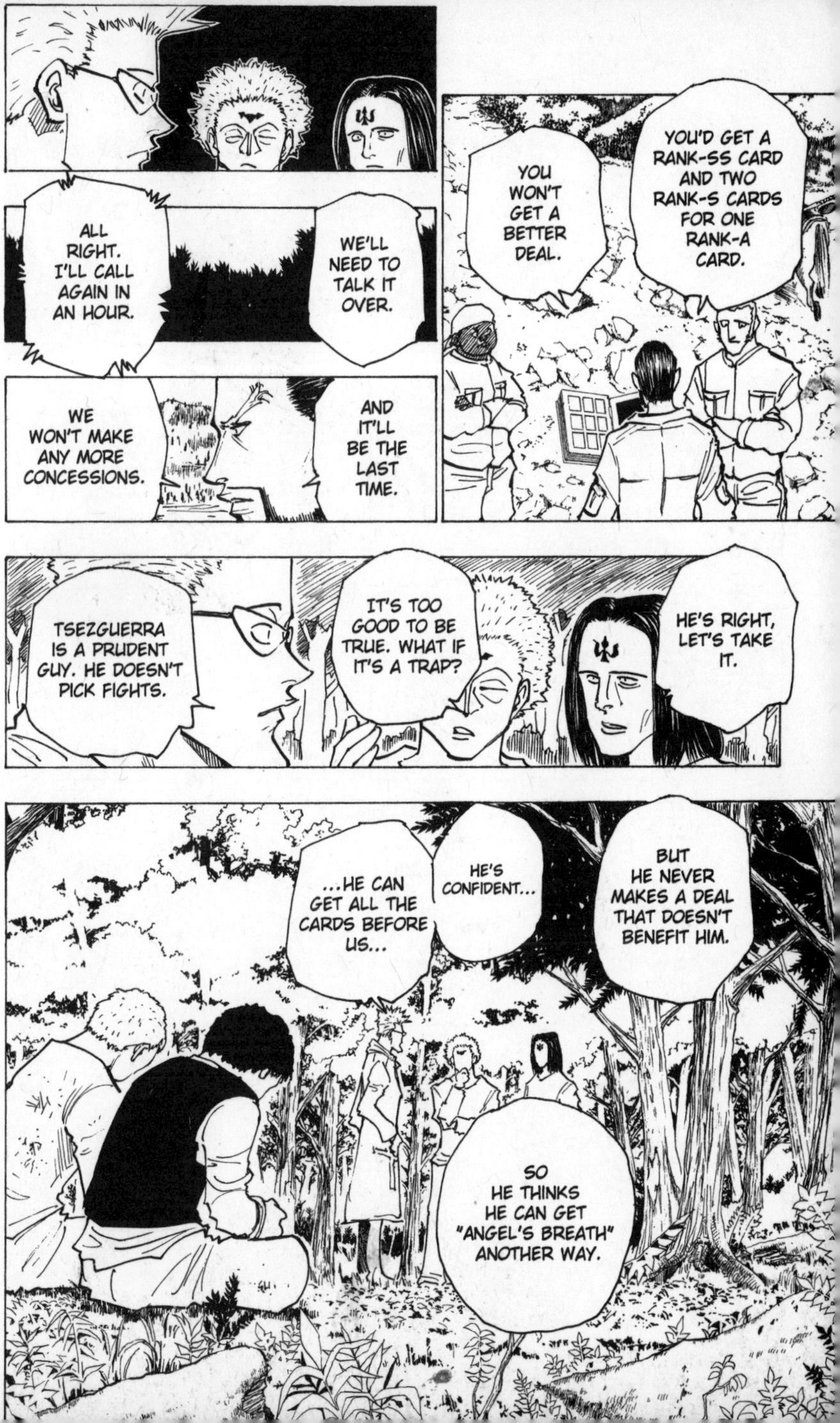
YOU'D GET A RANK-SS CARD AND TWO RANK-S CARDS FOR ONE RANK-A CARD.
YOU WON'T GET A BETTER DEAL.
WE'LL NEED TO TALK IT OVER.
ALL RIGHT. I'LL CALL AGAIN IN AN HOUR.
AND IT'LL BE THE LAST TIME.
WE WON'T MAKE ANY MORE CONCESSIONS.
HE'S RIGHT, LET'S TAKE IT.
IT'S TOO GOOD TO BE TRUE. WHAT IF IT'S A TRAP?
TSEZGUERRA IS A PRUDENT GUY. HE DOESN'T PICK FIGHTS.
BUT HE NEVER MAKES A DEAL THAT DOESN'T BENEFIT HIM.
HE'S CONFIDENT...
...HE CAN GET ALL THE CARDS BEFORE US...
SO HE THINKS HE CAN GET "ANGEL'S BREATH" ANOTHER WAY.

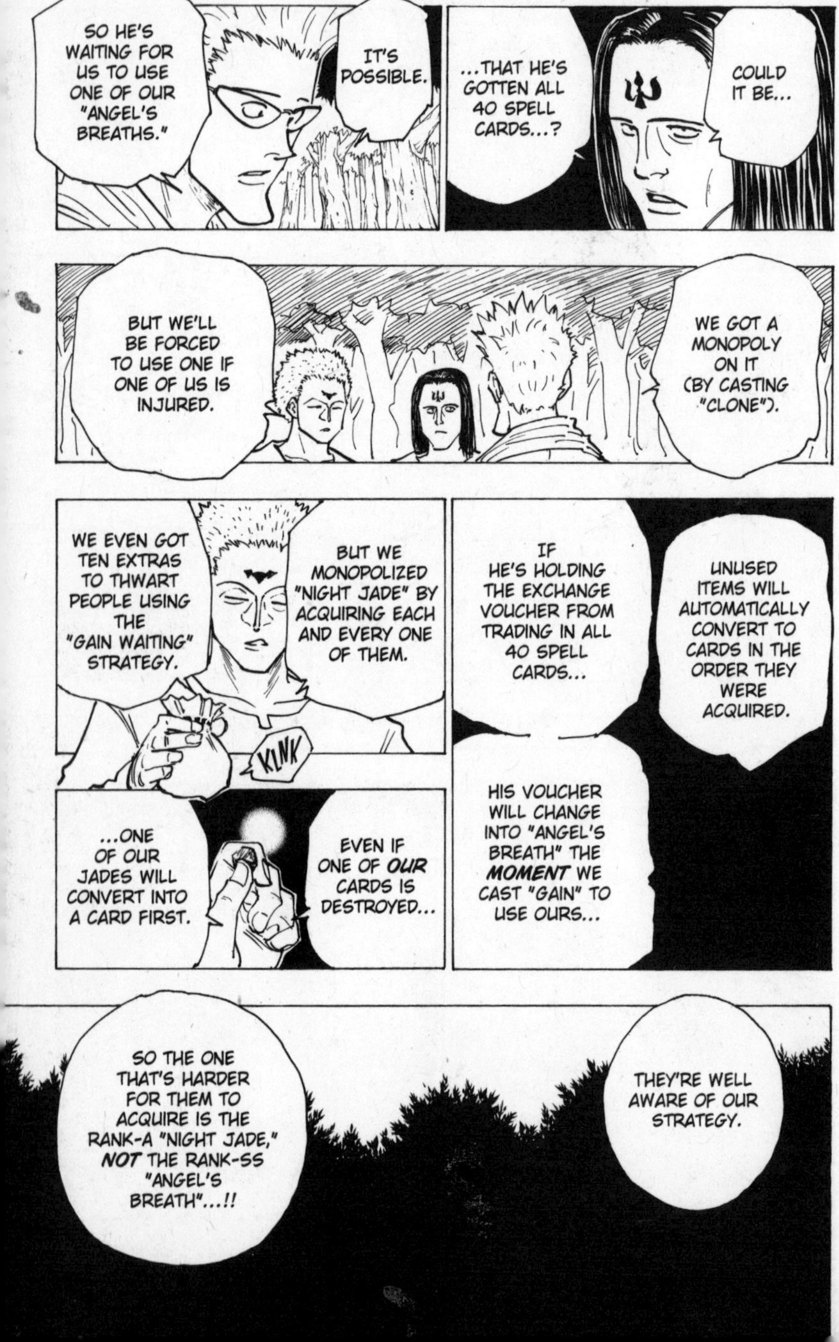
COULD IT BE...
...THAT HE'S GOTTEN ALL 40 SPELL CARDS...?
IT'S POSSIBLE.
SO HE'S WAITING FOR US TO USE ONE OF OUR "ANGEL'S BREATHS."
WE GOT A MONOPOLY ON IT (BY CASTING "CLONE").
BUT WE'LL BE FORCED TO USE ONE IF ONE OF US IS INJURED.
UNUSED ITEMS WILL AUTOMATICALLY CONVERT TO CARDS IN THE ORDER THEY WERE ACQUIRED.
IF HE'S HOLDING THE EXCHANGE VOUCHER FROM TRADING IN ALL 40 SPELL CARDS...
HIS VOUCHER WILL CHANGE INTO "ANGEL'S BREATH" THE *MOMENT* WE CAST "GAIN" TO USE OURS...
BUT WE MONOPOLIZED "NIGHT JADE" BY ACQUIRING EACH AND EVERY ONE OF THEM.
WE EVEN GOT TEN EXTRAS TO THWART PEOPLE USING THE "GAIN WAITING" STRATEGY.
KLINK
EVEN IF ONE OF *OUR* CARDS IS DESTROYED...
...ONE OF OUR JADES WILL CONVERT INTO A CARD FIRST.
THEY'RE WELL AWARE OF OUR STRATEGY.
SO THE ONE THAT'S HARDER FOR THEM TO ACQUIRE IS THE RANK-A "NIGHT JADE," *NOT* THE RANK-SS "ANGEL'S BREATH"...!!

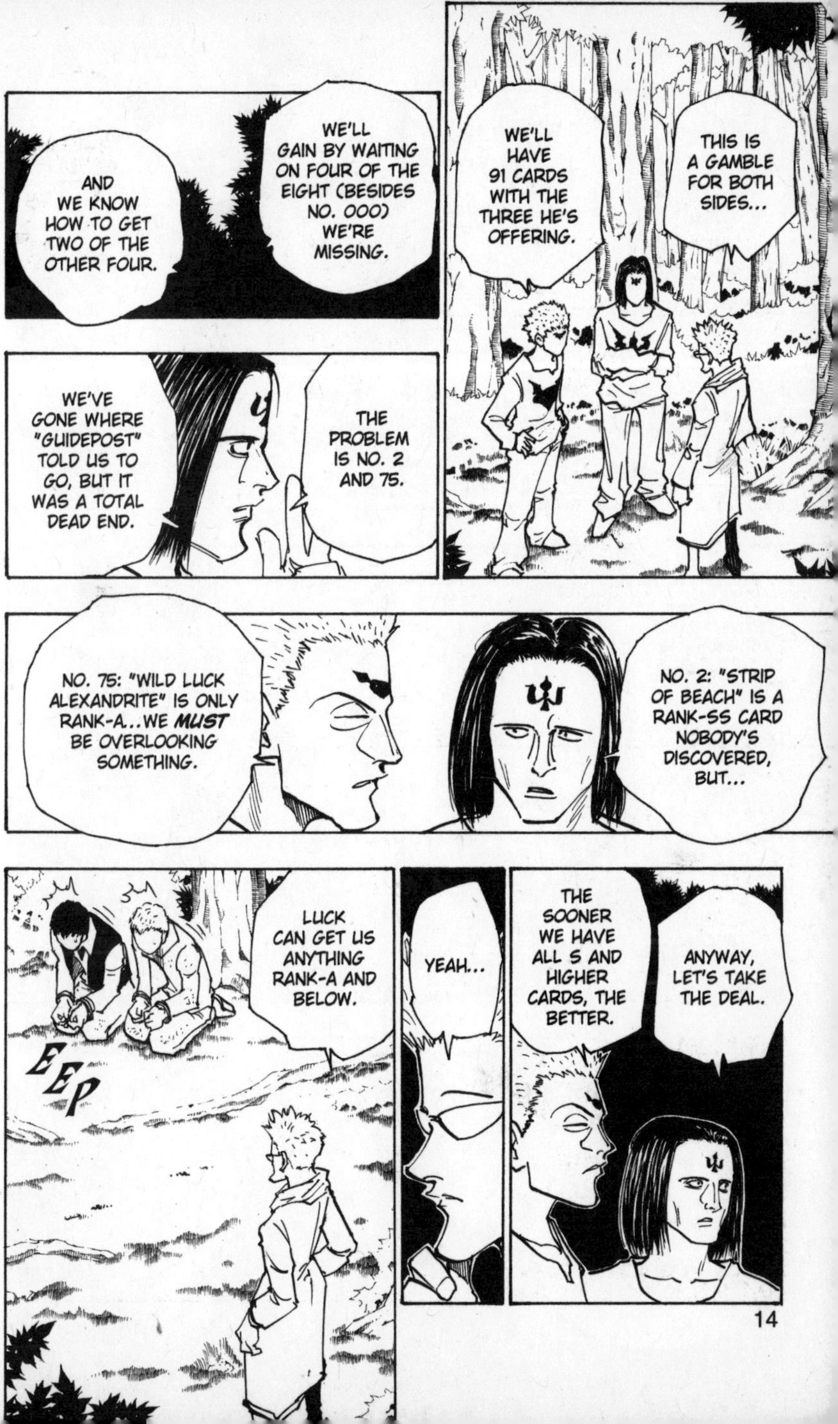
THIS IS A GAMBLE FOR BOTH SIDES...
WE'LL HAVE 91 CARDS WITH THE THREE HE'S OFFERING.
WE'LL GAIN BY WAITING ON FOUR OF THE EIGHT (BESIDES NO. 000) WE'RE MISSING.
AND WE KNOW HOW TO GET TWO OF THE OTHER FOUR.
THE PROBLEM IS NO. 2 AND 75.
WE'VE GONE WHERE "GUIDEPOST" TOLD US TO GO, BUT IT WAS A TOTAL DEAD END.
NO. 2: "STRIP OF BEACH" IS A RANK-SS CARD NOBODY'S DISCOVERED, BUT...
NO. 75: "WILD LUCK ALEXANDRITE" IS ONLY RANK-A...WE *MUST* BE OVERLOOKING SOMETHING.
ANYWAY, LET'S TAKE THE DEAL.
THE SOONER WE HAVE ALL S AND HIGHER CARDS, THE BETTER.
YEAH...
LUCK CAN GET US ANYTHING RANK-A AND BELOW.
EEP

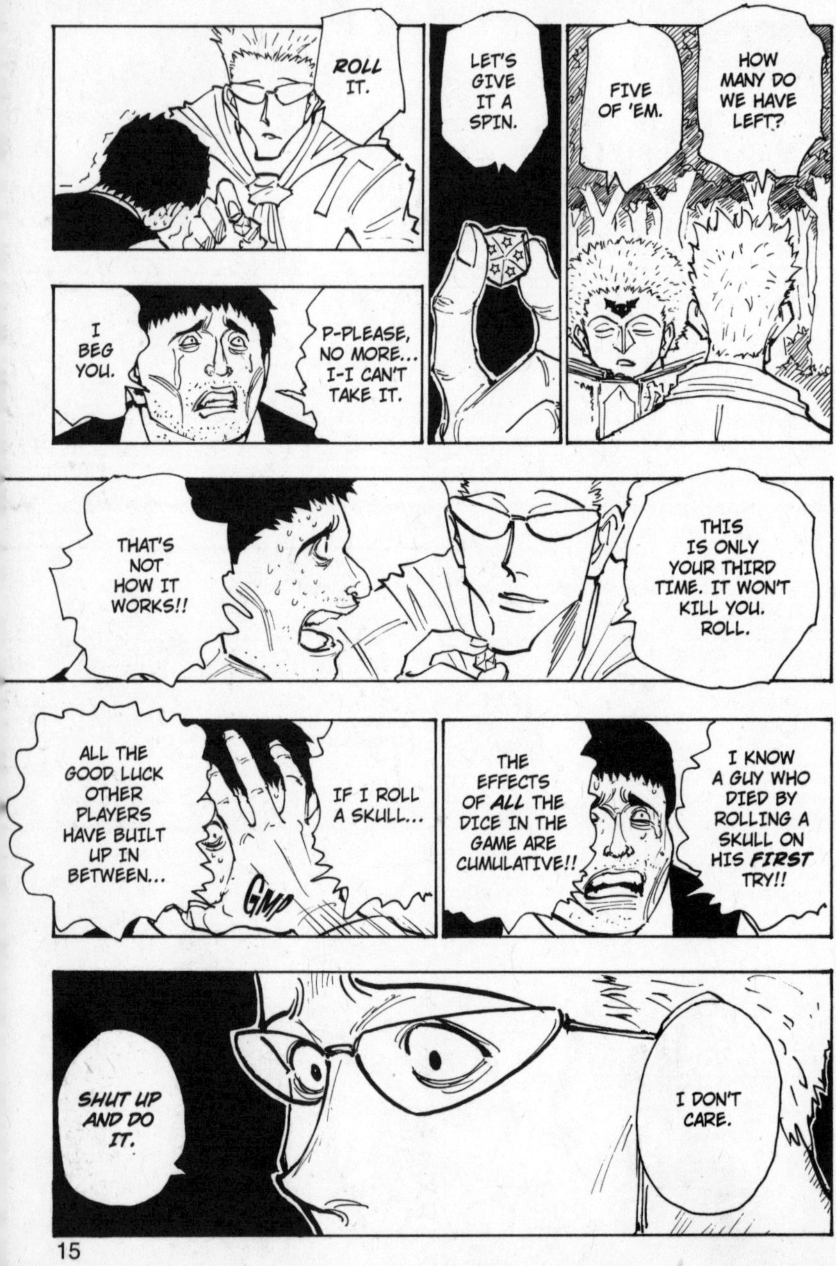
HOW MANY DO WE HAVE LEFT?
FIVE OF 'EM.
LET'S GIVE IT A SPIN.
ROLL IT.
P-PLEASE, NO MORE... I-I CAN'T TAKE IT.
I BEG YOU.
THIS IS ONLY YOUR THIRD TIME. IT WON'T KILL YOU. ROLL.
THAT'S NOT HOW IT WORKS!!
I KNOW A GUY WHO DIED BY ROLLING A SKULL ON HIS FIRST TRY!!
THE EFFECTS OF ALL THE DICE IN THE GAME ARE CUMULATIVE!!
IF I ROLL A SKULL...
ALL THE GOOD LUCK OTHER PLAYERS HAVE BUILT UP IN BETWEEN...
GMP
I DON'T CARE.
SHUT UP AND DO IT.

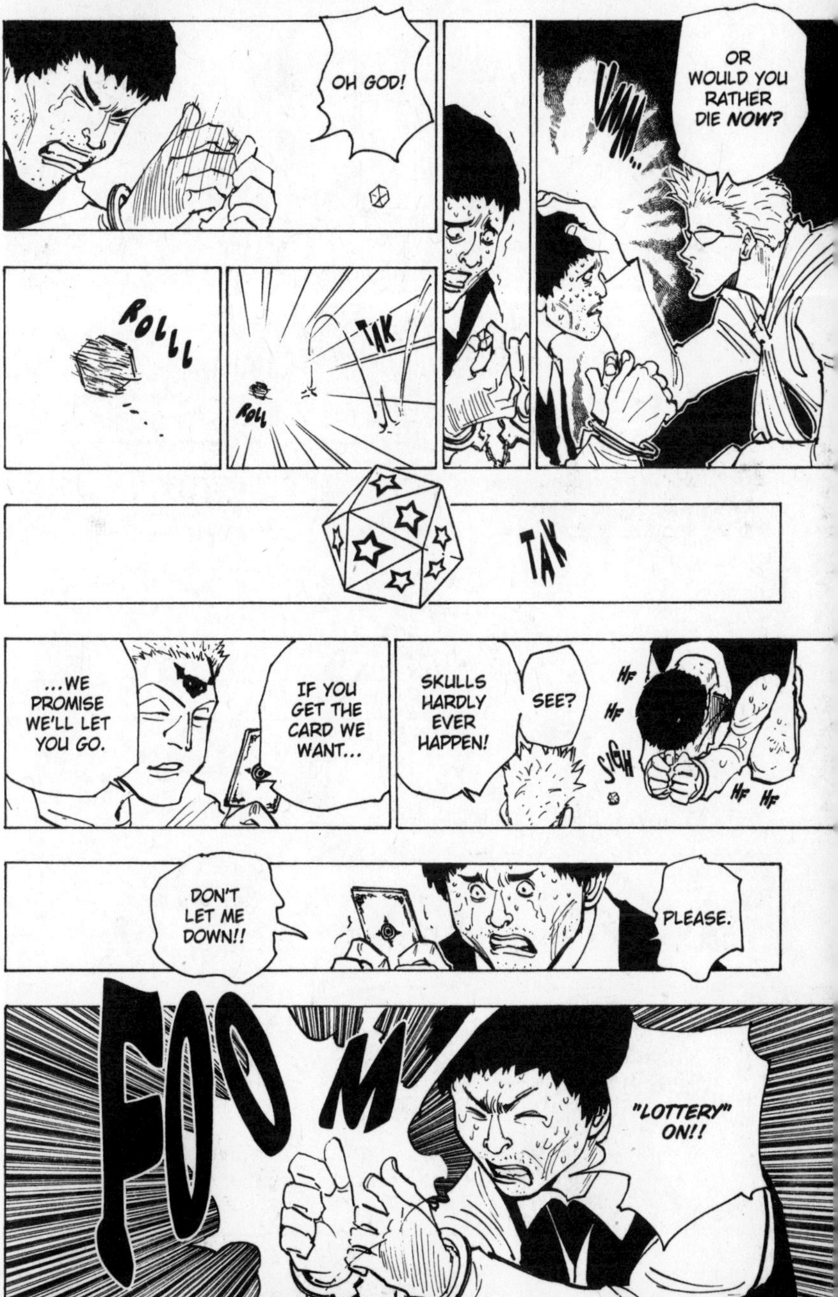
VMM...
OR WOULD YOU RATHER DIE *NOW?*
OH GOD!
TAK
ROLL
ROLLL
TAK
HF HF
SIGH
HF HF
SEE?
SKULLS HARDLY EVER HAPPEN!
IF YOU GET THE CARD WE WANT...
...WE PROMISE WE'LL LET YOU GO.
PLEASE.
DON'T LET ME DOWN!!
FOOM
"LOTTERY" ON!!

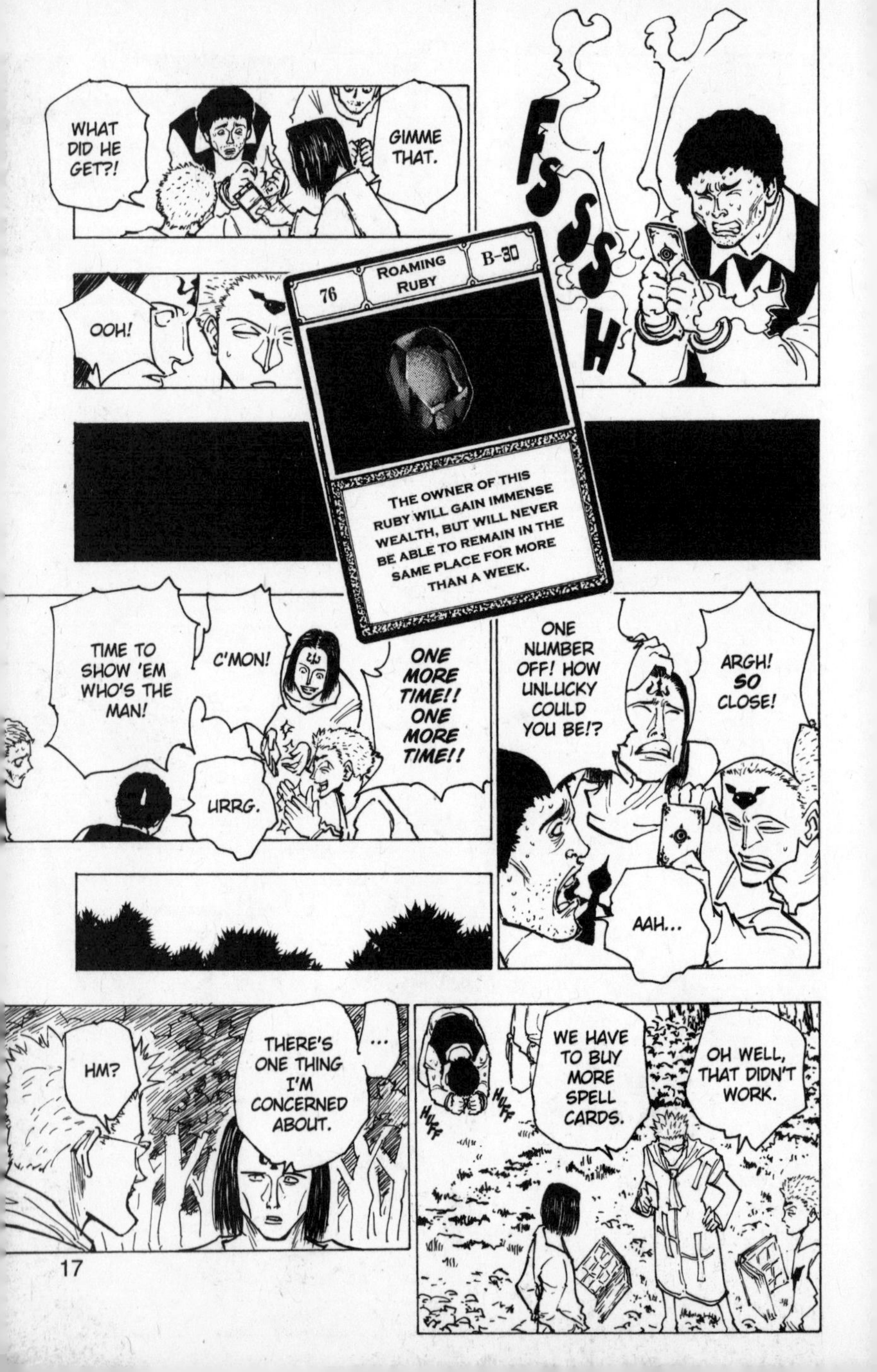
FSSSH
GIMME THAT.
WHAT DID HE GET?!
OOH!
76
ROAMING RUBY
B-30
THE OWNER OF THIS RUBY WILL GAIN IMMENSE WEALTH, BUT WILL NEVER BE ABLE TO REMAIN IN THE SAME PLACE FOR MORE THAN A WEEK.
ARGH! SO CLOSE!
ONE NUMBER OFF! HOW UNLUCKY COULD YOU BE!?
AAH...
ONE MORE TIME!! ONE MORE TIME!!
C'MON!
TIME TO SHOW 'EM WHO'S THE MAN!
URRG.
OH WELL, THAT DIDN'T WORK.
WE HAVE TO BUY MORE SPELL CARDS.
HUFF
HUFF
...
THERE'S ONE THING I'M CONCERNED ABOUT.
HM?

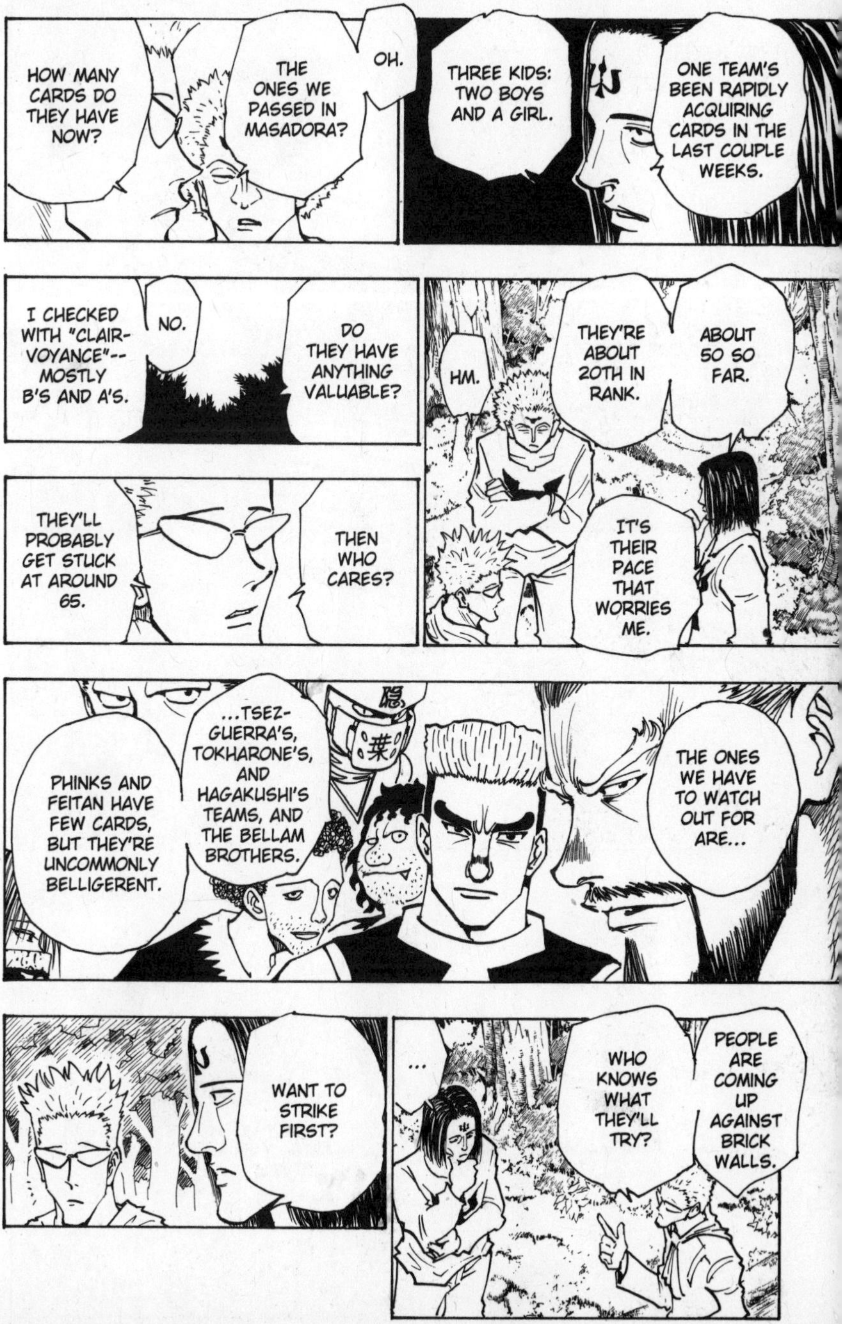
ONE TEAM'S BEEN RAPIDLY ACQUIRING CARDS IN THE LAST COUPLE WEEKS.
THREE KIDS: TWO BOYS AND A GIRL.
OH.
THE ONES WE PASSED IN MASADORA?
HOW MANY CARDS DO THEY HAVE NOW?
ABOUT 50 SO FAR.
THEY'RE ABOUT 20TH IN RANK.
HM.
IT'S THEIR PACE THAT WORRIES ME.
DO THEY HAVE ANYTHING VALUABLE?
NO.
I CHECKED WITH "CLAIR-VOYANCE"-- MOSTLY B'S AND A'S.
THEN WHO CARES?
THEY'LL PROBABLY GET STUCK AT AROUND 65.
THE ONES WE HAVE TO WATCH OUT FOR ARE...
...TSEZ-GUERRA'S, TOKHARONE'S, AND HAGAKUSHI'S TEAMS, AND THE BELLAM BROTHERS.
PHINKS AND FEITAN HAVE FEW CARDS, BUT THEY'RE UNCOMMONLY BELLIGERENT.
PEOPLE ARE COMING UP AGAINST BRICK WALLS.
WHO KNOWS WHAT THEY'LL TRY?
...
WANT TO STRIKE FIRST?

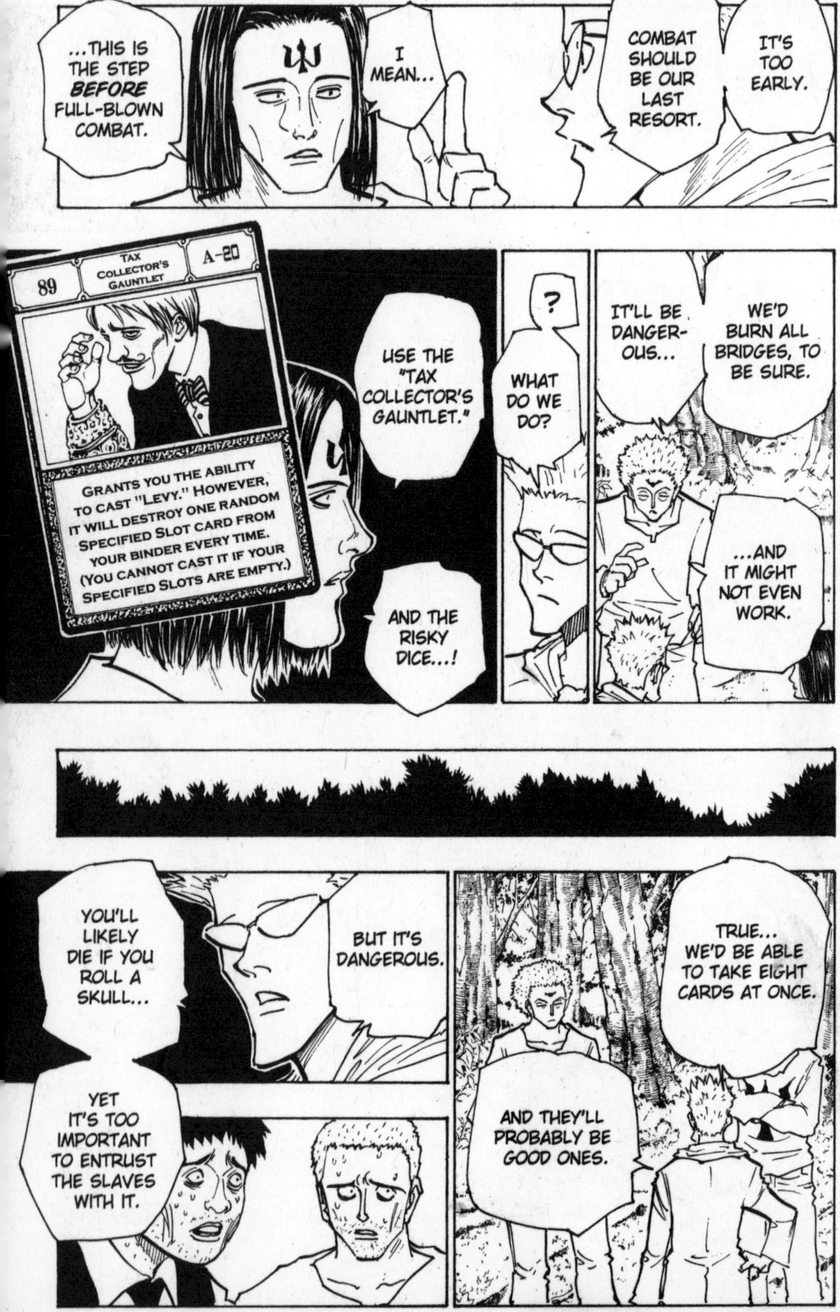
IT'S TOO EARLY.
COMBAT SHOULD BE OUR LAST RESORT.
I MEAN...
...THIS IS THE STEP *BEFORE* FULL-BLOWN COMBAT.
WE'D BURN ALL BRIDGES, TO BE SURE.
IT'LL BE DANGER-OUS...
...AND IT MIGHT NOT EVEN WORK.
?
WHAT DO WE DO?
USE THE "TAX COLLECTOR'S GAUNTLET."
AND THE RISKY DICE...!
A-20
TAX COLLECTOR'S GAUNTLET
89
GRANTS YOU THE ABILITY TO CAST "LEVY." HOWEVER, IT WILL DESTROY ONE RANDOM SPECIFIED SLOT CARD FROM YOUR BINDER EVERY TIME. (YOU CANNOT CAST IT IF YOUR SPECIFIED SLOTS ARE EMPTY.)
TRUE... WE'D BE ABLE TO TAKE EIGHT CARDS AT ONCE.
AND THEY'LL PROBABLY BE GOOD ONES.
BUT IT'S DANGEROUS.
YOU'LL LIKELY DIE IF YOU ROLL A SKULL...
YET IT'S TOO IMPORTANT TO ENTRUST THE SLAVES WITH IT.

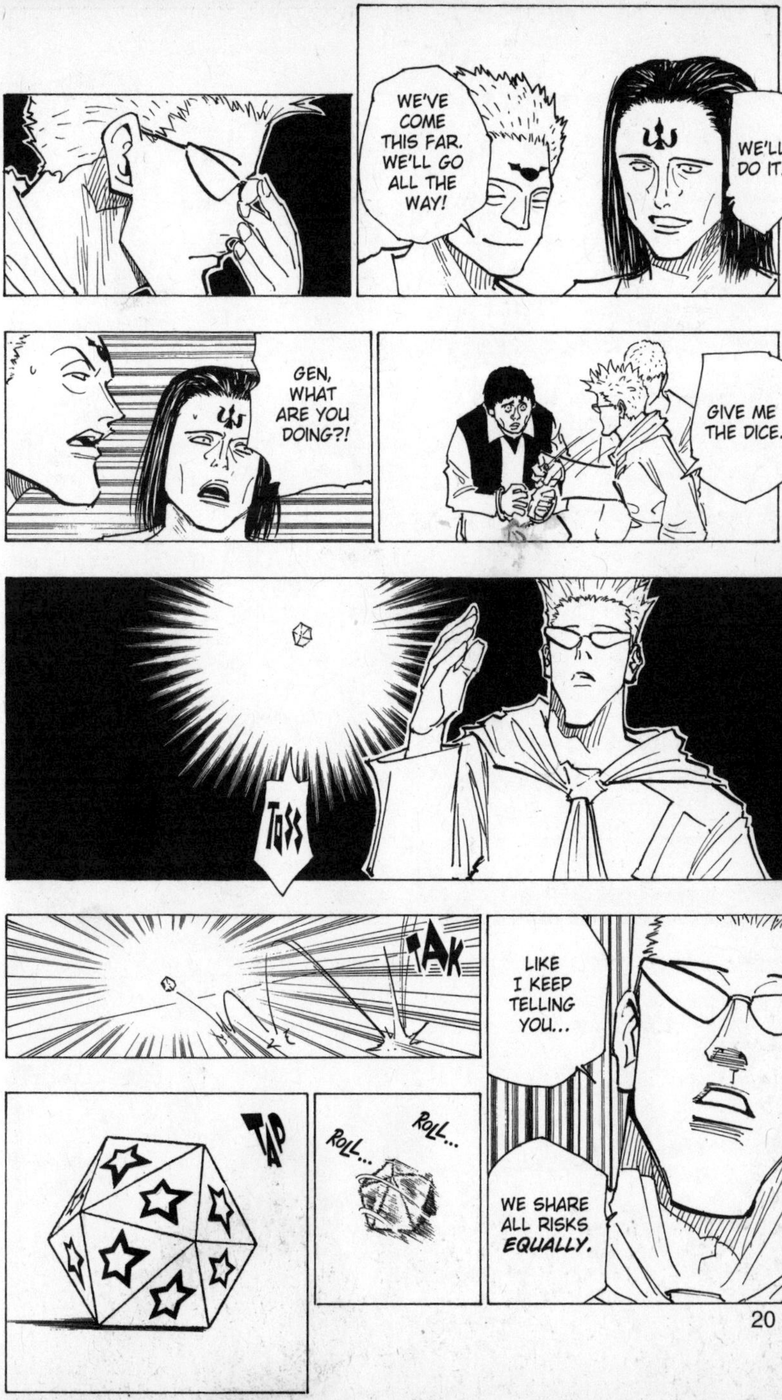
WE'LL DO IT!
WE'VE COME THIS FAR. WE'LL GO ALL THE WAY!
GIVE ME THE DICE.
GEN, WHAT ARE YOU DOING?!
TOSS
LIKE I KEEP TELLING YOU...
WE SHARE ALL RISKS *EQUALLY.*
TAK
ROLL... ROLL...
TAP

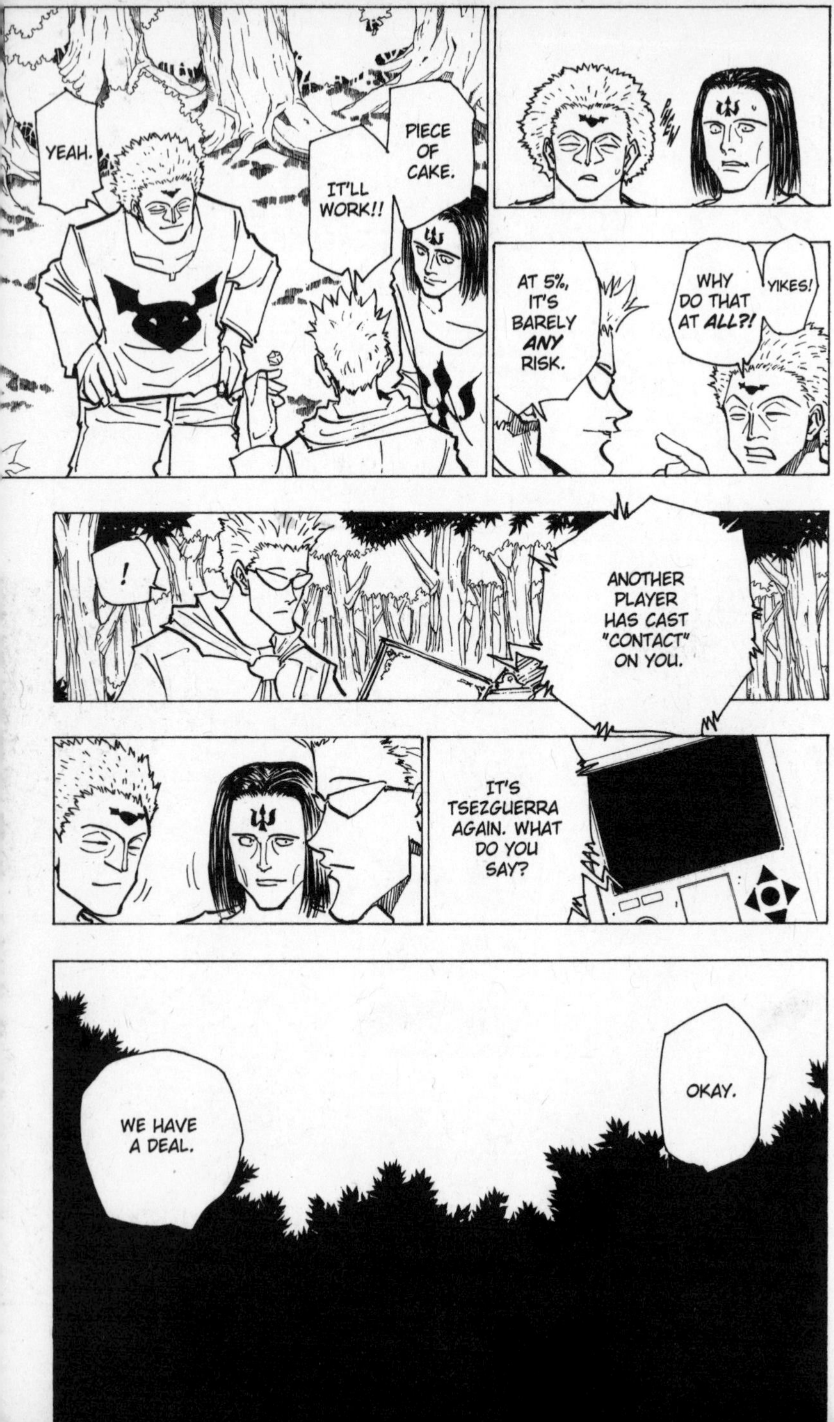
PHEW
YIKES!
WHY DO THAT AT ALL?!
AT 5%, IT'S BARELY ANY RISK.
PIECE OF CAKE.
IT'LL WORK!!
YEAH.
ANOTHER PLAYER HAS CAST "CONTACT" ON YOU.
!
IT'S TSEZGUERRA AGAIN. WHAT DO YOU SAY?
OKAY.
WE HAVE A DEAL.

PART 3 COULD NOT BE SHOWN
FOR COPYRIGHT REASONS...

T. Inoue

DRAW WITHOUT LOOKING: PART 4

JOHNESS

Chapter 153: Success

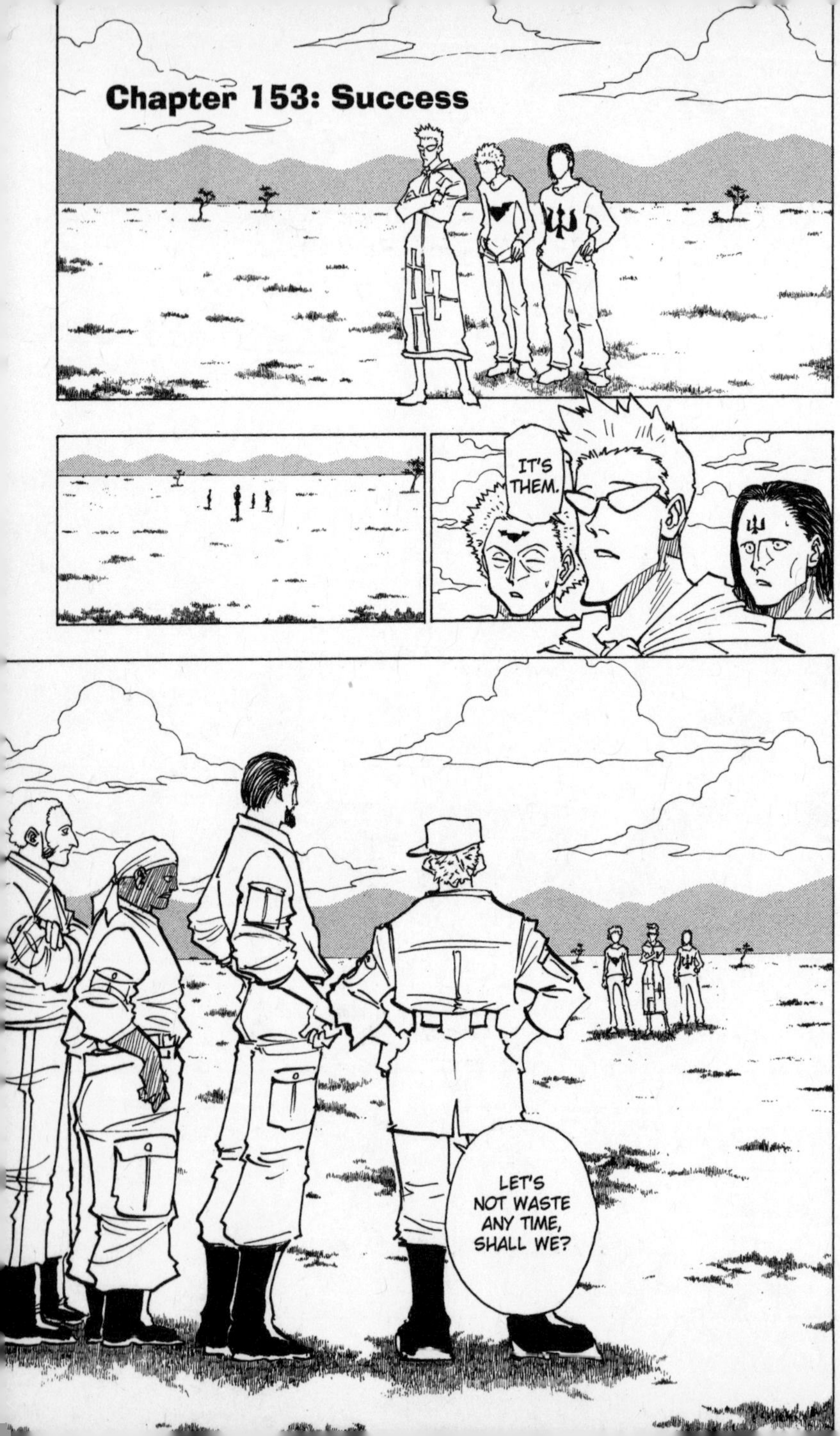
IT'S THEM.
LET'S NOT WASTE ANY TIME, SHALL WE?

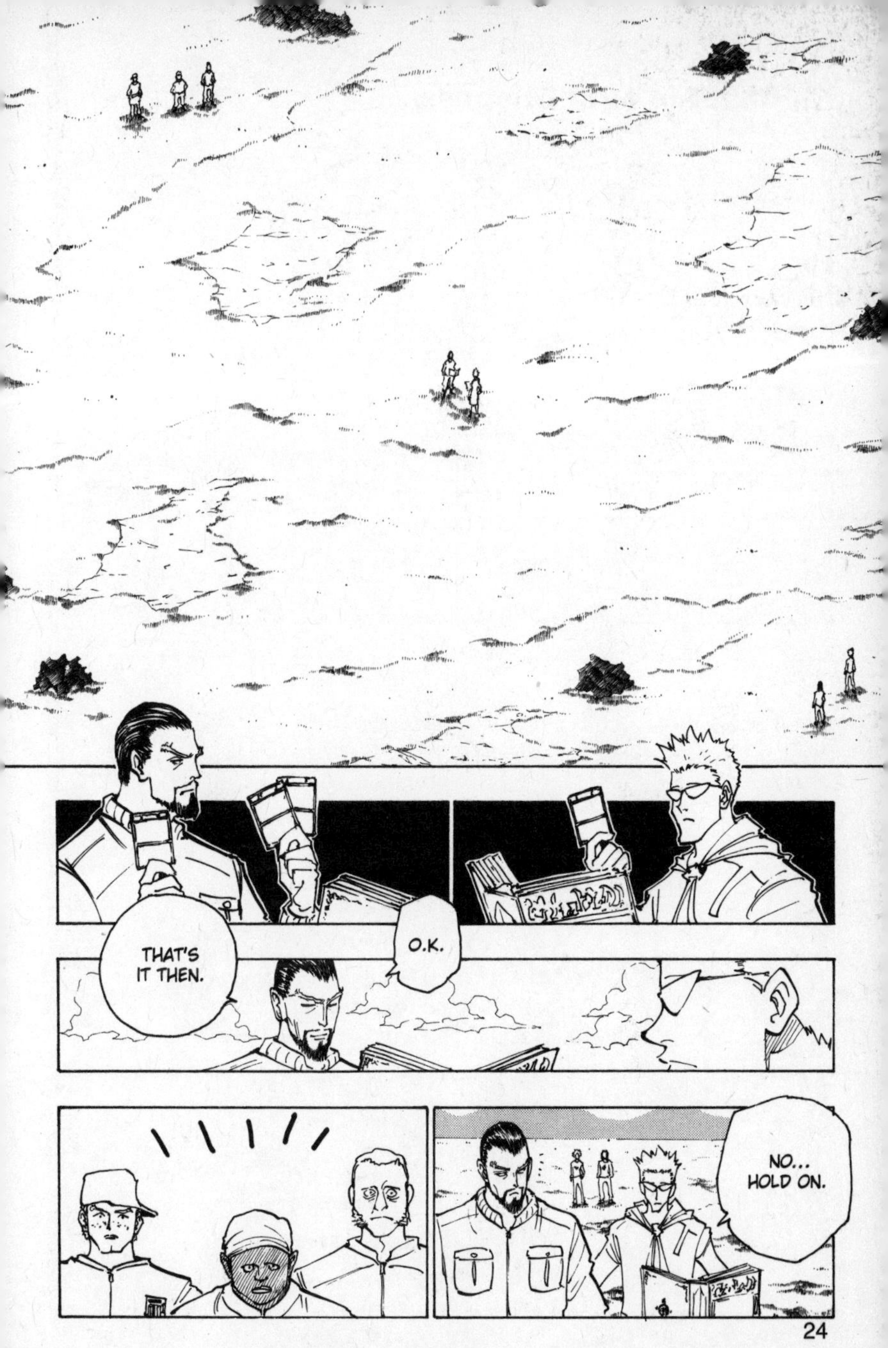
O.K.
THAT'S IT THEN.
NO... HOLD ON.

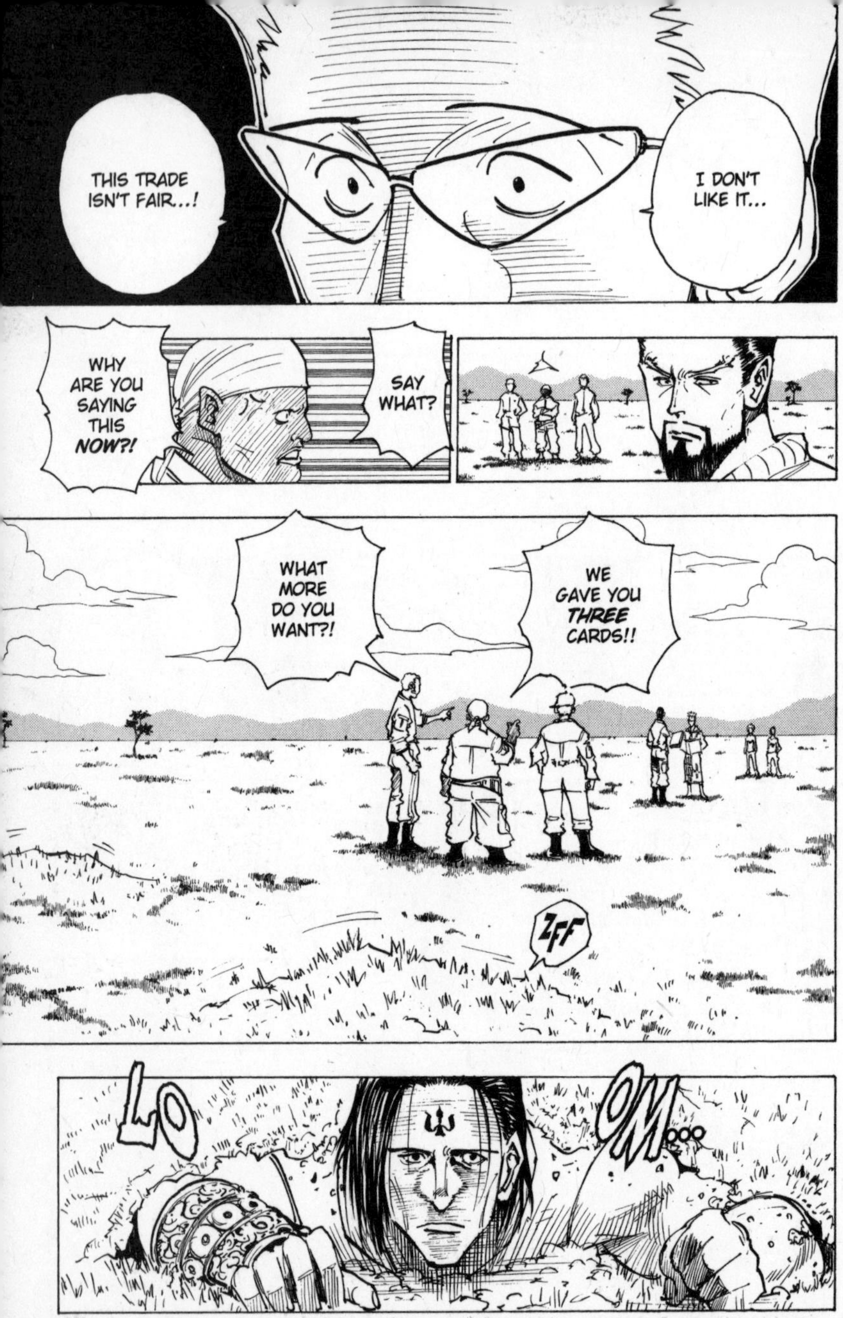
I DON'T LIKE IT...
THIS TRADE ISN'T FAIR...!
SAY WHAT?
WHY ARE YOU SAYING THIS *NOW?!*
WE GAVE YOU *THREE* CARDS!!
WHAT MORE DO YOU WANT?!
ZFF
LO
OM...

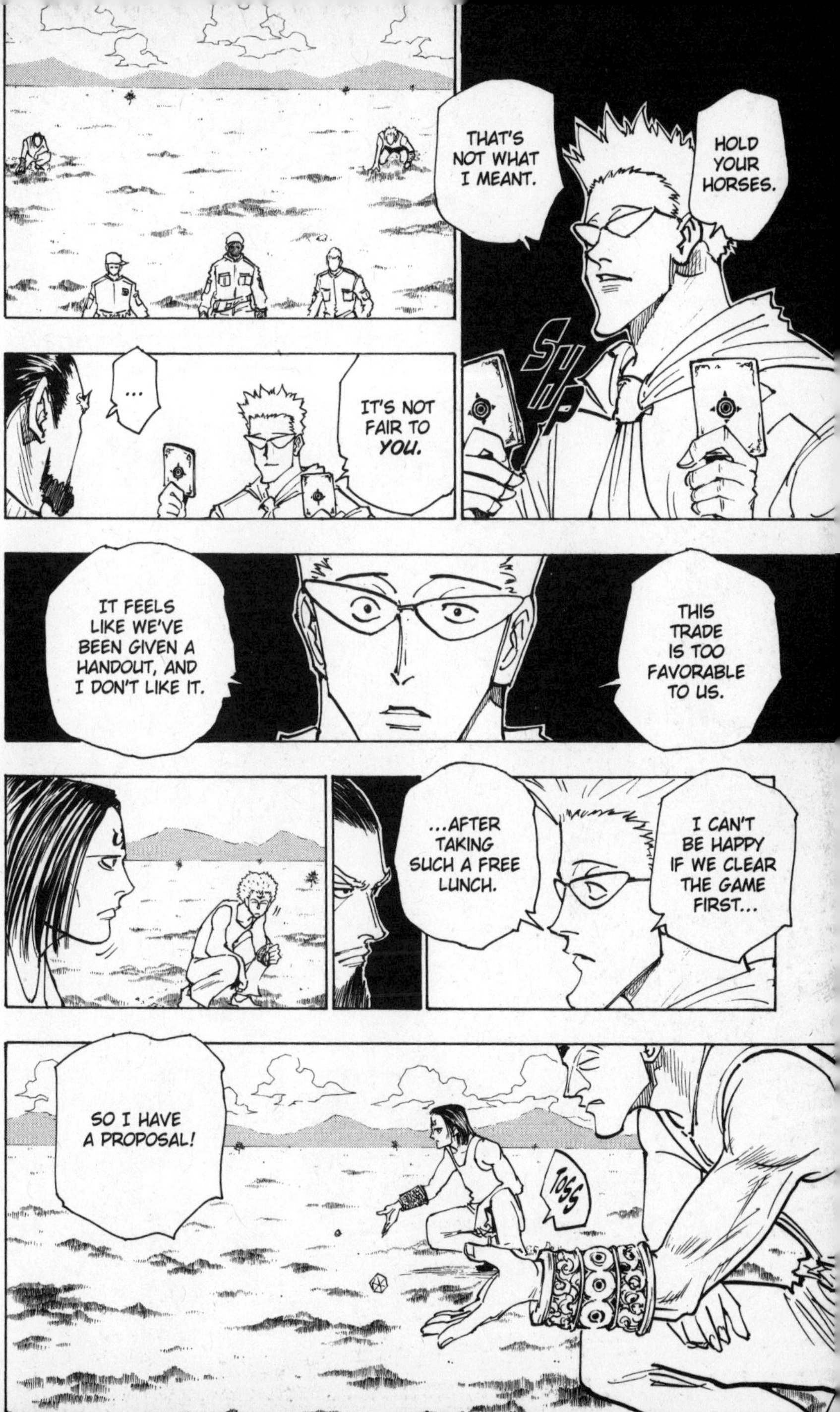
HOLD YOUR HORSES.
THAT'S NOT WHAT I MEANT.
IT'S NOT FAIR TO *YOU.*
...
THIS TRADE IS TOO FAVORABLE TO US.
IT FEELS LIKE WE'VE BEEN GIVEN A HANDOUT, AND I DON'T LIKE IT.
I CAN'T BE HAPPY IF WE CLEAR THE GAME FIRST...
...AFTER TAKING SUCH A FREE LUNCH.
SO I HAVE A PROPOSAL!
TOSS

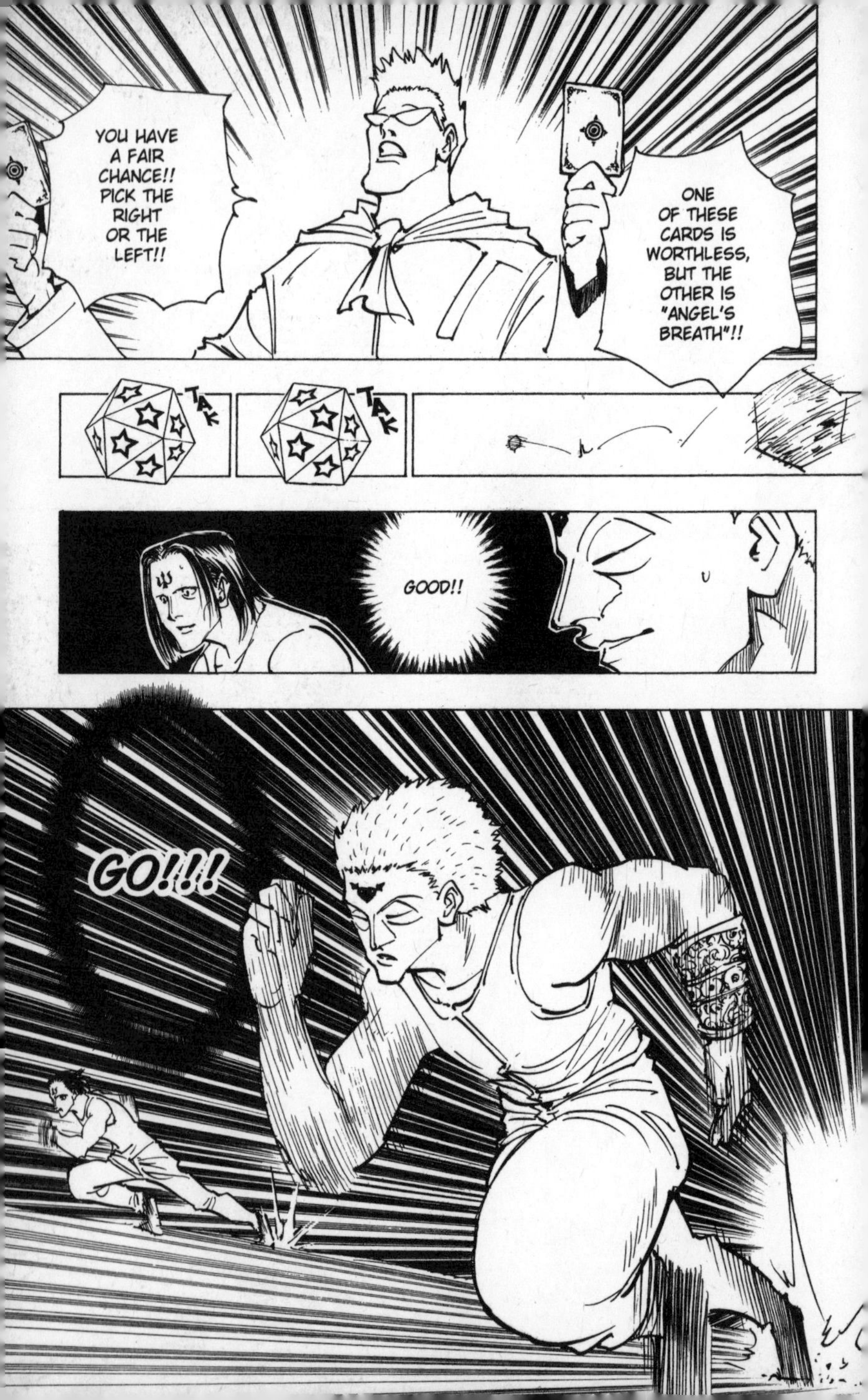
ONE OF THESE CARDS IS WORTHLESS, BUT THE OTHER IS "ANGEL'S BREATH"!!
YOU HAVE A FAIR CHANCE!! PICK THE RIGHT OR THE LEFT!!
TAK
TAK
GOOD!!
GO!!!

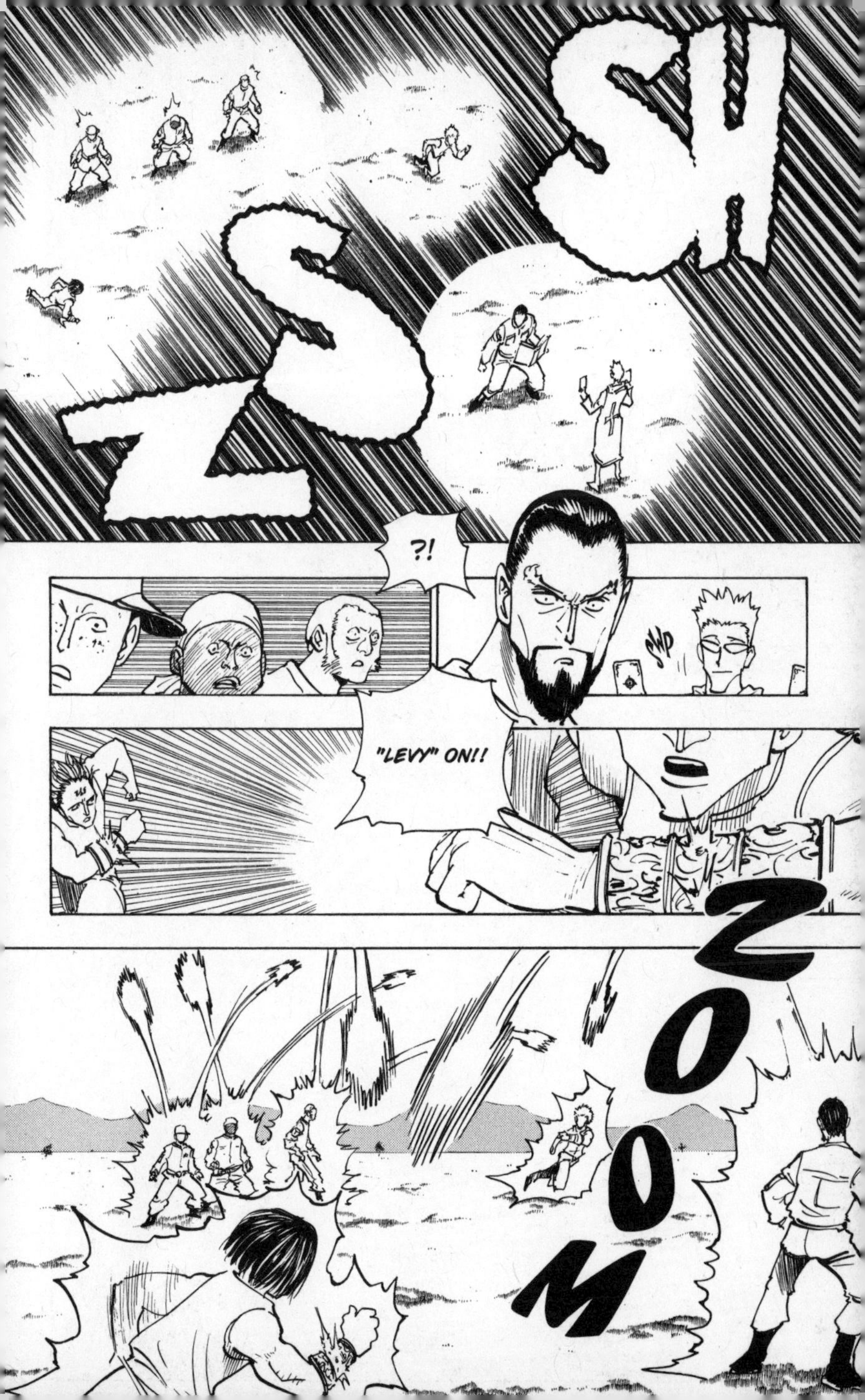

SZSCH
?!
SWP
"LEVY" ON!!
ZOOM

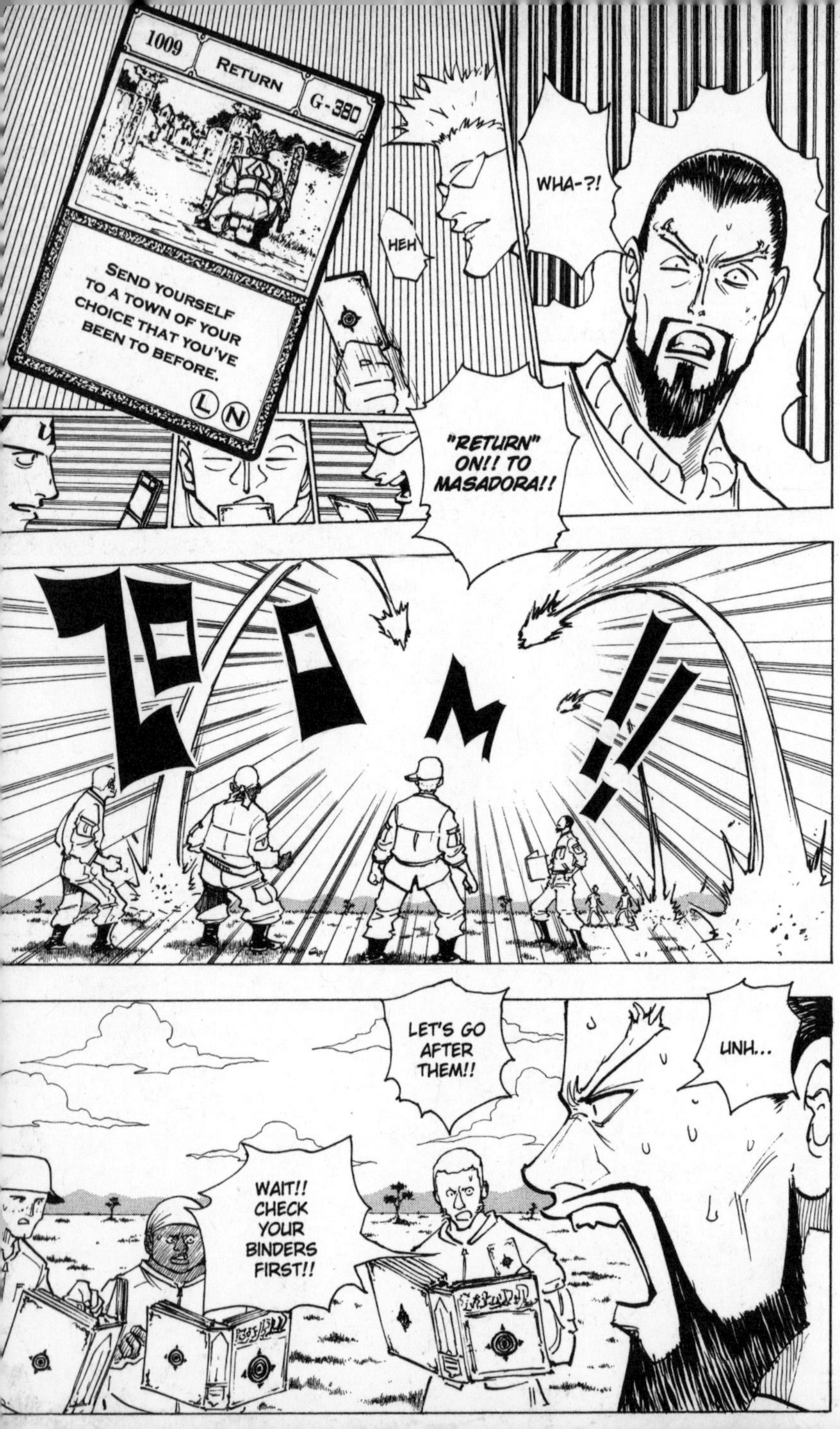
WHA-?!
HEH
1009
RETURN
G-380
SEND YOURSELF TO A TOWN OF YOUR CHOICE THAT YOU'VE BEEN TO BEFORE.
L N
"RETURN" ON!! TO MASADORA!!
UNH...
LET'S GO AFTER THEM!!
WAIT!! CHECK YOUR BINDERS FIRST!!

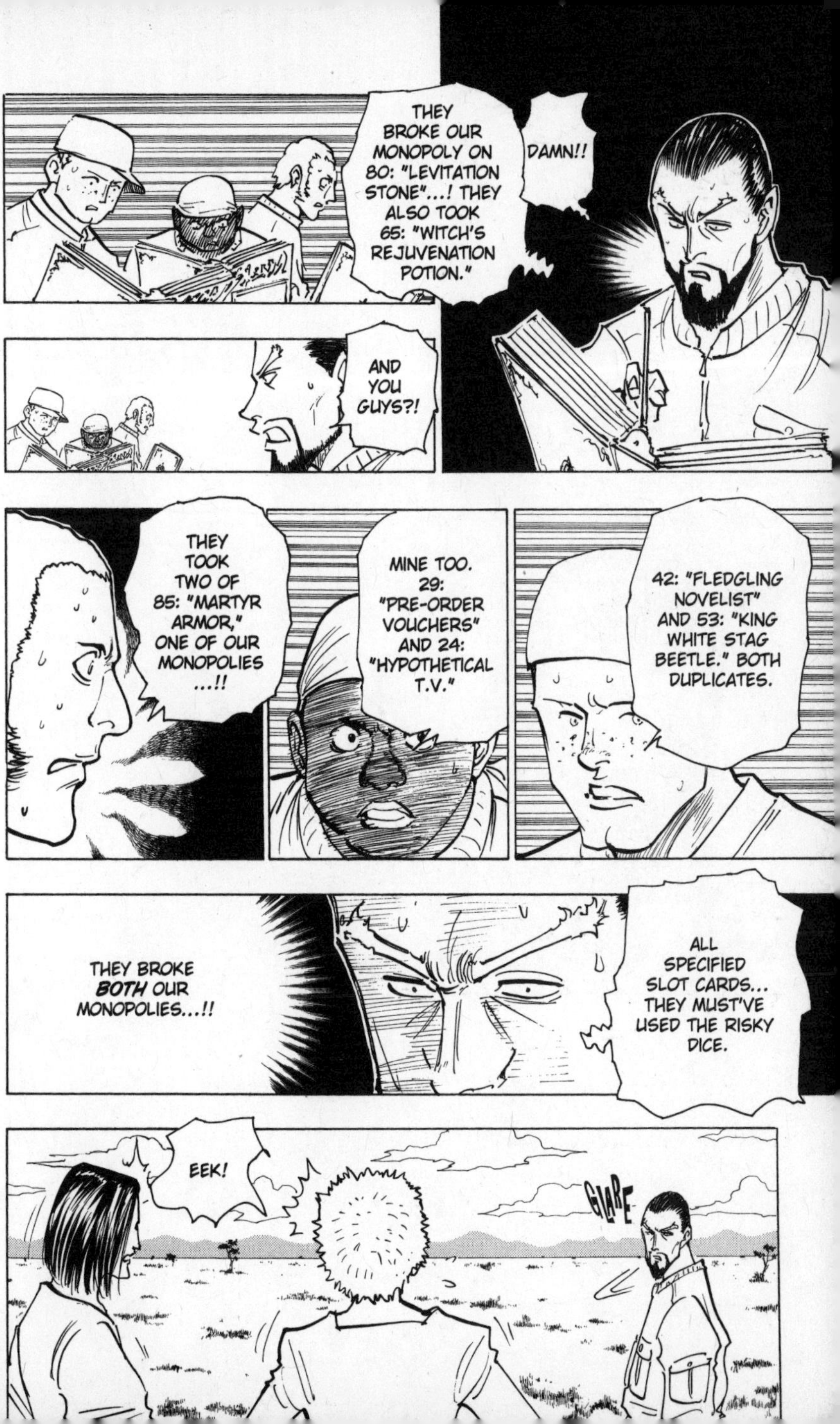
DAMN!!
THEY BROKE OUR MONOPOLY ON 80: "LEVITATION STONE"...! THEY ALSO TOOK 65: "WITCH'S REJUVENATION POTION."
AND YOU GUYS?!
42: "FLEDGLING NOVELIST" AND 53: "KING WHITE STAG BEETLE." BOTH DUPLICATES.
MINE TOO. 29: "PRE-ORDER VOUCHERS" AND 24: "HYPOTHETICAL T.V."
THEY TOOK TWO OF 85: "MARTYR ARMOR," ONE OF OUR MONOPOLIES ...!!
ALL SPECIFIED SLOT CARDS... THEY MUST'VE USED THE RISKY DICE.
THEY BROKE *BOTH* OUR MONOPOLIES...!!
GLARE
EEK!

READ THIS WAY

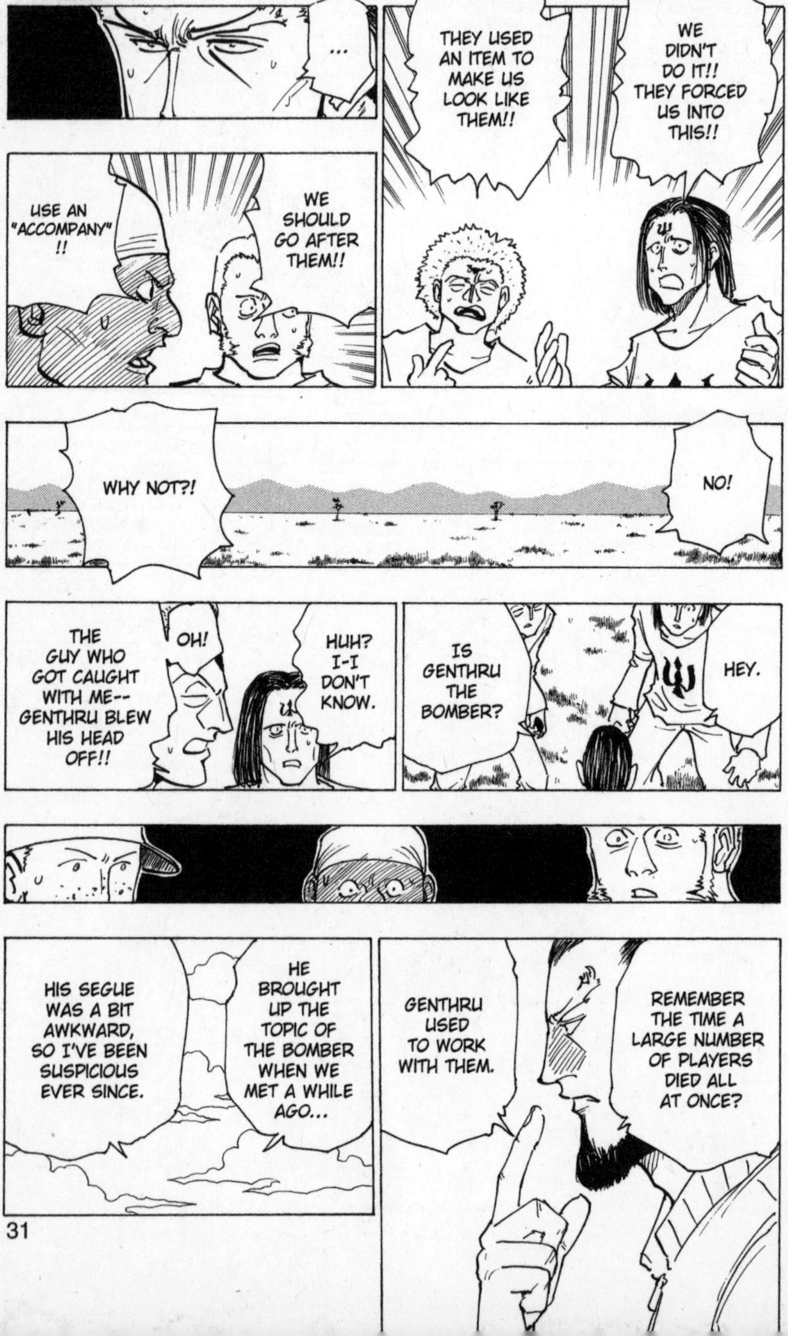

WE DIDN'T DO IT!! THEY FORCED US INTO THIS!!
THEY USED AN ITEM TO MAKE US LOOK LIKE THEM!!
...
WE SHOULD GO AFTER THEM!!
USE AN "ACCOMPANY" !!
NO!
WHY NOT?!
HEY.
IS GENTHRU THE BOMBER?
HUH? I-I DON'T KNOW.
OH!
THE GUY WHO GOT CAUGHT WITH ME-- GENTHRU BLEW HIS HEAD OFF!!
REMEMBER THE TIME A LARGE NUMBER OF PLAYERS DIED ALL AT ONCE?
GENTHRU USED TO WORK WITH THEM.
HE BROUGHT UP THE TOPIC OF THE BOMBER WHEN WE MET A WHILE AGO...
HIS SEGUE WAS A BIT AWKWARD, SO I'VE BEEN SUSPICIOUS EVER SINCE.

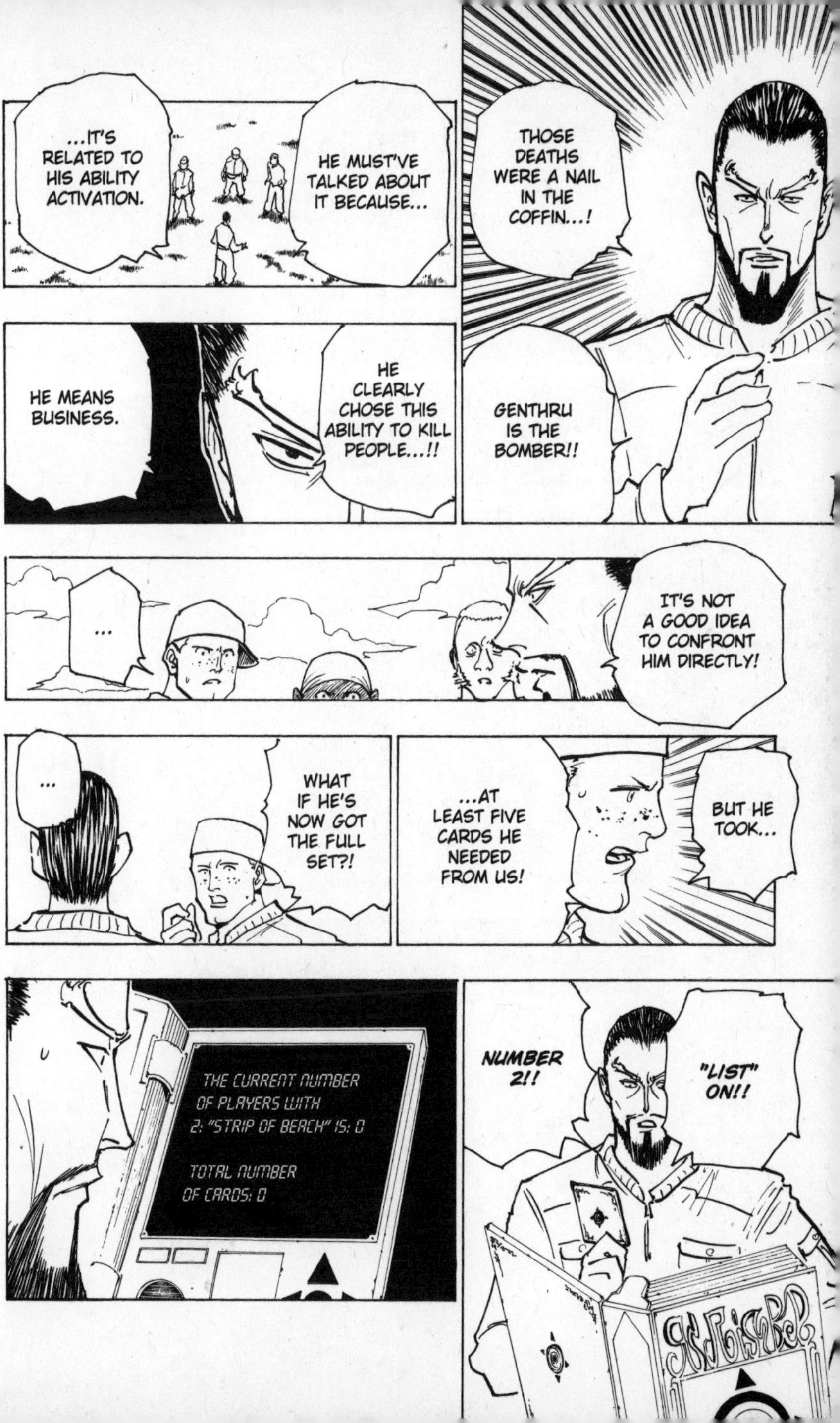
THOSE DEATHS WERE A NAIL IN THE COFFIN...!
GENTHRU IS THE BOMBER!!
HE MUST'VE TALKED ABOUT IT BECAUSE...
...IT'S RELATED TO HIS ABILITY ACTIVATION.
HE CLEARLY CHOSE THIS ABILITY TO KILL PEOPLE...!!
HE MEANS BUSINESS.
IT'S NOT A GOOD IDEA TO CONFRONT HIM DIRECTLY!
...
BUT HE TOOK...
...AT LEAST FIVE CARDS HE NEEDED FROM US!
WHAT IF HE'S NOW GOT THE FULL SET?!
...
"LIST" ON!!
NUMBER 2!!
THE CURRENT NUMBER OF PLAYERS WITH 2: "STRIP OF BEACH" IS: 0
TOTAL NUMBER OF CARDS: 0

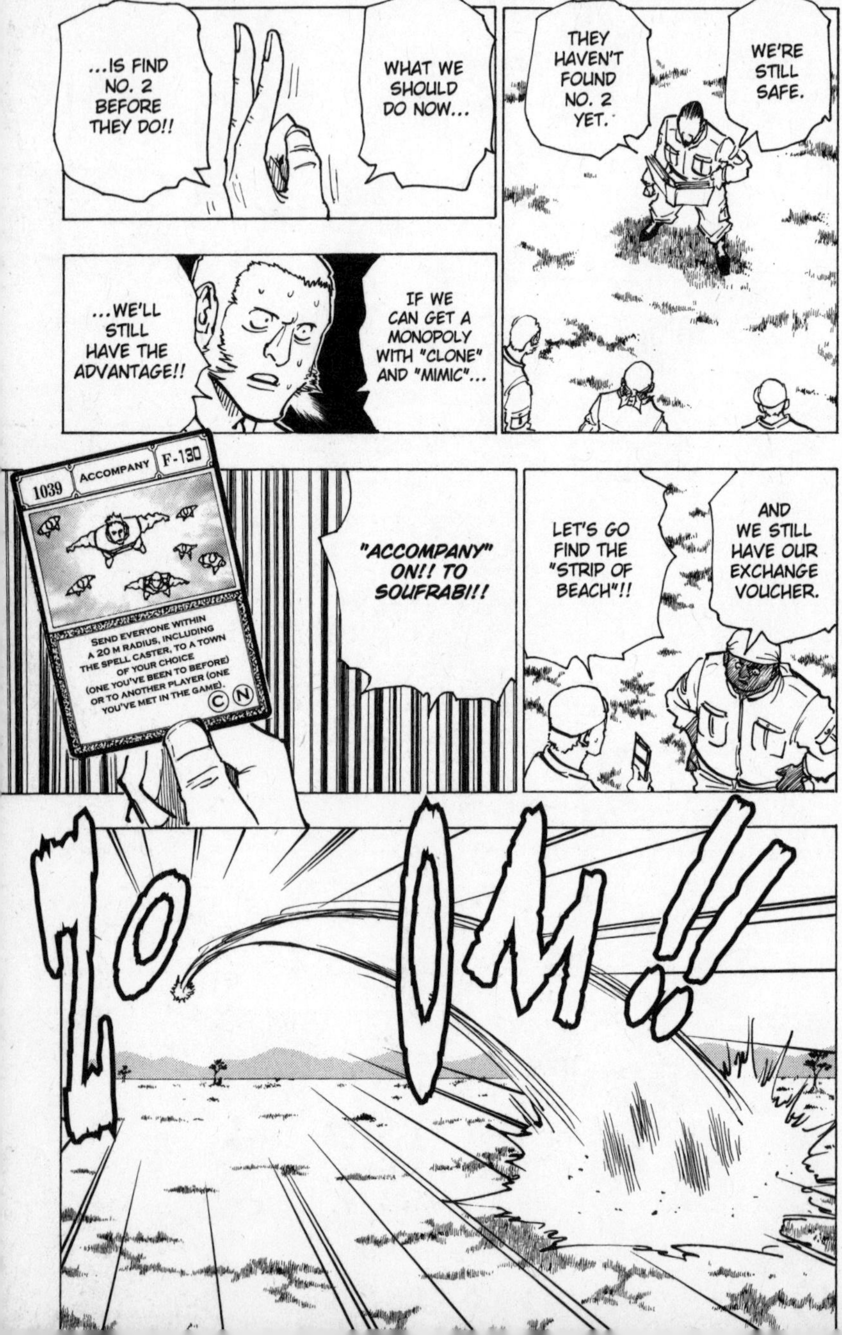
WE'RE STILL SAFE.
THEY HAVEN'T FOUND NO. 2 YET.
WHAT WE SHOULD DO NOW...
...IS FIND NO. 2 BEFORE THEY DO!!
IF WE CAN GET A MONOPOLY WITH "CLONE" AND "MIMIC"...
...WE'LL STILL HAVE THE ADVANTAGE!!
AND WE STILL HAVE OUR EXCHANGE VOUCHER.
LET'S GO FIND THE "STRIP OF BEACH"!!
"ACCOMPANY" ON!! TO SOUFRABI!!
1039
ACCOMPANY
F-130
SEND EVERYONE WITHIN A 20 M RADIUS, INCLUDING THE SPELL CASTER, TO A TOWN OF YOUR CHOICE (ONE YOU'VE BEEN TO BEFORE) OR TO ANOTHER PLAYER (ONE YOU'VE MET IN THE GAME).
C N
ZOOM!!

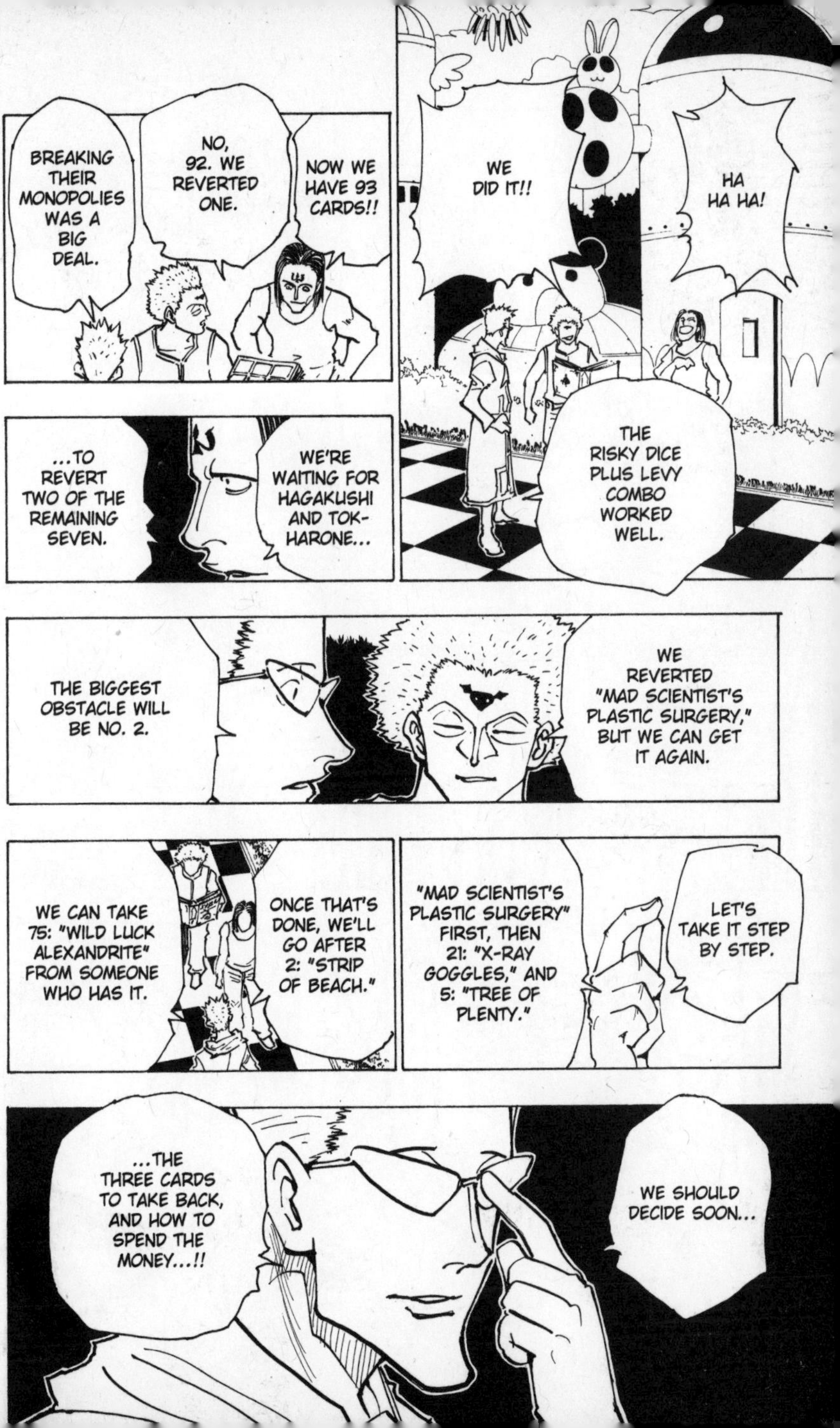
HA HA HA!
WE DID IT!!
THE RISKY DICE PLUS LEVY COMBO WORKED WELL.
NOW WE HAVE 93 CARDS!!
NO, 92. WE REVERTED ONE.
BREAKING THEIR MONOPOLIES WAS A BIG DEAL.
WE'RE WAITING FOR HAGAKUSHI AND TOK-HARONE...
...TO REVERT TWO OF THE REMAINING SEVEN.
WE REVERTED "MAD SCIENTIST'S PLASTIC SURGERY," BUT WE CAN GET IT AGAIN.
THE BIGGEST OBSTACLE WILL BE NO. 2.
LET'S TAKE IT STEP BY STEP.
"MAD SCIENTIST'S PLASTIC SURGERY" FIRST, THEN 21: "X-RAY GOGGLES," AND 5: "TREE OF PLENTY."
ONCE THAT'S DONE, WE'LL GO AFTER 2: "STRIP OF BEACH."
WE CAN TAKE 75: "WILD LUCK ALEXANDRITE" FROM SOMEONE WHO HAS IT.
WE SHOULD DECIDE SOON...
...THE THREE CARDS TO TAKE BACK, AND HOW TO SPEND THE MONEY...!!

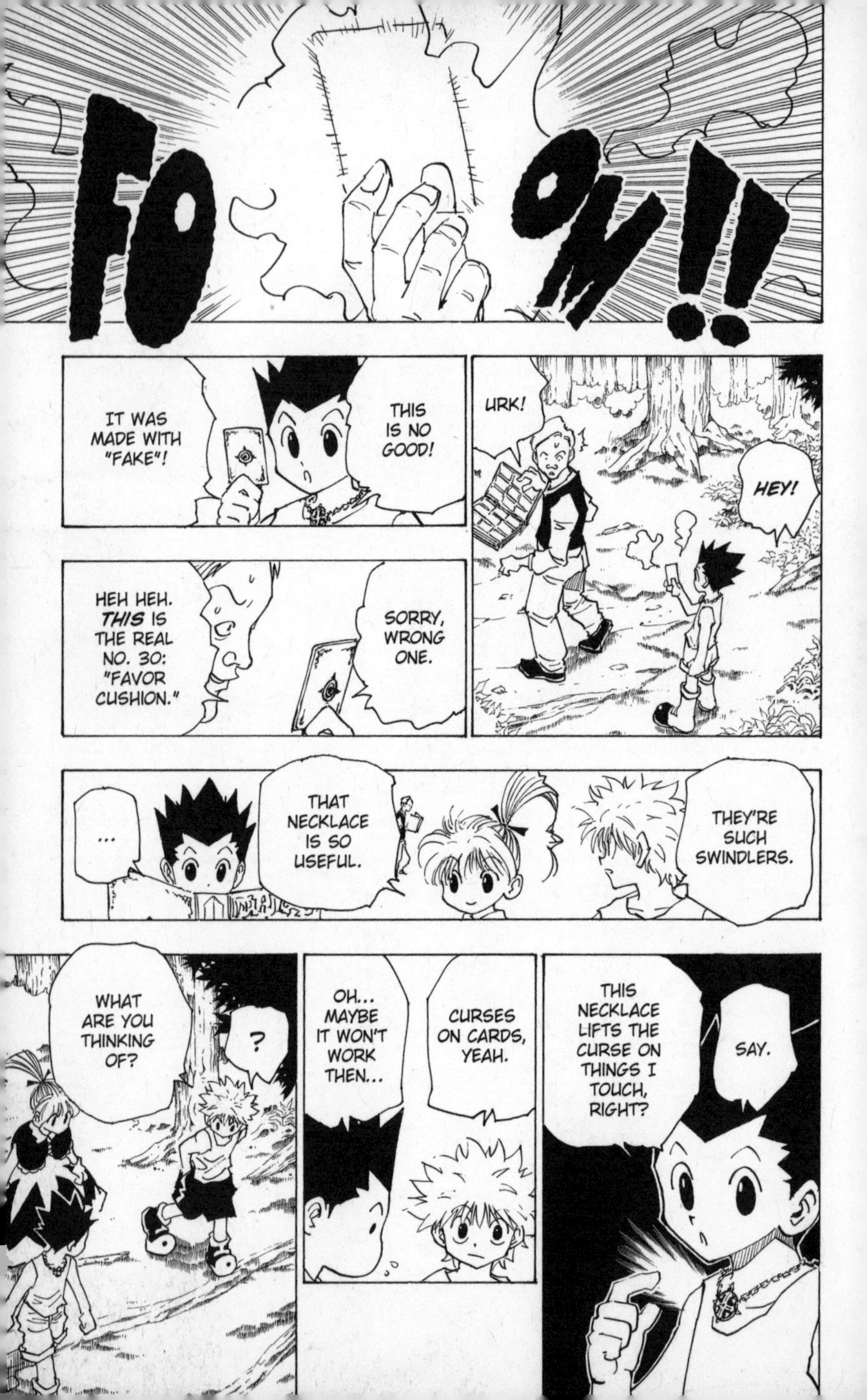
FOOM!!
HEY!
URK!
THIS IS NO GOOD!
IT WAS MADE WITH "FAKE"!
SORRY, WRONG ONE.
HEH HEH. *THIS* IS THE REAL NO. 30: "FAVOR CUSHION."
THEY'RE SUCH SWINDLERS.
THAT NECKLACE IS SO USEFUL.
...
SAY.
THIS NECKLACE LIFTS THE CURSE ON THINGS I TOUCH, RIGHT?
CURSES ON CARDS, YEAH.
OH... MAYBE IT WON'T WORK THEN...
?
WHAT ARE YOU THINKING OF?

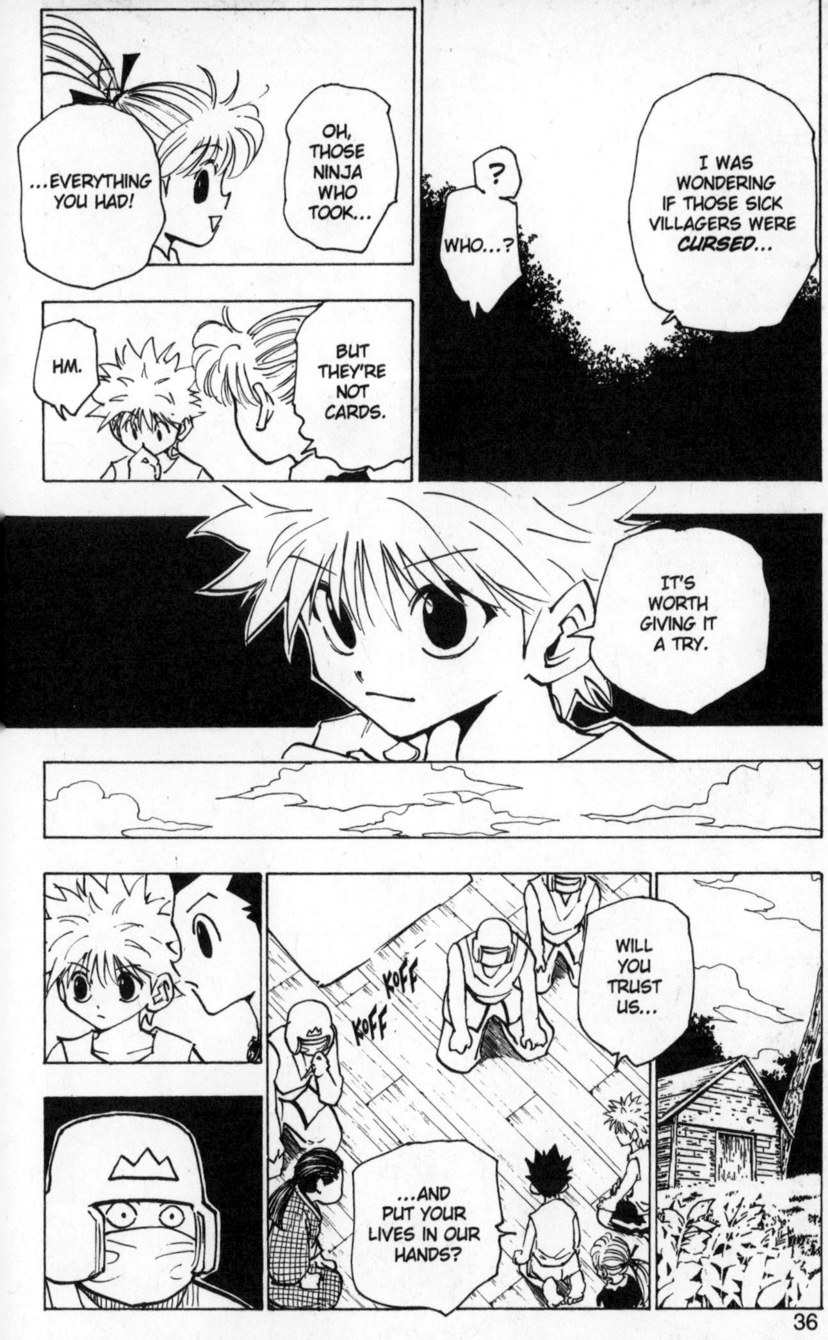
I WAS WONDERING IF THOSE SICK VILLAGERS WERE *CURSED*...
?
WHO...?
OH, THOSE NINJA WHO TOOK...
...EVERYTHING YOU HAD!
BUT THEY'RE NOT CARDS.
HM.
IT'S WORTH GIVING IT A TRY.
WILL YOU TRUST US...
KOFF
KOFF
...AND PUT YOUR LIVES IN OUR HANDS?

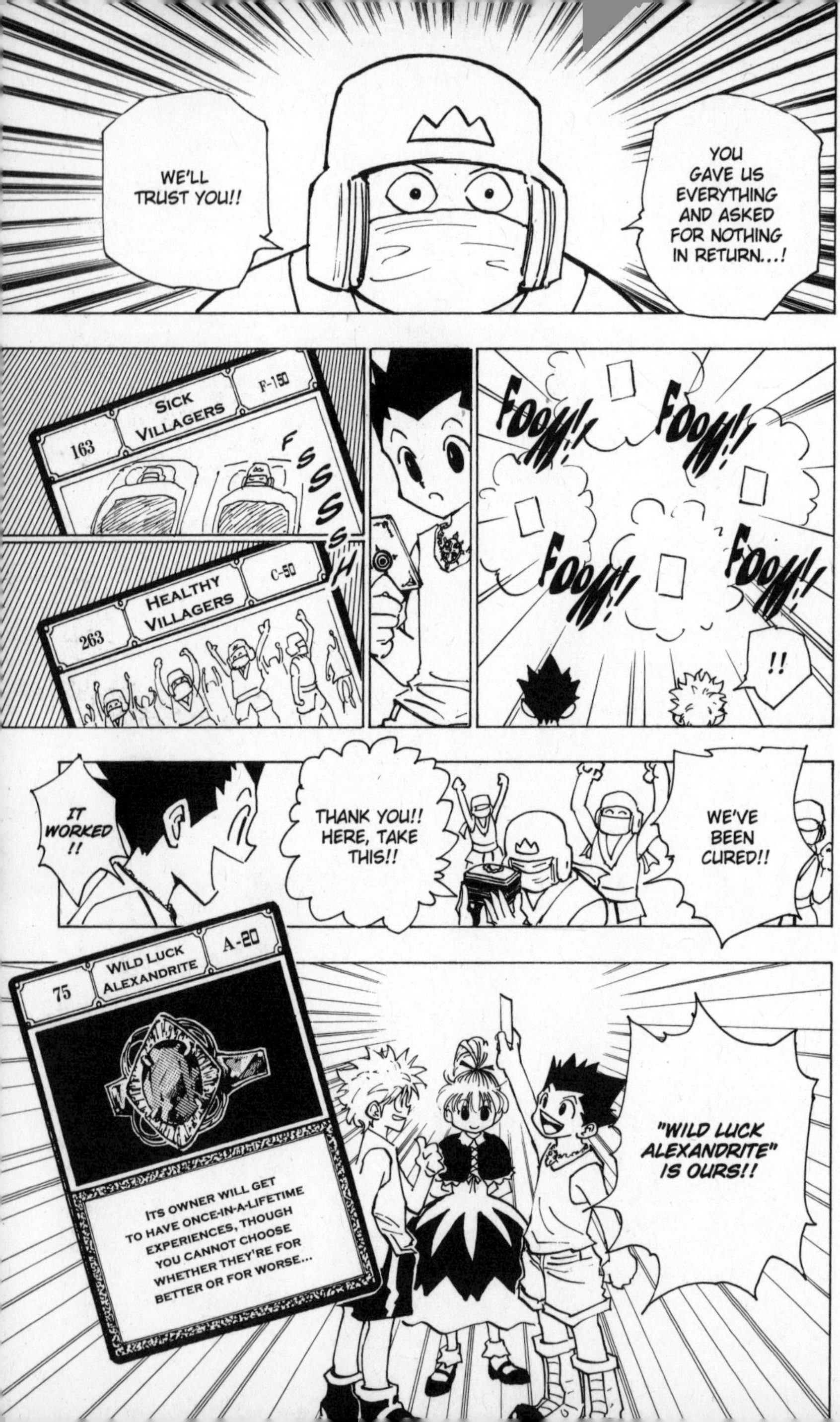
YOU GAVE US EVERYTHING AND ASKED FOR NOTHING IN RETURN...!
WE'LL TRUST YOU!!
FOOM!!
FOOM!!
FOOM!!
FOOM!!
!!
SICK VILLAGERS
F-150
163
FSSSSH
HEALTHY VILLAGERS
C-50
263
WE'VE BEEN CURED!!
THANK YOU!! HERE, TAKE THIS!!
IT WORKED!!
"WILD LUCK ALEXANDRITE" IS OURS!!
A-20
WILD LUCK ALEXANDRITE
75
ITS OWNER WILL GET TO HAVE ONCE-IN-A-LIFETIME EXPERIENCES, THOUGH YOU CANNOT CHOOSE WHETHER THEY'RE FOR BETTER OR FOR WORSE...

DRAW WITHOUT LOOKING: PART 4

JOHNESS

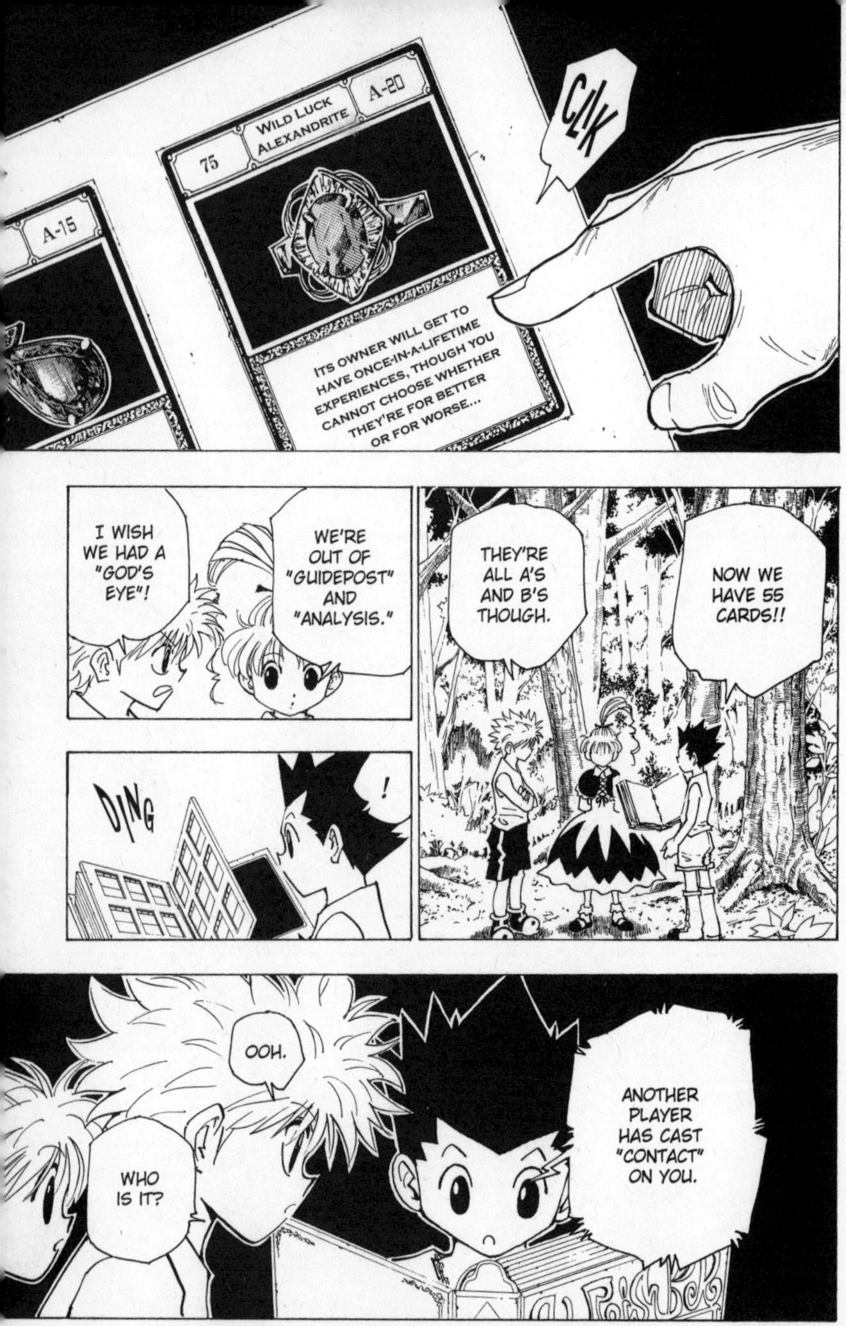
CLIK
75
WILD LUCK ALEXANDRITE
A-20
ITS OWNER WILL GET TO HAVE ONCE-IN-A-LIFETIME EXPERIENCES, THOUGH YOU CANNOT CHOOSE WHETHER THEY'RE FOR BETTER OR FOR WORSE...
A-15
NOW WE HAVE 55 CARDS!!
THEY'RE ALL A'S AND B'S THOUGH.
WE'RE OUT OF "GUIDEPOST" AND "ANALYSIS."
I WISH WE HAD A "GOD'S EYE"!
!
DING
ANOTHER PLAYER HAS CAST "CONTACT" ON YOU.
OOH.
WHO IS IT?

Chapter 154: Common Cause

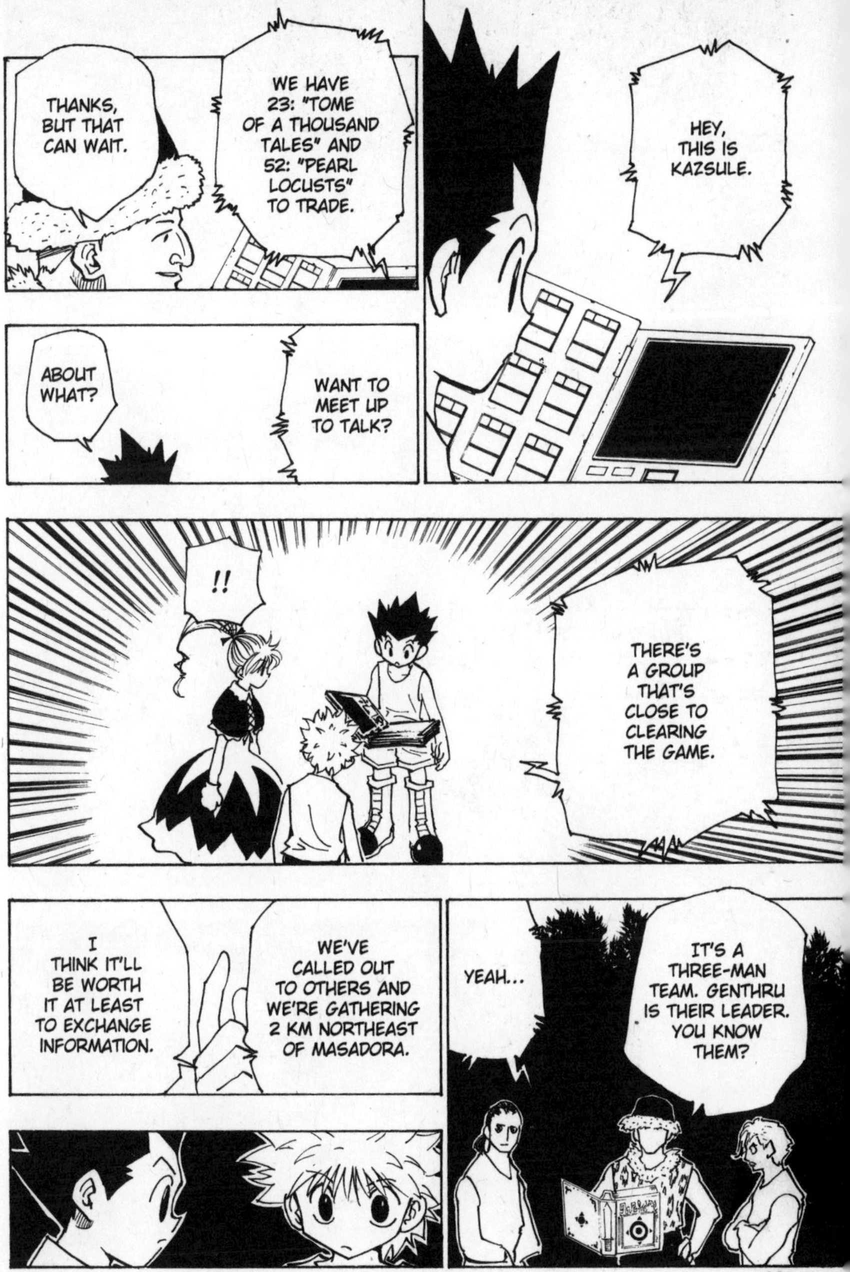
HEY, THIS IS KAZSULE.
WE HAVE 23: "TOME OF A THOUSAND TALES" AND 52: "PEARL LOCUSTS" TO TRADE.
THANKS, BUT THAT CAN WAIT.
WANT TO MEET UP TO TALK?
ABOUT WHAT?
THERE'S A GROUP THAT'S CLOSE TO CLEARING THE GAME.
!!
IT'S A THREE-MAN TEAM. GENTHRU IS THEIR LEADER. YOU KNOW THEM?
YEAH...
WE'VE CALLED OUT TO OTHERS AND WE'RE GATHERING 2 KM NORTHEAST OF MASADORA.
I THINK IT'LL BE WORTH IT AT LEAST TO EXCHANGE INFORMATION.

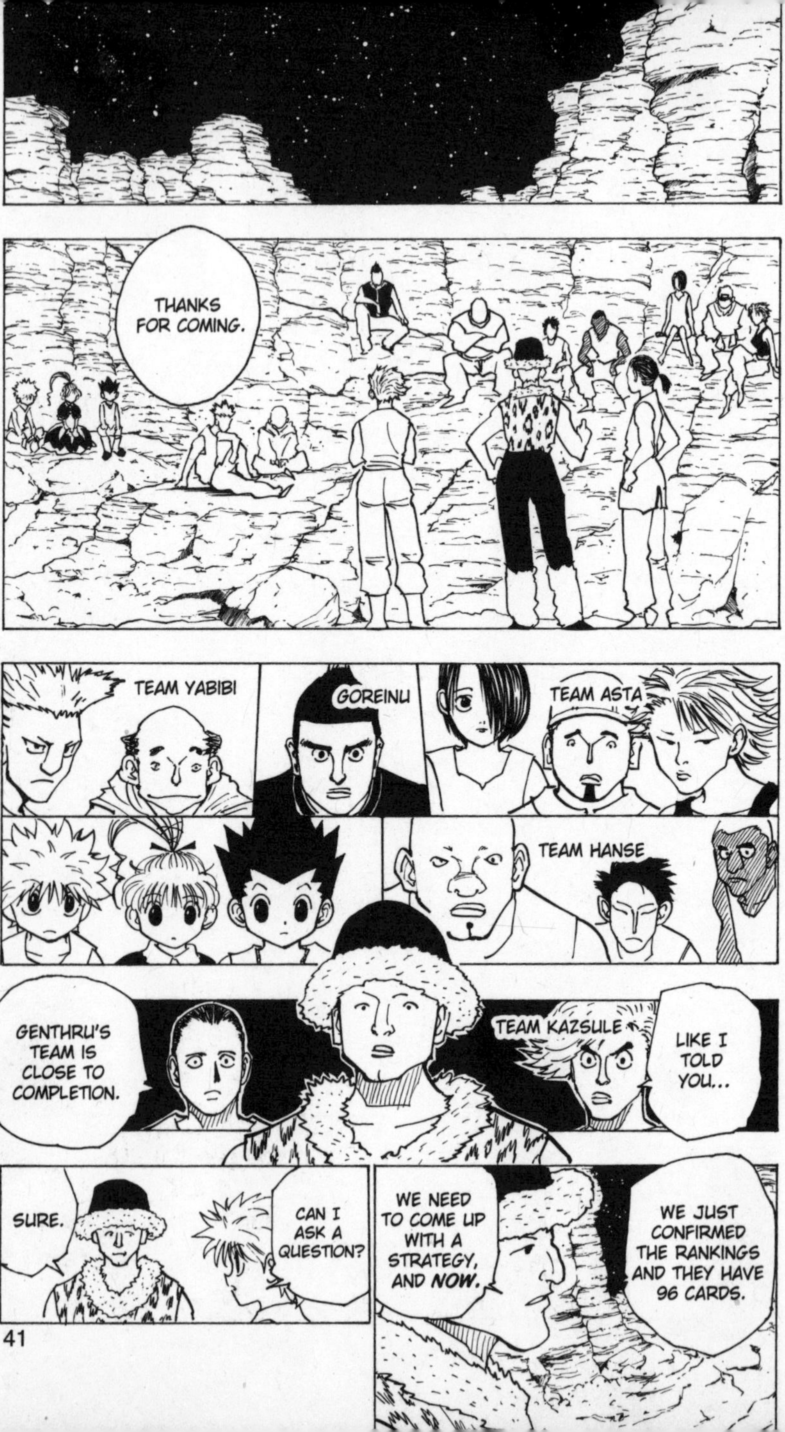
THANKS FOR COMING.
TEAM ASTA
GOREINU
TEAM YABIBI
TEAM HANSE
LIKE I TOLD YOU...
TEAM KAZSULE
GENTHRU'S TEAM IS CLOSE TO COMPLETION.
WE JUST CONFIRMED THE RANKINGS AND THEY HAVE 96 CARDS.
WE NEED TO COME UP WITH A STRATEGY, AND ***NOW***.
CAN I ASK A QUESTION?
SURE.

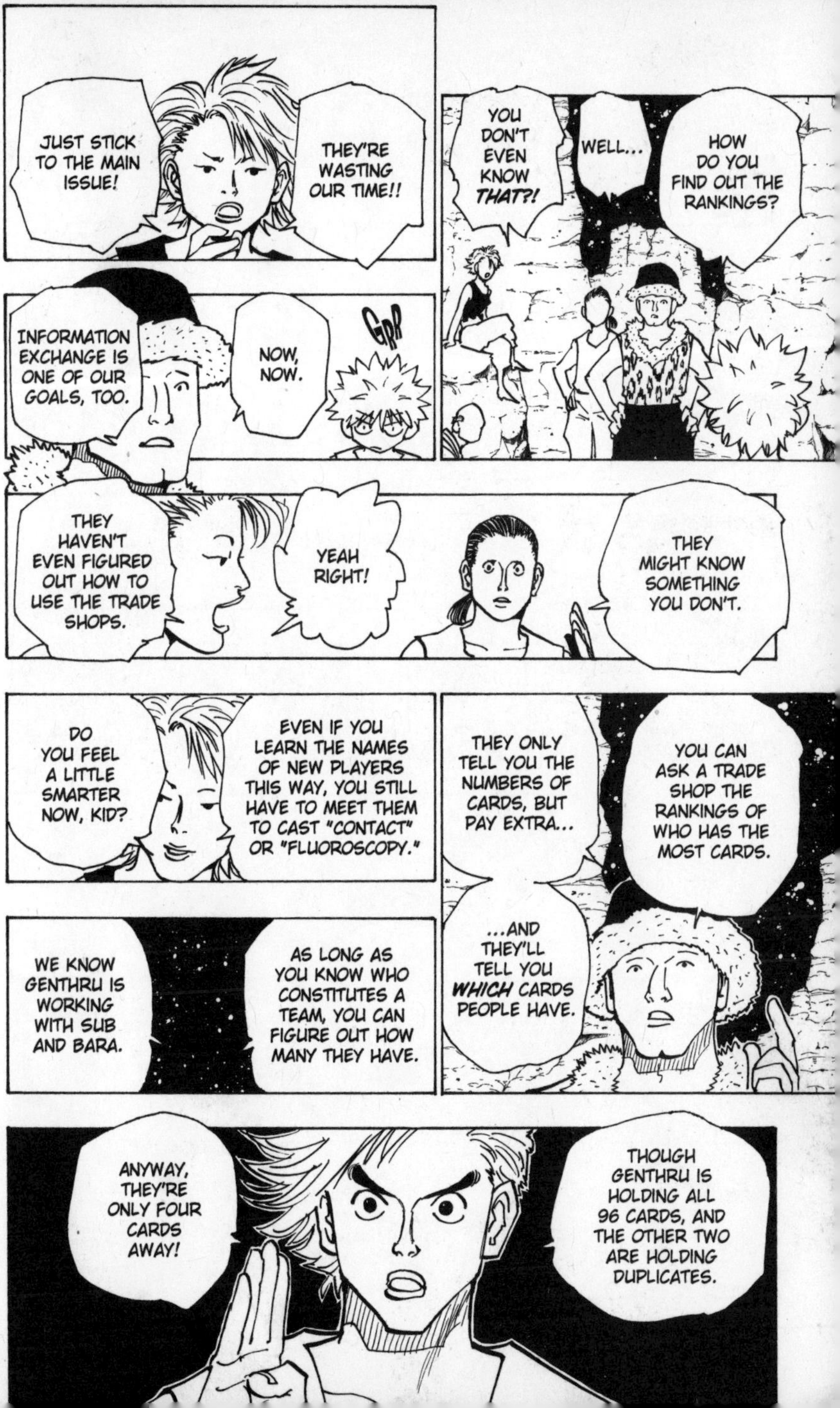
HOW DO YOU FIND OUT THE RANKINGS?
WELL...
YOU DON'T EVEN KNOW *THAT?!*
THEY'RE WASTING OUR TIME!!
JUST STICK TO THE MAIN ISSUE!
GRR
NOW, NOW.
INFORMATION EXCHANGE IS ONE OF OUR GOALS, TOO.
THEY MIGHT KNOW SOMETHING YOU DON'T.
YEAH RIGHT!
THEY HAVEN'T EVEN FIGURED OUT HOW TO USE THE TRADE SHOPS.
YOU CAN ASK A TRADE SHOP THE RANKINGS OF WHO HAS THE MOST CARDS.
THEY ONLY TELL YOU THE NUMBERS OF CARDS, BUT PAY EXTRA...
...AND THEY'LL TELL YOU *WHICH* CARDS PEOPLE HAVE.
EVEN IF YOU LEARN THE NAMES OF NEW PLAYERS THIS WAY, YOU STILL HAVE TO MEET THEM TO CAST "CONTACT" OR "FLUOROSCOPY."
DO YOU FEEL A LITTLE SMARTER NOW, KID?
AS LONG AS YOU KNOW WHO CONSTITUTES A TEAM, YOU CAN FIGURE OUT HOW MANY THEY HAVE.
WE KNOW GENTHRU IS WORKING WITH SUB AND BARA.
THOUGH GENTHRU IS HOLDING ALL 96 CARDS, AND THE OTHER TWO ARE HOLDING DUPLICATES.
ANYWAY, THEY'RE ONLY FOUR CARDS AWAY!

READ THIS WAY

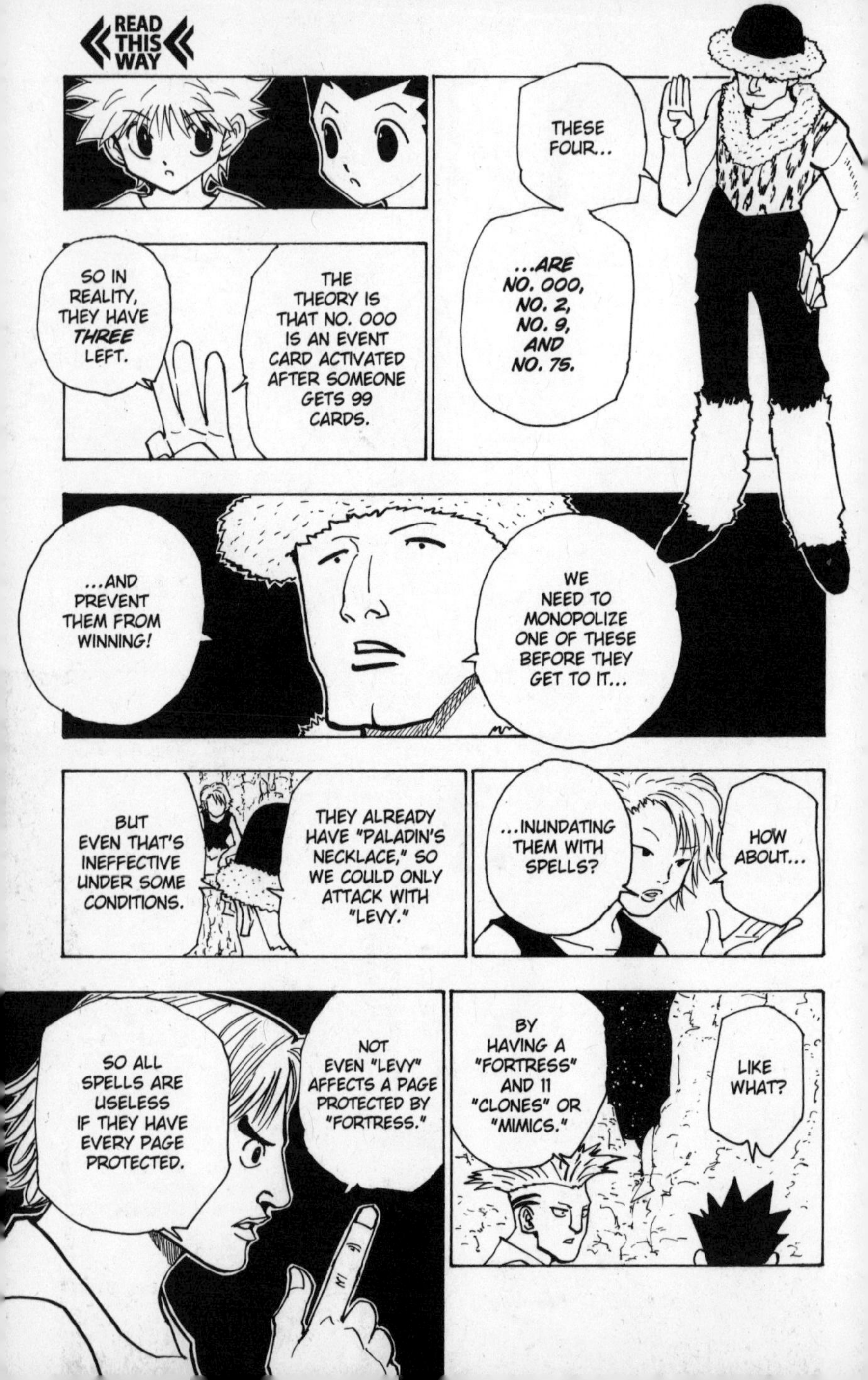
THESE FOUR...
...ARE NO. 000, NO. 2, NO. 9, AND NO. 75.
THE THEORY IS THAT NO. 000 IS AN EVENT CARD ACTIVATED AFTER SOMEONE GETS 99 CARDS.
SO IN REALITY, THEY HAVE *THREE* LEFT.
WE NEED TO MONOPOLIZE ONE OF THESE BEFORE THEY GET TO IT...
...AND PREVENT THEM FROM WINNING!
HOW ABOUT...
...INUNDATING THEM WITH SPELLS?
THEY ALREADY HAVE "PALADIN'S NECKLACE," SO WE COULD ONLY ATTACK WITH "LEVY."
BUT EVEN THAT'S INEFFECTIVE UNDER SOME CONDITIONS.
LIKE WHAT?
BY HAVING A "FORTRESS" AND 11 "CLONES" OR "MIMICS."
NOT EVEN "LEVY" AFFECTS A PAGE PROTECTED BY "FORTRESS."
SO ALL SPELLS ARE USELESS IF THEY HAVE EVERY PAGE PROTECTED.

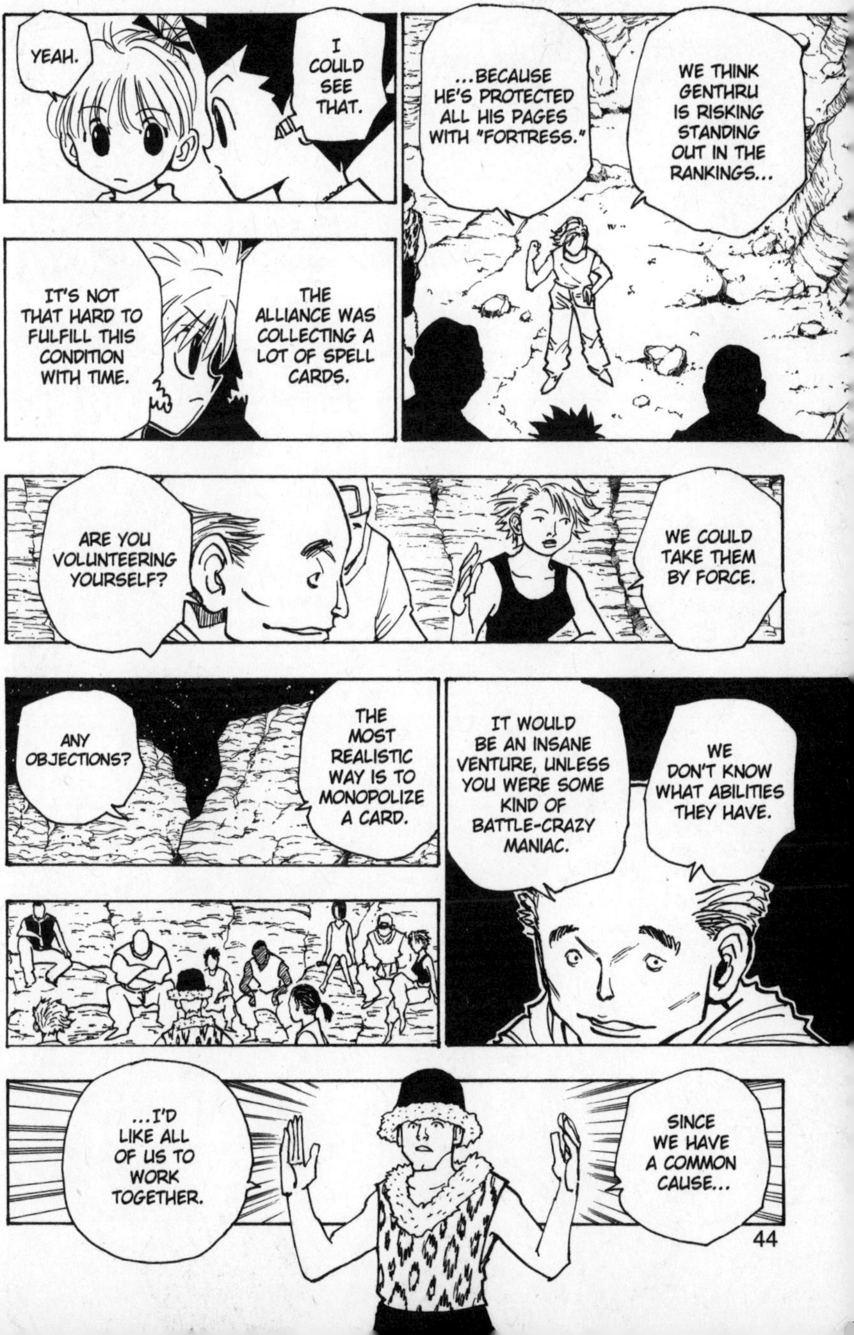
WE THINK GENTHRU IS RISKING STANDING OUT IN THE RANKINGS...
...BECAUSE HE'S PROTECTED ALL HIS PAGES WITH "FORTRESS."
I COULD SEE THAT.
YEAH.
THE ALLIANCE WAS COLLECTING A LOT OF SPELL CARDS.
IT'S NOT THAT HARD TO FULFILL THIS CONDITION WITH TIME.
WE COULD TAKE THEM BY FORCE.
ARE YOU VOLUNTEERING YOURSELF?
WE DON'T KNOW WHAT ABILITIES THEY HAVE.
IT WOULD BE AN INSANE VENTURE, UNLESS YOU WERE SOME KIND OF BATTLE-CRAZY MANIAC.
THE MOST REALISTIC WAY IS TO MONOPOLIZE A CARD.
ANY OBJECTIONS?
SINCE WE HAVE A COMMON CAUSE...
...I'D LIKE ALL OF US TO WORK TOGETHER.

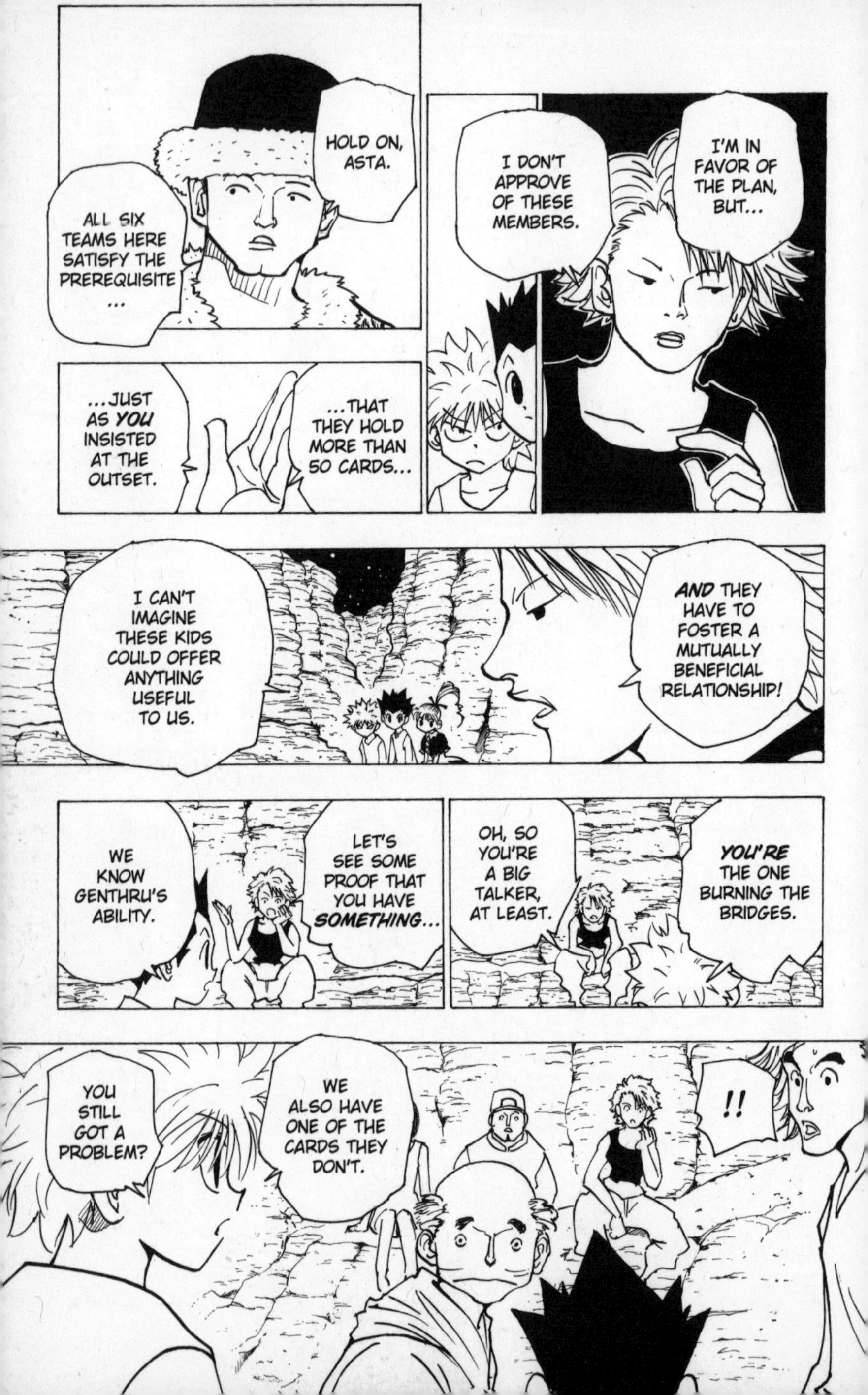
I'M IN FAVOR OF THE PLAN, BUT...
I DON'T APPROVE OF THESE MEMBERS.
HOLD ON, ASTA.
ALL SIX TEAMS HERE SATISFY THE PREREQUISITE ...
...THAT THEY HOLD MORE THAN 50 CARDS...
...JUST AS *YOU* INSISTED AT THE OUTSET.
AND THEY HAVE TO FOSTER A MUTUALLY BENEFICIAL RELATIONSHIP!
I CAN'T IMAGINE THESE KIDS COULD OFFER ANYTHING USEFUL TO US.
YOU'RE THE ONE BURNING THE BRIDGES.
OH, SO YOU'RE A BIG TALKER, AT LEAST.
LET'S SEE SOME PROOF THAT YOU HAVE *SOMETHING*...
WE KNOW GENTHRU'S ABILITY.
!!
WE ALSO HAVE ONE OF THE CARDS THEY DON'T.
YOU STILL GOT A PROBLEM?

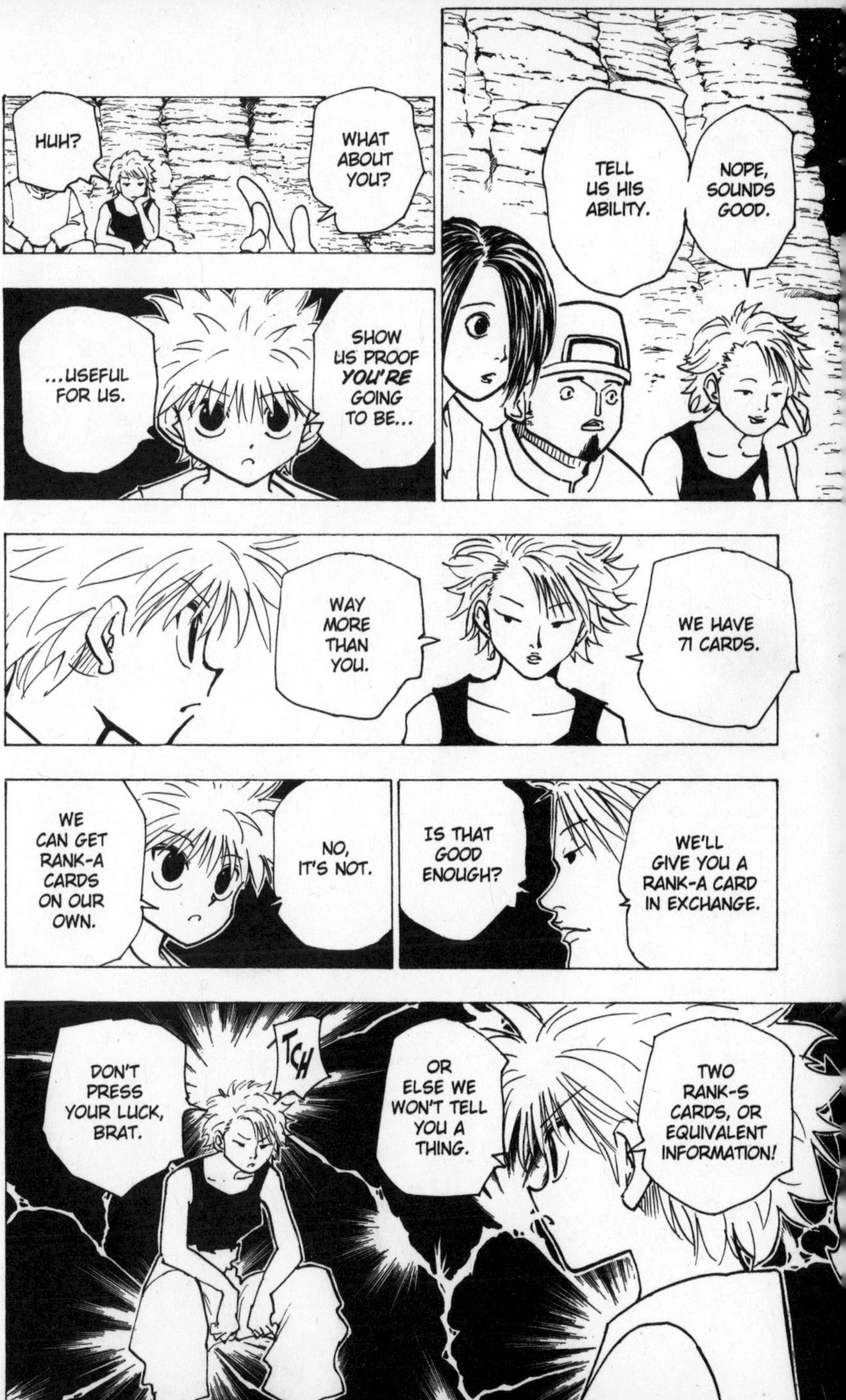
NOPE, SOUNDS GOOD.
TELL US HIS ABILITY.
WHAT ABOUT YOU?
HUH?
SHOW US PROOF ***YOU'RE*** GOING TO BE...
...USEFUL FOR US.
WE HAVE 71 CARDS.
WAY MORE THAN YOU.
WE'LL GIVE YOU A RANK-A CARD IN EXCHANGE.
IS THAT GOOD ENOUGH?
NO, IT'S NOT.
WE CAN GET RANK-A CARDS ON OUR OWN.
TWO RANK-S CARDS, OR EQUIVALENT INFORMATION!
OR ELSE WE WON'T TELL YOU A THING.
TCH
DON'T PRESS YOUR LUCK, BRAT.

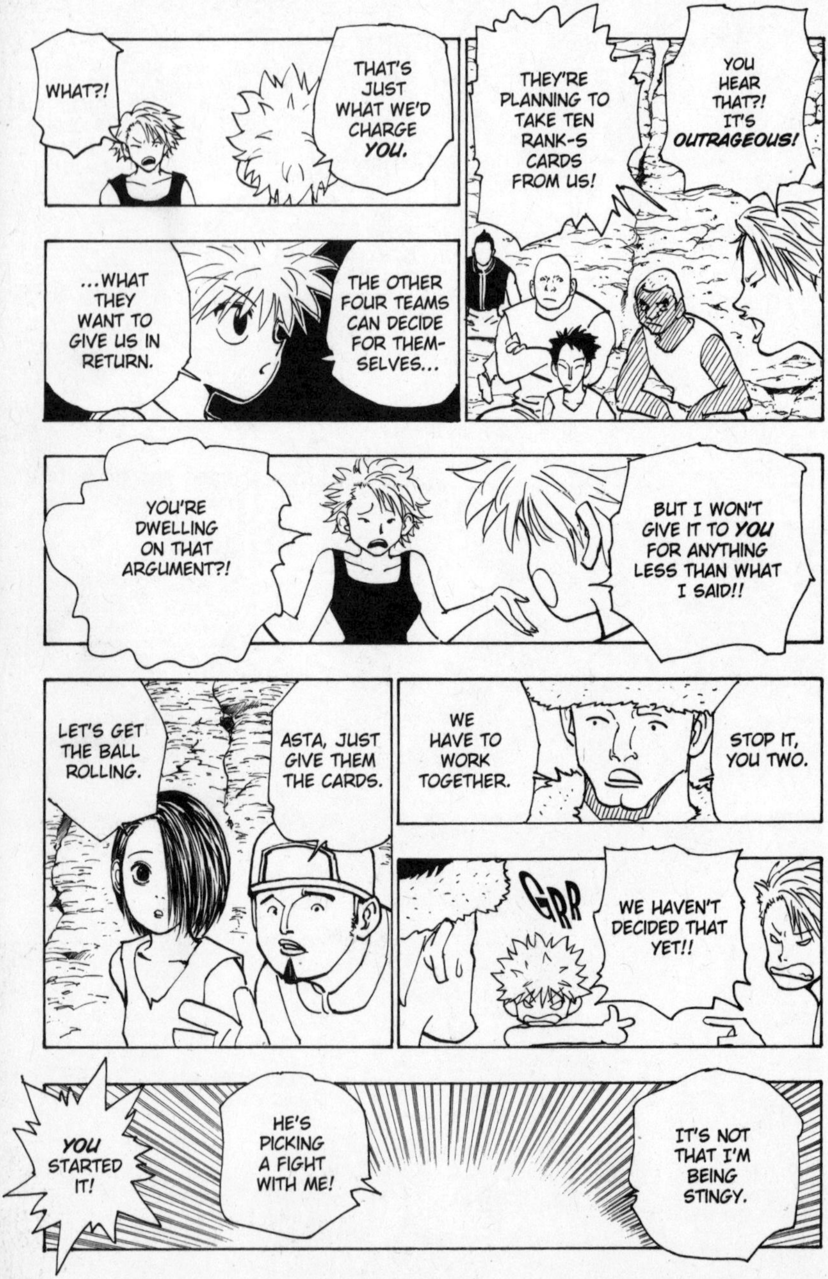
YOU HEAR THAT?! IT'S OUTRAGEOUS!
THEY'RE PLANNING TO TAKE TEN RANK-S CARDS FROM US!
THAT'S JUST WHAT WE'D CHARGE YOU.
WHAT?!
THE OTHER FOUR TEAMS CAN DECIDE FOR THEM-SELVES...
...WHAT THEY WANT TO GIVE US IN RETURN.
BUT I WON'T GIVE IT TO YOU FOR ANYTHING LESS THAN WHAT I SAID!!
YOU'RE DWELLING ON THAT ARGUMENT?!
STOP IT, YOU TWO.
WE HAVE TO WORK TOGETHER.
WE HAVEN'T DECIDED THAT YET!!
GRR
ASTA, JUST GIVE THEM THE CARDS.
LET'S GET THE BALL ROLLING.
IT'S NOT THAT I'M BEING STINGY.
HE'S PICKING A FIGHT WITH ME!
YOU STARTED IT!

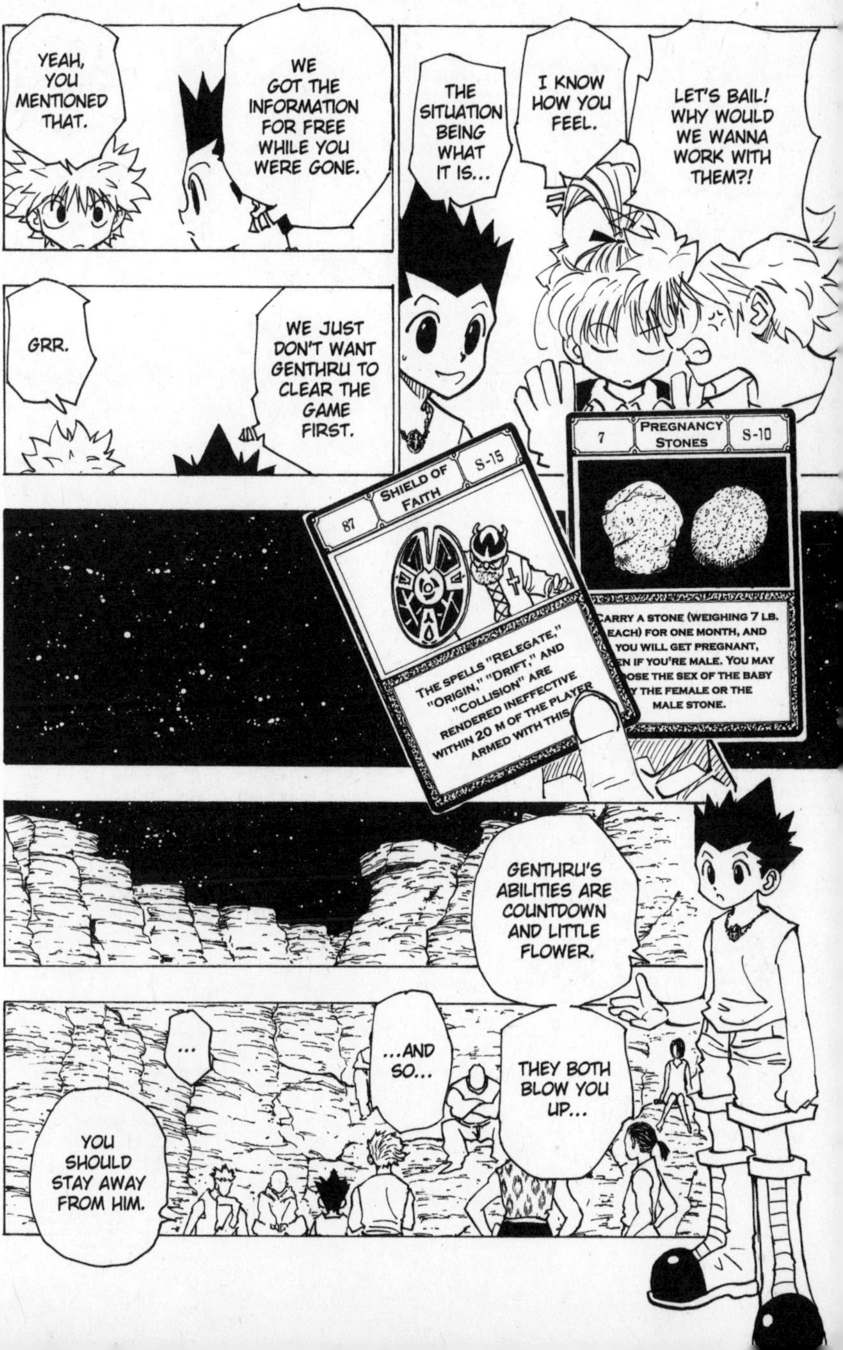
LET'S BAIL! WHY WOULD WE WANNA WORK WITH THEM?!
I KNOW HOW YOU FEEL.
THE SITUATION BEING WHAT IT IS...
WE GOT THE INFORMATION FOR FREE WHILE YOU WERE GONE.
YEAH, YOU MENTIONED THAT.
WE JUST DON'T WANT GENTHRU TO CLEAR THE GAME FIRST.
GRR.
7
PREGNANCY STONES
S-10
CARRY A STONE (WEIGHING 7 LB. EACH) FOR ONE MONTH, AND YOU WILL GET PREGNANT, EN IF YOU'RE MALE. YOU MAY OOSE THE SEX OF THE BABY Y THE FEMALE OR THE MALE STONE.
87
SHIELD OF FAITH
S-15
THE SPELLS "RELEGATE," "ORIGIN," "DRIFT," AND "COLLISION" ARE RENDERED INEFFECTIVE WITHIN 20 M OF THE PLAYER ARMED WITH THIS
GENTHRU'S ABILITIES ARE COUNTDOWN AND LITTLE FLOWER.
THEY BOTH BLOW YOU UP...
...AND SO...
...
YOU SHOULD STAY AWAY FROM HIM.

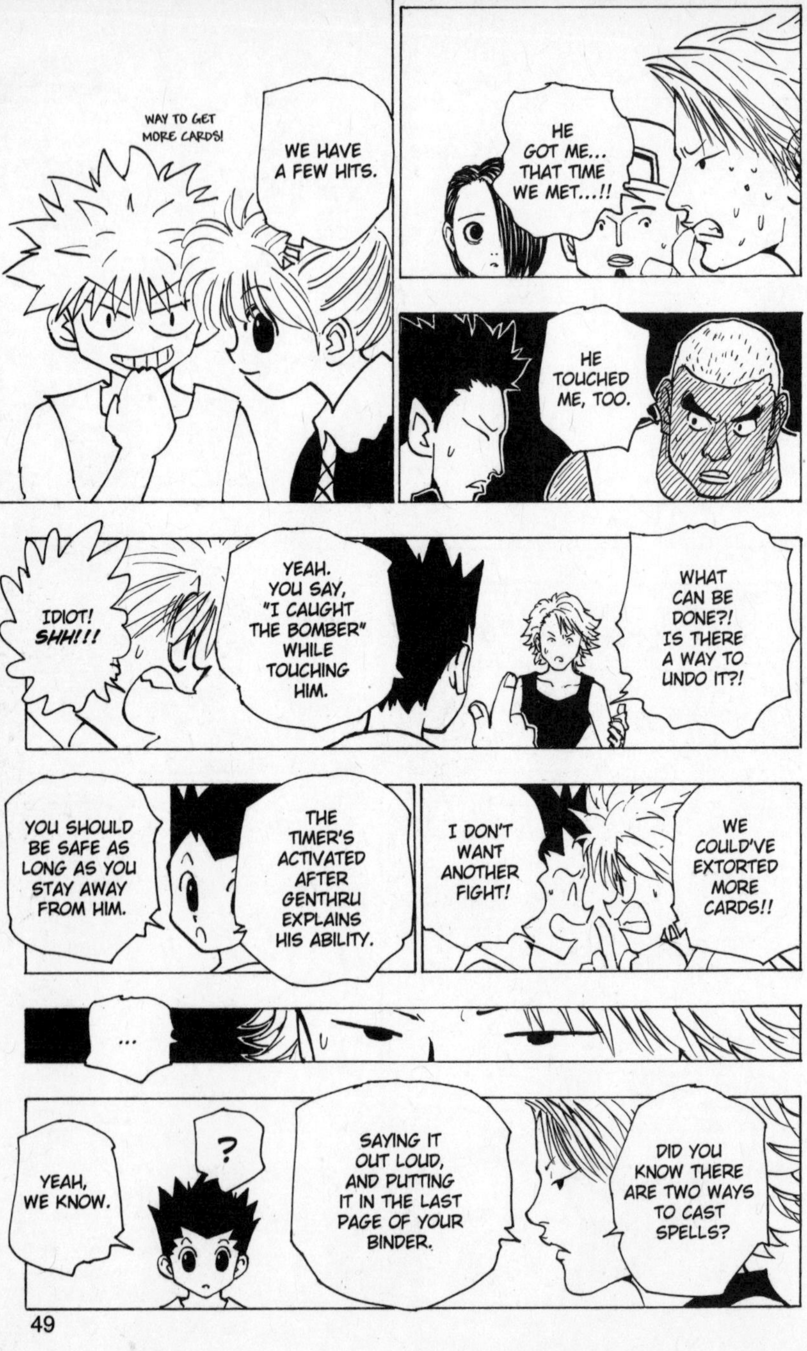
HE GOT ME... THAT TIME WE MET...!!
HE TOUCHED ME, TOO.
WE HAVE A FEW HITS.
WAY TO GET MORE CARDS!
WHAT CAN BE DONE?! IS THERE A WAY TO UNDO IT?!
YEAH. YOU SAY, "I CAUGHT THE BOMBER" WHILE TOUCHING HIM.
IDIOT! **SHH!!!**
WE COULD'VE EXTORTED MORE CARDS!!
I DON'T WANT ANOTHER FIGHT!
THE TIMER'S ACTIVATED AFTER GENTHRU EXPLAINS HIS ABILITY.
YOU SHOULD BE SAFE AS LONG AS YOU STAY AWAY FROM HIM.
...
DID YOU KNOW THERE ARE TWO WAYS TO CAST SPELLS?
SAYING IT OUT LOUD, AND PUTTING IT IN THE LAST PAGE OF YOUR BINDER.
?
YEAH, WE KNOW.

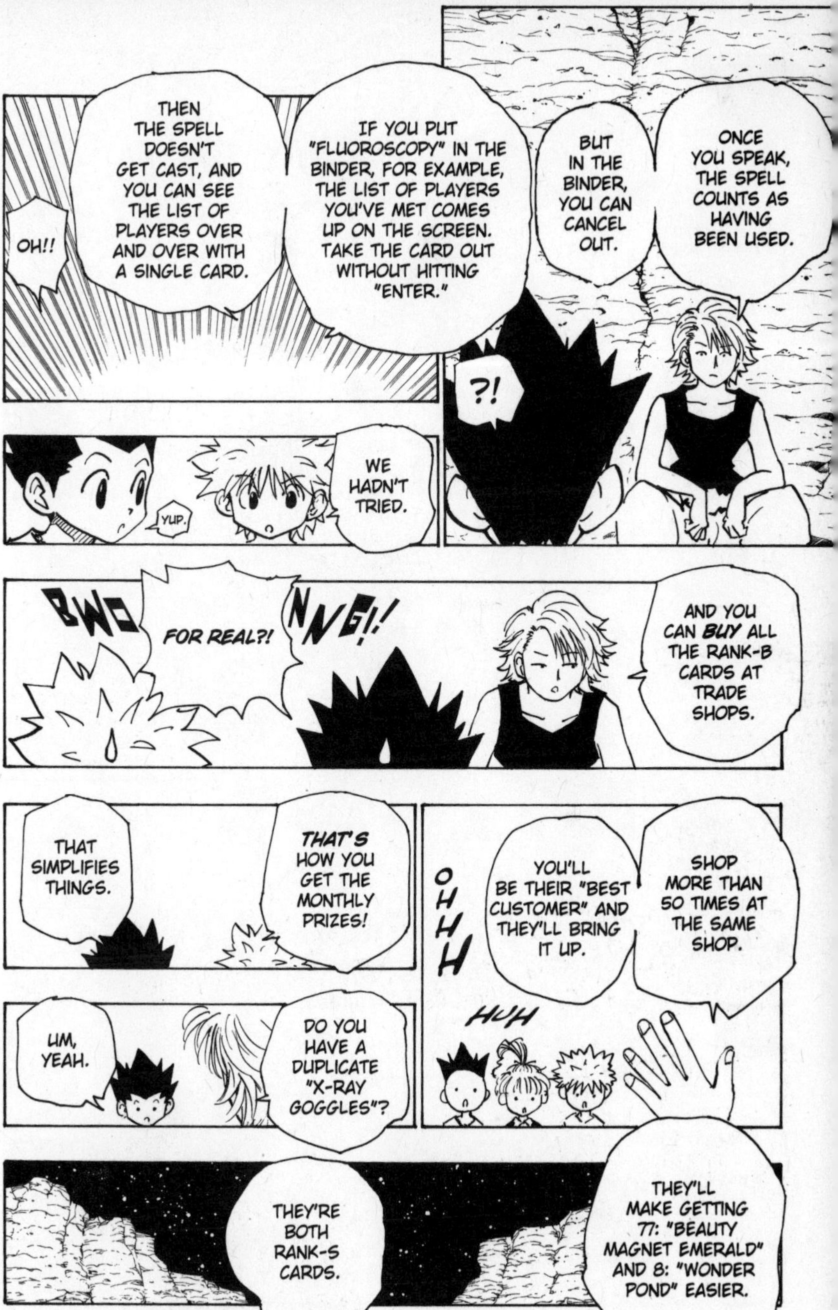
ONCE YOU SPEAK, THE SPELL COUNTS AS HAVING BEEN USED.
BUT IN THE BINDER, YOU CAN CANCEL OUT.
?!
IF YOU PUT "FLUOROSCOPY" IN THE BINDER, FOR EXAMPLE, THE LIST OF PLAYERS YOU'VE MET COMES UP ON THE SCREEN. TAKE THE CARD OUT WITHOUT HITTING "ENTER."
THEN THE SPELL DOESN'T GET CAST, AND YOU CAN SEE THE LIST OF PLAYERS OVER AND OVER WITH A SINGLE CARD.
OH!!
WE HADN'T TRIED.
YUP.
AND YOU CAN ***BUY*** ALL THE RANK-B CARDS AT TRADE SHOPS.
BWONNG!!
FOR REAL?!
SHOP MORE THAN 50 TIMES AT THE SAME SHOP.
YOU'LL BE THEIR "BEST CUSTOMER" AND THEY'LL BRING IT UP.
OHHH
HUH
THAT'S HOW YOU GET THE MONTHLY PRIZES!
THAT SIMPLIFIES THINGS.
DO YOU HAVE A DUPLICATE "X-RAY GOGGLES"?
UM, YEAH.
THEY'LL MAKE GETTING 77: "BEAUTY MAGNET EMERALD" AND 8: "WONDER POND" EASIER.
THEY'RE BOTH RANK-S CARDS.

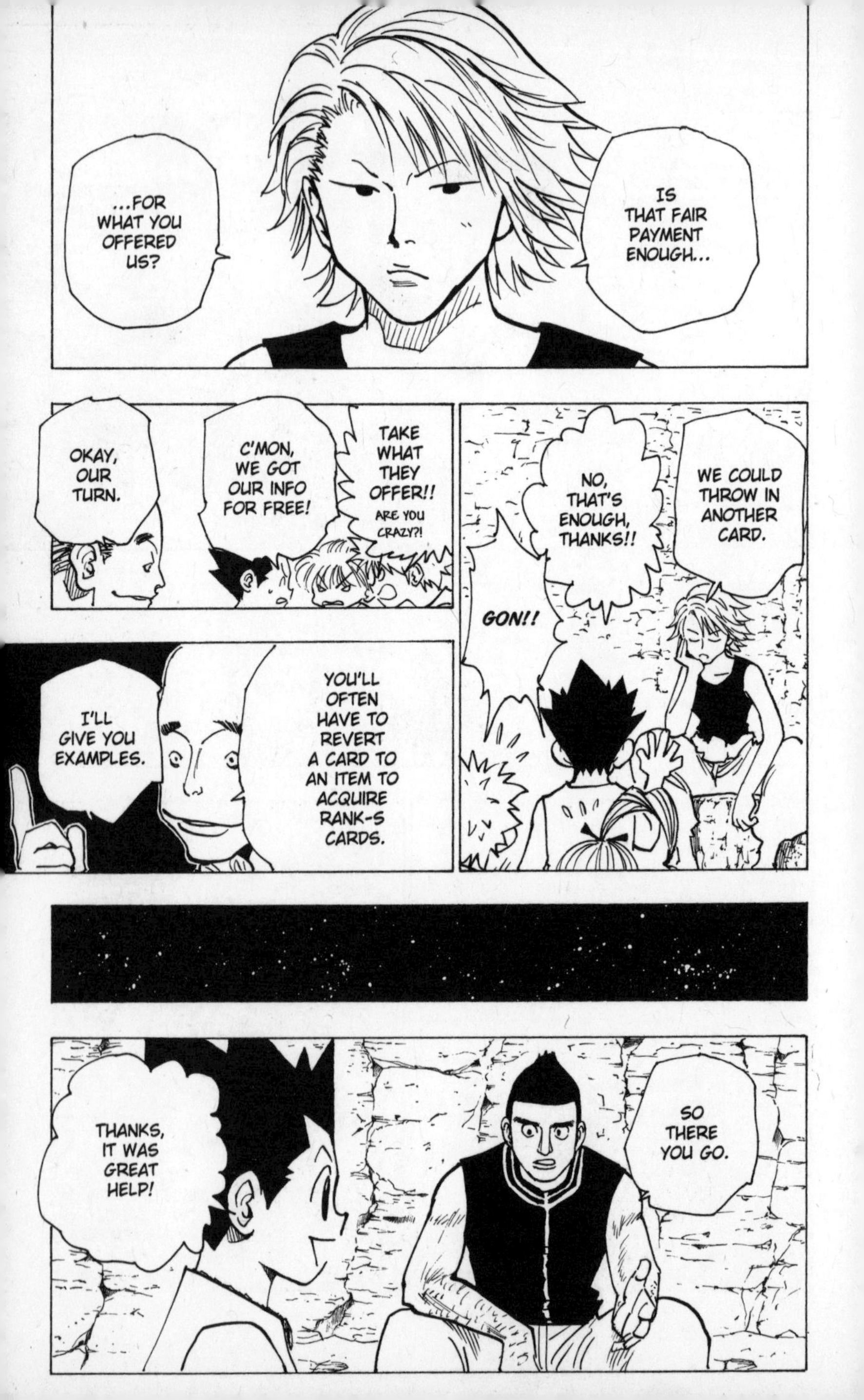
IS THAT FAIR PAYMENT ENOUGH...
...FOR WHAT YOU OFFERED US?
WE COULD THROW IN ANOTHER CARD.
NO, THAT'S ENOUGH, THANKS!!
GON!!
TAKE WHAT THEY OFFER!!
ARE YOU CRAZY?!
C'MON, WE GOT OUR INFO FOR FREE!
OKAY, OUR TURN.
YOU'LL OFTEN HAVE TO REVERT A CARD TO AN ITEM TO ACQUIRE RANK-S CARDS.
I'LL GIVE YOU EXAMPLES.
SO THERE YOU GO.
THANKS, IT WAS GREAT HELP!

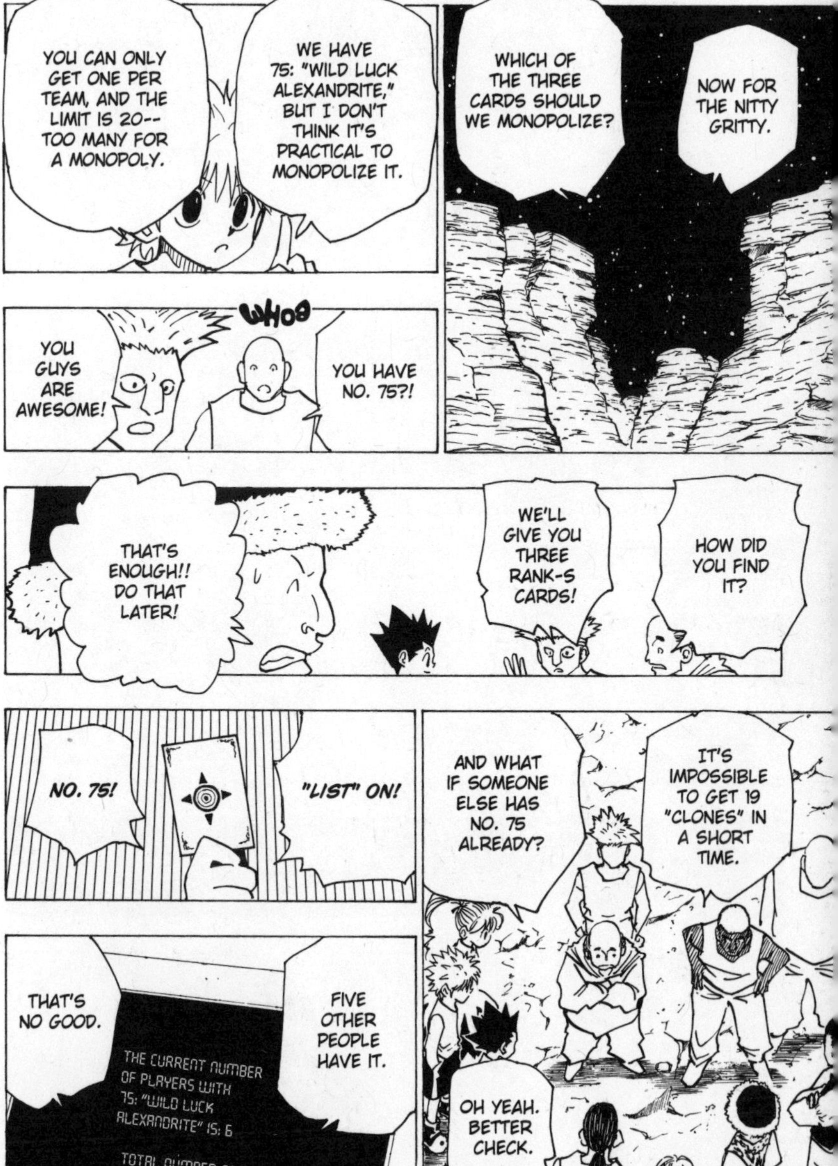
NOW FOR THE NITTY GRITTY.
WHICH OF THE THREE CARDS SHOULD WE MONOPOLIZE?
WE HAVE 75: "WILD LUCK ALEXANDRITE," BUT I DON'T THINK IT'S PRACTICAL TO MONOPOLIZE IT.
YOU CAN ONLY GET ONE PER TEAM, AND THE LIMIT IS 20-- TOO MANY FOR A MONOPOLY.
YOU HAVE NO. 75?!
WHOA
YOU GUYS ARE AWESOME!
HOW DID YOU FIND IT?
WE'LL GIVE YOU THREE RANK-S CARDS!
THAT'S ENOUGH!! DO THAT LATER!
IT'S IMPOSSIBLE TO GET 19 "CLONES" IN A SHORT TIME.
AND WHAT IF SOMEONE ELSE HAS NO. 75 ALREADY?
OH YEAH. BETTER CHECK.
"LIST" ON!
NO. 75!
FIVE OTHER PEOPLE HAVE IT.
THE CURRENT NUMBER OF PLAYERS WITH 75: "WILD LUCK ALEXANDRITE" IS: 6
TOTAL NUMBER OF CARDS: 6
THAT'S NO GOOD.

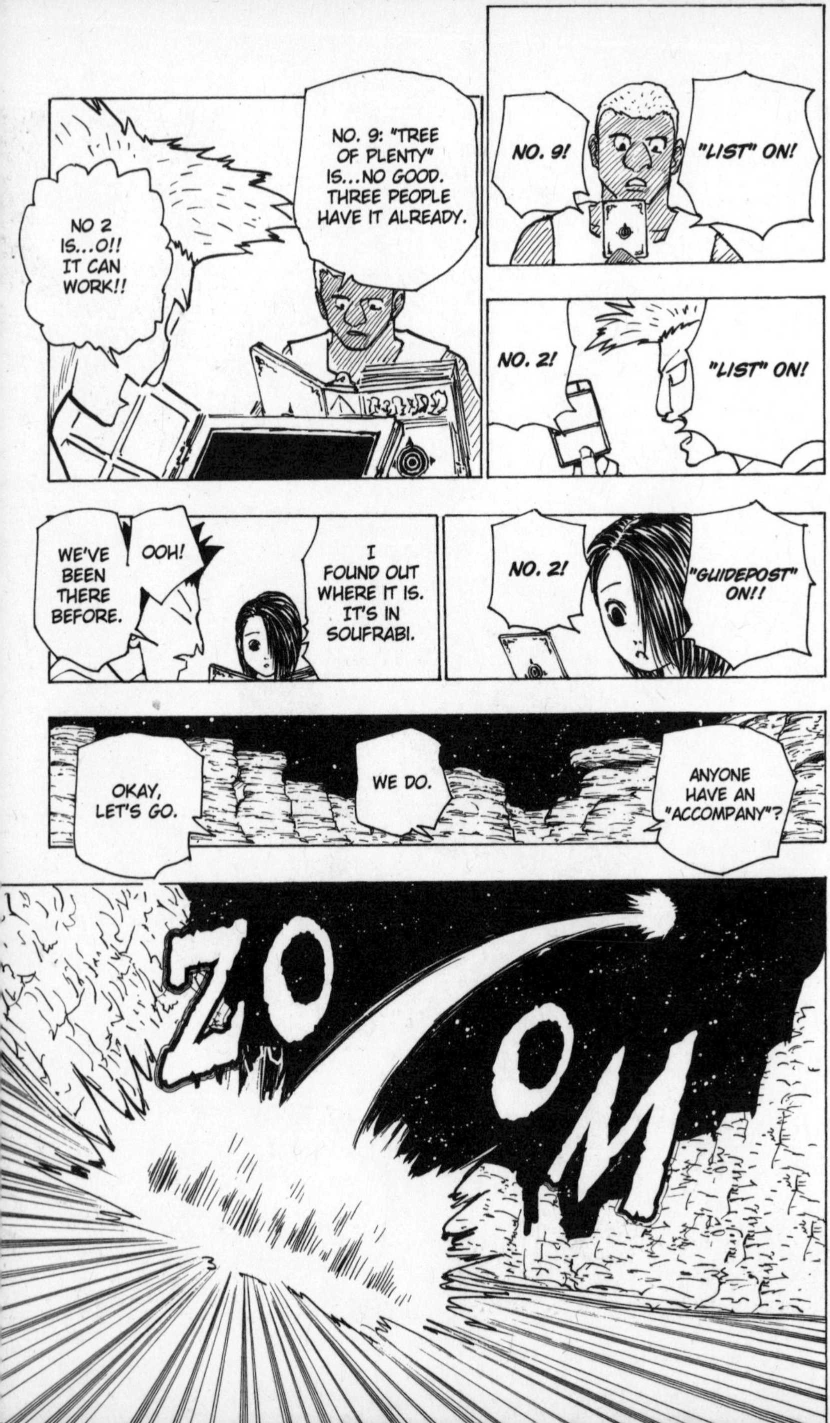

"LIST" ON!
NO. 9!
NO. 9: "TREE OF PLENTY" IS...NO GOOD. THREE PEOPLE HAVE IT ALREADY.
NO 2 IS...0!! IT CAN WORK!!
"LIST" ON!
NO. 2!
"GUIDEPOST" ON!!
NO. 2!
I FOUND OUT WHERE IT IS. IT'S IN SOUFRABI.
OOH!
WE'VE BEEN THERE BEFORE.
ANYONE HAVE AN "ACCOMPANY"?
WE DO.
OKAY, LET'S GO.
ZOOM

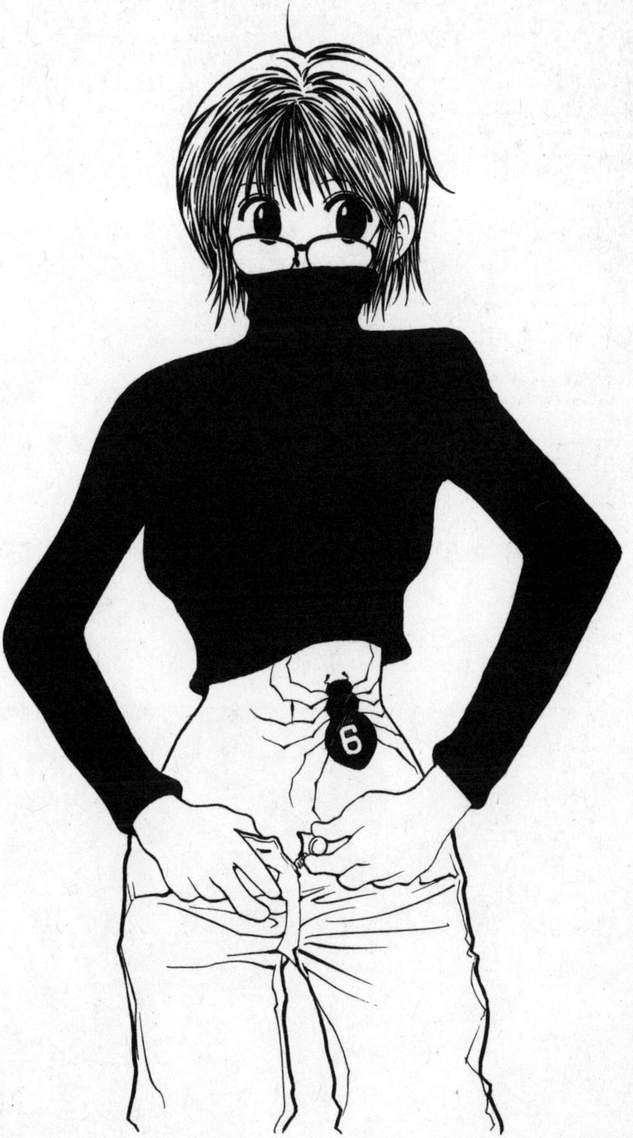
6

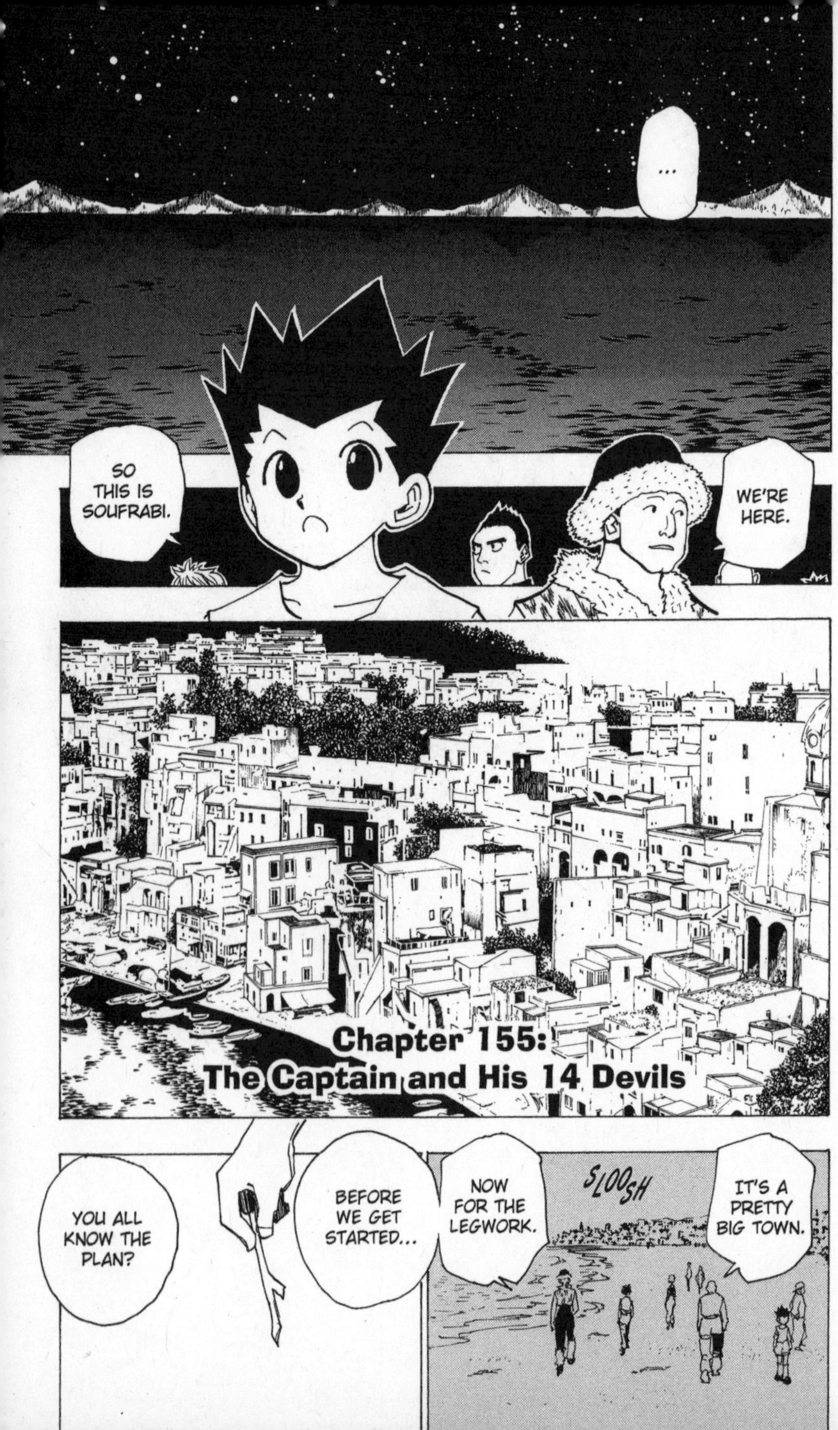
...
WE'RE HERE.
SO THIS IS SOUFRABI.
Chapter 155:
The Captain and His 14 Devils
IT'S A PRETTY BIG TOWN.
SLOOSH
NOW FOR THE LEGWORK.
BEFORE WE GET STARTED...
YOU ALL KNOW THE PLAN?

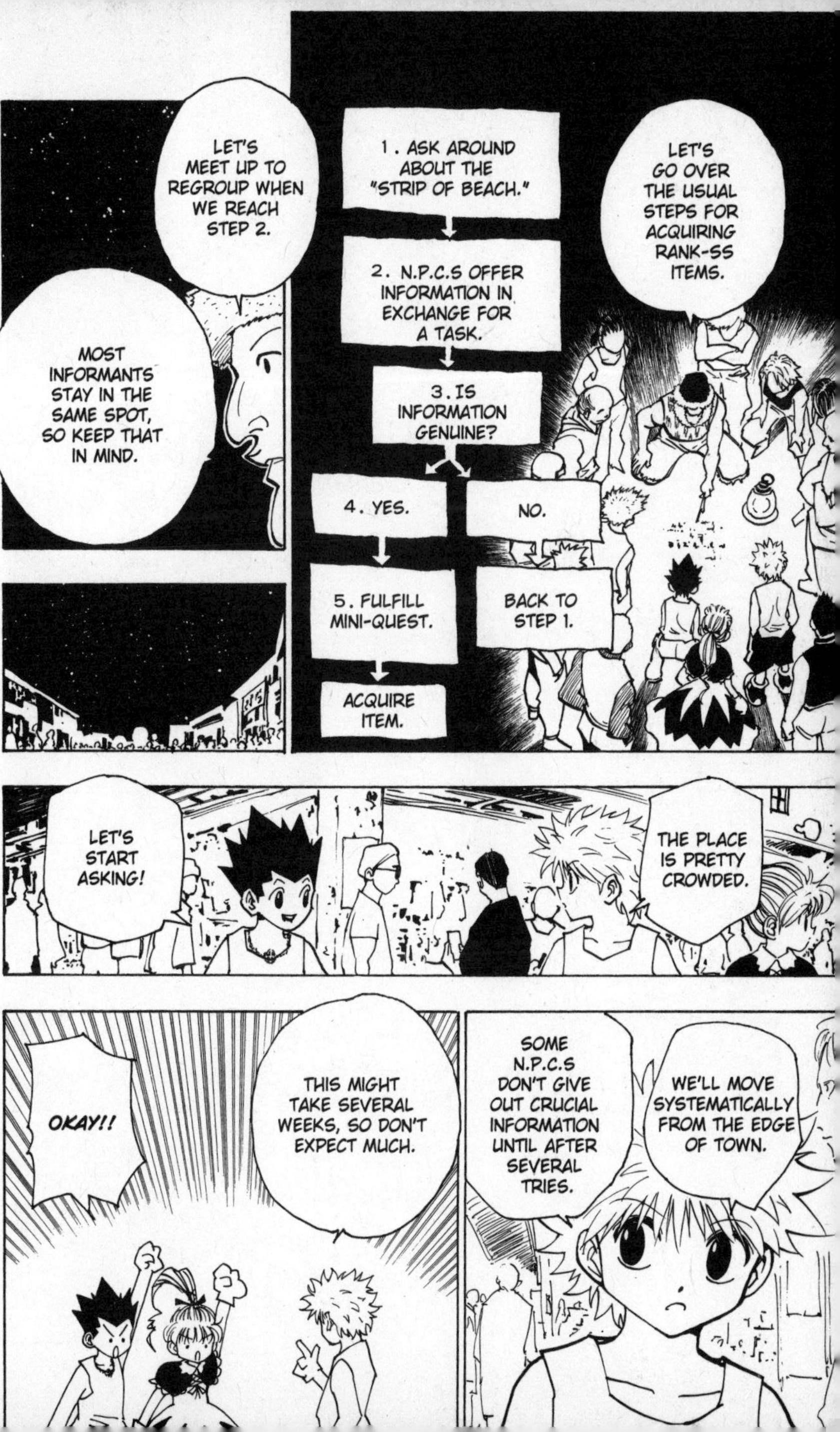
LET'S GO OVER THE USUAL STEPS FOR ACQUIRING RANK-SS ITEMS.
1. ASK AROUND ABOUT THE "STRIP OF BEACH."
2. N.P.C.S OFFER INFORMATION IN EXCHANGE FOR A TASK.
3. IS INFORMATION GENUINE?
4. YES.
NO.
5. FULFILL MINI-QUEST.
BACK TO STEP 1.
ACQUIRE ITEM.
LET'S MEET UP TO REGROUP WHEN WE REACH STEP 2.
MOST INFORMANTS STAY IN THE SAME SPOT, SO KEEP THAT IN MIND.
THE PLACE IS PRETTY CROWDED.
LET'S START ASKING!
WE'LL MOVE SYSTEMATICALLY FROM THE EDGE OF TOWN.
SOME N.P.C.S DON'T GIVE OUT CRUCIAL INFORMATION UNTIL AFTER SEVERAL TRIES.
THIS MIGHT TAKE SEVERAL WEEKS, SO DON'T EXPECT MUCH.
OKAY!!

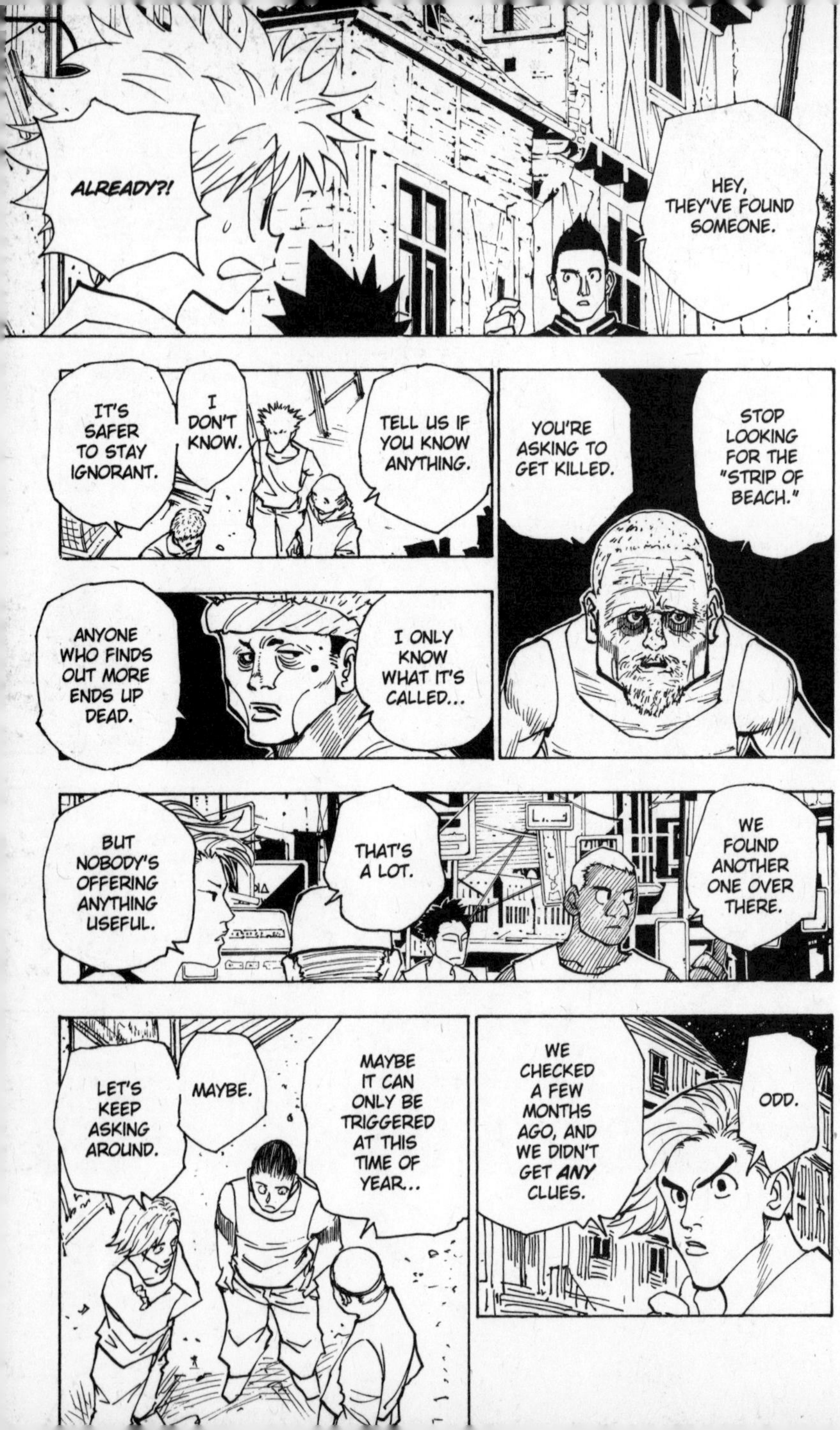

HEY, THEY'VE FOUND SOMEONE.
ALREADY?!
STOP LOOKING FOR THE "STRIP OF BEACH."
YOU'RE ASKING TO GET KILLED.
TELL US IF YOU KNOW ANYTHING.
I DON'T KNOW.
IT'S SAFER TO STAY IGNORANT.
I ONLY KNOW WHAT IT'S CALLED...
ANYONE WHO FINDS OUT MORE ENDS UP DEAD.
WE FOUND ANOTHER ONE OVER THERE.
THAT'S A LOT.
BUT NOBODY'S OFFERING ANYTHING USEFUL.
ODD.
WE CHECKED A FEW MONTHS AGO, AND WE DIDN'T GET *ANY* CLUES.
MAYBE IT CAN ONLY BE TRIGGERED AT THIS TIME OF YEAR...
MAYBE.
LET'S KEEP ASKING AROUND.

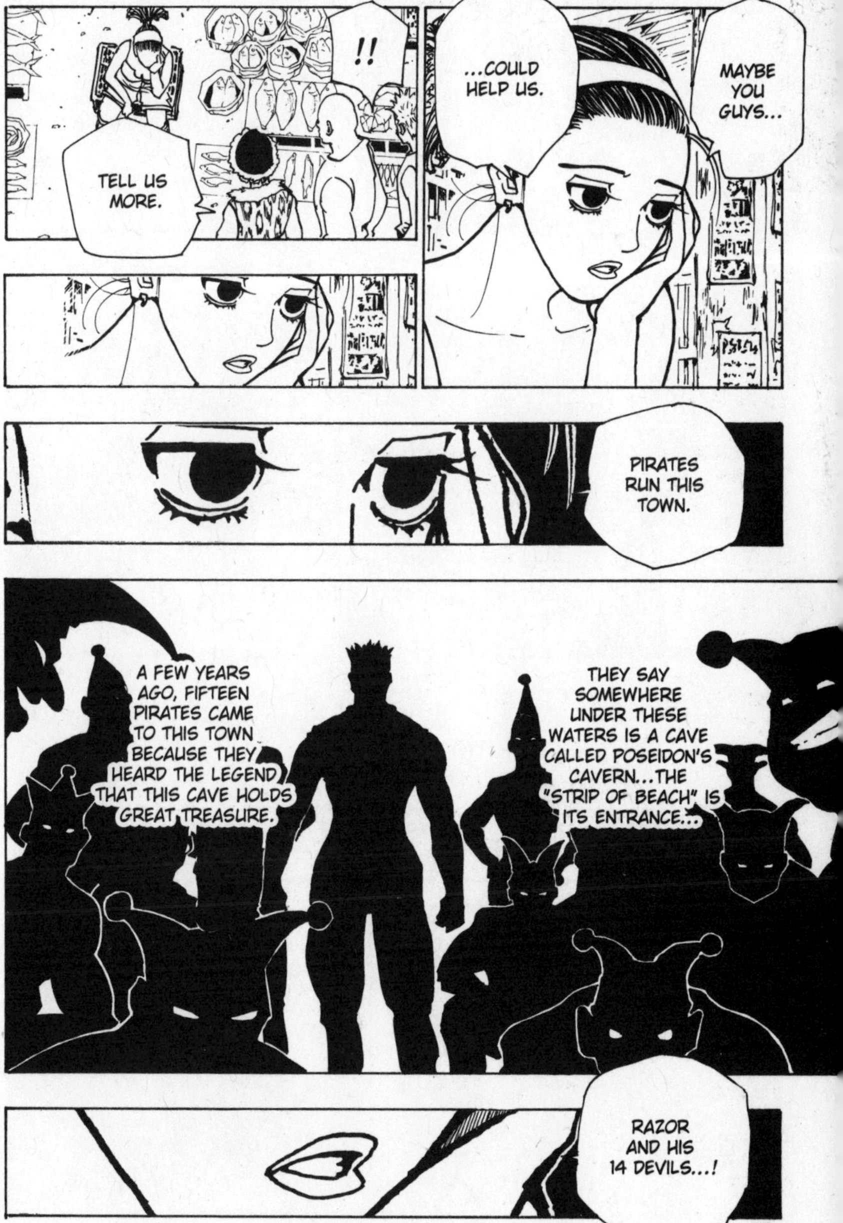
MAYBE YOU GUYS...
...COULD HELP US.
!!
TELL US MORE.
PIRATES RUN THIS TOWN.
THEY SAY SOMEWHERE UNDER THESE WATERS IS A CAVE CALLED POSEIDON'S CAVERN...THE "STRIP OF BEACH" IS ITS ENTRANCE...
A FEW YEARS AGO, FIFTEEN PIRATES CAME TO THIS TOWN BECAUSE THEY HEARD THE LEGEND THAT THIS CAVE HOLDS GREAT TREASURE.
RAZOR AND HIS 14 DEVILS...!

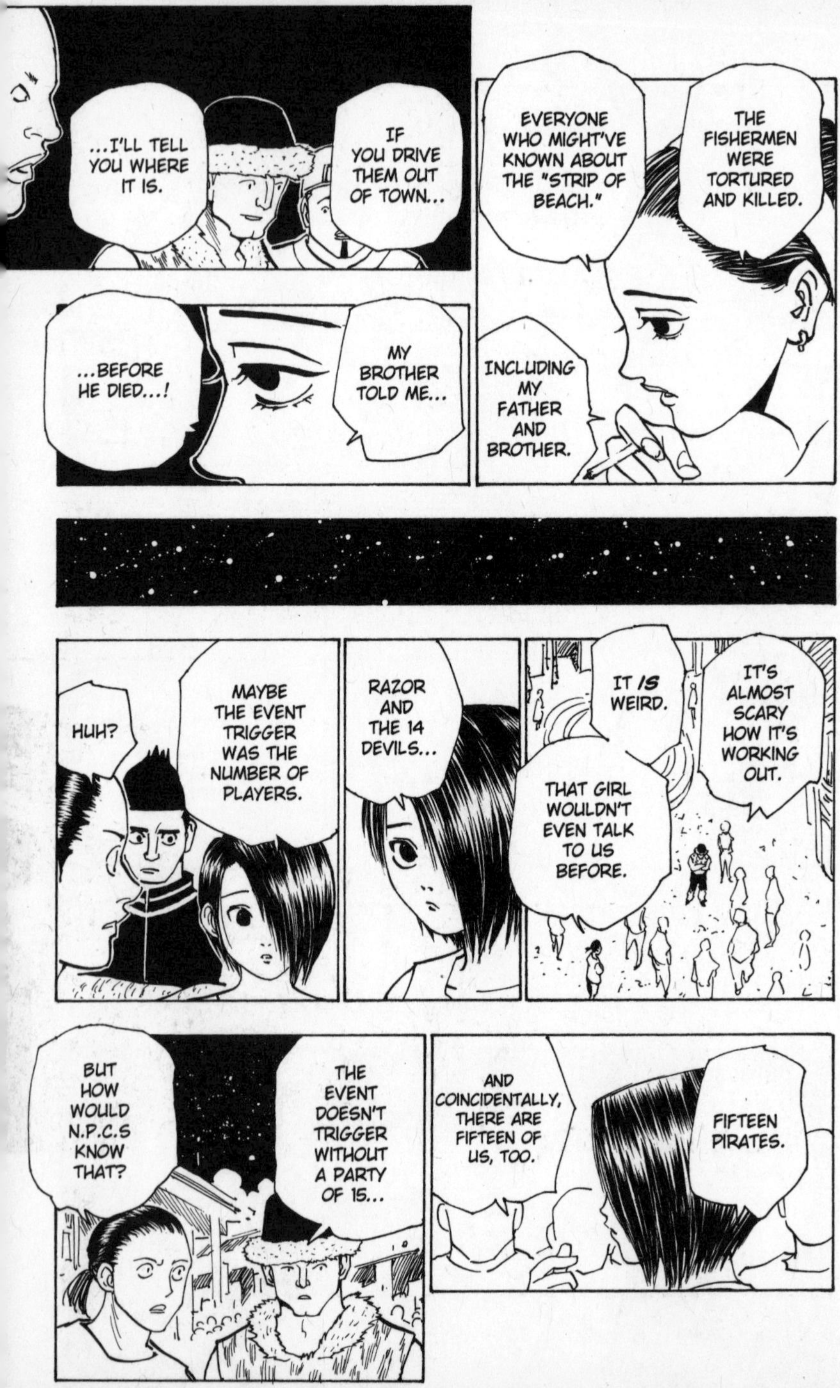
THE FISHERMEN WERE TORTURED AND KILLED.
EVERYONE WHO MIGHT'VE KNOWN ABOUT THE "STRIP OF BEACH."
INCLUDING MY FATHER AND BROTHER.
IF YOU DRIVE THEM OUT OF TOWN...
...I'LL TELL YOU WHERE IT IS.
MY BROTHER TOLD ME...
...BEFORE HE DIED...!
IT'S ALMOST SCARY HOW IT'S WORKING OUT.
IT *IS* WEIRD.
THAT GIRL WOULDN'T EVEN TALK TO US BEFORE.
RAZOR AND THE 14 DEVILS...
MAYBE THE EVENT TRIGGER WAS THE NUMBER OF PLAYERS.
HUH?
FIFTEEN PIRATES.
AND COINCIDENTALLY, THERE ARE FIFTEEN OF US, TOO.
THE EVENT DOESN'T TRIGGER WITHOUT A PARTY OF 15...
BUT HOW WOULD N.P.C.S KNOW THAT?

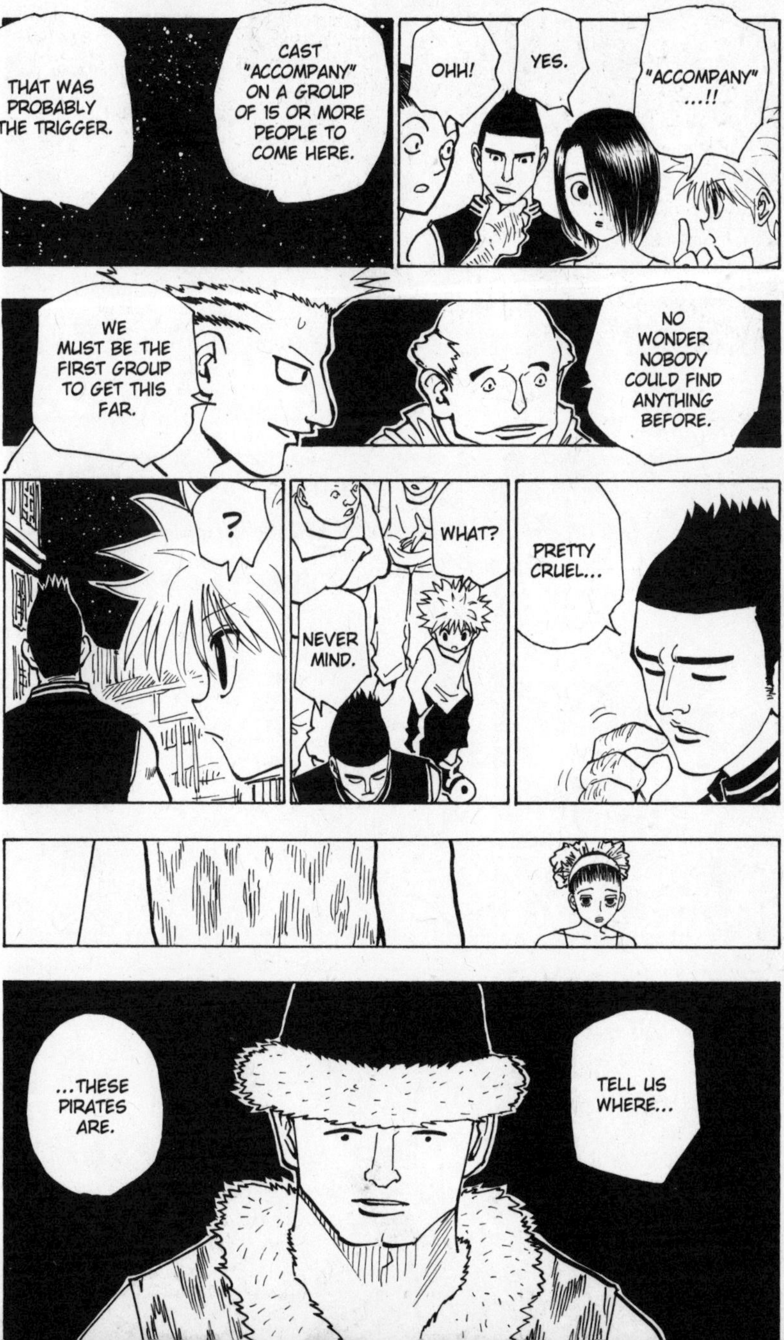
"ACCOMPANY" ...!!
YES.
OHH!
CAST "ACCOMPANY" ON A GROUP OF 15 OR MORE PEOPLE TO COME HERE.
THAT WAS PROBABLY THE TRIGGER.
NO WONDER NOBODY COULD FIND ANYTHING BEFORE.
WE MUST BE THE FIRST GROUP TO GET THIS FAR.
PRETTY CRUEL...
WHAT?
NEVER MIND.
?
TELL US WHERE...
...THESE PIRATES ARE.

READ THIS WAY

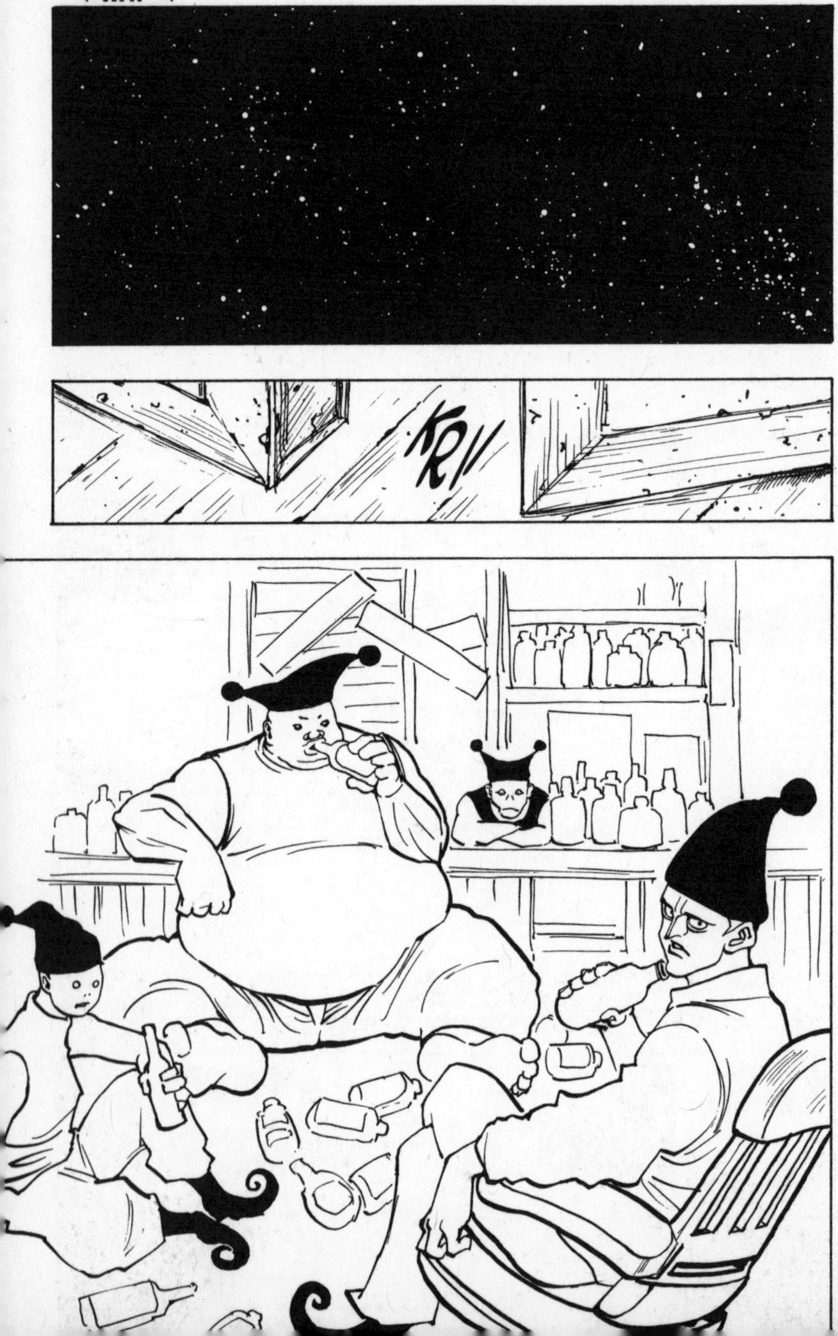
KRII

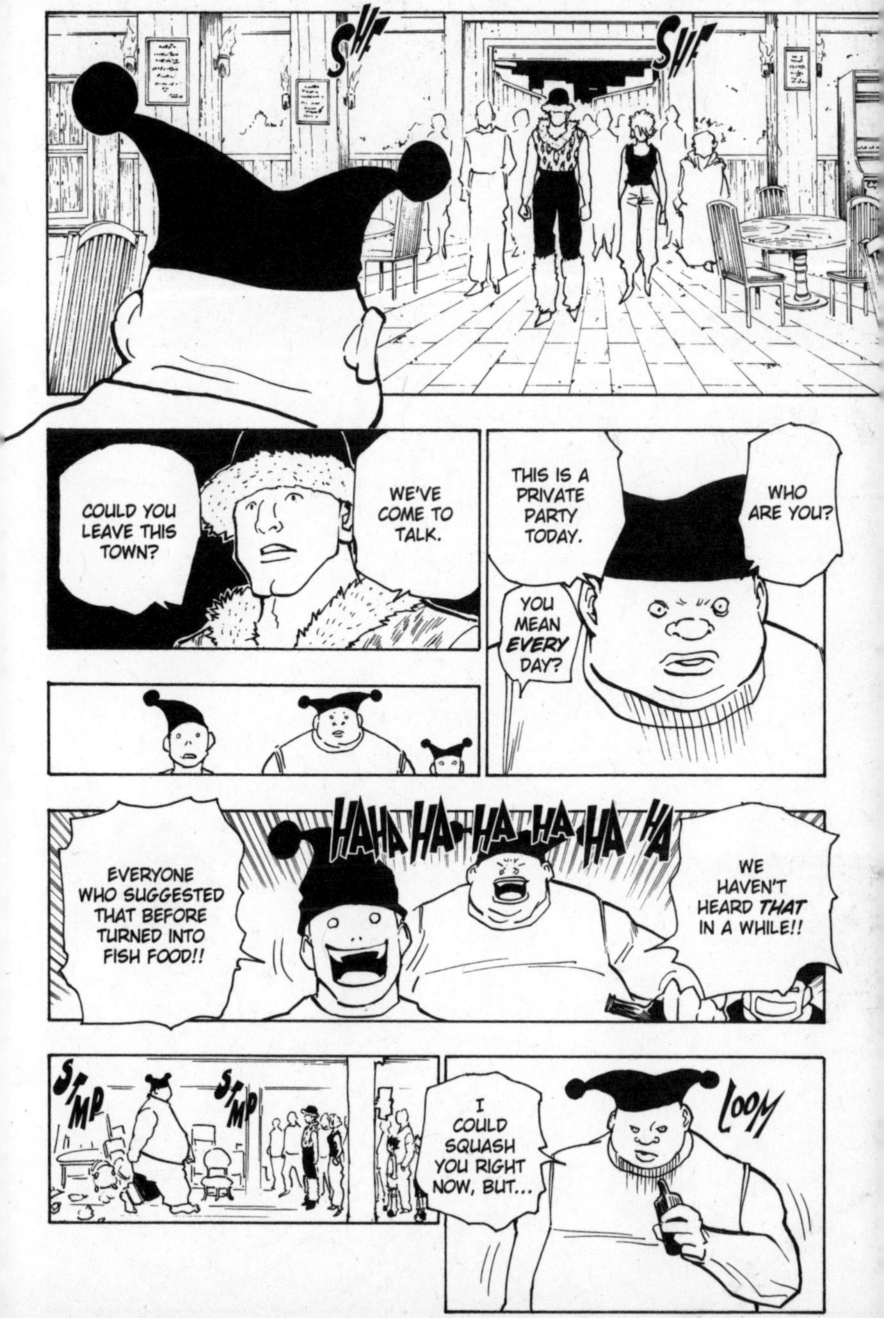
SHF
SHF
WHO ARE YOU?
THIS IS A PRIVATE PARTY TODAY.
YOU MEAN EVERY DAY?
WE'VE COME TO TALK.
COULD YOU LEAVE THIS TOWN?
HAHAHA HA HA HA HA HA
WE HAVEN'T HEARD THAT IN A WHILE!!
EVERYONE WHO SUGGESTED THAT BEFORE TURNED INTO FISH FOOD!!
LOOM
I COULD SQUASH YOU RIGHT NOW, BUT...
STMP
STMP

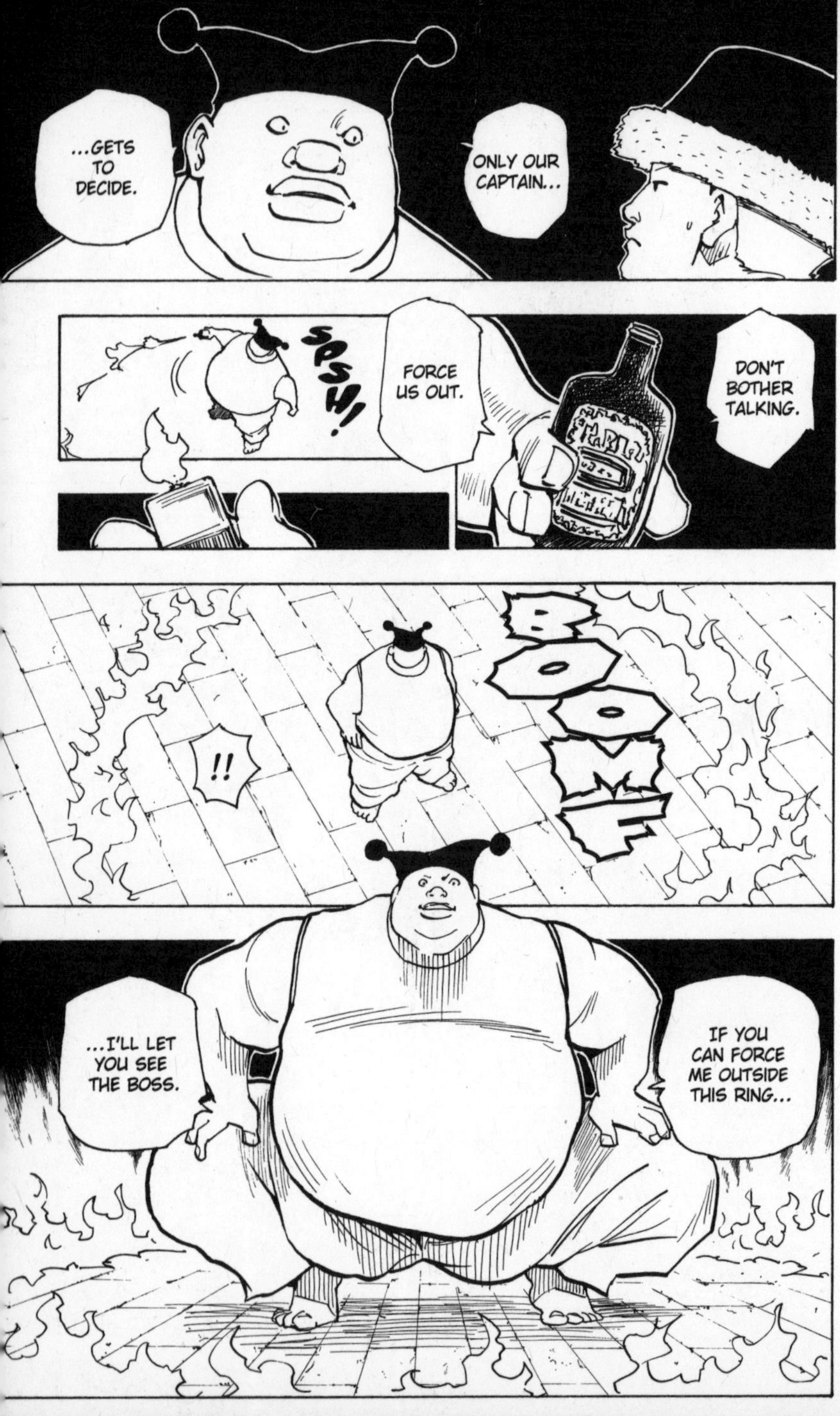
ONLY OUR CAPTAIN...
...GETS TO DECIDE.
DON'T BOTHER TALKING.
FORCE US OUT.
SPSH!
BOOOMF
!!
IF YOU CAN FORCE ME OUTSIDE THIS RING...
...I'LL LET YOU SEE THE BOSS.

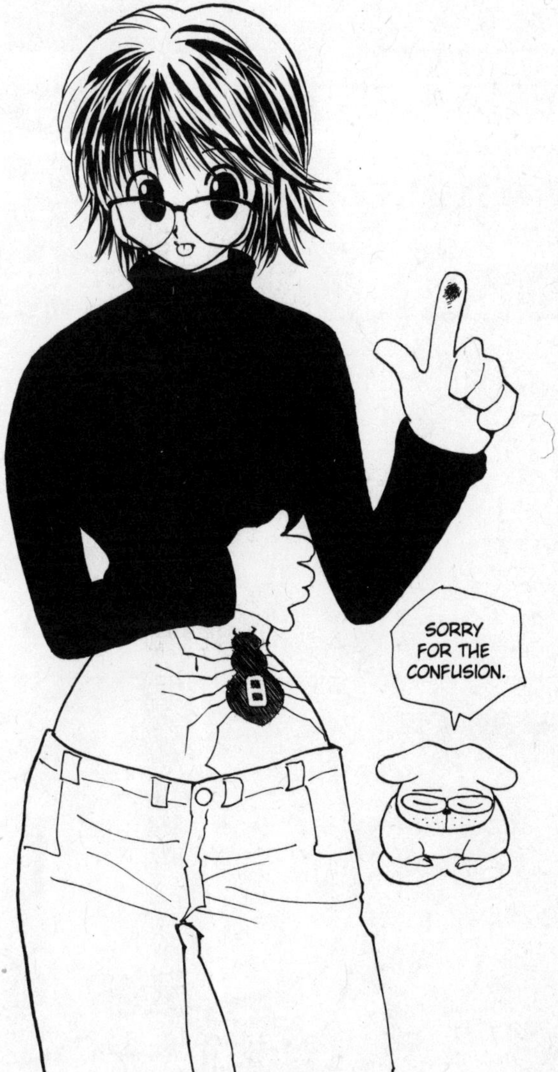
SORRY FOR THE CONFUSION.

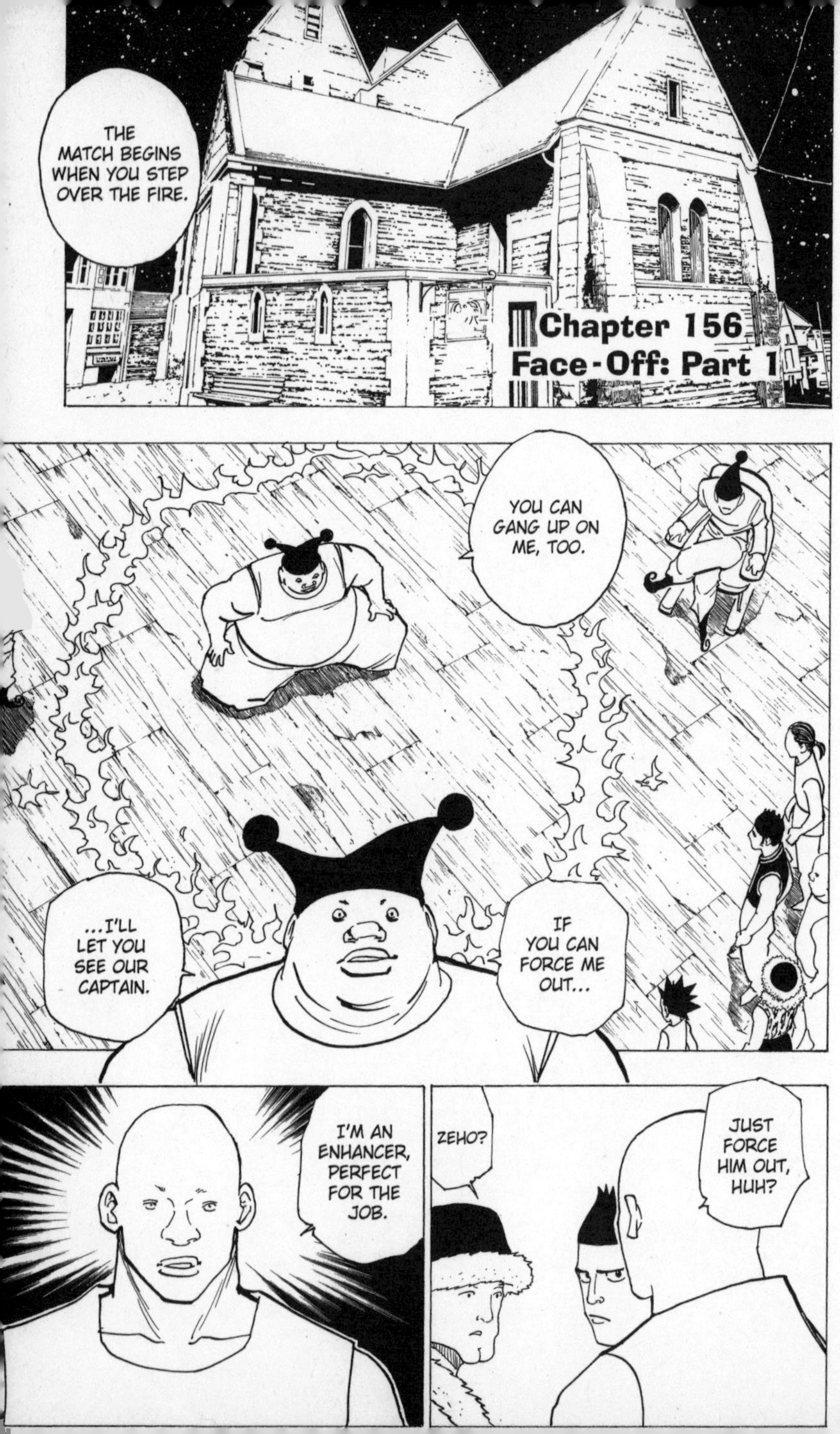
Chapter 156
Face-Off: Part 1
THE MATCH BEGINS WHEN YOU STEP OVER THE FIRE.
YOU CAN GANG UP ON ME, TOO.
IF YOU CAN FORCE ME OUT...
...I'LL LET YOU SEE OUR CAPTAIN.
JUST FORCE HIM OUT, HUH?
ZEHO?
I'M AN ENHANCER, PERFECT FOR THE JOB.

PHEW...
POP
POP
HAAH!
RRG...
VMMM
HE'S NO GOOD.
OUT OF PRACTICE.
HE TOOK WAY TOO LONG FOR THAT PALTRY REN.
TP
HAH!!
DW
DW
DW
GMP

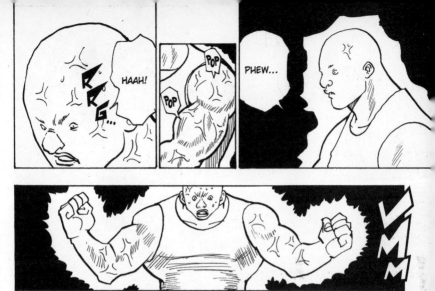

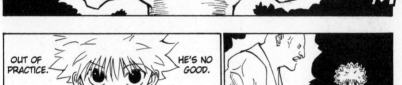

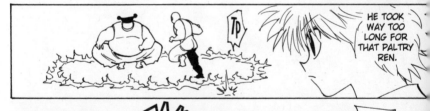

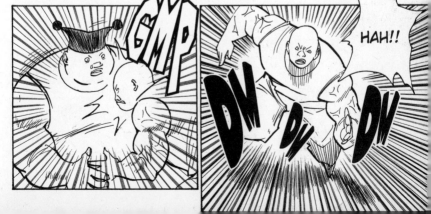

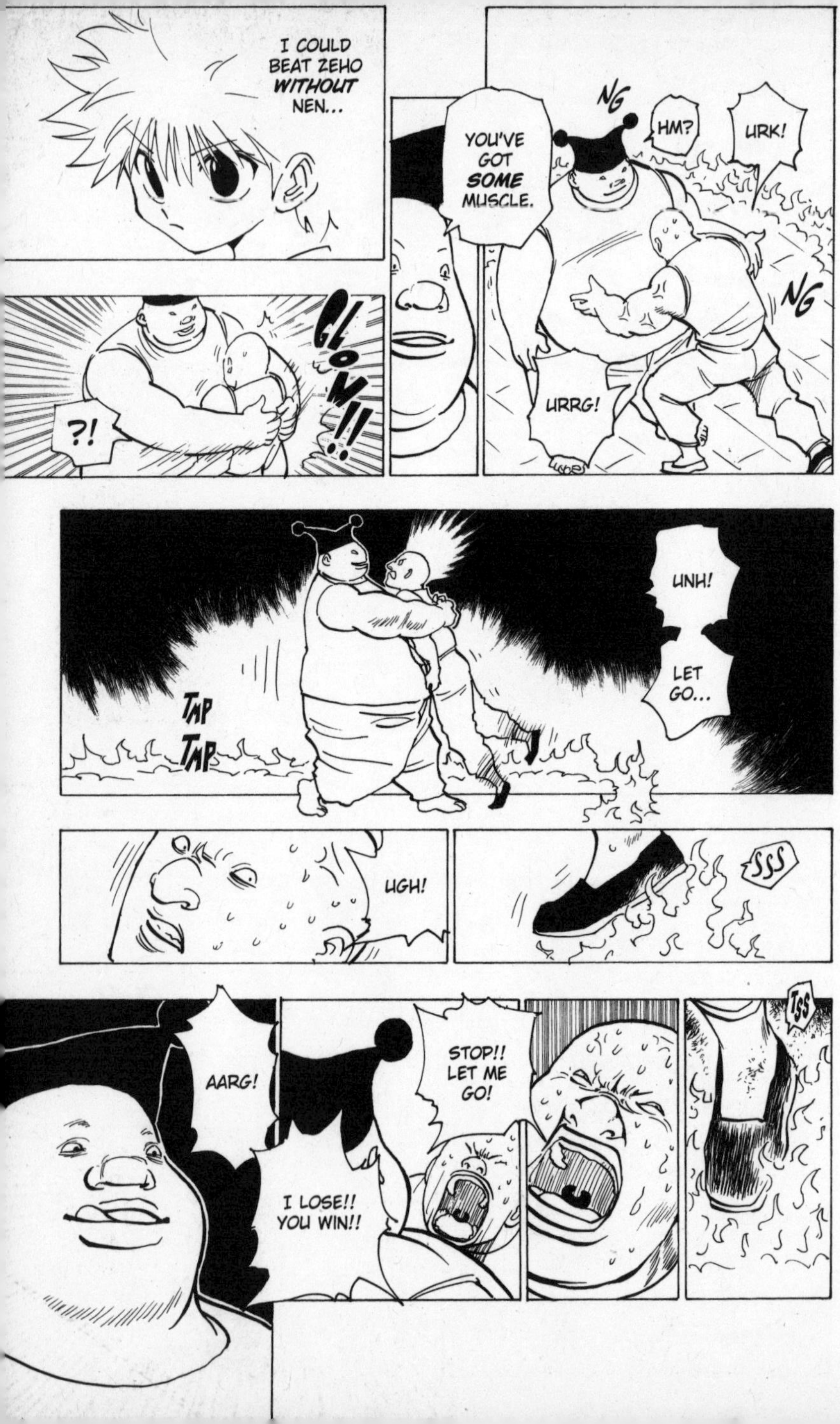
URK!
HM?
NG
NG
URRG!
YOU'VE GOT SOME MUSCLE.
I COULD BEAT ZEHO WITHOUT NEN...
GLOW!!
?!
UNH!
LET GO...
TMP TMP
SSS
UGH!
TSS
STOP!! LET ME GO!
I LOSE!! YOU WIN!!
AARG!

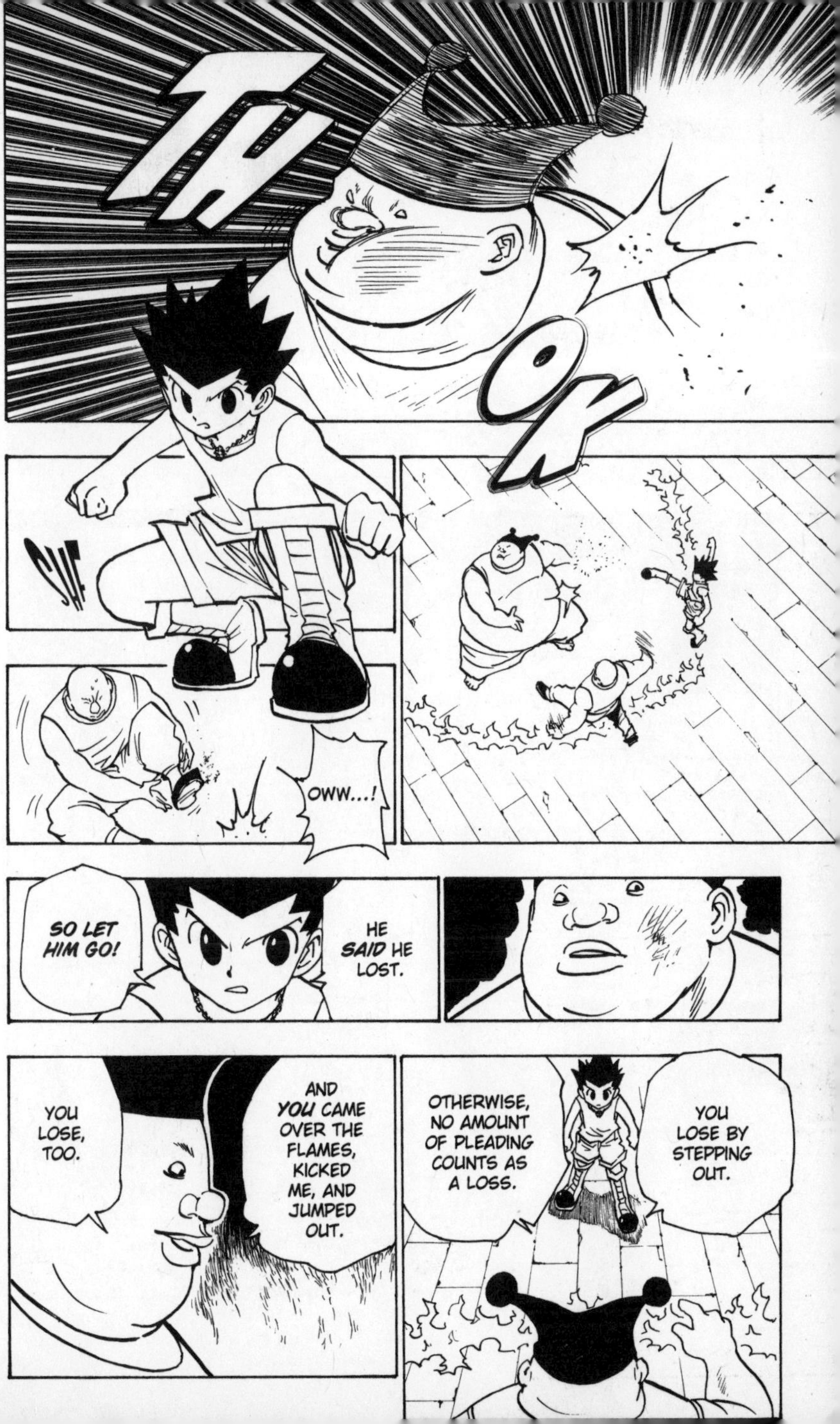
THOK
SHF
OWW...!
HE *SAID* HE LOST.
SO LET HIM GO!
YOU LOSE BY STEPPING OUT.
OTHERWISE, NO AMOUNT OF PLEADING COUNTS AS A LOSS.
AND *YOU* CAME OVER THE FLAMES, KICKED ME, AND JUMPED OUT.
YOU LOSE, TOO.

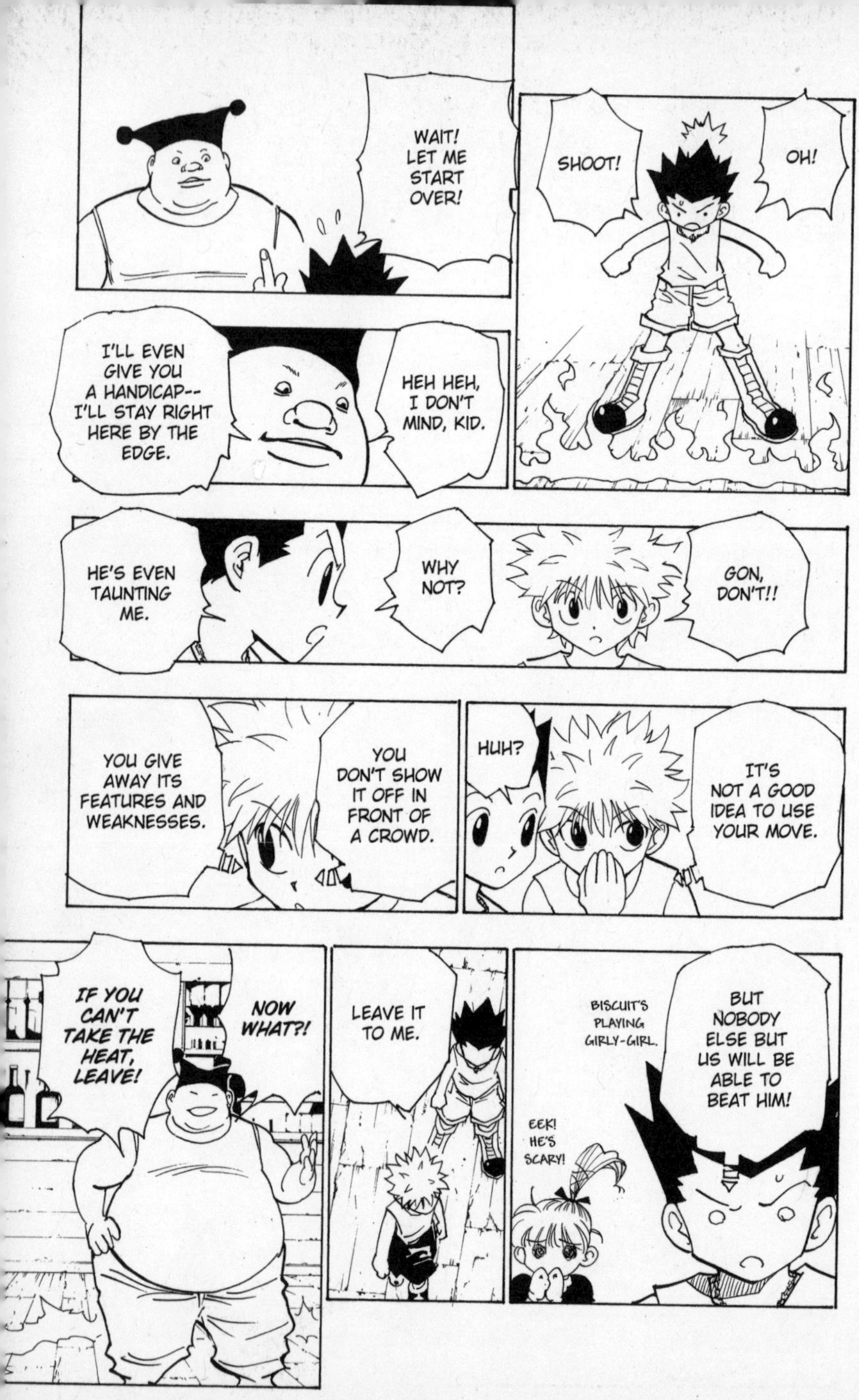
OH!
SHOOT!
WAIT! LET ME START OVER!
HEH HEH, I DON'T MIND, KID.
I'LL EVEN GIVE YOU A HANDICAP-- I'LL STAY RIGHT HERE BY THE EDGE.
GON, DON'T!!
WHY NOT?
HE'S EVEN TAUNTING ME.
IT'S NOT A GOOD IDEA TO USE YOUR MOVE.
HUH?
YOU DON'T SHOW IT OFF IN FRONT OF A CROWD.
YOU GIVE AWAY ITS FEATURES AND WEAKNESSES.
BUT NOBODY ELSE BUT US WILL BE ABLE TO BEAT HIM!
BISCUIT'S PLAYING GIRLY-GIRL.
EEK! HE'S SCARY!
LEAVE IT TO ME.
NOW WHAT?!
IF YOU CAN'T TAKE THE HEAT, LEAVE!

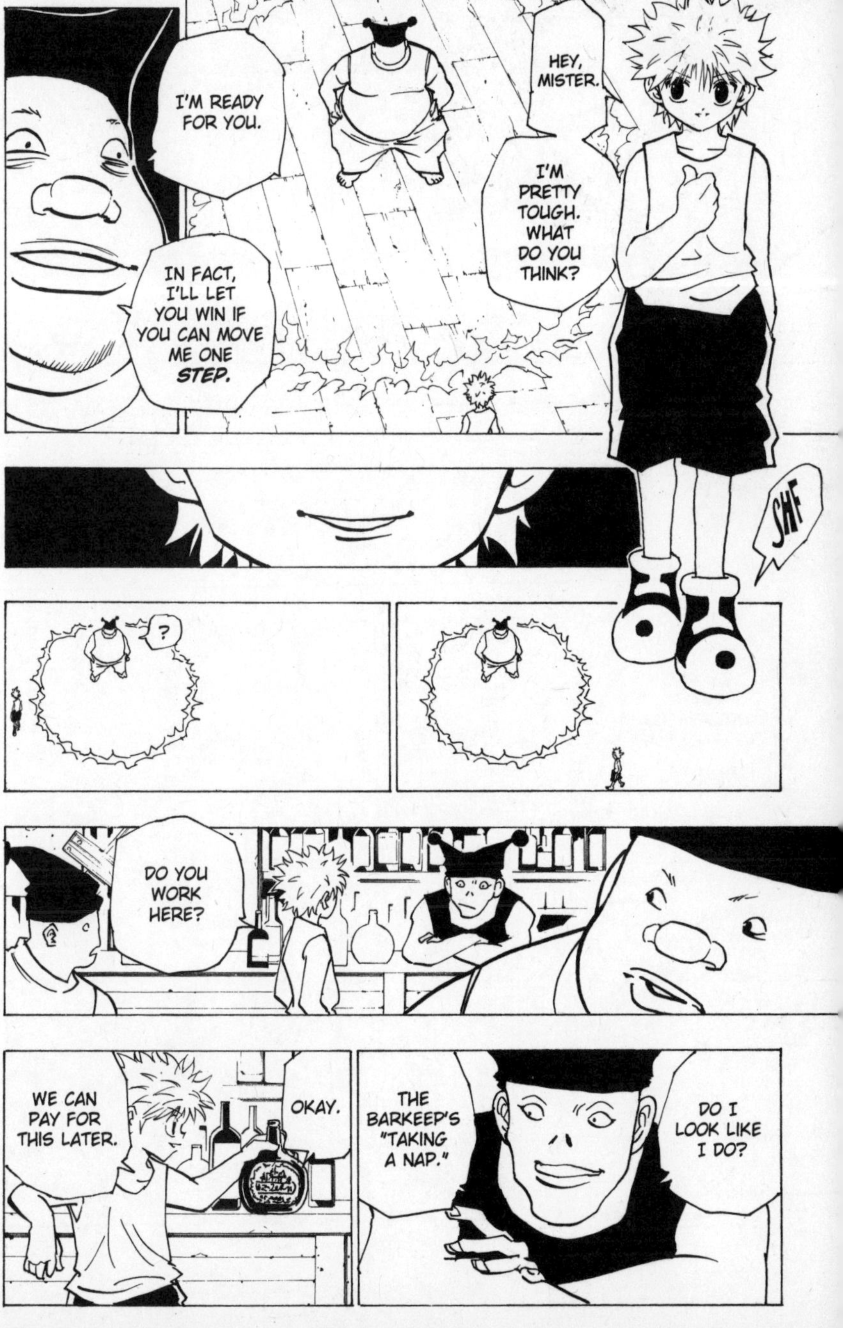
HEY, MISTER.
I'M PRETTY TOUGH. WHAT DO YOU THINK?
SHF
I'M READY FOR YOU.
IN FACT, I'LL LET YOU WIN IF YOU CAN MOVE ME ONE *STEP.*
?
DO YOU WORK HERE?
DO I LOOK LIKE I DO?
THE BARKEEP'S "TAKING A NAP."
OKAY.
WE CAN PAY FOR THIS LATER.

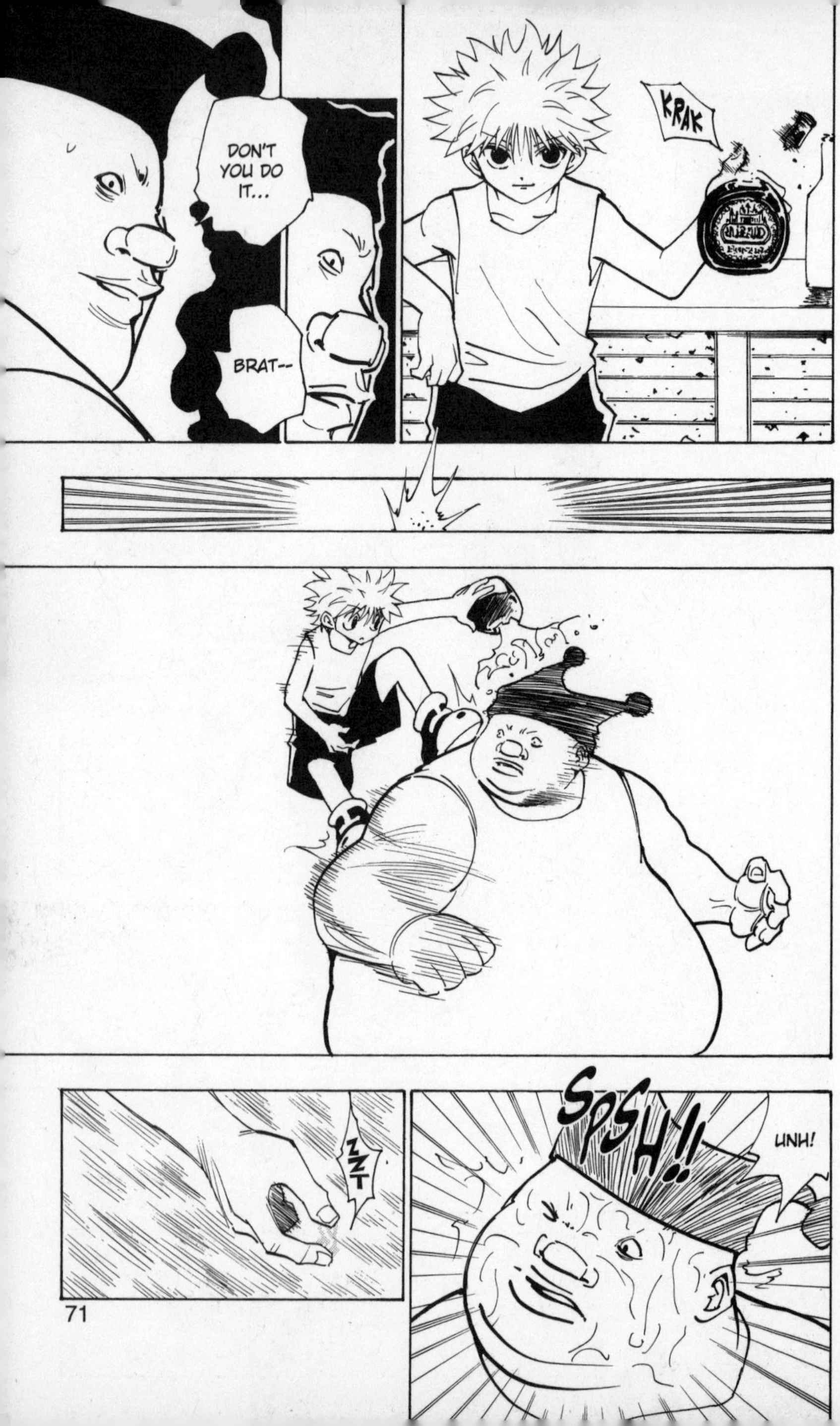
KRAK
DON'T YOU DO IT...
BRAT--
SPSH!!
UNH!
ZZT

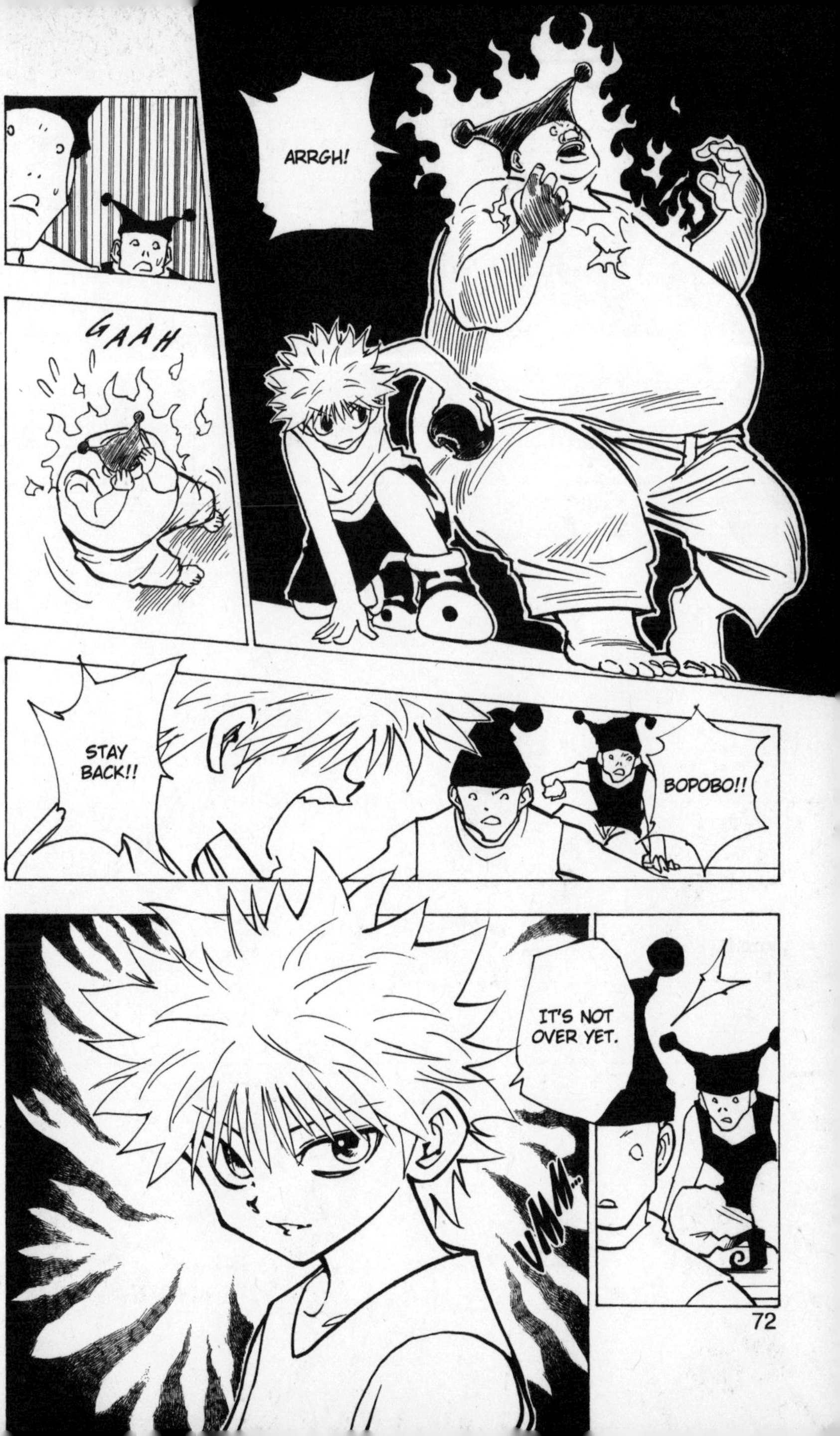

ARRGH!
GAAH
BOPOBO!!
STAY BACK!!
IT'S NOT OVER YET.

READ THIS WAY

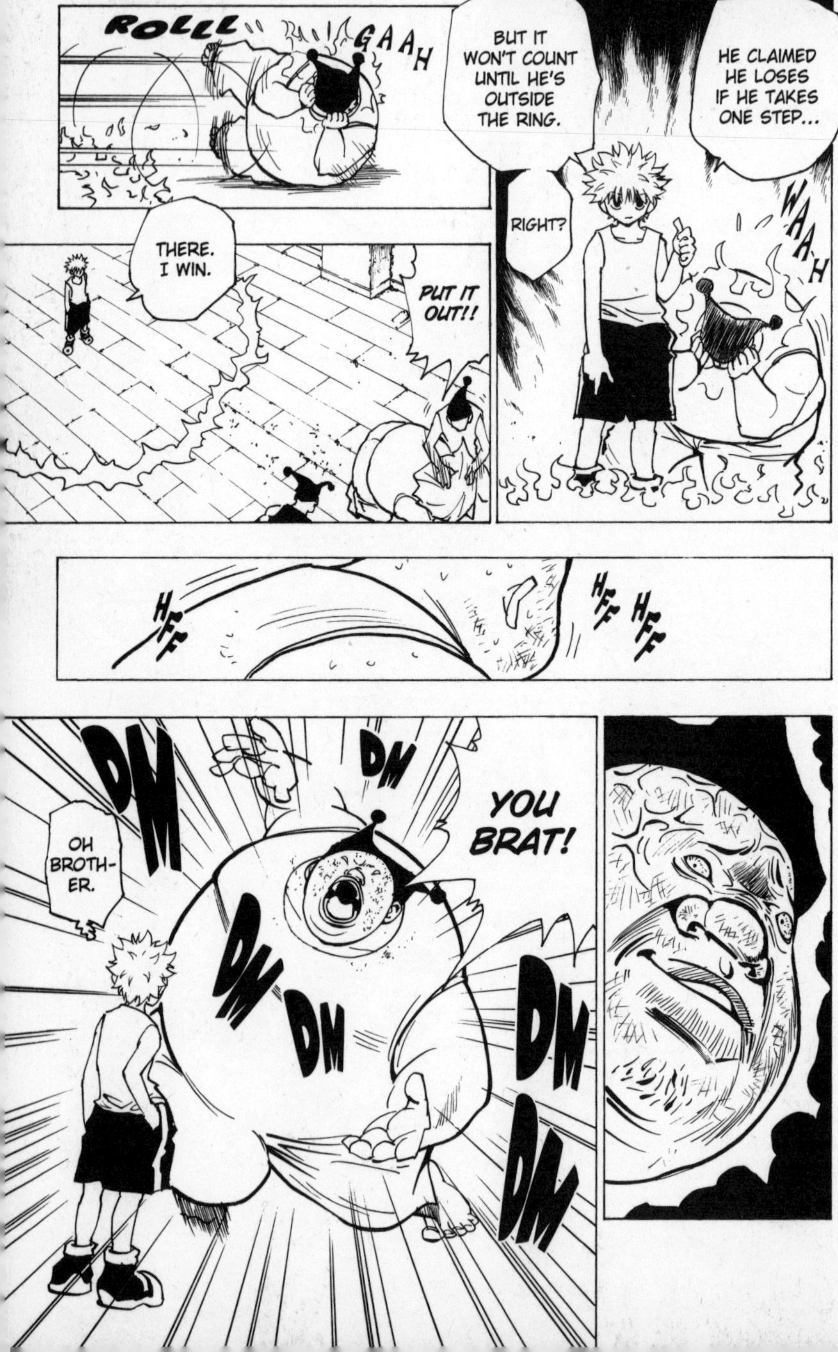
HE CLAIMED HE LOSES IF HE TAKES ONE STEP...
BUT IT WON'T COUNT UNTIL HE'S OUTSIDE THE RING.
RIGHT?
WAAAH
ROLLL
GAAAH
THERE. I WIN.
PUT IT OUT!!
HFF
HFF
HFF
DM
DM
YOU BRAT!
DM
DM
DM
DM
OH BROTHER.

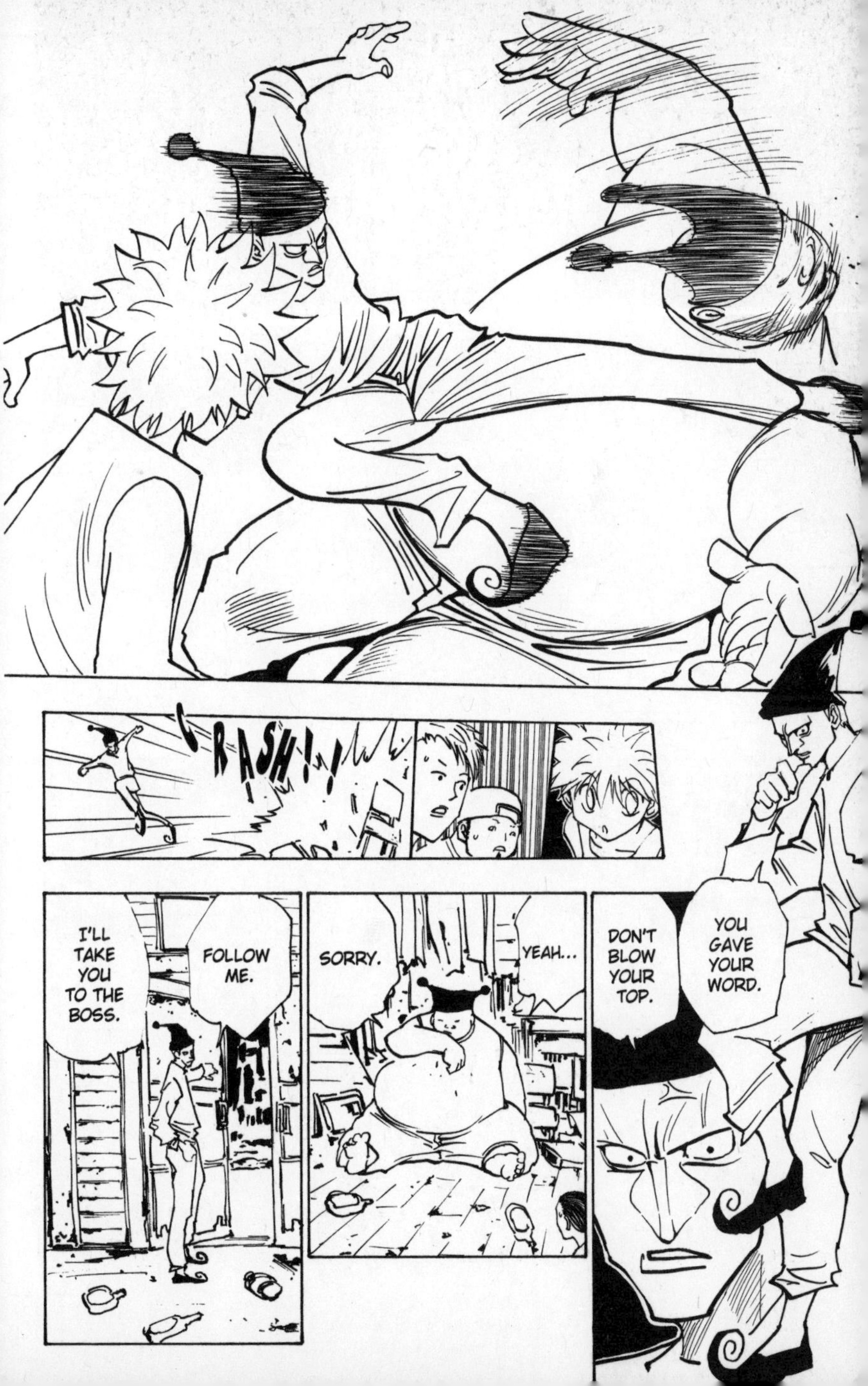
CRASH!!
YOU GAVE YOUR WORD.
DON'T BLOW YOUR TOP.
YEAH...
SORRY.
FOLLOW ME.
I'LL TAKE YOU TO THE BOSS.

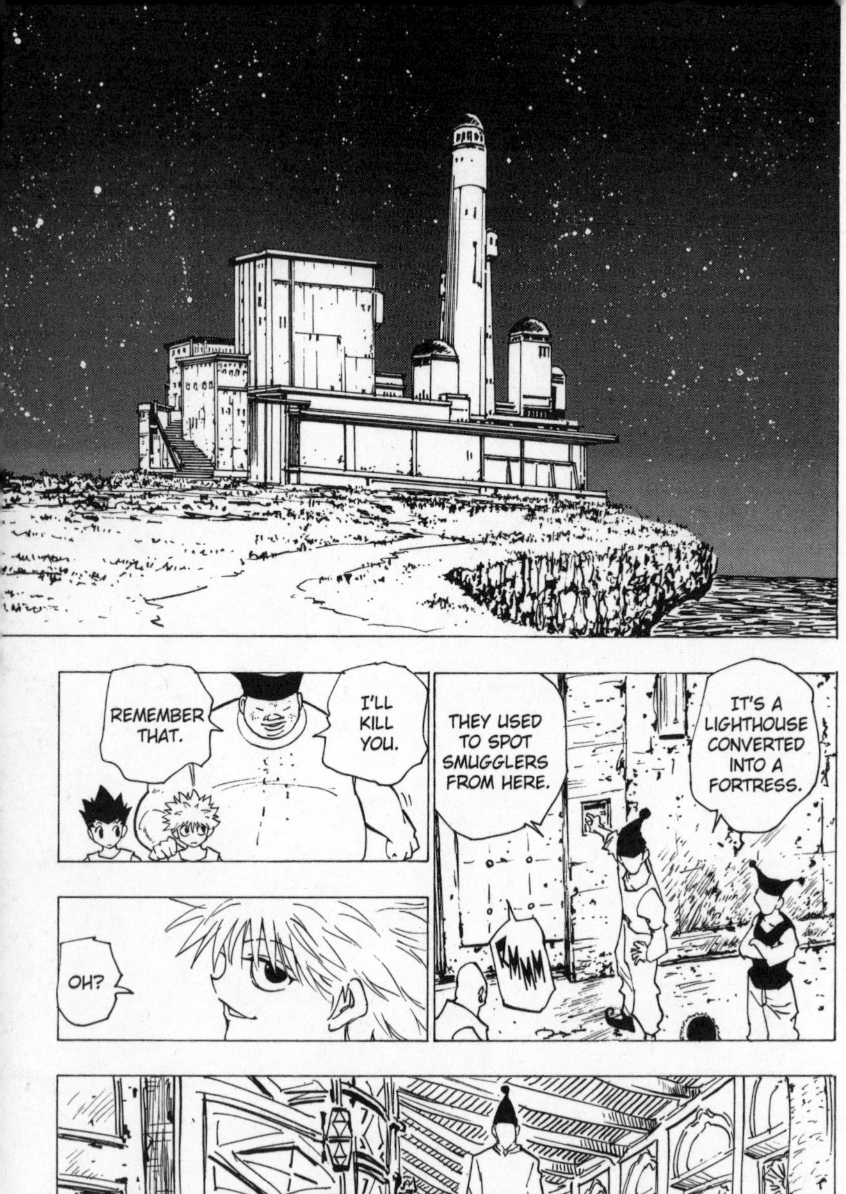
IT'S A LIGHTHOUSE CONVERTED INTO A FORTRESS.
THEY USED TO SPOT SMUGGLERS FROM HERE.
I'LL KILL YOU.
REMEMBER THAT.
OH?

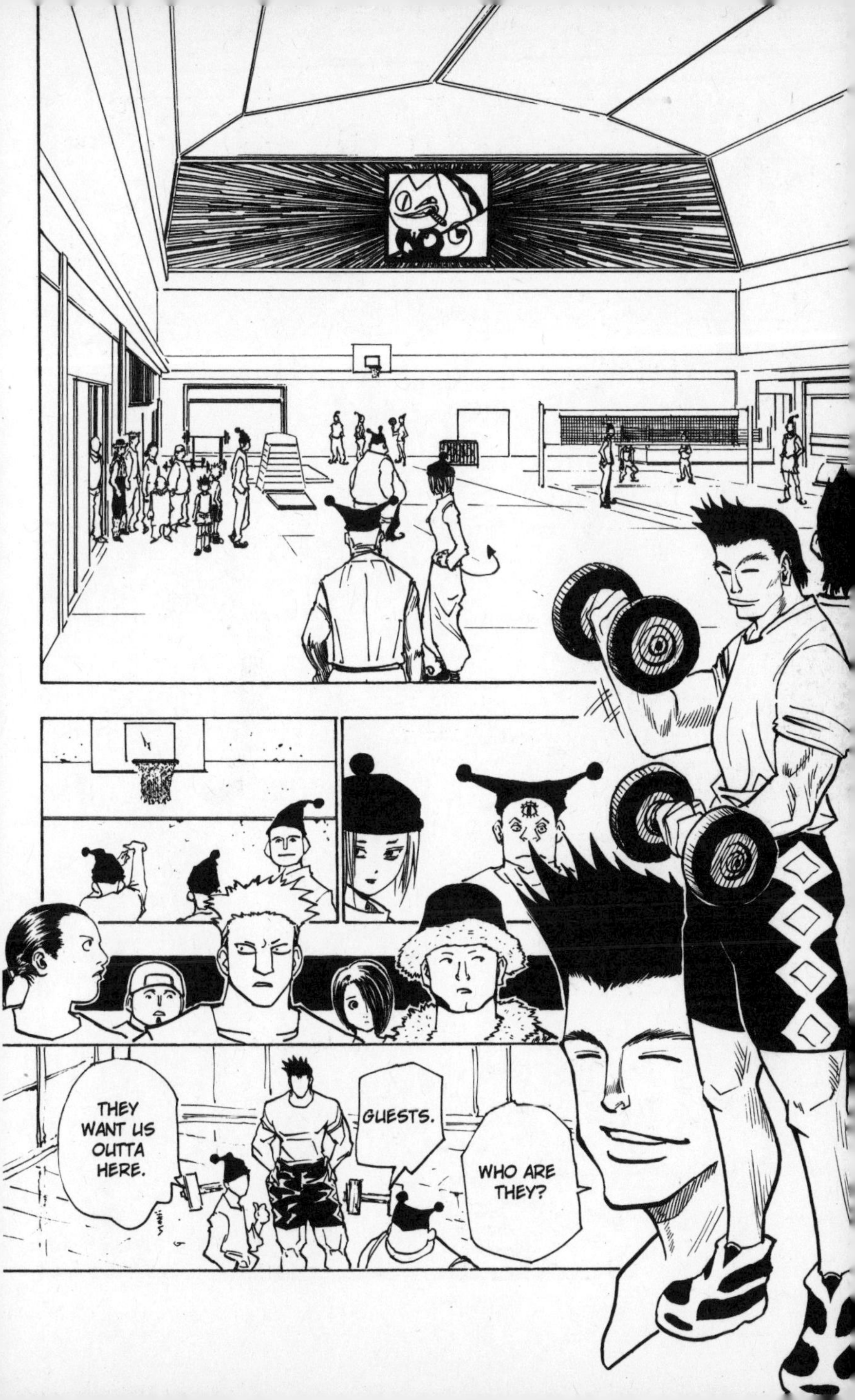
WHO ARE THEY?
GUESTS.
THEY WANT US OUTTA HERE.

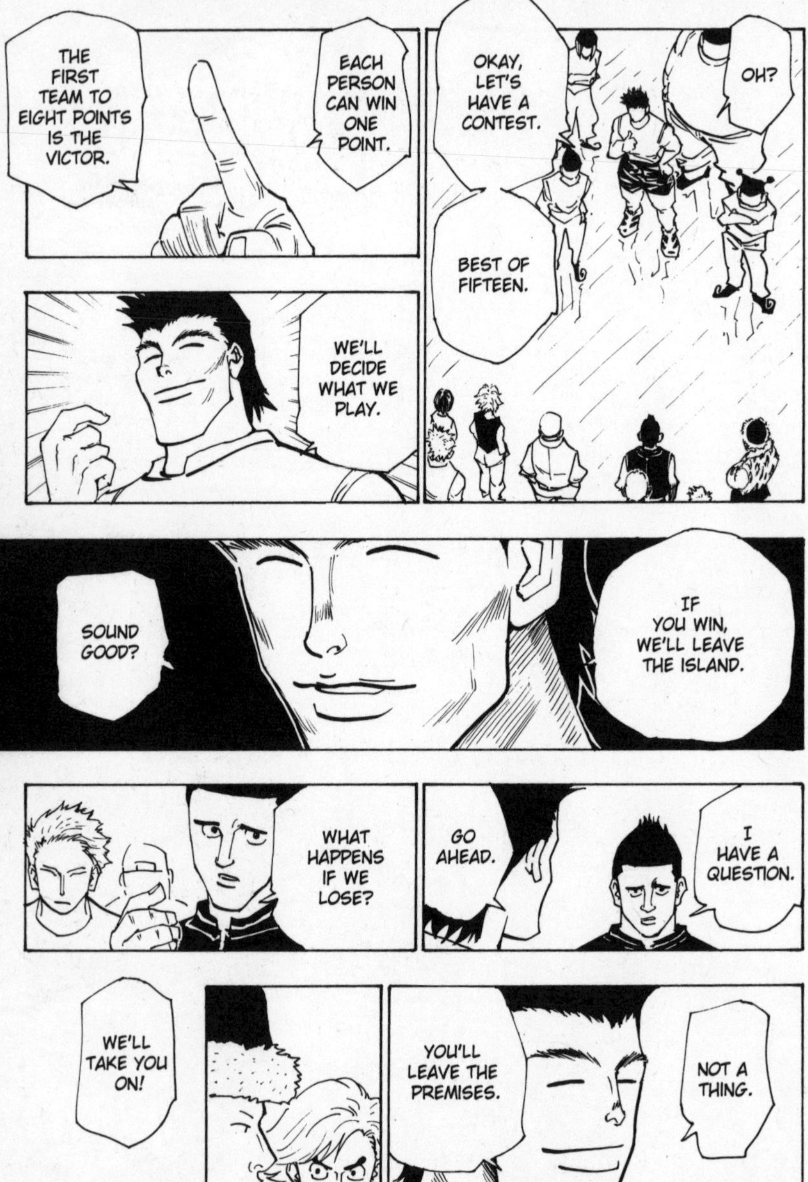
OH?
OKAY, LET'S HAVE A CONTEST.
BEST OF FIFTEEN.
EACH PERSON CAN WIN ONE POINT.
THE FIRST TEAM TO EIGHT POINTS IS THE VICTOR.
WE'LL DECIDE WHAT WE PLAY.
IF YOU WIN, WE'LL LEAVE THE ISLAND.
SOUND GOOD?
I HAVE A QUESTION.
GO AHEAD.
WHAT HAPPENS IF WE LOSE?
NOT A THING.
YOU'LL LEAVE THE PREMISES.
WE'LL TAKE YOU ON!

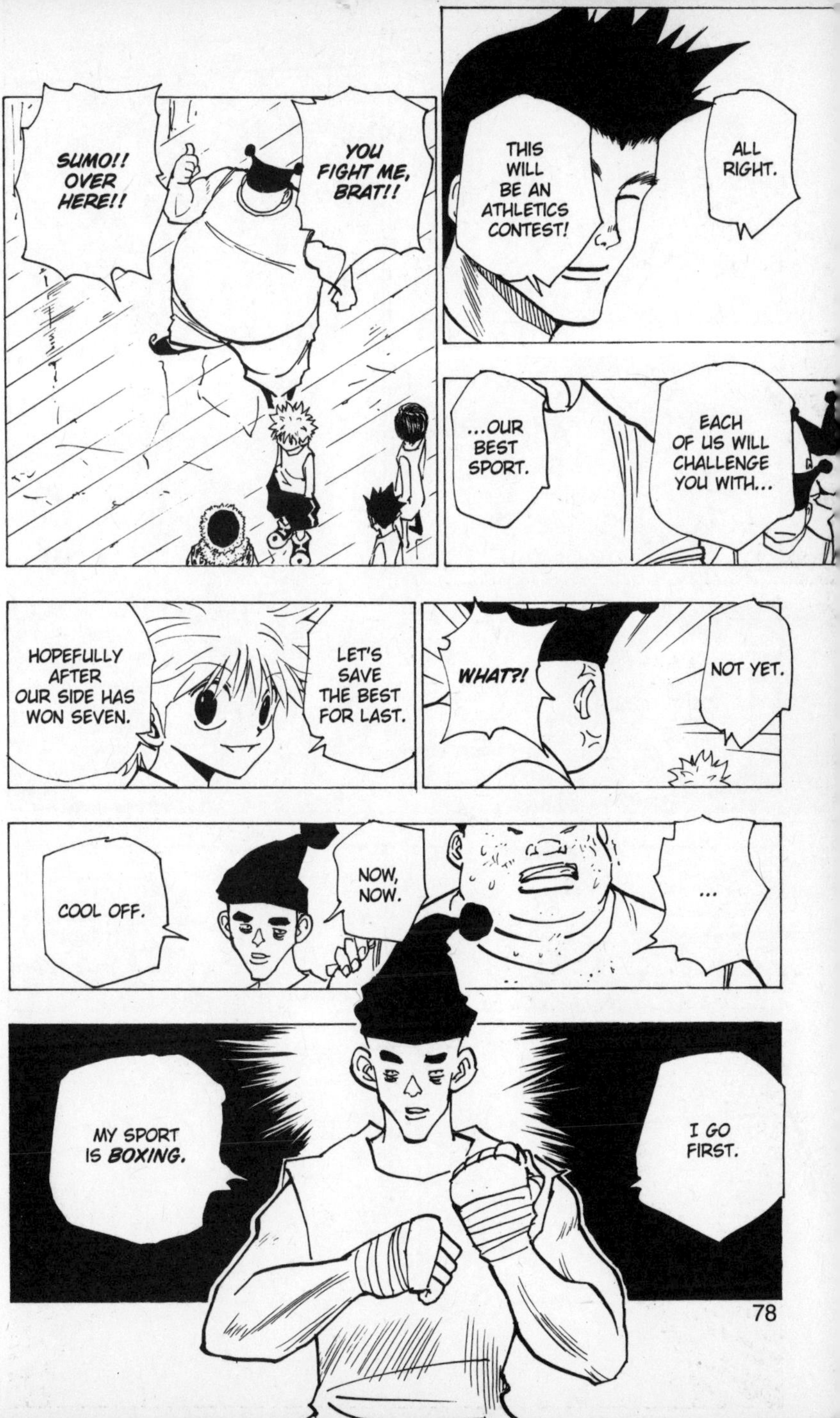
ALL RIGHT.
THIS WILL BE AN ATHLETICS CONTEST!
EACH OF US WILL CHALLENGE YOU WITH...
...OUR BEST SPORT.
YOU FIGHT ME, BRAT!!
SUMO!! OVER HERE!!
NOT YET.
WHAT?!
LET'S SAVE THE BEST FOR LAST.
HOPEFULLY AFTER OUR SIDE HAS WON SEVEN.
...
NOW, NOW.
COOL OFF.
I GO FIRST.
MY SPORT IS BOXING.

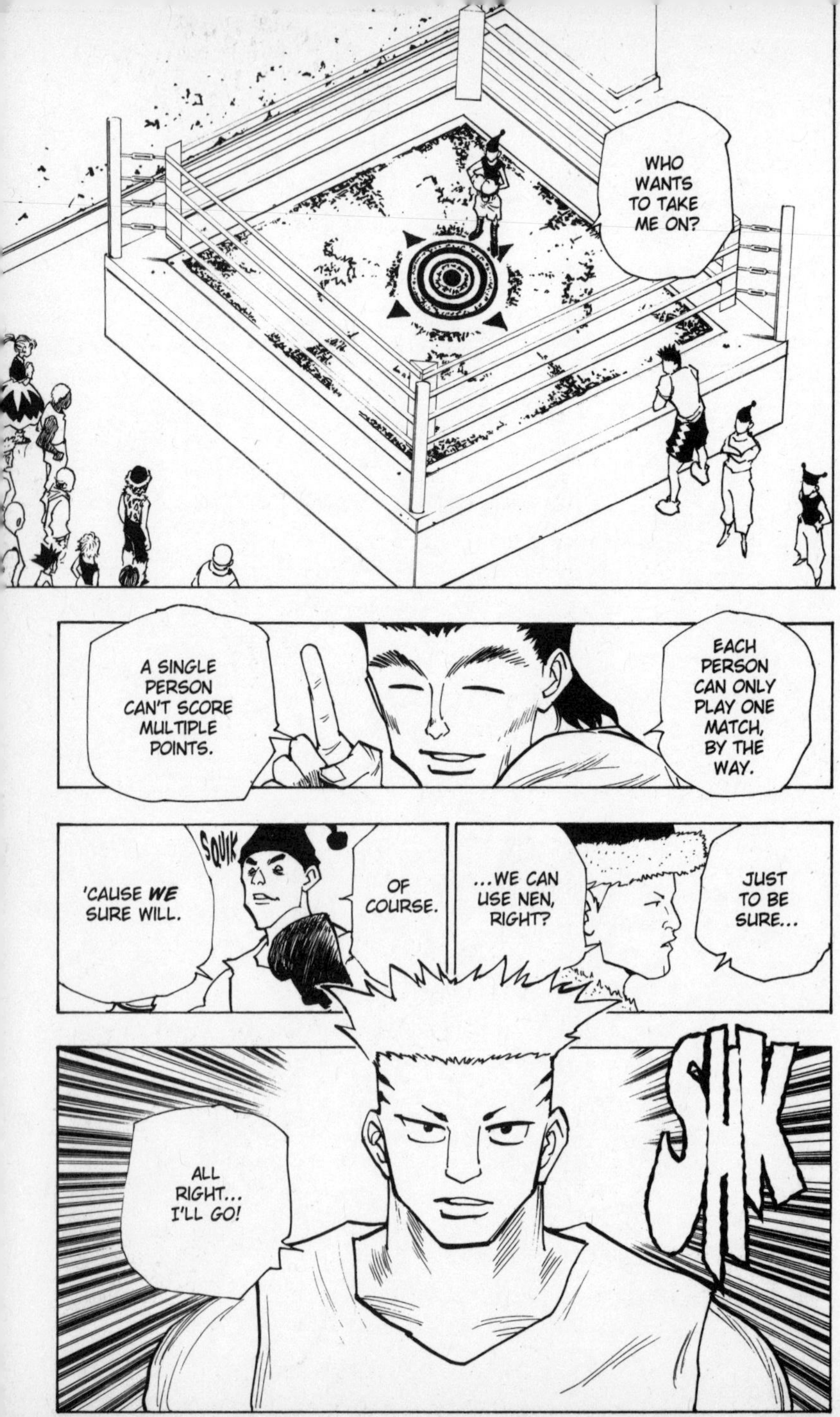
WHO WANTS TO TAKE ME ON?
EACH PERSON CAN ONLY PLAY ONE MATCH, BY THE WAY.
A SINGLE PERSON CAN'T SCORE MULTIPLE POINTS.
JUST TO BE SURE...
...WE CAN USE NEN, RIGHT?
OF COURSE.
SQUIK
'CAUSE *WE* SURE WILL.
SHK
ALL RIGHT... I'LL GO!

DRAW WITHOUT LOOKING: PART 4
JOHNESS

Chapter 157
Face-Off: Part 2

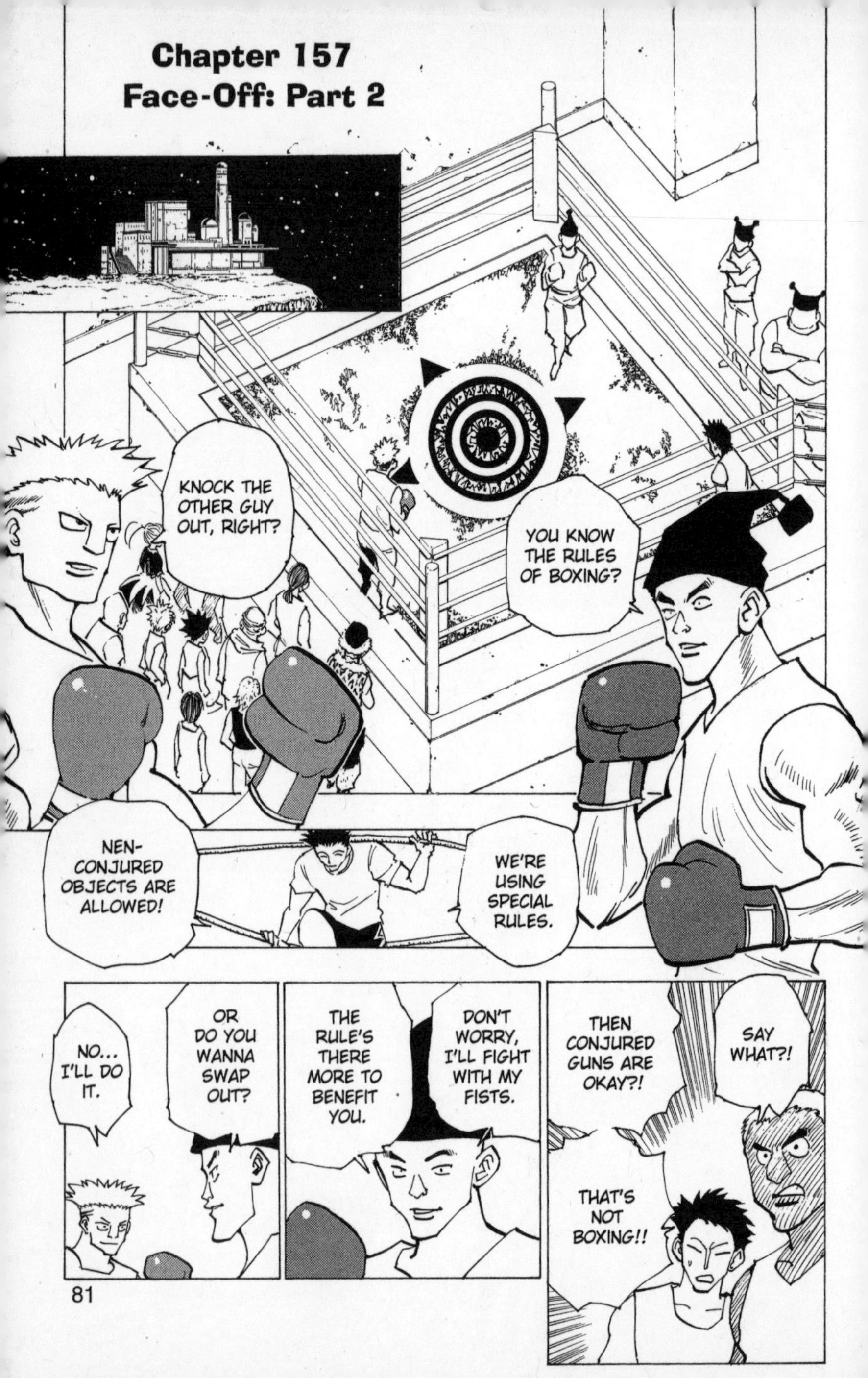
YOU KNOW THE RULES OF BOXING?
KNOCK THE OTHER GUY OUT, RIGHT?
WE'RE USING SPECIAL RULES.
NEN-CONJURED OBJECTS ARE ALLOWED!
SAY WHAT?!
THEN CONJURED GUNS ARE OKAY?!
THAT'S NOT BOXING!!
DON'T WORRY, I'LL FIGHT WITH MY FISTS.
THE RULE'S THERE MORE TO BENEFIT YOU.
OR DO YOU WANNA SWAP OUT?
NO... I'LL DO IT.

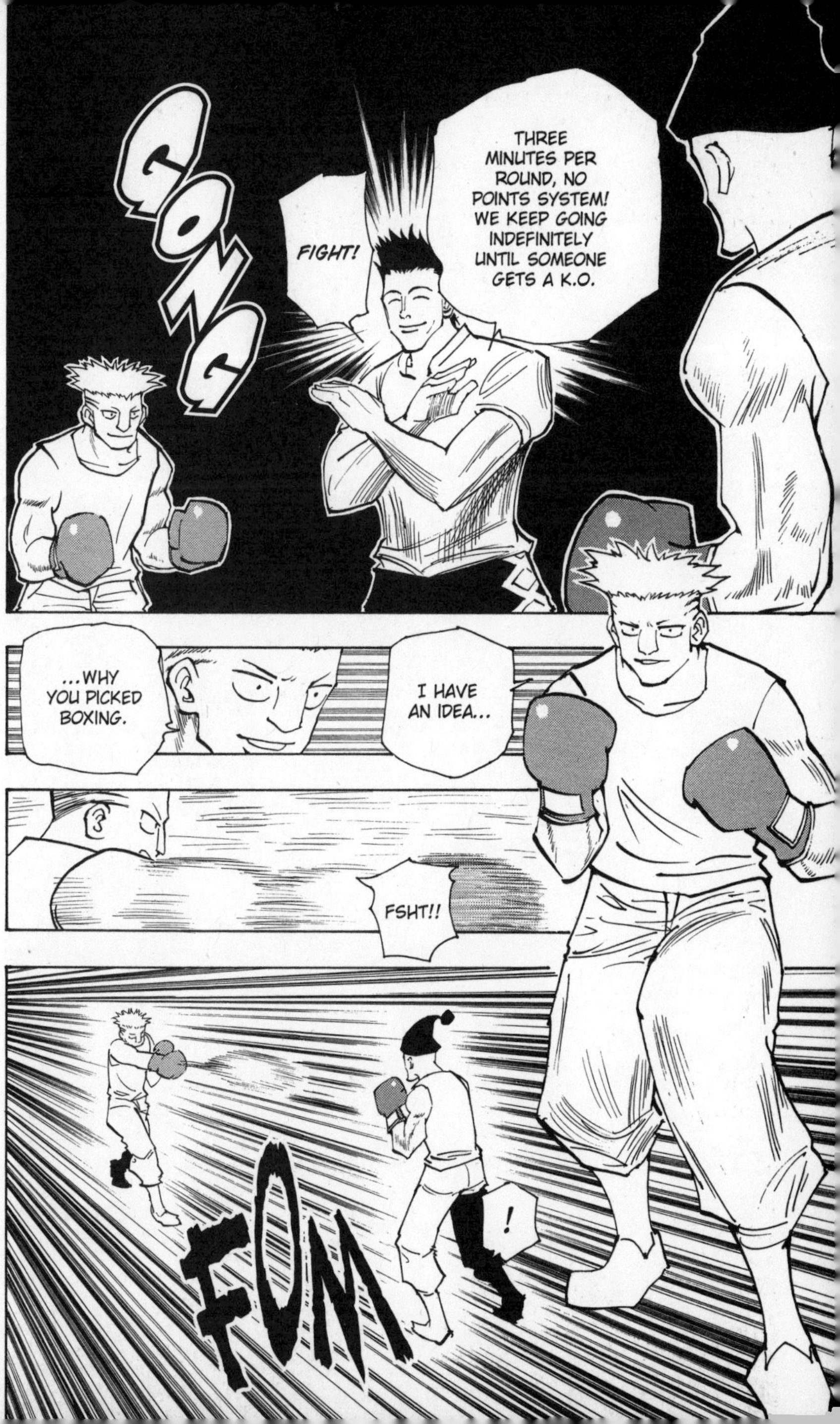
THREE MINUTES PER ROUND, NO POINTS SYSTEM! WE KEEP GOING INDEFINITELY UNTIL SOMEONE GETS A K.O.
FIGHT!
GONG
I HAVE AN IDEA...
...WHY YOU PICKED BOXING.
FSHT!!
!
FOM

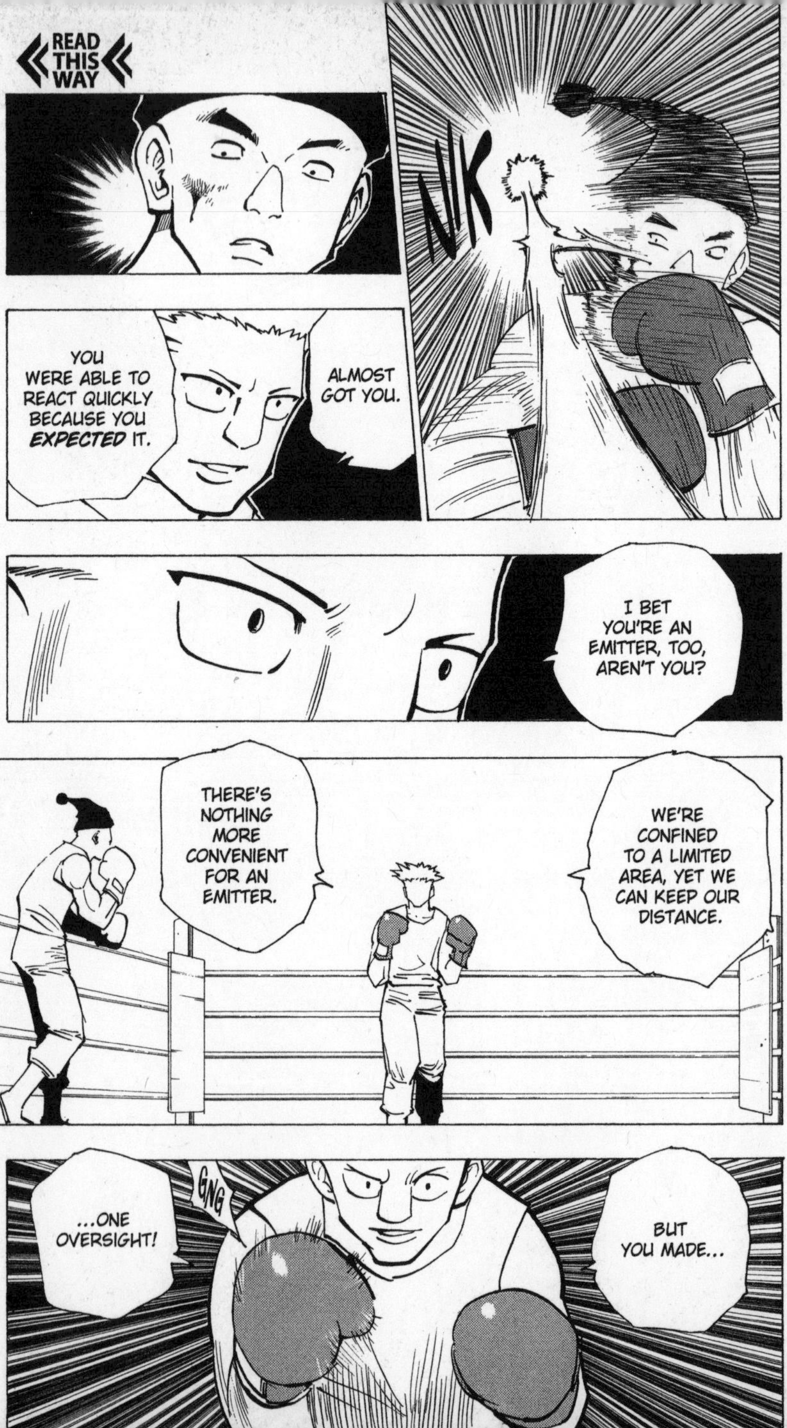
READ THIS WAY
NK
ALMOST GOT YOU.
YOU WERE ABLE TO REACT QUICKLY BECAUSE YOU *EXPECTED* IT.
I BET YOU'RE AN EMITTER, TOO, AREN'T YOU?
WE'RE CONFINED TO A LIMITED AREA, YET WE CAN KEEP OUR DISTANCE.
THERE'S NOTHING MORE CONVENIENT FOR AN EMITTER.
GNG
BUT YOU MADE...
...ONE OVERSIGHT!

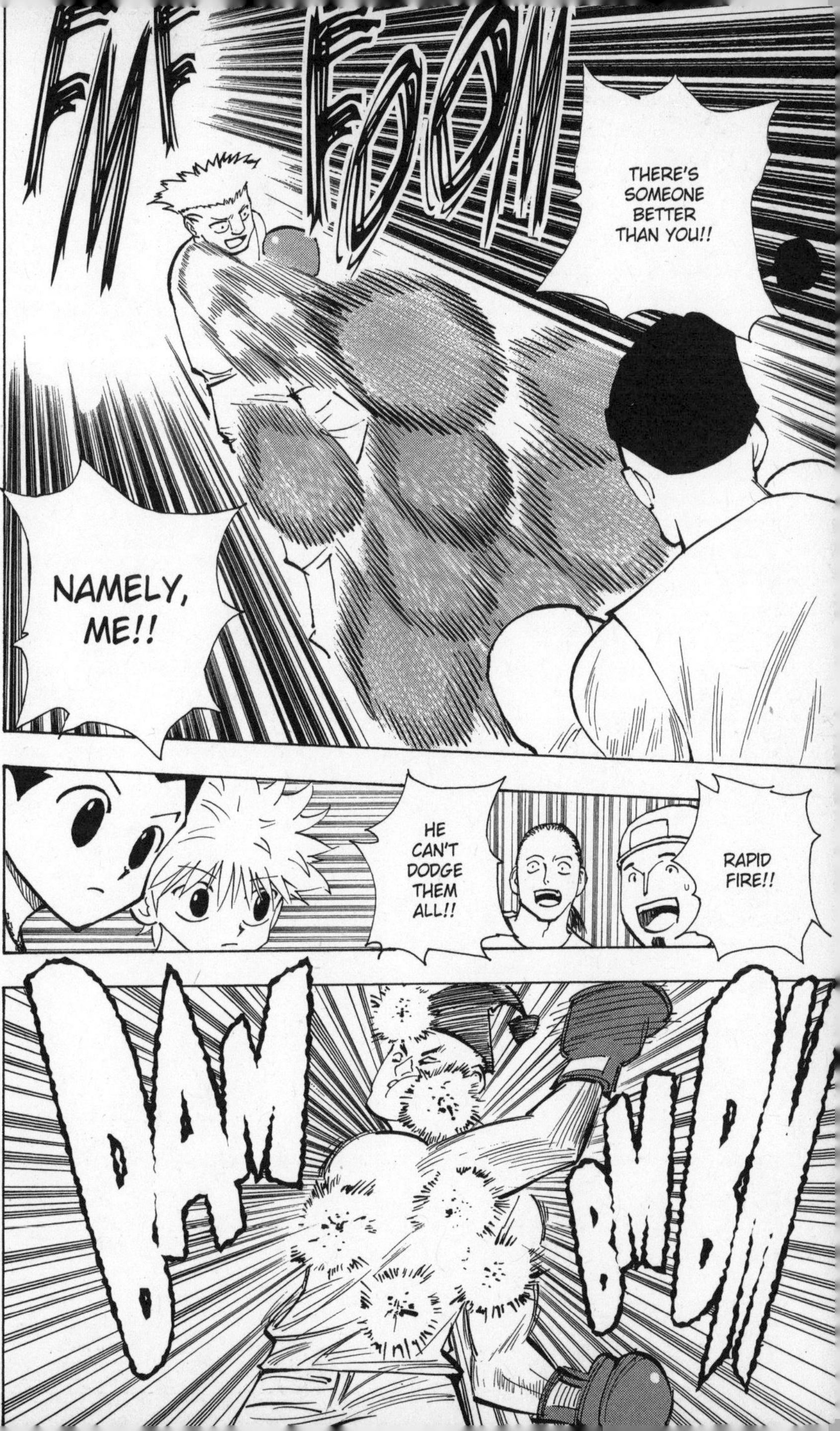
FOOM
THERE'S SOMEONE BETTER THAN YOU!!
FWF
NAMELY, ME!!
RAPID FIRE!!
HE CAN'T DODGE THEM ALL!!
BAM BAM
BAM

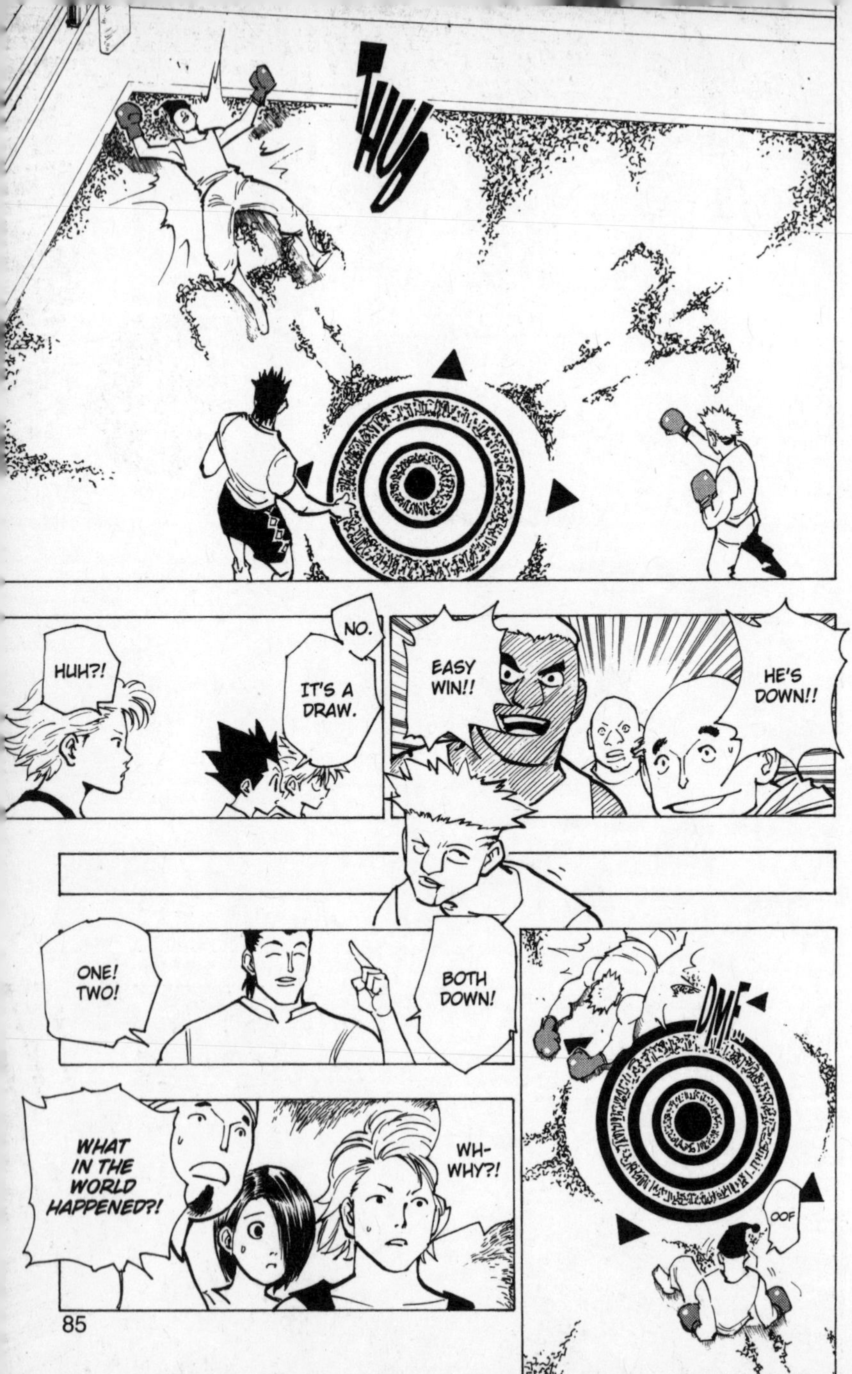
THUD
HE'S DOWN!!
EASY WIN!!
NO.
IT'S A DRAW.
HUH?!
DMF...
OOF
BOTH DOWN!
ONE! TWO!
WH- WHY?!
WHAT IN THE WORLD HAPPENED?!

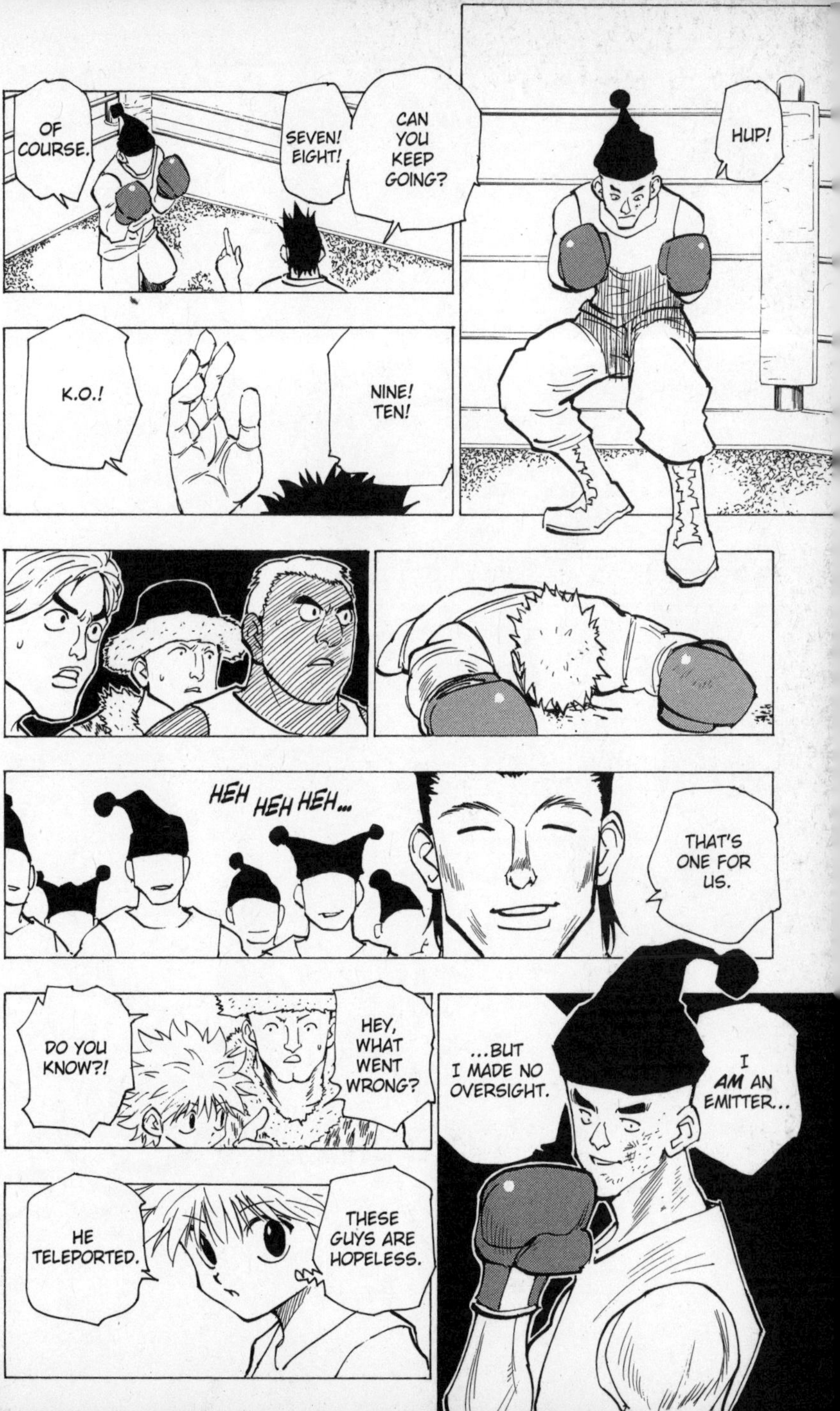
HUP!
CAN YOU KEEP GOING?
SEVEN! EIGHT!
OF COURSE.
NINE! TEN!
K.O.!
THAT'S ONE FOR US.
HEH HEH HEH...
I AM AN EMITTER...
...BUT I MADE NO OVERSIGHT.
HEY, WHAT WENT WRONG?
DO YOU KNOW?!
THESE GUYS ARE HOPELESS.
HE TELEPORTED.

READ THIS WAY

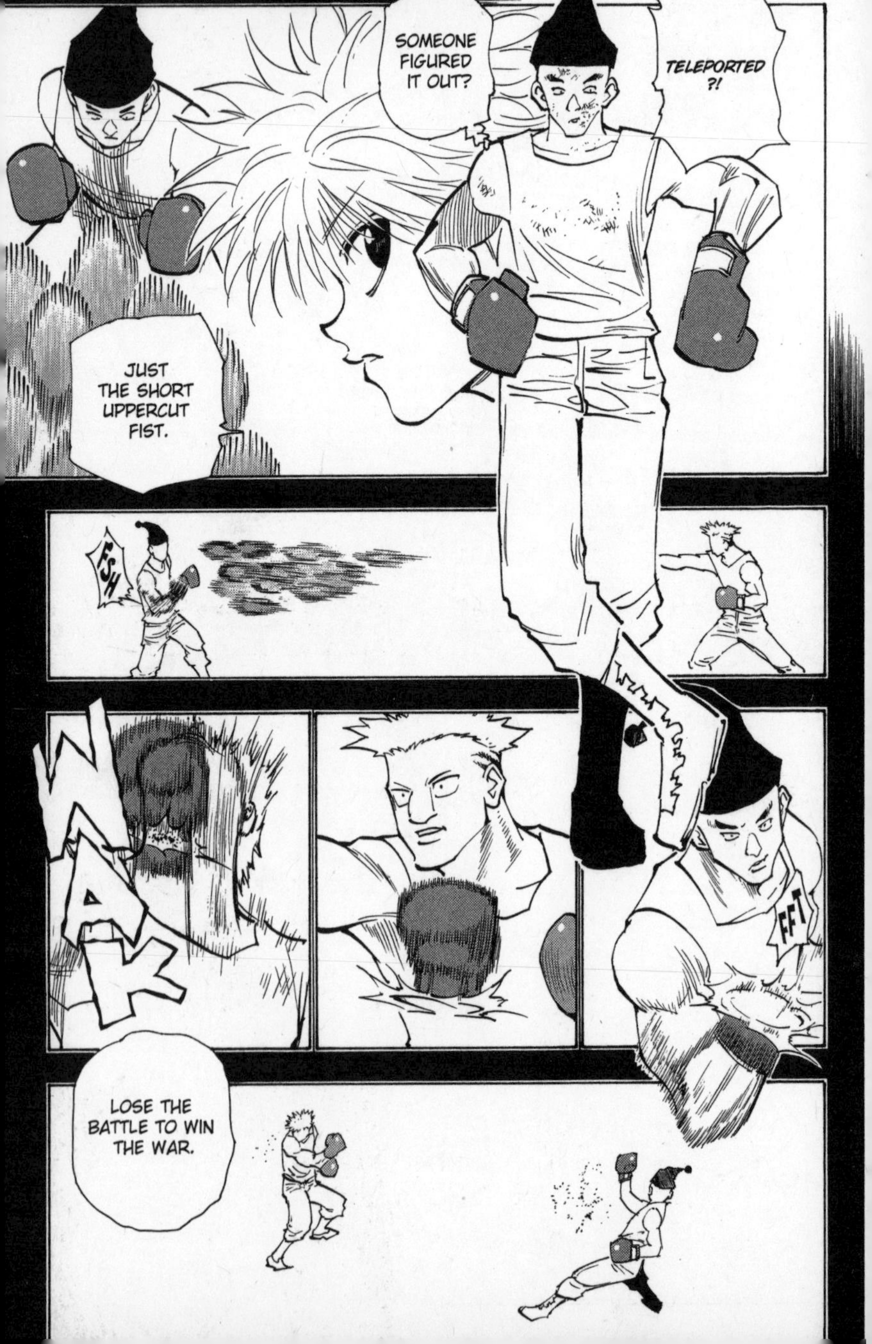
TELEPORTED ?!
SOMEONE FIGURED IT OUT?
JUST THE SHORT UPPERCUT FIST.
FSH
FFT
WHAK
LOSE THE BATTLE TO WIN THE WAR.

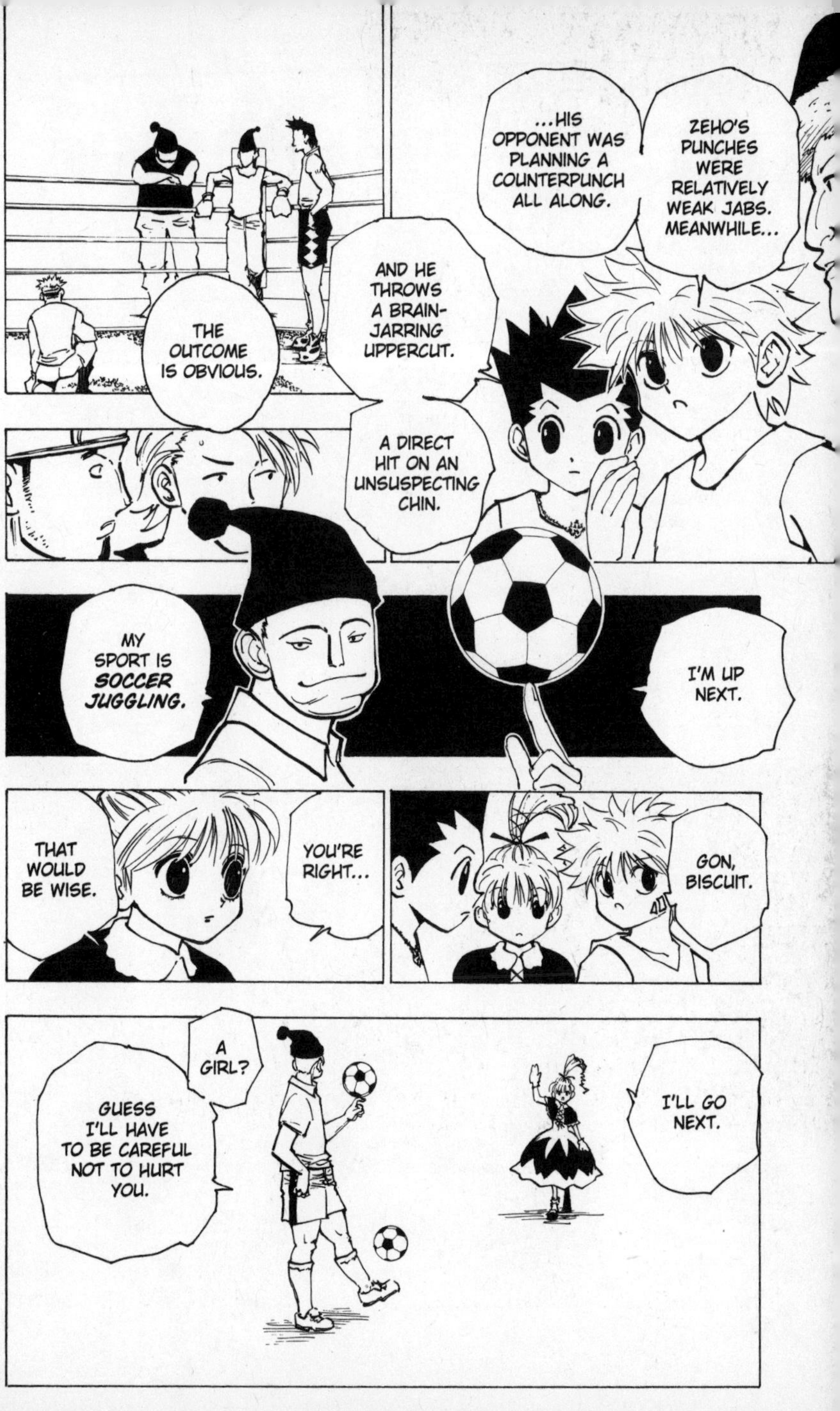
ZEHO'S PUNCHES WERE RELATIVELY WEAK JABS. MEANWHILE...
...HIS OPPONENT WAS PLANNING A COUNTERPUNCH ALL ALONG.
AND HE THROWS A BRAIN-JARRING UPPERCUT.
A DIRECT HIT ON AN UNSUSPECTING CHIN.
THE OUTCOME IS OBVIOUS.
I'M UP NEXT.
MY SPORT IS *SOCCER JUGGLING.*
GON, BISCUIT.
YOU'RE RIGHT...
THAT WOULD BE WISE.
I'LL GO NEXT.
A GIRL?
GUESS I'LL HAVE TO BE CAREFUL NOT TO HURT YOU.

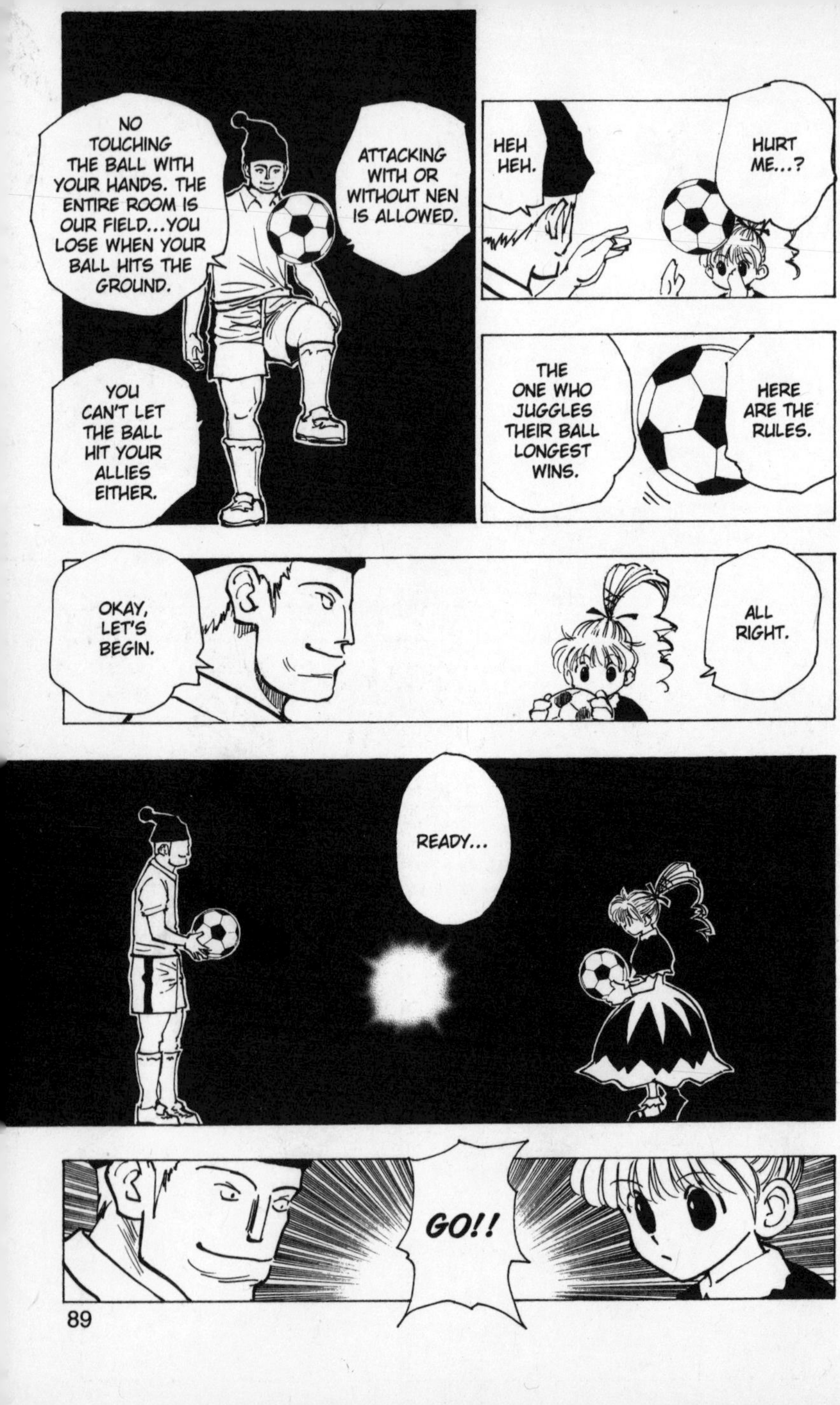
HURT ME...?
HEH HEH.
HERE ARE THE RULES.
THE ONE WHO JUGGLES THEIR BALL LONGEST WINS.
ATTACKING WITH OR WITHOUT NEN IS ALLOWED.
NO TOUCHING THE BALL WITH YOUR HANDS. THE ENTIRE ROOM IS OUR FIELD...YOU LOSE WHEN YOUR BALL HITS THE GROUND.
YOU CAN'T LET THE BALL HIT YOUR ALLIES EITHER.
ALL RIGHT.
OKAY, LET'S BEGIN.
READY...
GO!!

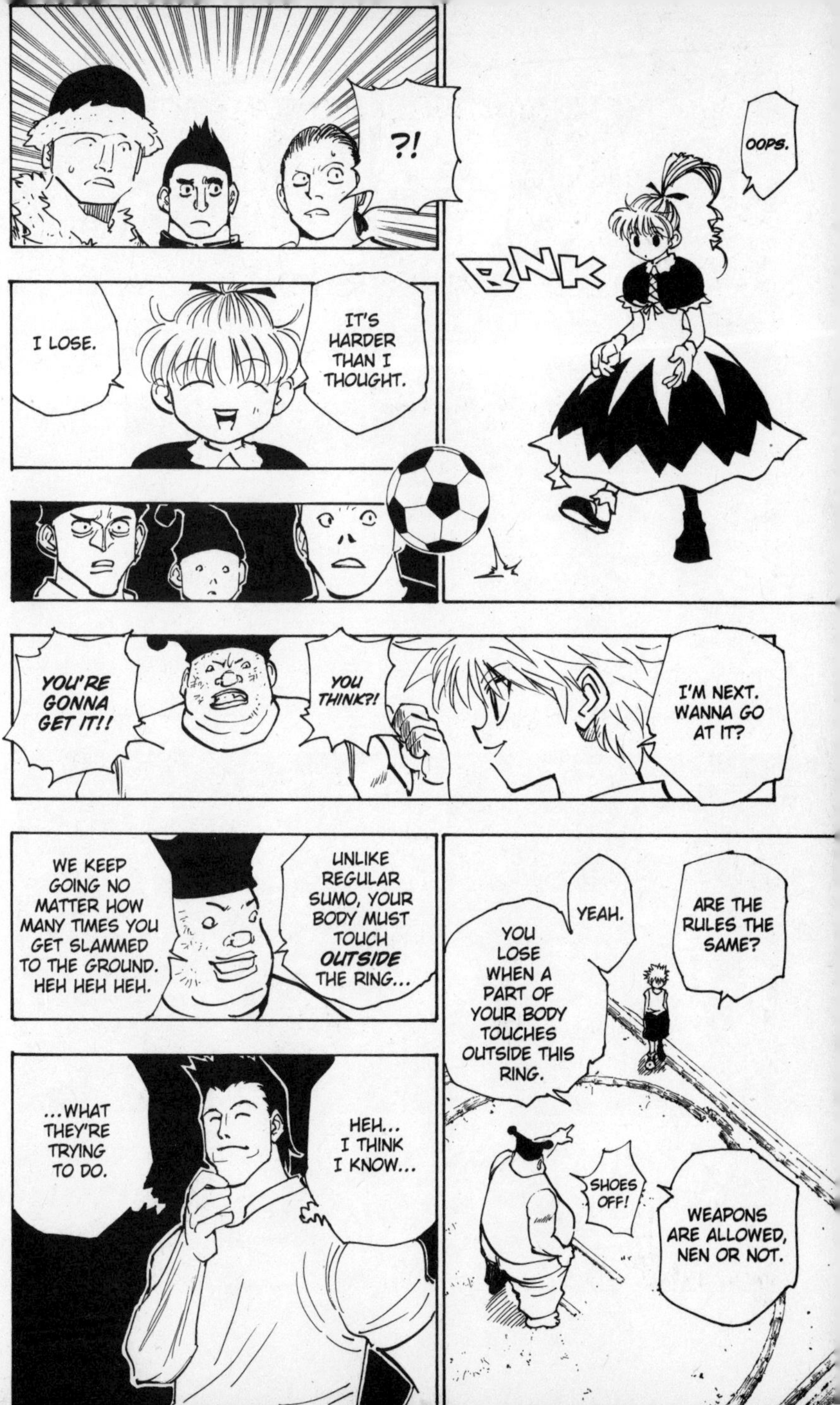
OOPS.
BNK
?!
IT'S HARDER THAN I THOUGHT.
I LOSE.
I'M NEXT. WANNA GO AT IT?
YOU THINK?!
YOU'RE GONNA GET IT!!
ARE THE RULES THE SAME?
YEAH.
YOU LOSE WHEN A PART OF YOUR BODY TOUCHES OUTSIDE THIS RING.
WEAPONS ARE ALLOWED, NEN OR NOT.
SHOES OFF!
UNLIKE REGULAR SUMO, YOUR BODY MUST TOUCH OUTSIDE THE RING...
WE KEEP GOING NO MATTER HOW MANY TIMES YOU GET SLAMMED TO THE GROUND. HEH HEH HEH.
HEH... I THINK I KNOW...
...WHAT THEY'RE TRYING TO DO.

READ THIS WAY

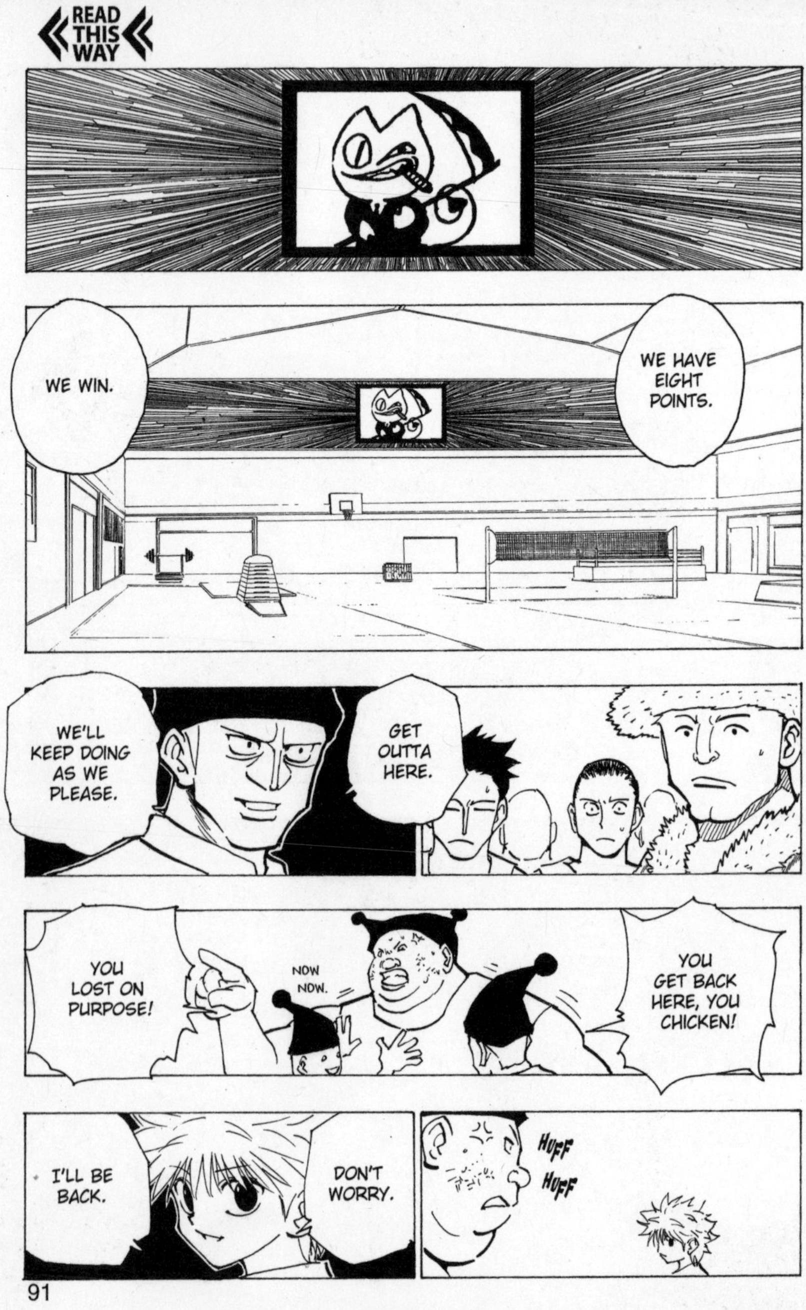

WE HAVE EIGHT POINTS.
WE WIN.
GET OUTTA HERE.
WE'LL KEEP DOING AS WE PLEASE.
YOU GET BACK HERE, YOU CHICKEN!
NOW NOW.
YOU LOST ON PURPOSE!
HUFF
HUFF
DON'T WORRY.
I'LL BE BACK.

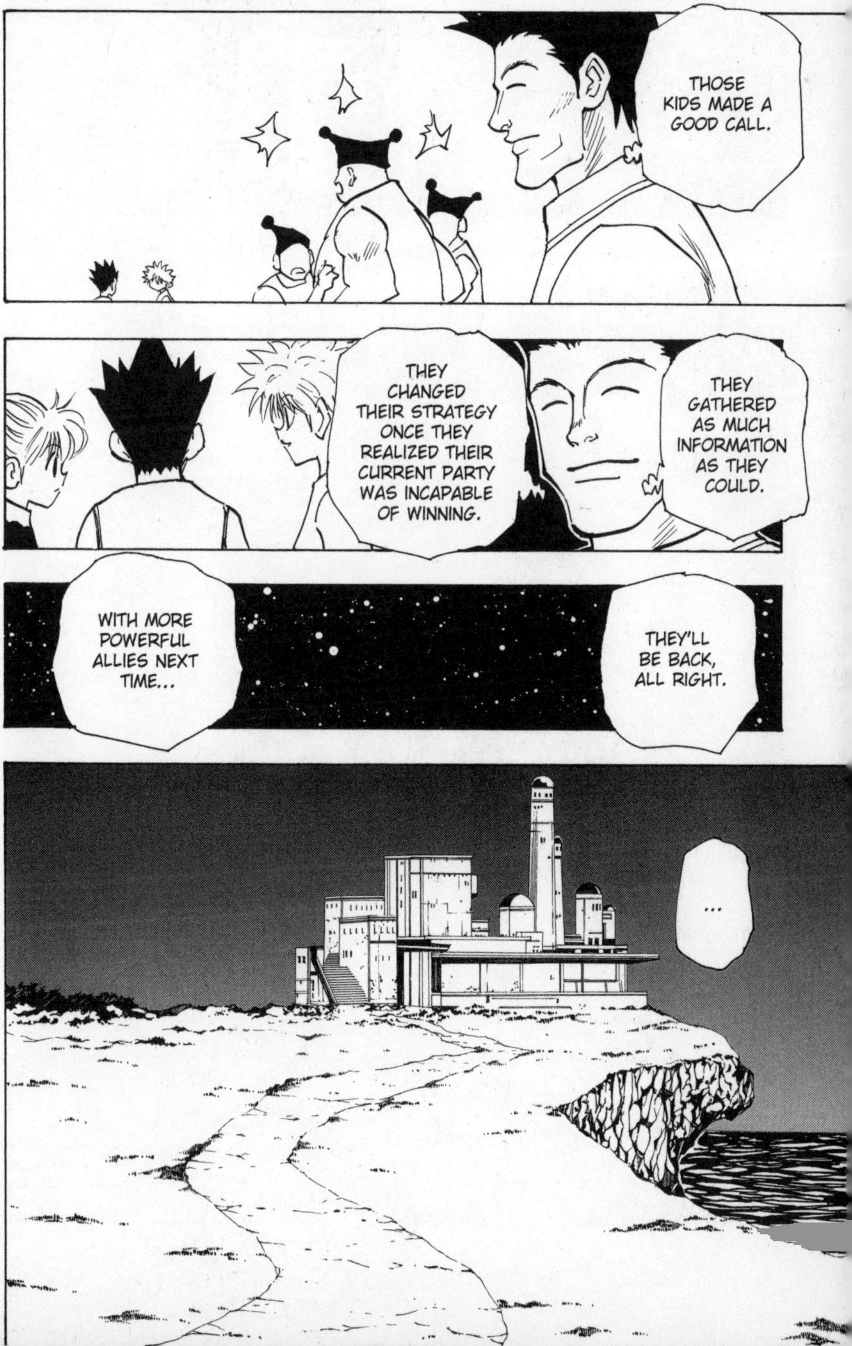
THOSE KIDS MADE A GOOD CALL.
THEY GATHERED AS MUCH INFORMATION AS THEY COULD.
THEY CHANGED THEIR STRATEGY ONCE THEY REALIZED THEIR CURRENT PARTY WAS INCAPABLE OF WINNING.
THEY'LL BE BACK, ALL RIGHT.
WITH MORE POWERFUL ALLIES NEXT TIME...
...

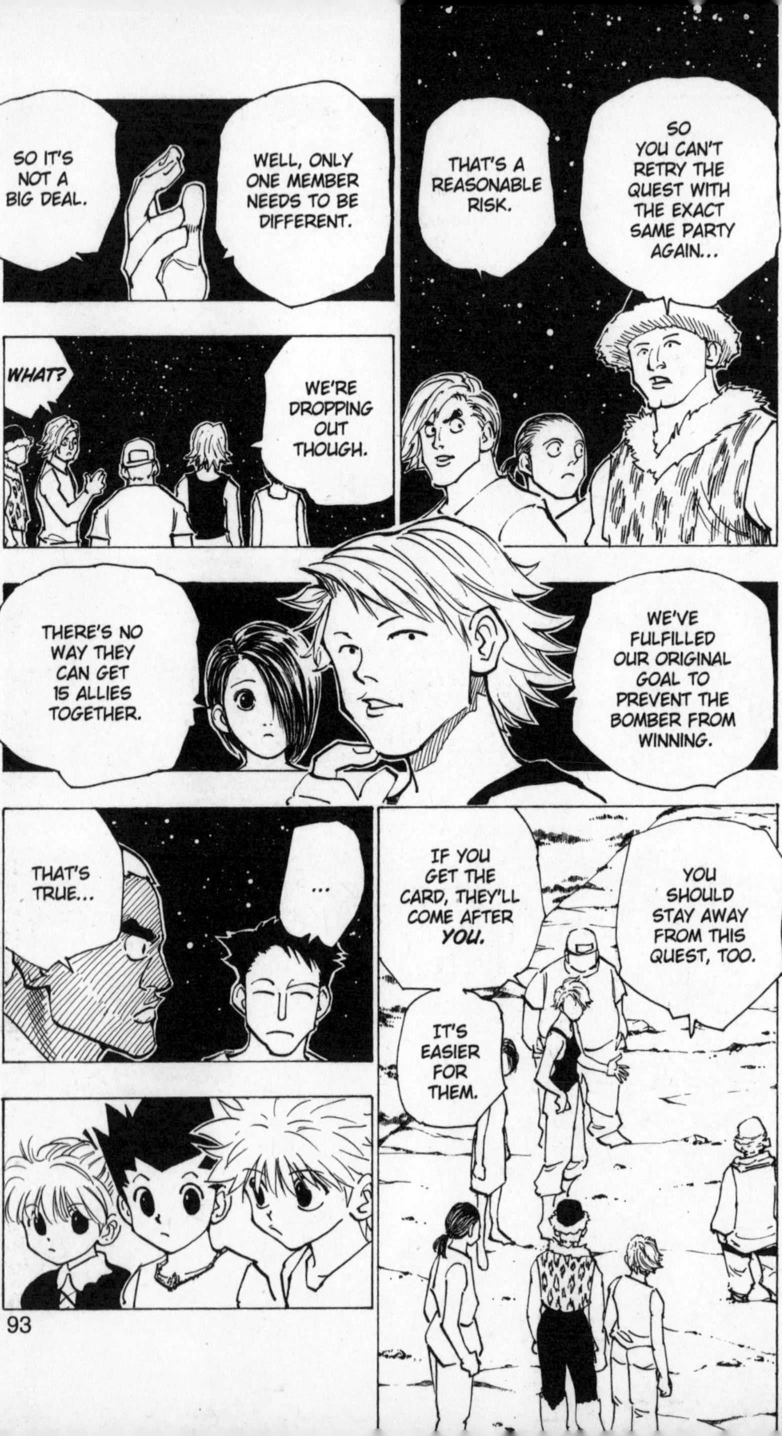
SO YOU CAN'T RETRY THE QUEST WITH THE EXACT SAME PARTY AGAIN...
THAT'S A REASONABLE RISK.
WELL, ONLY ONE MEMBER NEEDS TO BE DIFFERENT.
SO IT'S NOT A BIG DEAL.
WE'RE DROPPING OUT THOUGH.
WHAT?
WE'VE FULFILLED OUR ORIGINAL GOAL TO PREVENT THE BOMBER FROM WINNING.
THERE'S NO WAY THEY CAN GET 15 ALLIES TOGETHER.
YOU SHOULD STAY AWAY FROM THIS QUEST, TOO.
IF YOU GET THE CARD, THEY'LL COME AFTER YOU.
IT'S EASIER FOR THEM.
...
THAT'S TRUE...

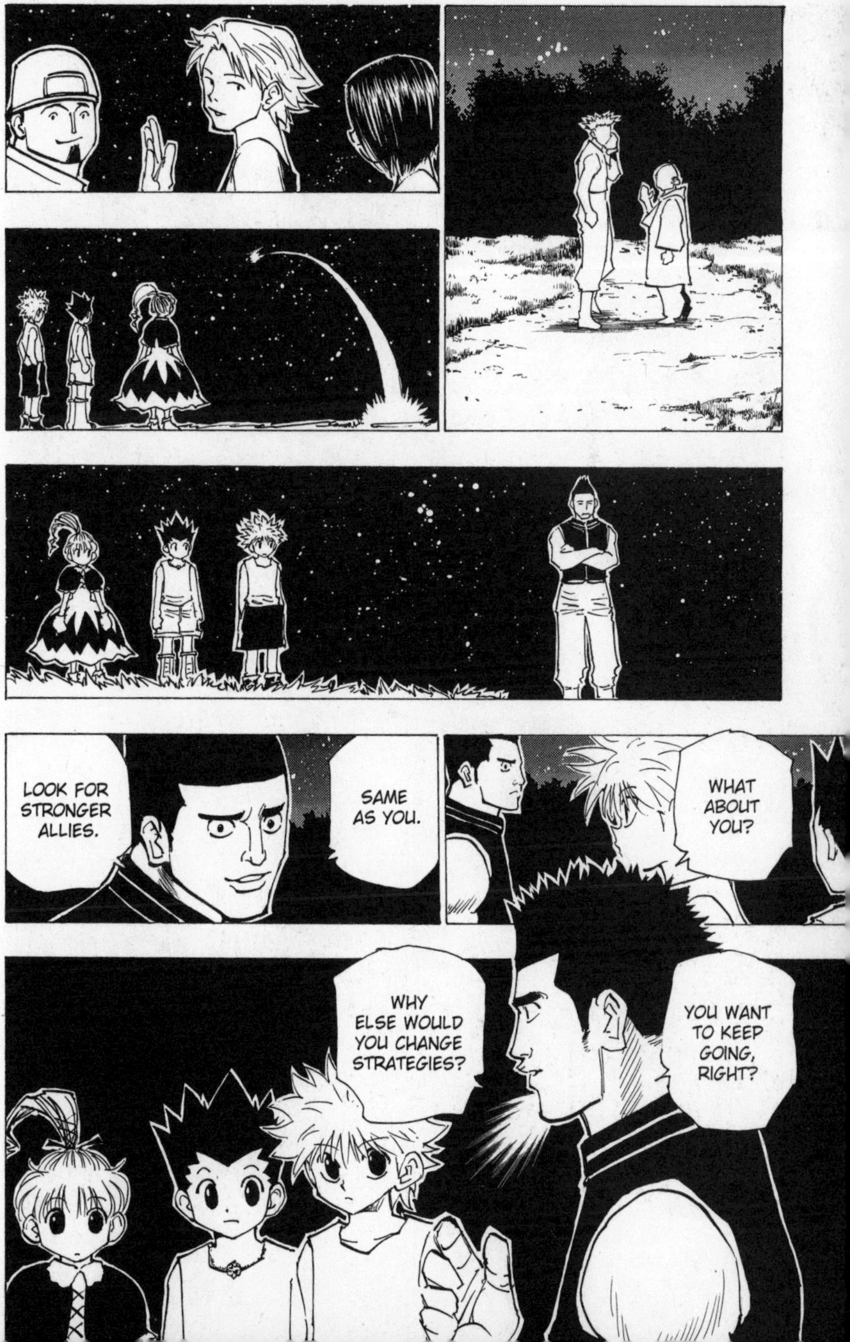
WHAT ABOUT YOU?
SAME AS YOU.
LOOK FOR STRONGER ALLIES.
YOU WANT TO KEEP GOING, RIGHT?
WHY ELSE WOULD YOU CHANGE STRATEGIES?

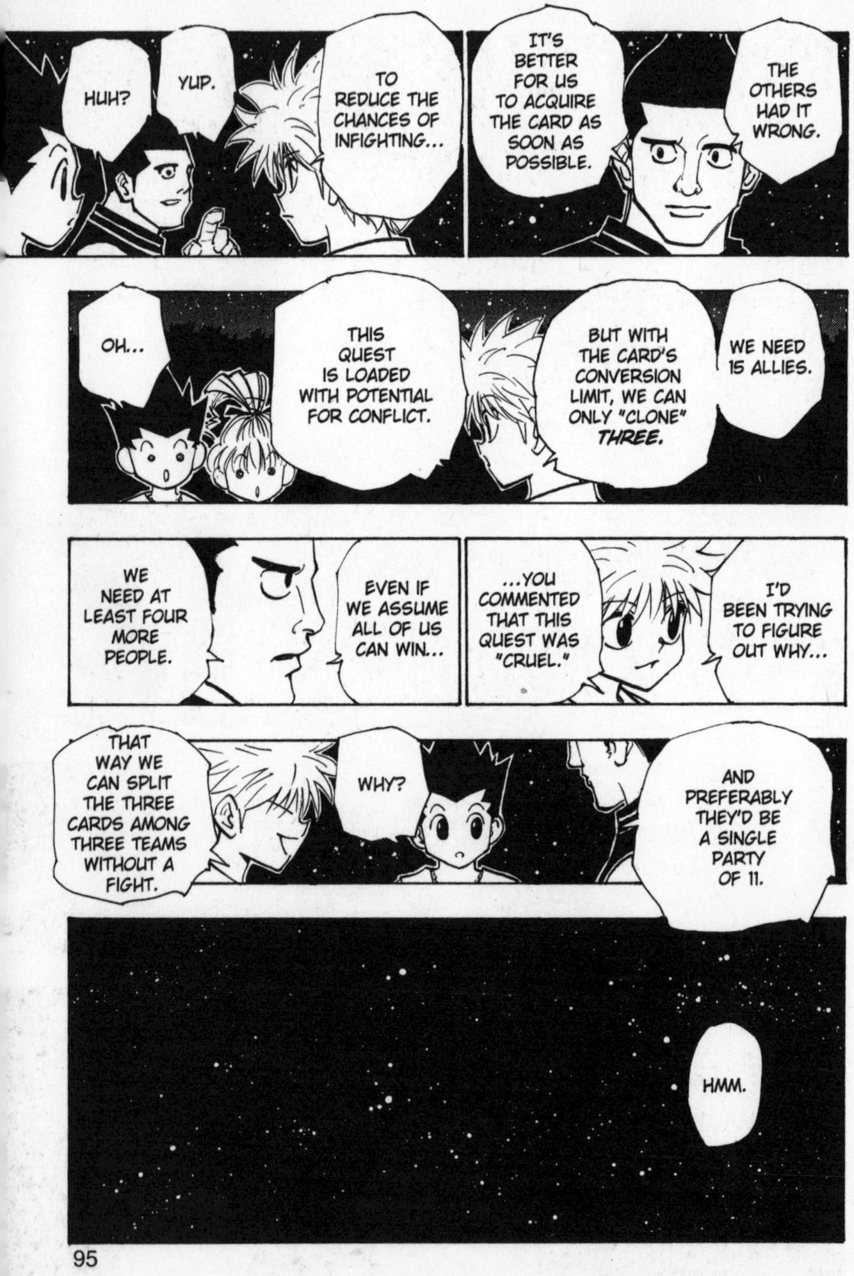
THE OTHERS HAD IT WRONG.
IT'S BETTER FOR US TO ACQUIRE THE CARD AS SOON AS POSSIBLE.
TO REDUCE THE CHANCES OF INFIGHTING...
YUP.
HUH?
WE NEED 15 ALLIES.
BUT WITH THE CARD'S CONVERSION LIMIT, WE CAN ONLY "CLONE" *THREE.*
THIS QUEST IS LOADED WITH POTENTIAL FOR CONFLICT.
OH...
I'D BEEN TRYING TO FIGURE OUT WHY...
...YOU COMMENTED THAT THIS QUEST WAS "CRUEL."
EVEN IF WE ASSUME ALL OF US CAN WIN...
WE NEED AT LEAST FOUR MORE PEOPLE.
AND PREFERABLY THEY'D BE A SINGLE PARTY OF 11.
WHY?
THAT WAY WE CAN SPLIT THE THREE CARDS AMONG THREE TEAMS WITHOUT A FIGHT.
HMM.

DRAW WITHOUT LOOKING: PART 5
RABID DOG

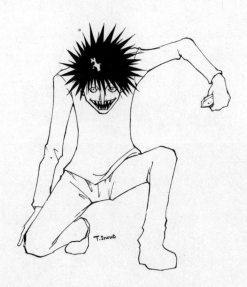

T.Inoue

Chapter 158: Two of a Kind +1

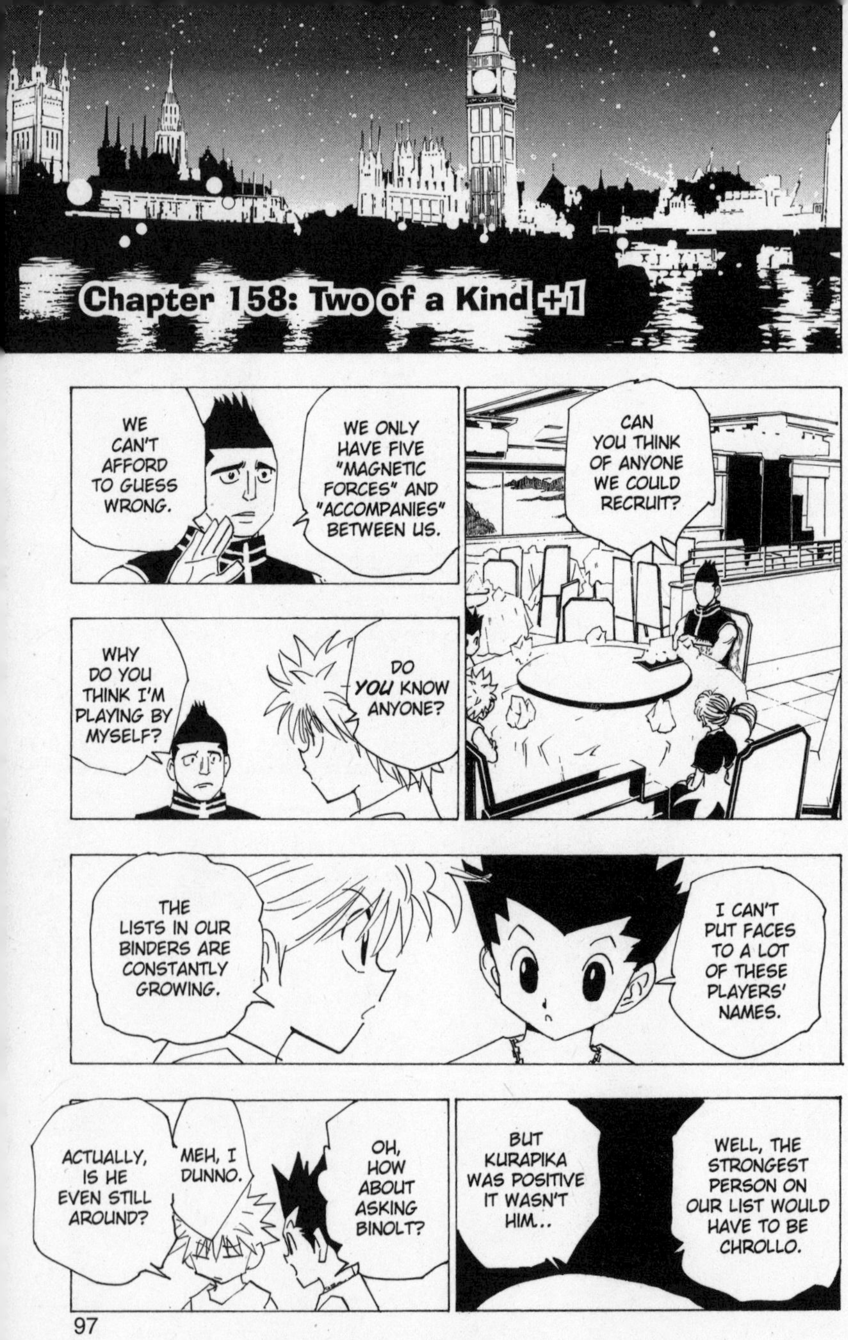

CAN YOU THINK OF ANYONE WE COULD RECRUIT?
WE ONLY HAVE FIVE "MAGNETIC FORCES" AND "ACCOMPANIES" BETWEEN US.
WE CAN'T AFFORD TO GUESS WRONG.
DO *YOU* KNOW ANYONE?
WHY DO YOU THINK I'M PLAYING BY MYSELF?
I CAN'T PUT FACES TO A LOT OF THESE PLAYERS' NAMES.
THE LISTS IN OUR BINDERS ARE CONSTANTLY GROWING.
WELL, THE STRONGEST PERSON ON OUR LIST WOULD HAVE TO BE CHROLLO.
BUT KURAPIKA WAS POSITIVE IT WASN'T HIM..
OH, HOW ABOUT ASKING BINOLT?
MEH, I DUNNO.
ACTUALLY, IS HE EVEN STILL AROUND?

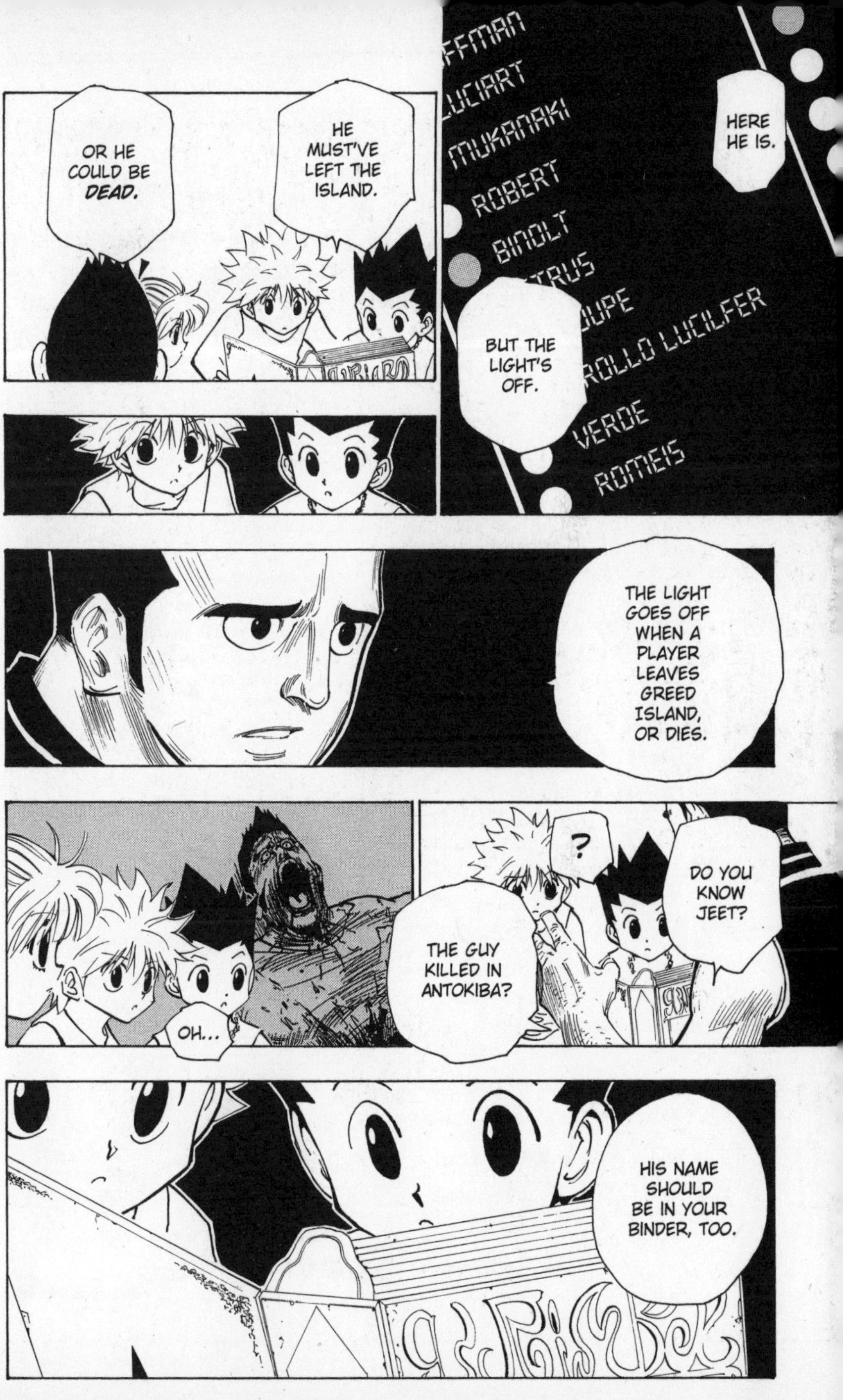
HERE HE IS.
LUCIART
MUKANAKI
ROBERT
BINOLT
ROLLO LUCILFER
VERDE
ROMEIS
BUT THE LIGHT'S OFF.
HE MUST'VE LEFT THE ISLAND.
OR HE COULD BE *DEAD.*
THE LIGHT GOES OFF WHEN A PLAYER LEAVES GREED ISLAND, OR DIES.
DO YOU KNOW JEET?
?
THE GUY KILLED IN ANTOKIBA?
OH...
HIS NAME SHOULD BE IN YOUR BINDER, TOO.

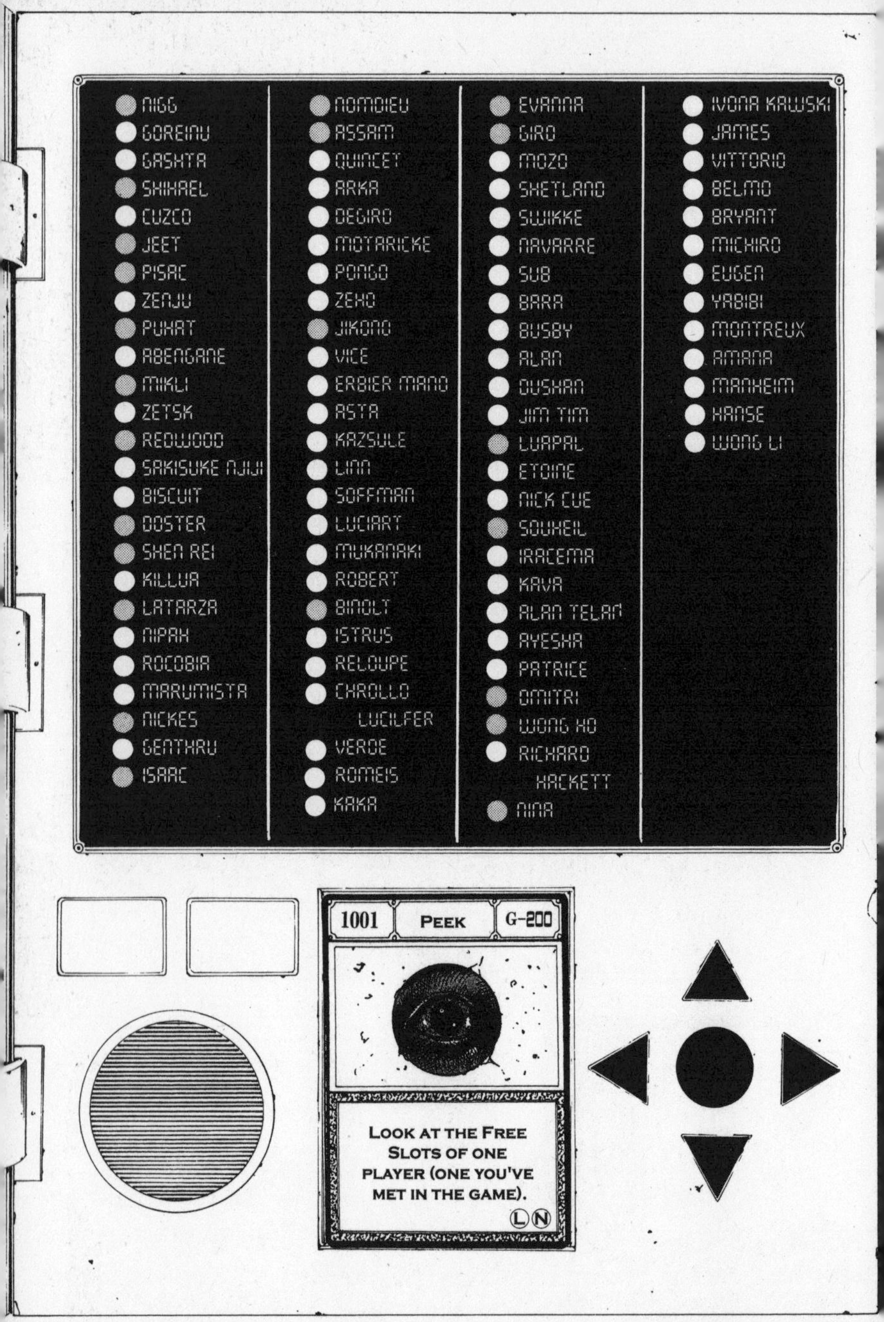

NIGG	NOMDIEU	EVANNA	IVONA KRWSKI
GOREINU	ASSAM	GIRO	JAMES
GASHTA	QUINCET	MOZO	VITTORIO
SHIMAEL	ARKA	SHETLAND	BELMO
CUZCO	DEGIRO	SWIKKE	BRYANT
JEET	MOTRRICKE	NAVARRE	MICHIRO
PISAC	PONGO	SUB	EUGEN
ZENJU	ZEKO	BARA	YABIBI
PUHAT	JIKONO	BUSBY	MONTREUX
ABENGANE	VICE	ALAN	AMANA
MIKLI	ERBIER MANO	DUSHAN	MANHEIM
ZETSK	ASTA	JIM TIM	HANSE
REDWOOD	KAZSULE	LUAPAL	WONG LI
SAKISUKE NJIJI	LINN	ETOINE	
BISCUIT	SOFFMAN	NICK CUE	
DOSTER	LUCIART	SOUHEIL	
SHEN REI	MUKANAKI	IRACEMA	
KILLUA	ROBERT	KAVA	
LATARZA	BINOLT	ALAN TELAN	
NIPAH	ISTRUS	AYESHA	
ROCOBIA	RELOUPE	PATRICE	
MARUMISTA	CHROLLO	DMITRI	
NICKES	LUCILFER	WONG HO	
GENTHRU	VERDE	RICHARD	
ISAAC	ROMEIS	HACKETT	
	KAKA	NINA	

1001   PEEK   G-200

LOOK AT THE FREE SLOTS OF ONE PLAYER (ONE YOU'VE MET IN THE GAME).

Ⓛ Ⓝ

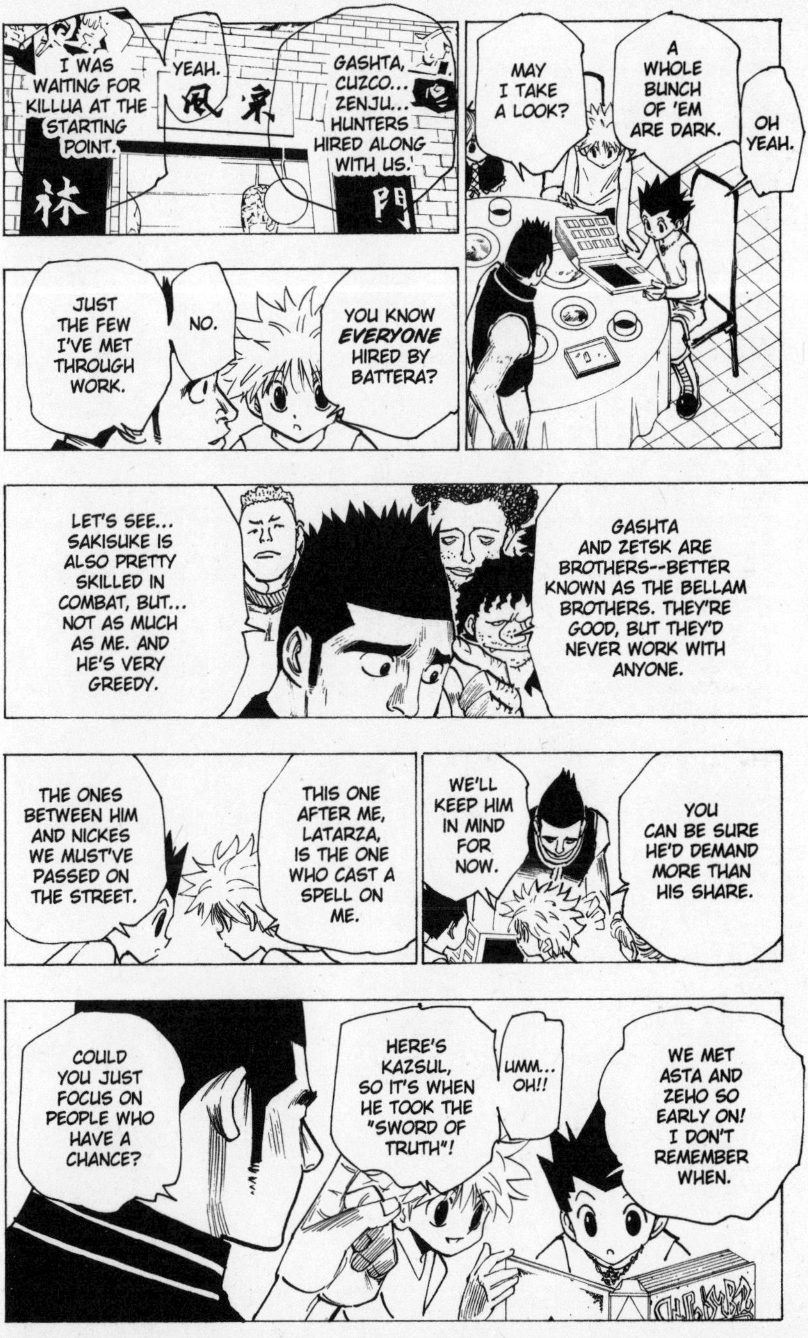
OH YEAH.
A WHOLE BUNCH OF 'EM ARE DARK.
MAY I TAKE A LOOK?
GASHTA, CUZCO... ZENJU... HUNTERS HIRED ALONG WITH US.
YEAH.
I WAS WAITING FOR KILLUA AT THE STARTING POINT.
YOU KNOW *EVERYONE* HIRED BY BATTERA?
NO.
JUST THE FEW I'VE MET THROUGH WORK.
GASHTA AND ZETSK ARE BROTHERS--BETTER KNOWN AS THE BELLAM BROTHERS. THEY'RE GOOD, BUT THEY'D NEVER WORK WITH ANYONE.
LET'S SEE... SAKISUKE IS ALSO PRETTY SKILLED IN COMBAT, BUT... NOT AS MUCH AS ME. AND HE'S VERY GREEDY.
YOU CAN BE SURE HE'D DEMAND MORE THAN HIS SHARE.
WE'LL KEEP HIM IN MIND FOR NOW.
THIS ONE AFTER ME, LATARZA, IS THE ONE WHO CAST A SPELL ON ME.
THE ONES BETWEEN HIM AND NICKES WE MUST'VE PASSED ON THE STREET.
WE MET ASTA AND ZEHO SO EARLY ON! I DON'T REMEMBER WHEN.
UMM... OH!!
HERE'S KAZSUL, SO IT'S WHEN HE TOOK THE "SWORD OF TRUTH"!
COULD YOU JUST FOCUS ON PEOPLE WHO HAVE A CHANCE?

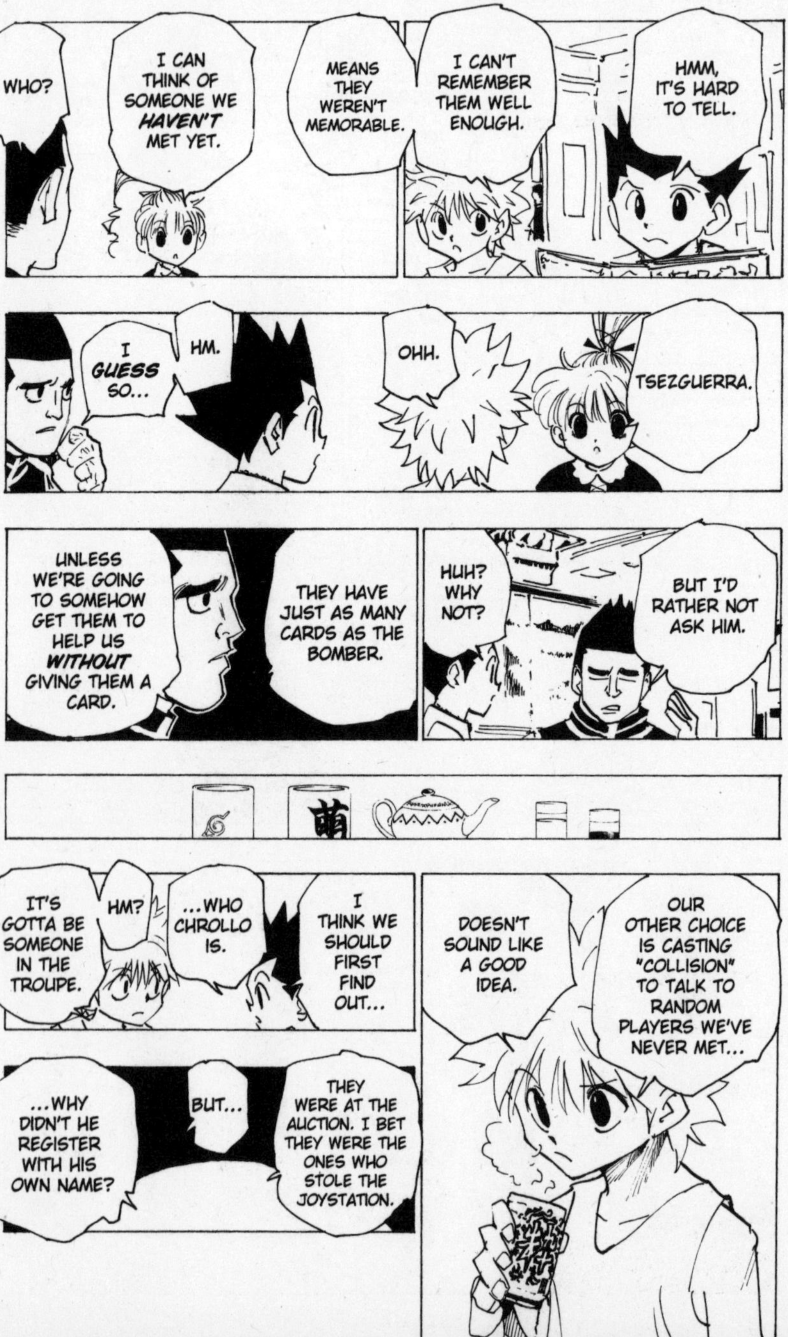
HMM, IT'S HARD TO TELL.
I CAN'T REMEMBER THEM WELL ENOUGH.
MEANS THEY WEREN'T MEMORABLE.
I CAN THINK OF SOMEONE WE *HAVEN'T* MET YET.
WHO?
TSEZGUERRA.
OHH.
HM.
I *GUESS* SO...
BUT I'D RATHER NOT ASK HIM.
HUH? WHY NOT?
THEY HAVE JUST AS MANY CARDS AS THE BOMBER.
UNLESS WE'RE GOING TO SOMEHOW GET THEM TO HELP US *WITHOUT* GIVING THEM A CARD.
萌
OUR OTHER CHOICE IS CASTING "COLLISION" TO TALK TO RANDOM PLAYERS WE'VE NEVER MET...
DOESN'T SOUND LIKE A GOOD IDEA.
I THINK WE SHOULD FIRST FIND OUT...
...WHO CHROLLO IS.
HM?
IT'S GOTTA BE SOMEONE IN THE TROUPE.
THEY WERE AT THE AUCTION. I BET THEY WERE THE ONES WHO STOLE THE JOYSTATION.
BUT...
...WHY DIDN'T HE REGISTER WITH HIS OWN NAME?

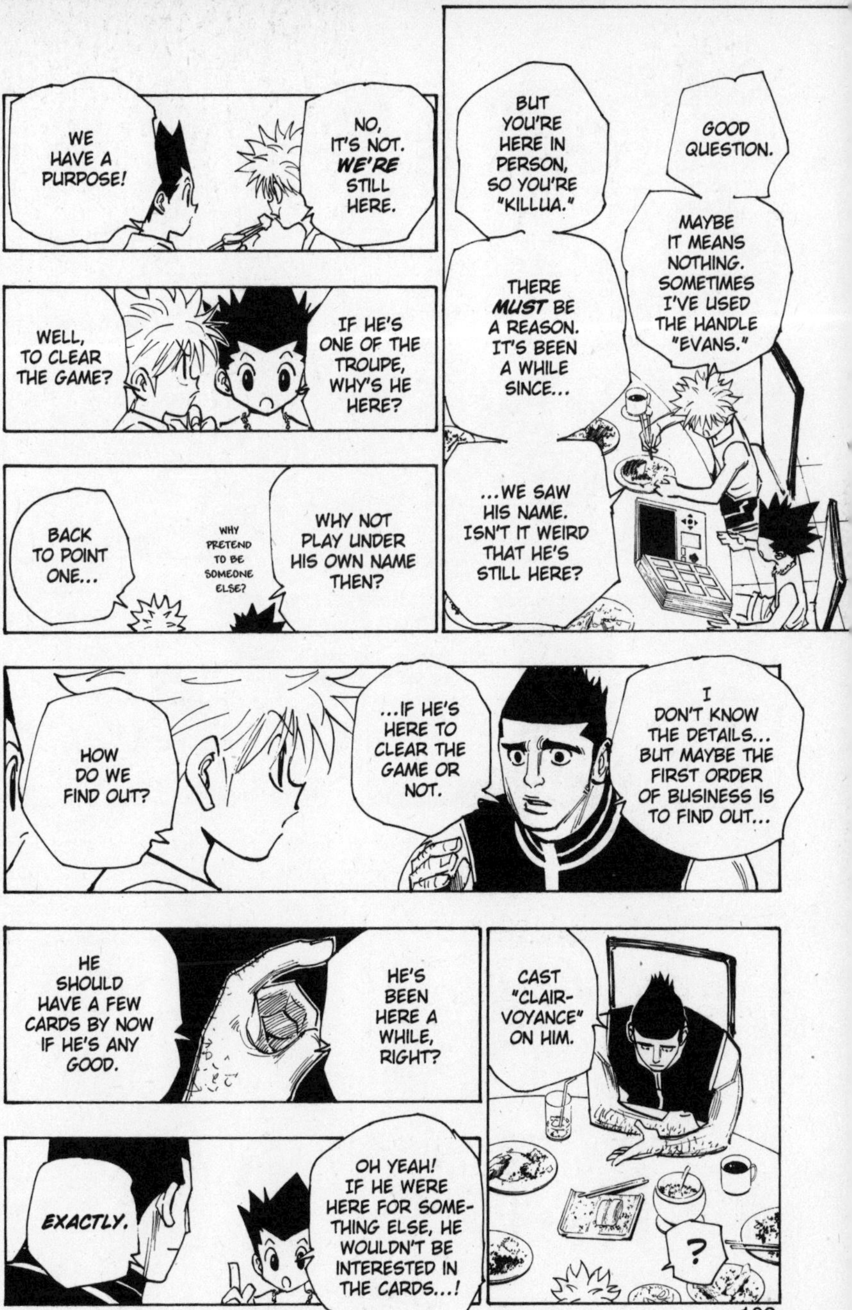
GOOD QUESTION.
MAYBE IT MEANS NOTHING. SOMETIMES I'VE USED THE HANDLE "EVANS."
BUT YOU'RE HERE IN PERSON, SO YOU'RE "KILLUA."
THERE *MUST* BE A REASON. IT'S BEEN A WHILE SINCE...
...WE SAW HIS NAME. ISN'T IT WEIRD THAT HE'S STILL HERE?
NO, IT'S NOT. *WE'RE* STILL HERE.
WE HAVE A PURPOSE!
IF HE'S ONE OF THE TROUPE, WHY'S HE HERE?
WELL, TO CLEAR THE GAME?
WHY NOT PLAY UNDER HIS OWN NAME THEN?
WHY PRETEND TO BE SOMEONE ELSE?
BACK TO POINT ONE...
I DON'T KNOW THE DETAILS... BUT MAYBE THE FIRST ORDER OF BUSINESS IS TO FIND OUT...
...IF HE'S HERE TO CLEAR THE GAME OR NOT.
HOW DO WE FIND OUT?
CAST "CLAIR-VOYANCE" ON HIM.
?
HE'S BEEN HERE A WHILE, RIGHT?
HE SHOULD HAVE A FEW CARDS BY NOW IF HE'S ANY GOOD.
OH YEAH! IF HE WERE HERE FOR SOME-THING ELSE, HE WOULDN'T BE INTERESTED IN THE CARDS...!
EXACTLY.

READ THIS WAY

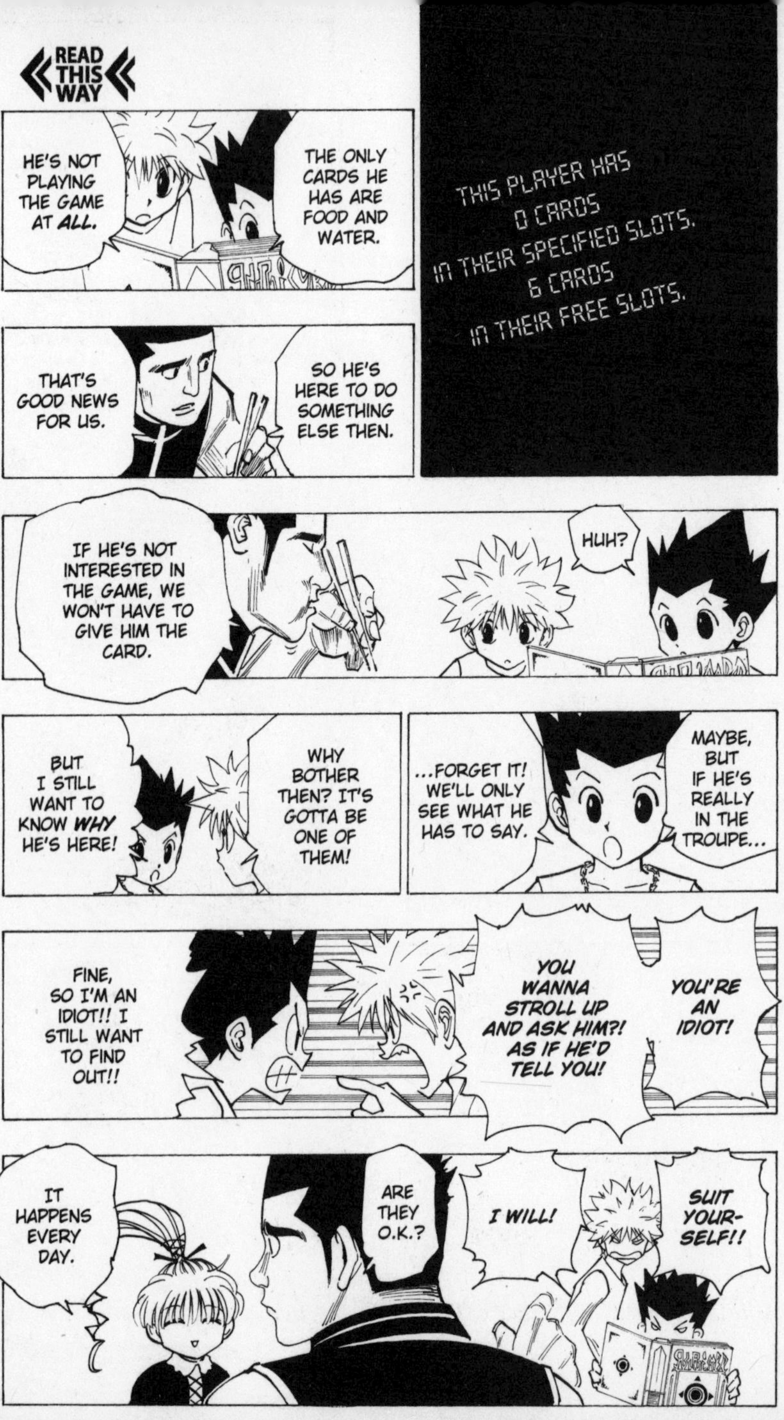
THIS PLAYER HAS 0 CARDS IN THEIR SPECIFIED SLOTS. 6 CARDS IN THEIR FREE SLOTS.
THE ONLY CARDS HE HAS ARE FOOD AND WATER.
HE'S NOT PLAYING THE GAME AT ALL.
SO HE'S HERE TO DO SOMETHING ELSE THEN.
THAT'S GOOD NEWS FOR US.
HUH?
IF HE'S NOT INTERESTED IN THE GAME, WE WON'T HAVE TO GIVE HIM THE CARD.
MAYBE, BUT IF HE'S REALLY IN THE TROUPE...
...FORGET IT! WE'LL ONLY SEE WHAT HE HAS TO SAY.
WHY BOTHER THEN? IT'S GOTTA BE ONE OF THEM!
BUT I STILL WANT TO KNOW WHY HE'S HERE!
YOU'RE AN IDIOT!
YOU WANNA STROLL UP AND ASK HIM?! AS IF HE'D TELL YOU!
FINE, SO I'M AN IDIOT!! I STILL WANT TO FIND OUT!!
SUIT YOURSELF!!
I WILL!
ARE THEY O.K.?
IT HAPPENS EVERY DAY.

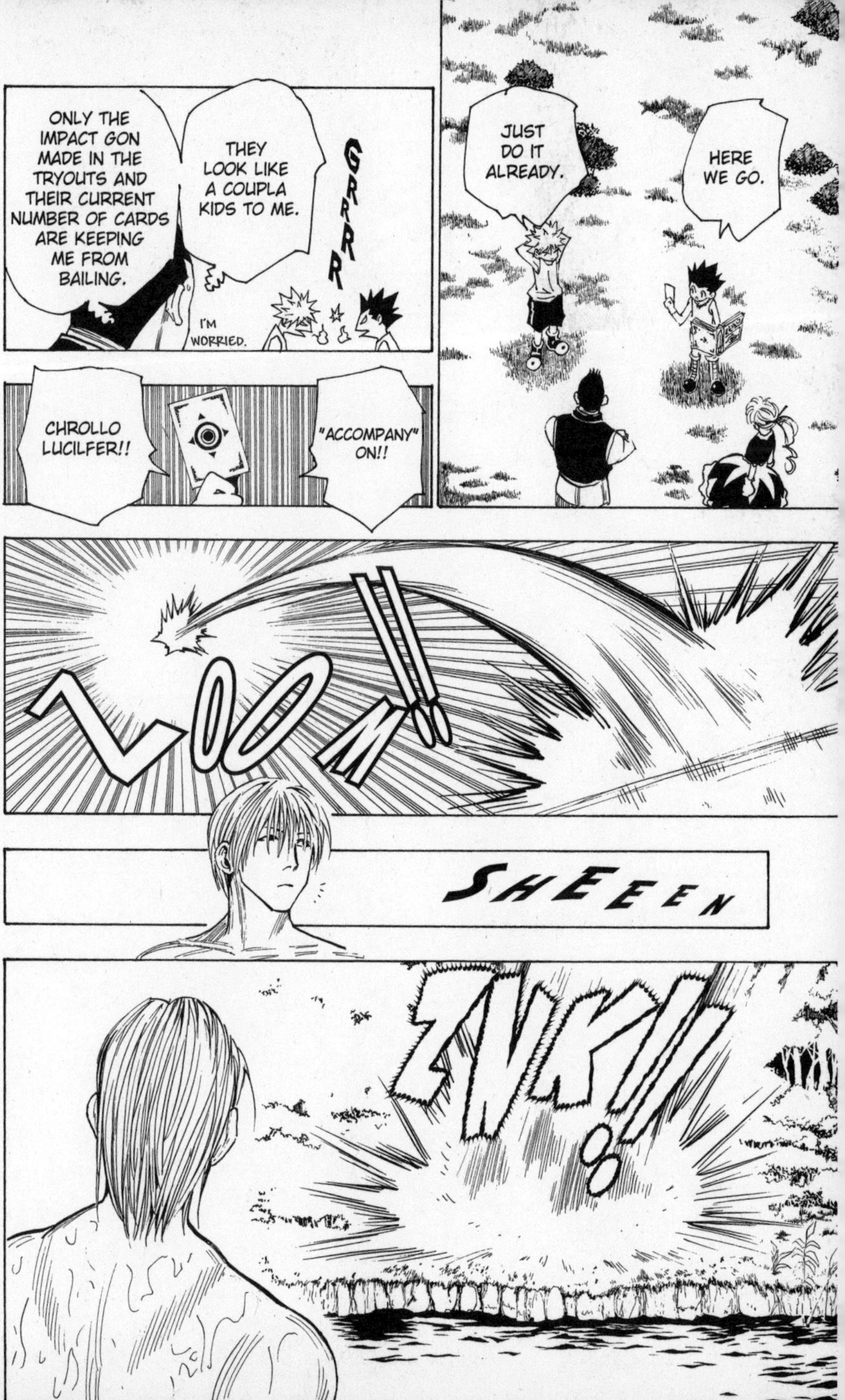
HERE WE GO.
JUST DO IT ALREADY.
GRRRR
THEY LOOK LIKE A COUPLA KIDS TO ME.
ONLY THE IMPACT GON MADE IN THE TRYOUTS AND THEIR CURRENT NUMBER OF CARDS ARE KEEPING ME FROM BAILING.
I'M WORRIED.
"ACCOMPANY" ON!!
CHROLLO LUCILFER!!
VOOOM!!
SHEEEN

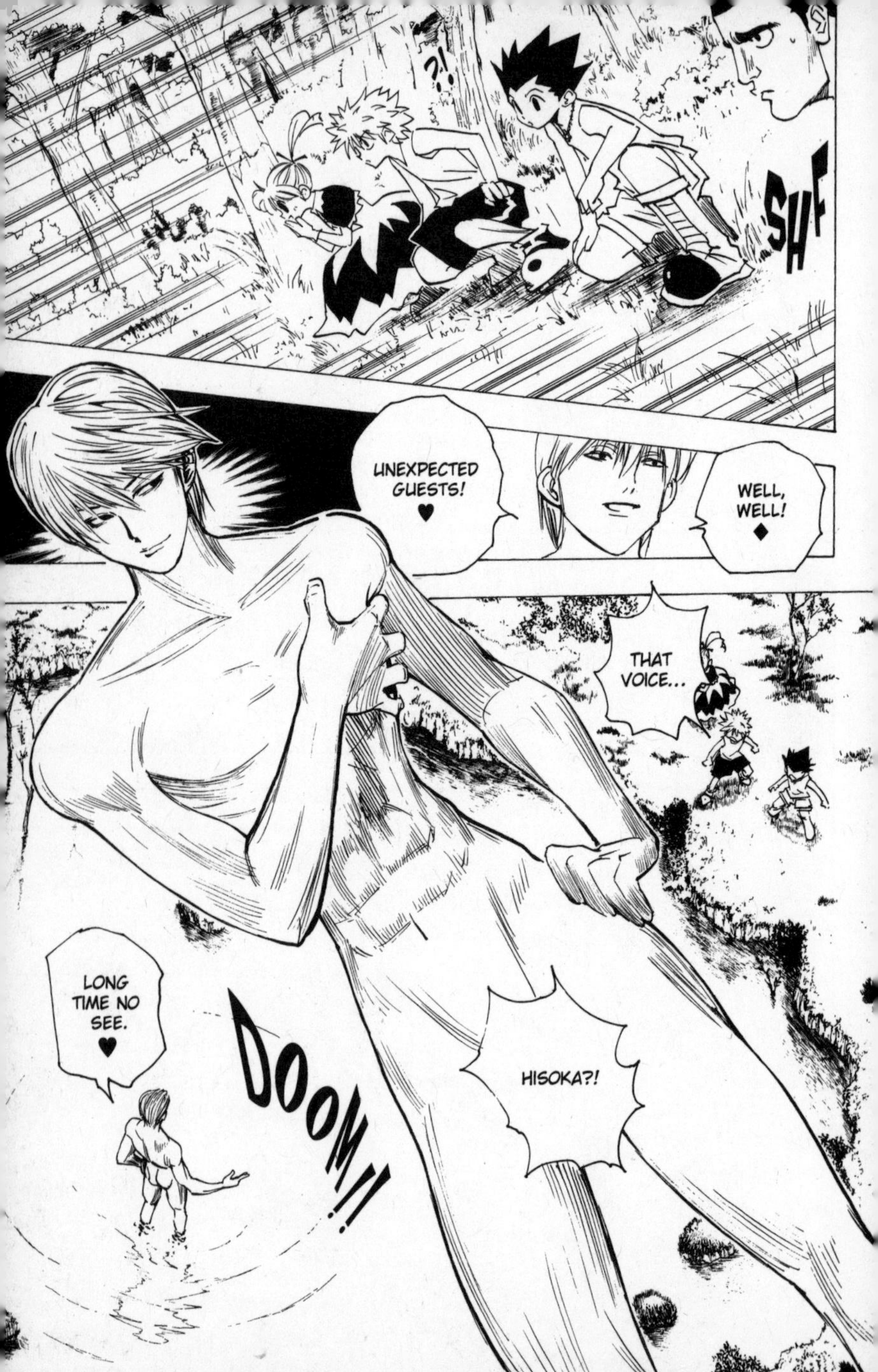
SHF
?!
WELL, WELL! ◆
UNEXPECTED GUESTS! ♥
THAT VOICE...
HISOKA?!
DOOM!!
LONG TIME NO SEE. ♥

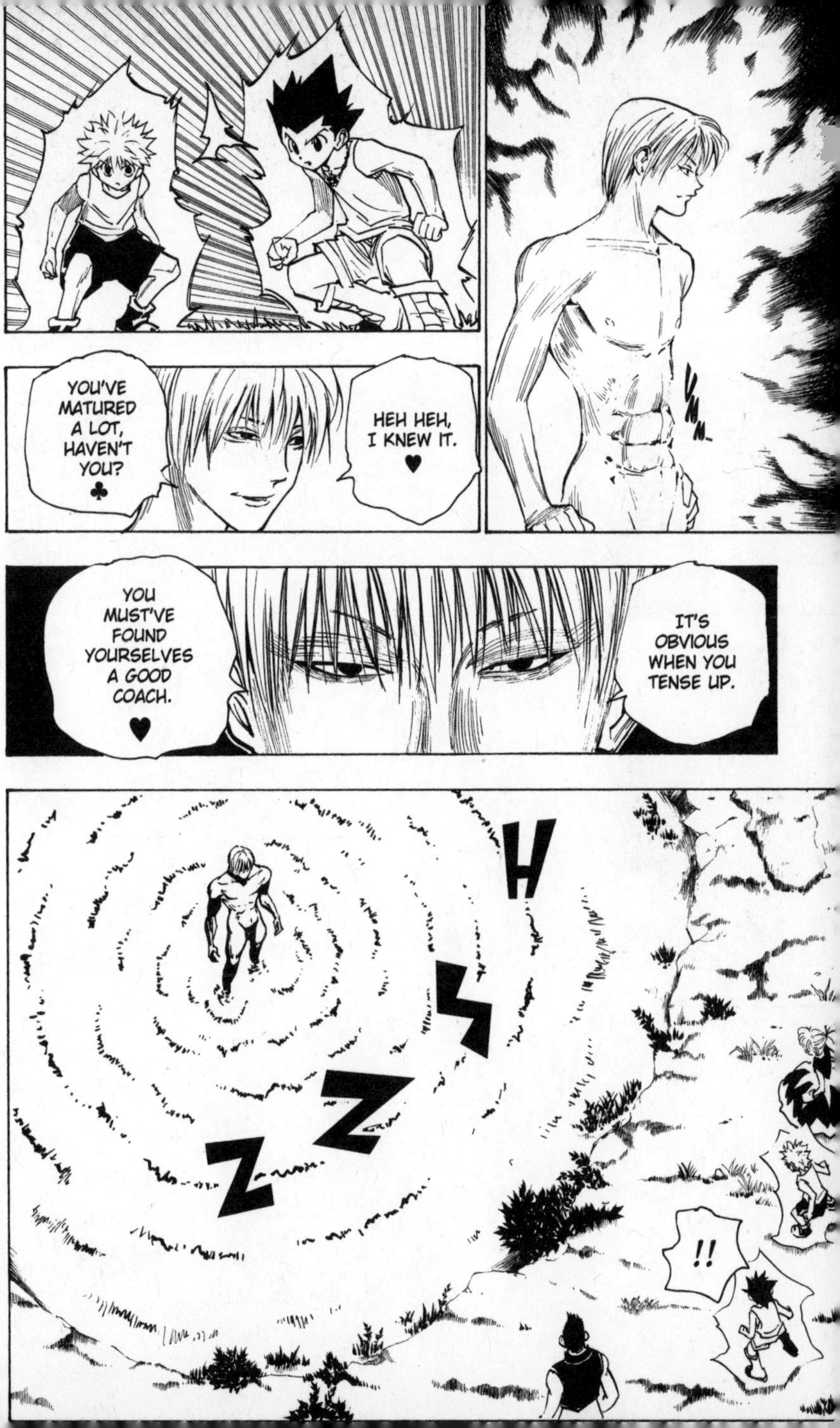
VMM..
HEH HEH, I KNEW IT. ♥
YOU'VE MATURED A LOT, HAVEN'T YOU? ♣
IT'S OBVIOUS WHEN YOU TENSE UP.
YOU MUST'VE FOUND YOURSELVES A GOOD COACH. ♥
HSZZ
!!

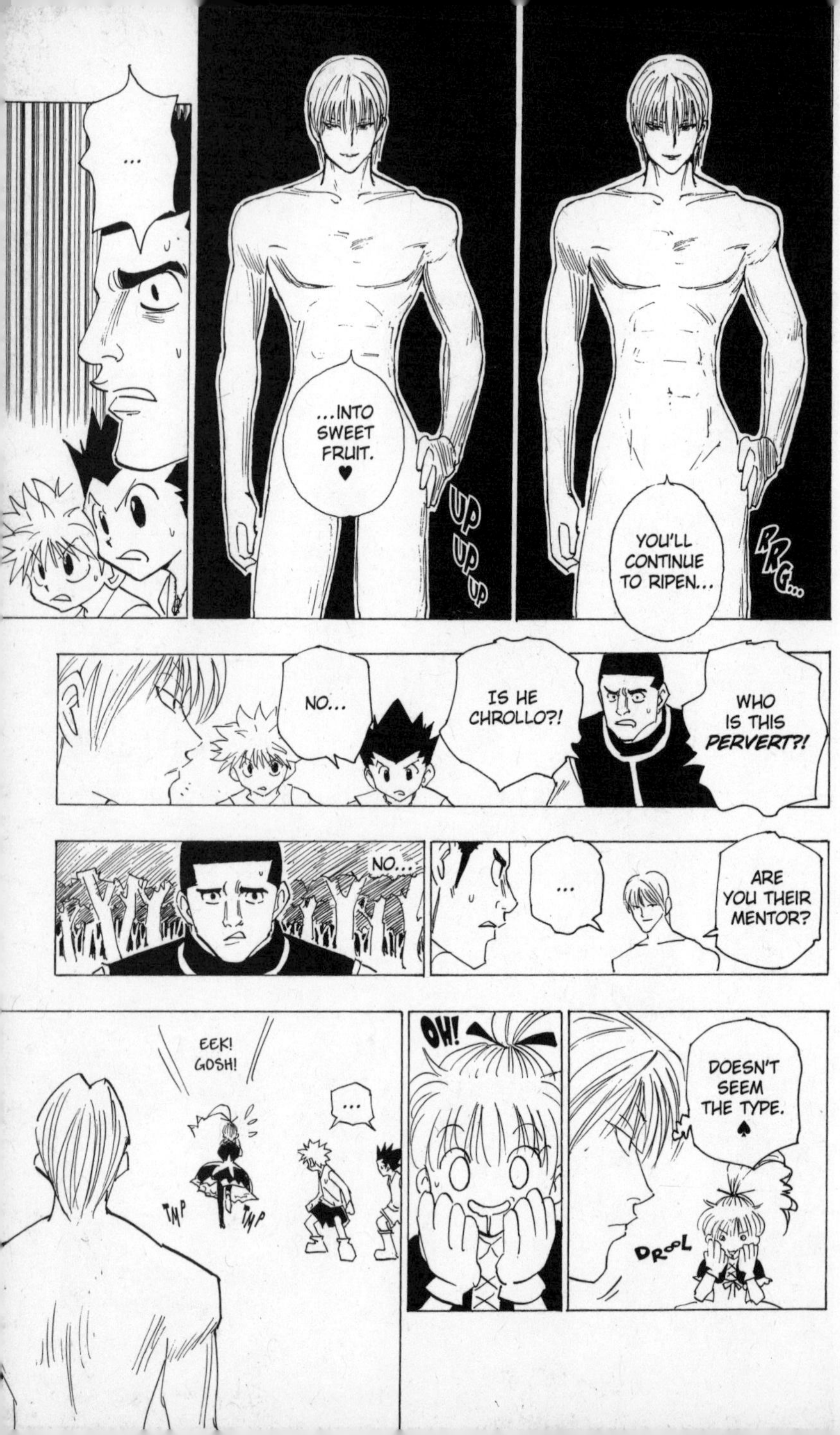
YOU'LL CONTINUE TO RIPEN...
RRG...
...INTO SWEET FRUIT. ♥
UP UP UP
...
WHO IS THIS PERVERT?!
IS HE CHROLLO?!
NO...
ARE YOU THEIR MENTOR?
...
NO...
DOESN'T SEEM THE TYPE. ♠
DROOL
OH!
EEK! GOSH!
...
TMP
TMP

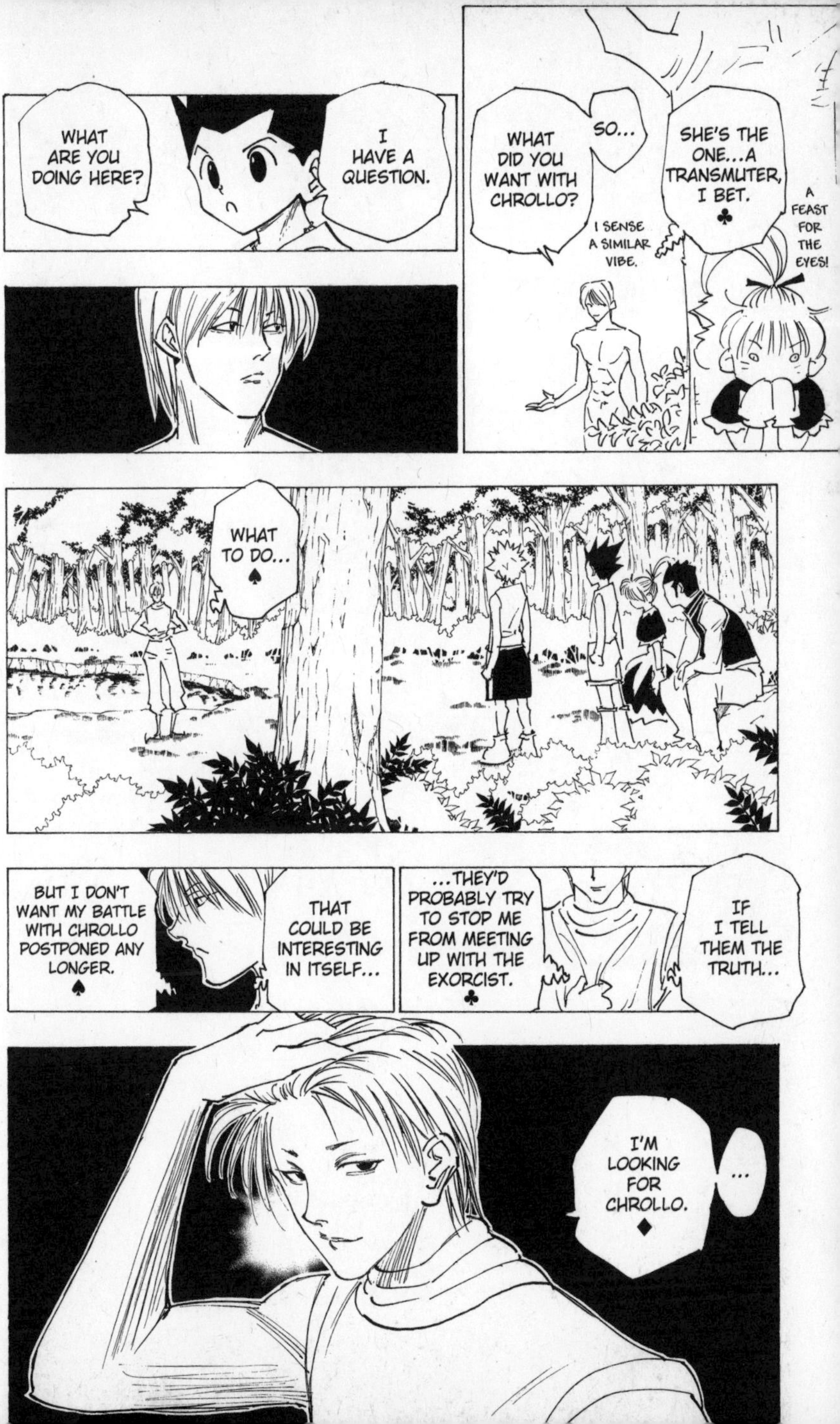
A FEAST FOR THE EYES!
SHE'S THE ONE...A TRANSMUTER, I BET. ♣
I SENSE A SIMILAR VIBE.
SO...
WHAT DID YOU WANT WITH CHROLLO?
I HAVE A QUESTION.
WHAT ARE YOU DOING HERE?
WHAT TO DO... ♠
IF I TELL THEM THE TRUTH...
...THEY'D PROBABLY TRY TO STOP ME FROM MEETING UP WITH THE EXORCIST. ♣
THAT COULD BE INTERESTING IN ITSELF...
BUT I DON'T WANT MY BATTLE WITH CHROLLO POSTPONED ANY LONGER. ♠
...
I'M LOOKING FOR CHROLLO. ♦

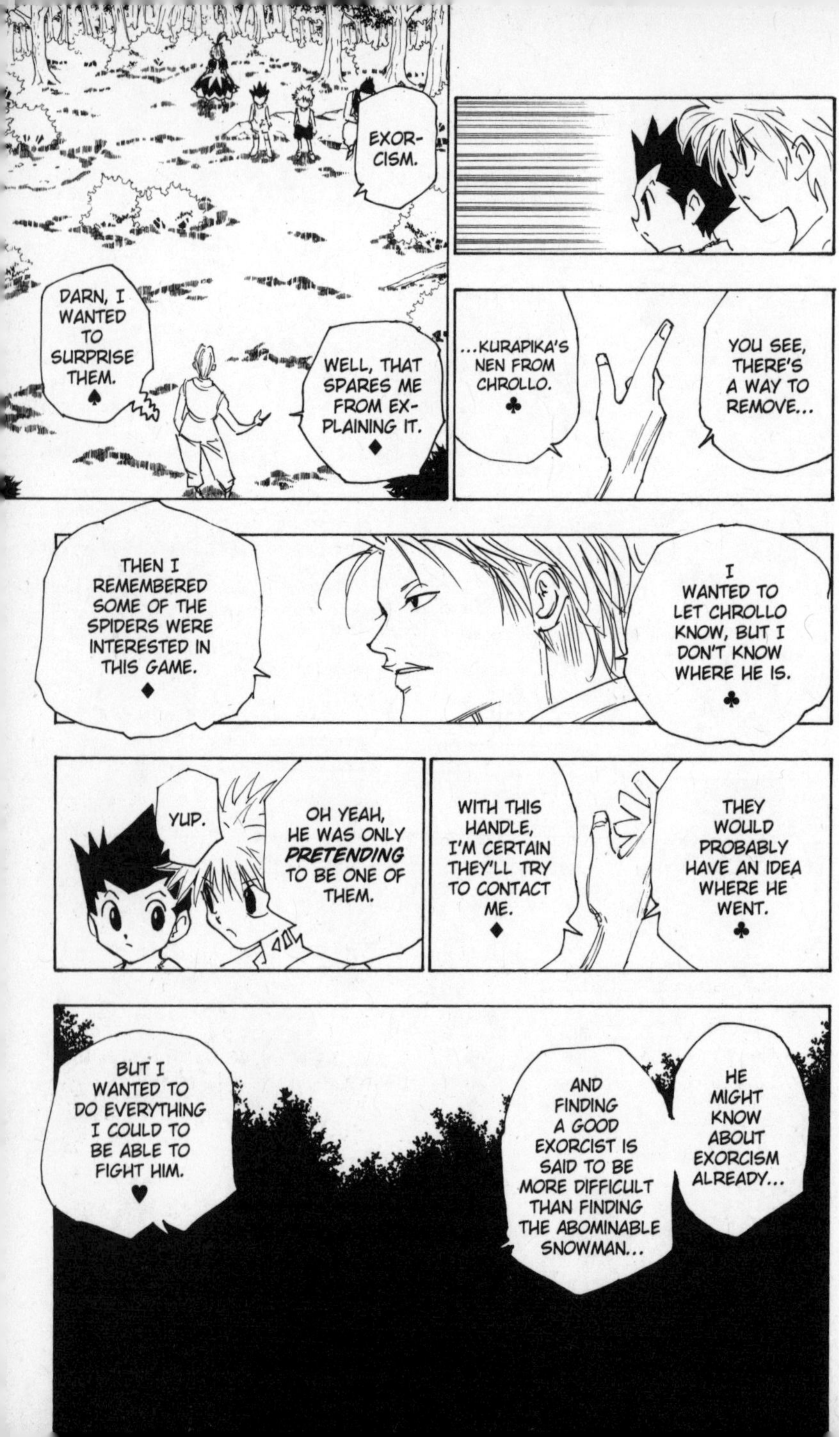
YOU SEE, THERE'S A WAY TO REMOVE...
...KURAPIKA'S NEN FROM CHROLLO. ♣
EXOR-CISM.
WELL, THAT SPARES ME FROM EX-PLAINING IT. ♦
DARN, I WANTED TO SURPRISE THEM. ♠
I WANTED TO LET CHROLLO KNOW, BUT I DON'T KNOW WHERE HE IS. ♣
THEN I REMEMBERED SOME OF THE SPIDERS WERE INTERESTED IN THIS GAME. ♦
THEY WOULD PROBABLY HAVE AN IDEA WHERE HE WENT. ♣
WITH THIS HANDLE, I'M CERTAIN THEY'LL TRY TO CONTACT ME. ♦
OH YEAH, HE WAS ONLY *PRETENDING* TO BE ONE OF THEM.
YUP.
HE MIGHT KNOW ABOUT EXORCISM ALREADY...
AND FINDING A GOOD EXORCIST IS SAID TO BE MORE DIFFICULT THAN FINDING THE ABOMINABLE SNOWMAN...
BUT I WANTED TO DO EVERYTHING I COULD TO BE ABLE TO FIGHT HIM. ♥

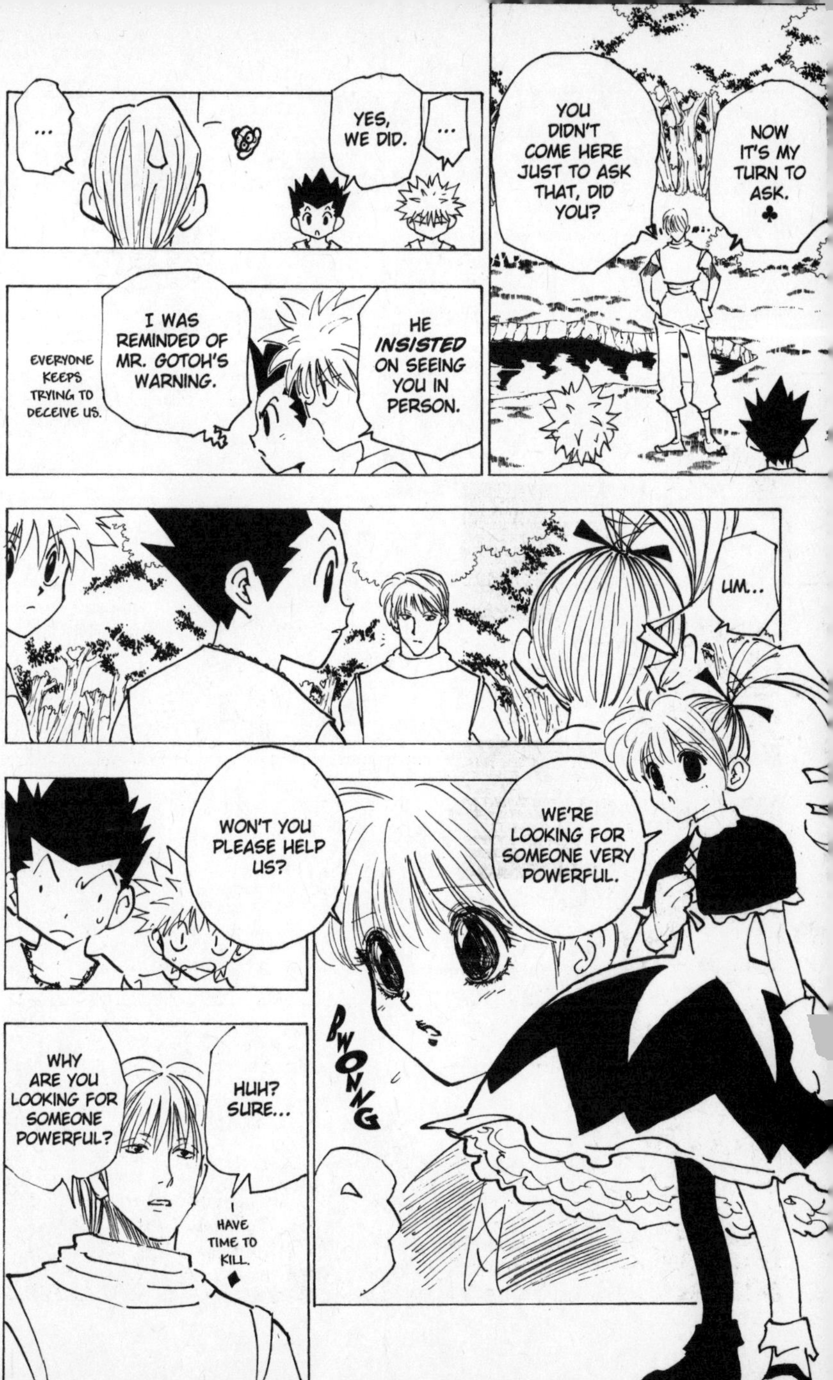
NOW IT'S MY TURN TO ASK. ♣
YOU DIDN'T COME HERE JUST TO ASK THAT, DID YOU?
...
YES, WE DID.
...
HE INSISTED ON SEEING YOU IN PERSON.
I WAS REMINDED OF MR. GOTOH'S WARNING.
EVERYONE KEEPS TRYING TO DECEIVE US.
UM...
WE'RE LOOKING FOR SOMEONE VERY POWERFUL.
WON'T YOU PLEASE HELP US?
BWONNG
HUH? SURE...
I HAVE TIME TO KILL. ♦
WHY ARE YOU LOOKING FOR SOMEONE POWERFUL?

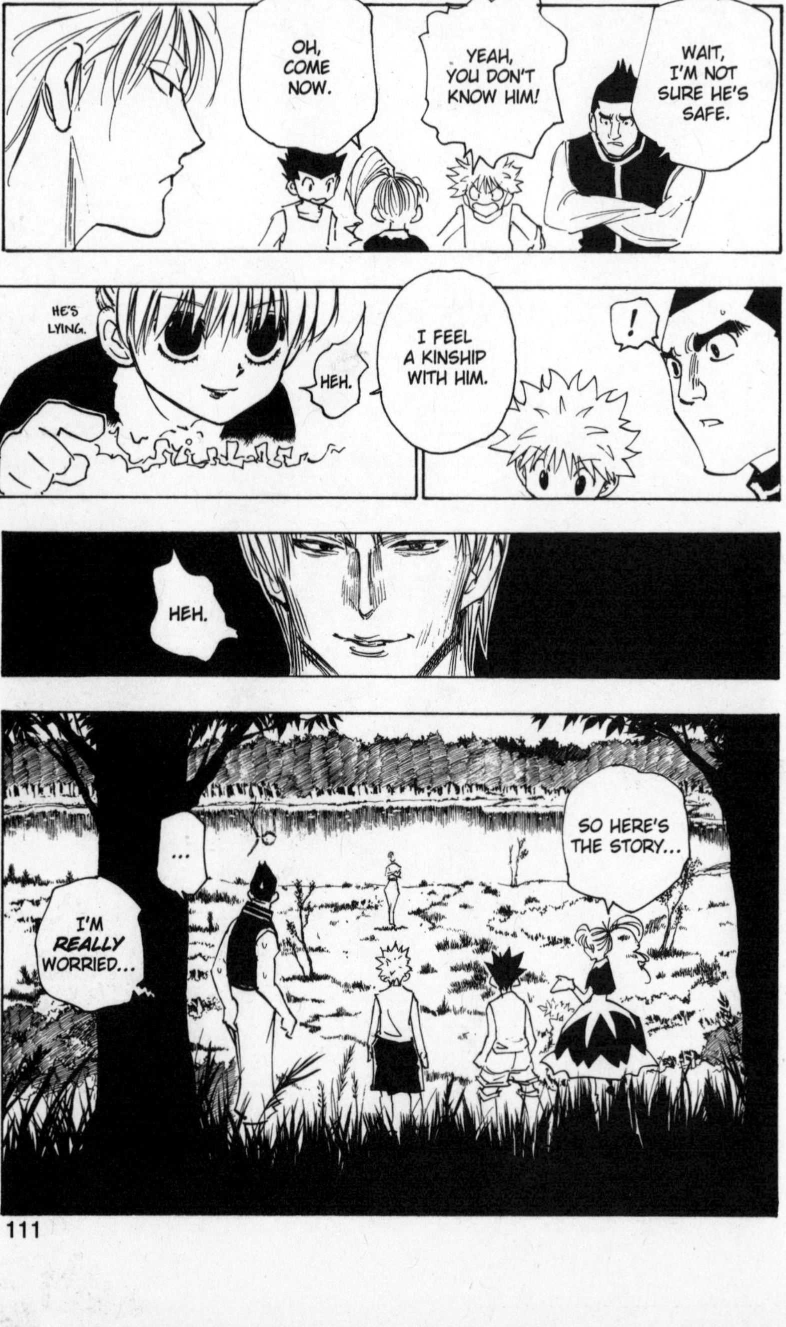
WAIT, I'M NOT SURE HE'S SAFE.
YEAH, YOU DON'T KNOW HIM!
OH, COME NOW.
!
I FEEL A KINSHIP WITH HIM.
HEH.
HE'S LYING.
HEH.
SO HERE'S THE STORY...
...
I'M *REALLY* WORRIED...

DRAW WITHOUT LOOKING 5:
RABID DOG

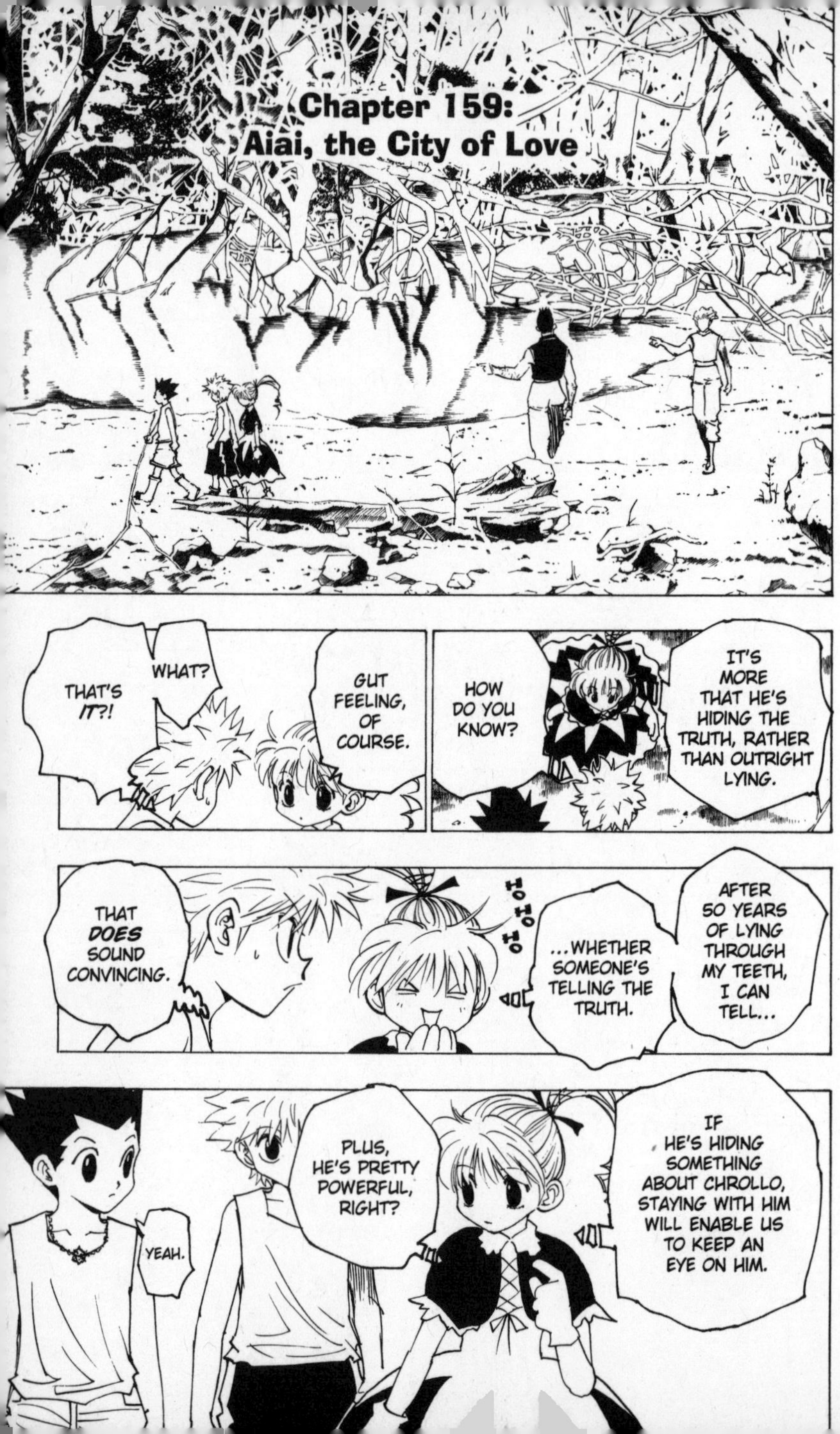
Chapter 159:
Aiai, the City of Love
IT'S MORE THAT HE'S HIDING THE TRUTH, RATHER THAN OUTRIGHT LYING.
HOW DO YOU KNOW?
GUT FEELING, OF COURSE.
WHAT?
THAT'S *IT?!*
AFTER 50 YEARS OF LYING THROUGH MY TEETH, I CAN TELL...
...WHETHER SOMEONE'S TELLING THE TRUTH.
HO HO HO
THAT **DOES** SOUND CONVINCING.
IF HE'S HIDING SOMETHING ABOUT CHROLLO, STAYING WITH HIM WILL ENABLE US TO KEEP AN EYE ON HIM.
PLUS, HE'S PRETTY POWERFUL, RIGHT?
YEAH.

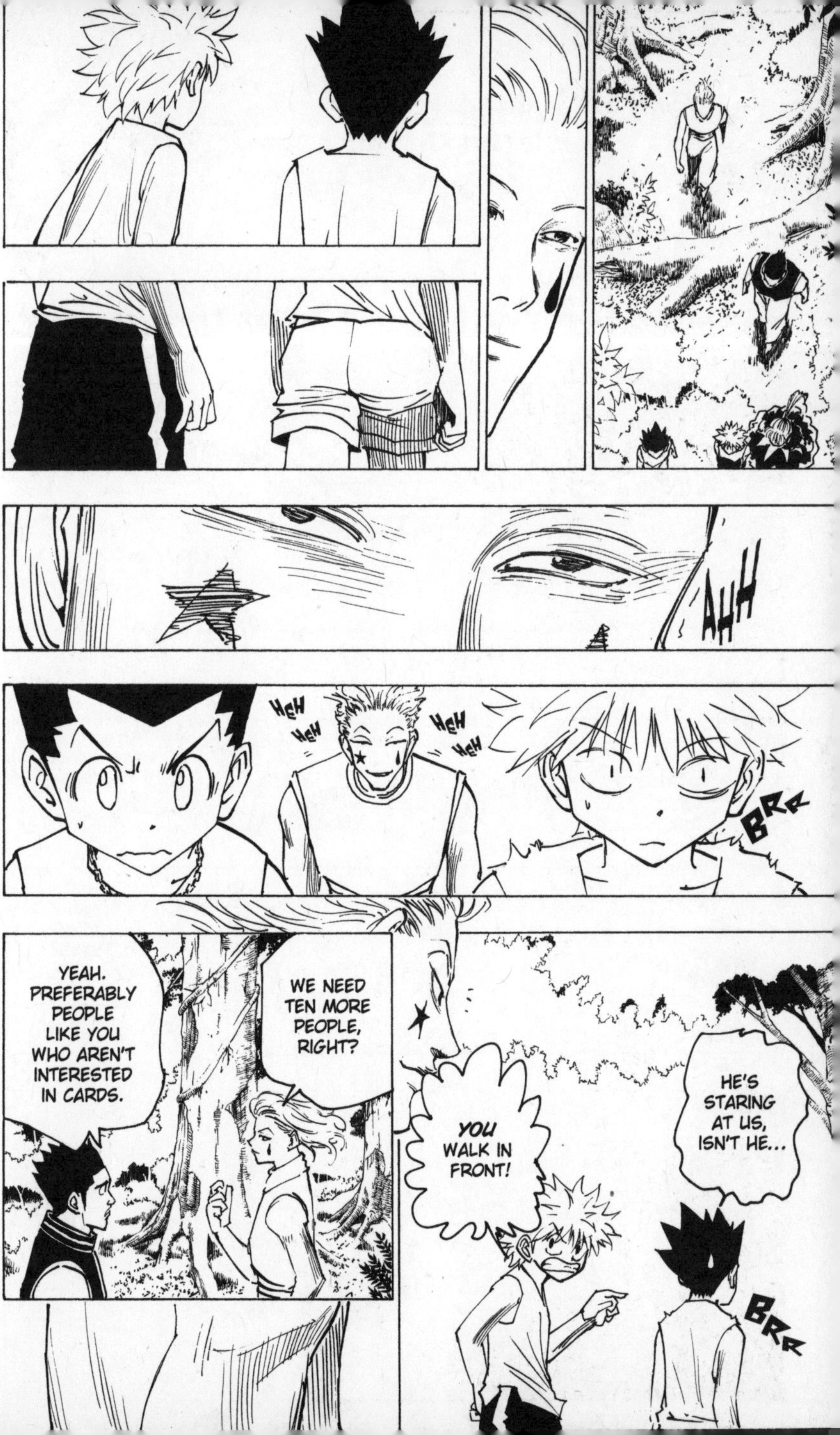
AHH
BRR
HEH HEH
HEH HEH
HE'S STARING AT US, ISN'T HE...
YOU WALK IN FRONT!
BRR
WE NEED TEN MORE PEOPLE, RIGHT?
YEAH. PREFERABLY PEOPLE LIKE YOU WHO AREN'T INTERESTED IN CARDS.

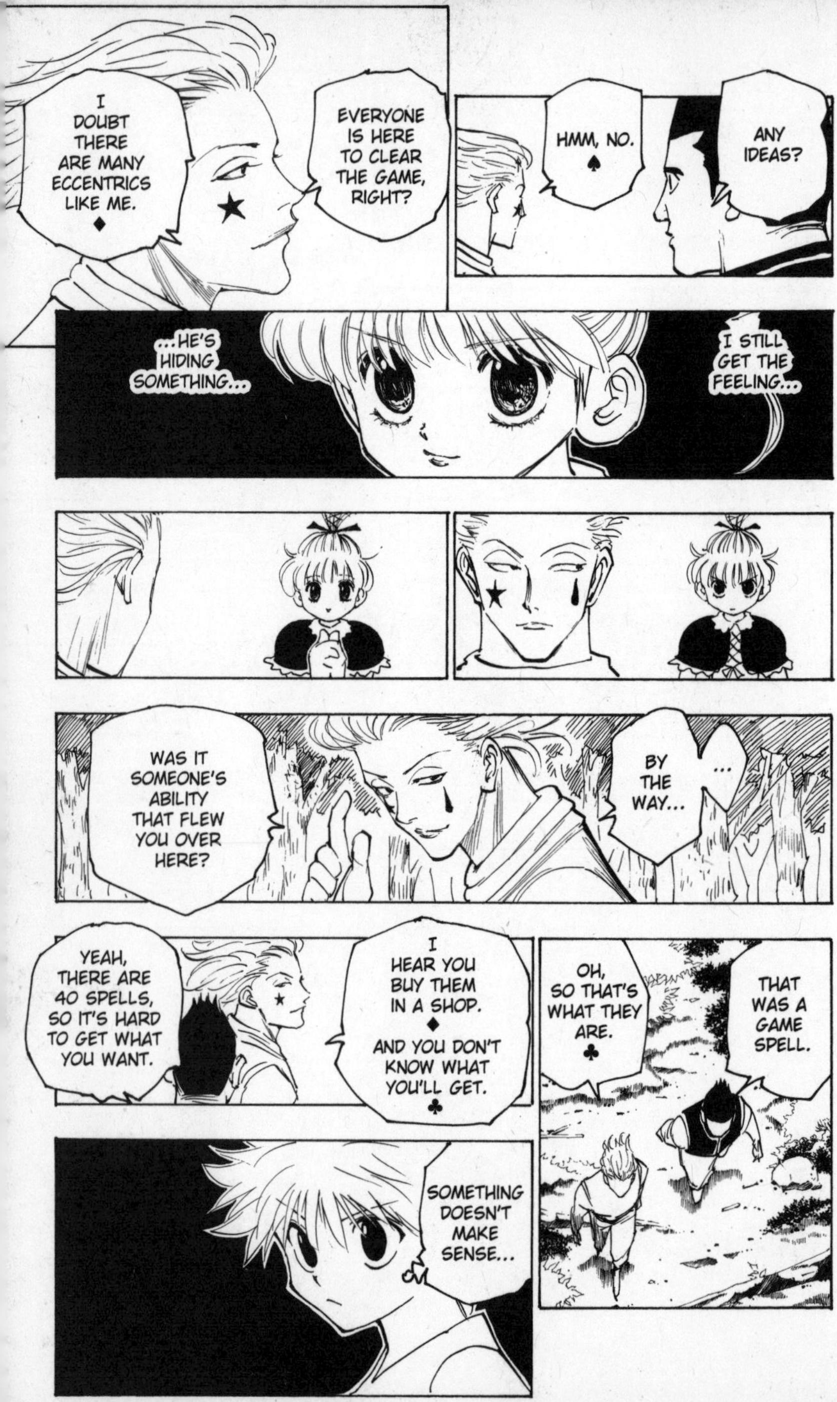
ANY IDEAS?
HMM, NO. ♠
EVERYONE IS HERE TO CLEAR THE GAME, RIGHT?
I DOUBT THERE ARE MANY ECCENTRICS LIKE ME. ♦
I STILL GET THE FEELING...
...HE'S HIDING SOMETHING...
...
BY THE WAY...
WAS IT SOMEONE'S ABILITY THAT FLEW YOU OVER HERE?
THAT WAS A GAME SPELL.
OH, SO THAT'S WHAT THEY ARE. ♣
I HEAR YOU BUY THEM IN A SHOP. ♦ AND YOU DON'T KNOW WHAT YOU'LL GET. ♣
YEAH, THERE ARE 40 SPELLS, SO IT'S HARD TO GET WHAT YOU WANT.
SOMETHING DOESN'T MAKE SENSE...

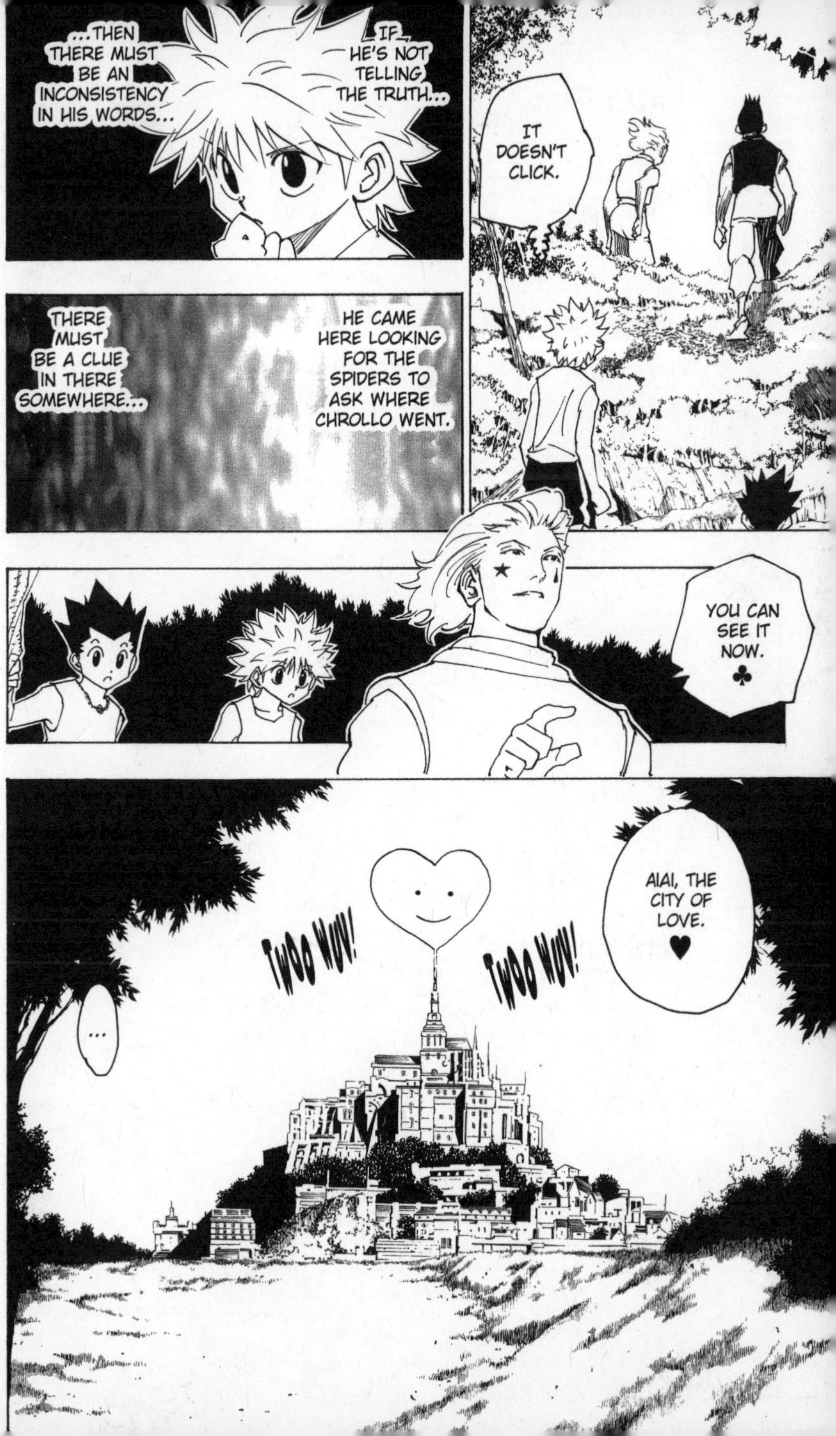
IT DOESN'T CLICK.
IF HE'S NOT TELLING THE TRUTH...
...THEN THERE MUST BE AN INCONSISTENCY IN HIS WORDS...
HE CAME HERE LOOKING FOR THE SPIDERS TO ASK WHERE CHROLLO WENT.
THERE MUST BE A CLUE IN THERE SOMEWHERE...
YOU CAN SEE IT NOW. ♣
AIAI, THE CITY OF LOVE. ♥
TWOO WUV!
TWOO WUV!
...

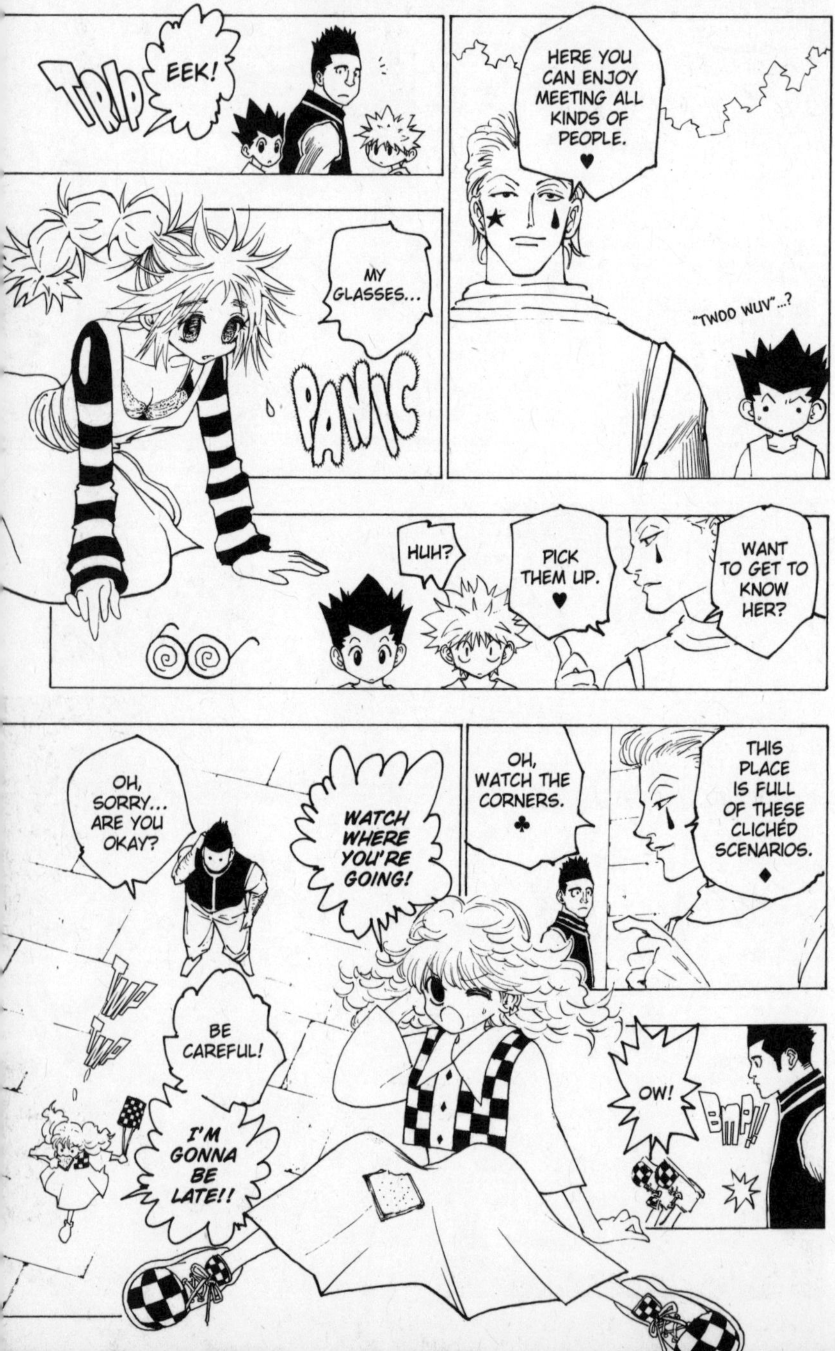
HERE YOU CAN ENJOY MEETING ALL KINDS OF PEOPLE. ♥
"TWOO WUV"...?
TRIP
EEK!
MY GLASSES...
PANIC
WANT TO GET TO KNOW HER?
PICK THEM UP. ♥
HUH?
THIS PLACE IS FULL OF THESE CLICHÉD SCENARIOS. ♦
OH, WATCH THE CORNERS. ♣
OW!
BMP!!
WATCH WHERE YOU'RE GOING!
OH, SORRY... ARE YOU OKAY?
BE CAREFUL!
I'M GONNA BE LATE!!

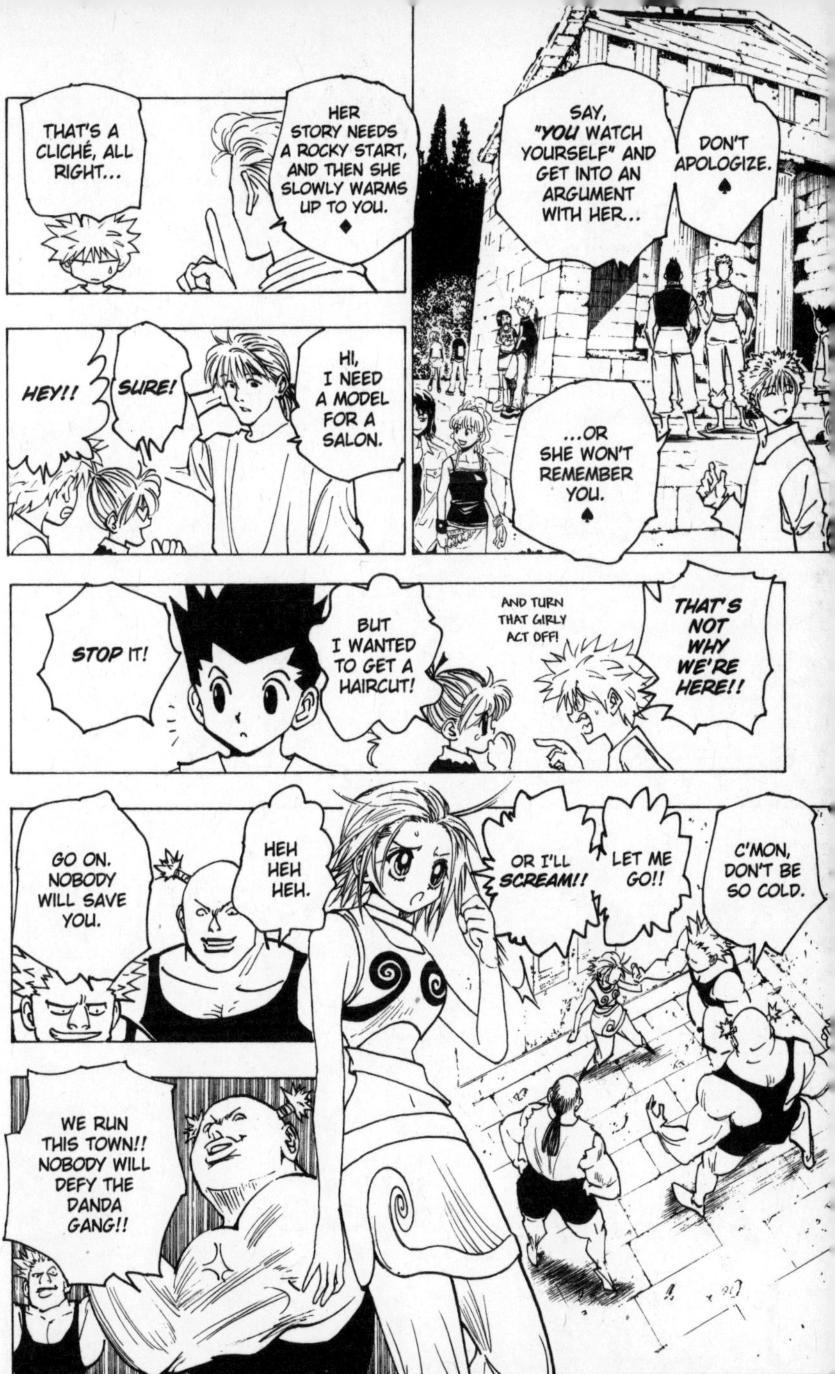
DON'T APOLOGIZE. ♠
SAY, "YOU WATCH YOURSELF" AND GET INTO AN ARGUMENT WITH HER...
...OR SHE WON'T REMEMBER YOU. ♠
HER STORY NEEDS A ROCKY START, AND THEN SHE SLOWLY WARMS UP TO YOU. ♦
THAT'S A CLICHÉ, ALL RIGHT...
HI, I NEED A MODEL FOR A SALON.
SURE!
HEY!!
THAT'S NOT WHY WE'RE HERE!!
AND TURN THAT GIRLY ACT OFF!
BUT I WANTED TO GET A HAIRCUT!
STOP IT!
C'MON, DON'T BE SO COLD.
LET ME GO!!
OR I'LL SCREAM!!
HEH HEH HEH.
GO ON. NOBODY WILL SAVE YOU.
WE RUN THIS TOWN!! NOBODY WILL DEFY THE DANDA GANG!!

READ THIS WAY

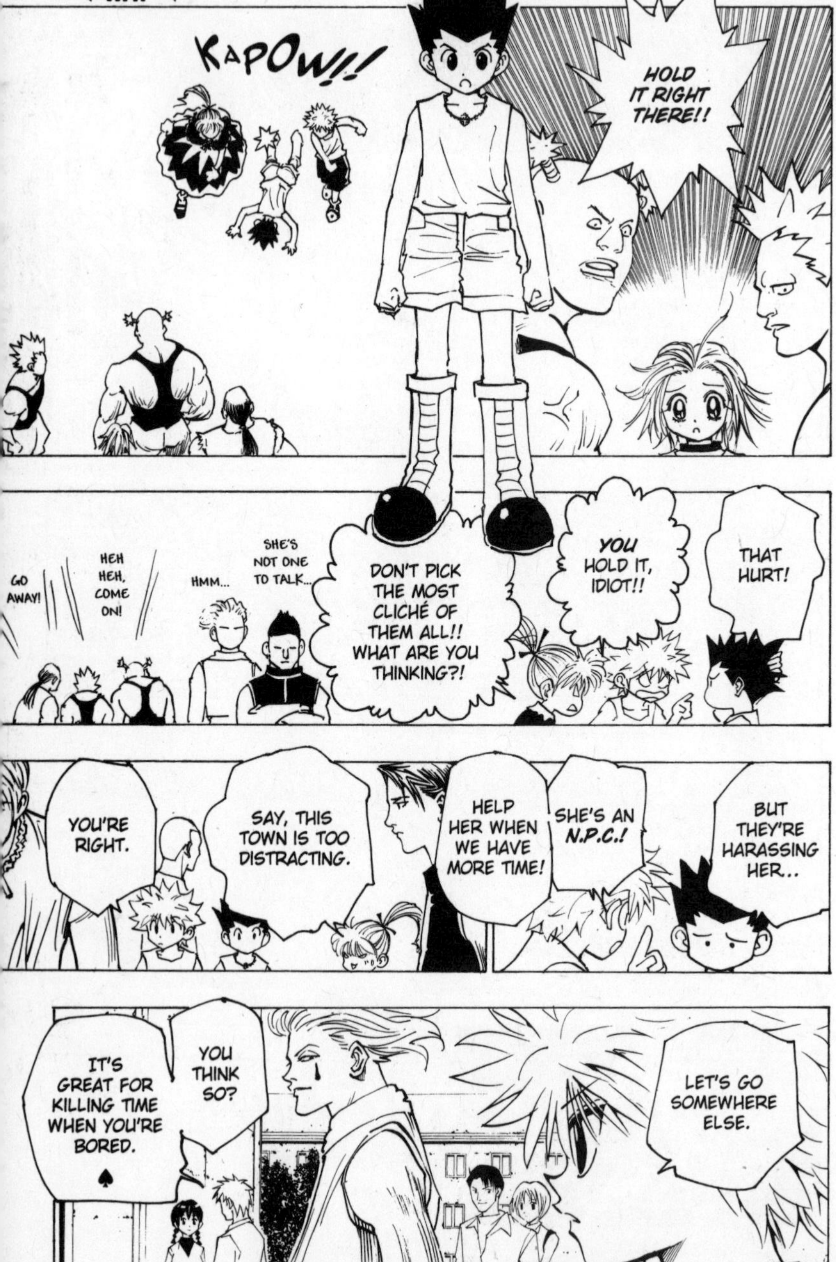
HOLD IT RIGHT THERE!!
KAPOW!!
THAT HURT!
YOU HOLD IT, IDIOT!!
DON'T PICK THE MOST CLICHÉ OF THEM ALL!! WHAT ARE YOU THINKING?!
SHE'S NOT ONE TO TALK...
HMM...
HEH HEH, COME ON!
GO AWAY!
BUT THEY'RE HARASSING HER...
SHE'S AN N.P.C.!
HELP HER WHEN WE HAVE MORE TIME!
SAY, THIS TOWN IS TOO DISTRACTING.
YOU'RE RIGHT.
LET'S GO SOMEWHERE ELSE.
YOU THINK SO?
IT'S GREAT FOR KILLING TIME WHEN YOU'RE BORED. ♠

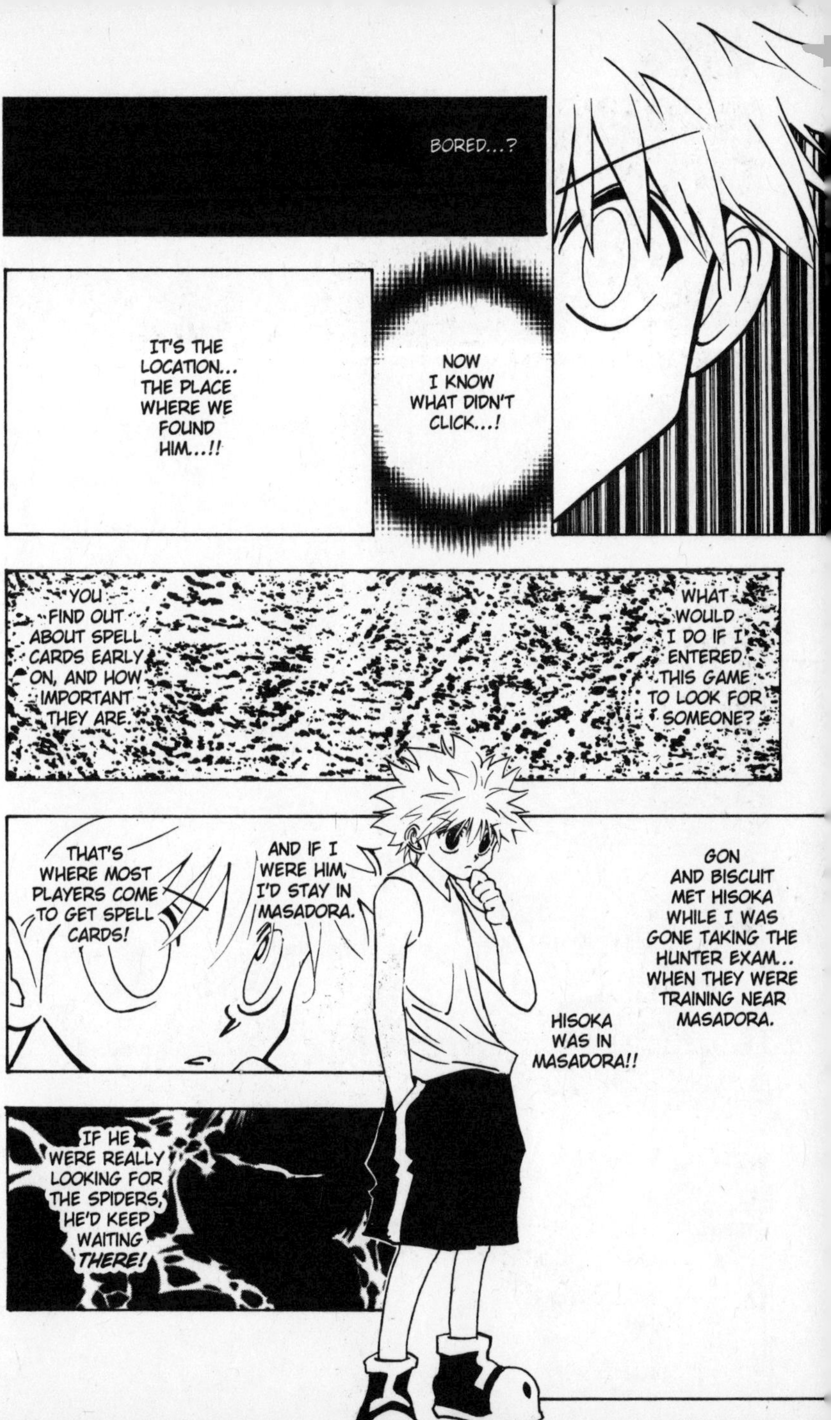
BORED...?
NOW I KNOW WHAT DIDN'T CLICK...!
IT'S THE LOCATION... THE PLACE WHERE WE FOUND HIM...!!
WHAT WOULD I DO IF I ENTERED THIS GAME TO LOOK FOR SOMEONE?
YOU FIND OUT ABOUT SPELL CARDS EARLY ON, AND HOW IMPORTANT THEY ARE.
GON AND BISCUIT MET HISOKA WHILE I WAS GONE TAKING THE HUNTER EXAM... WHEN THEY WERE TRAINING NEAR MASADORA.
HISOKA WAS IN MASADORA!!
AND IF I WERE HIM, I'D STAY IN MASADORA.
THAT'S WHERE MOST PLAYERS COME TO GET SPELL CARDS!
IF HE WERE REALLY LOOKING FOR THE SPIDERS, HE'D KEEP WAITING *THERE!*

READ THIS WAY

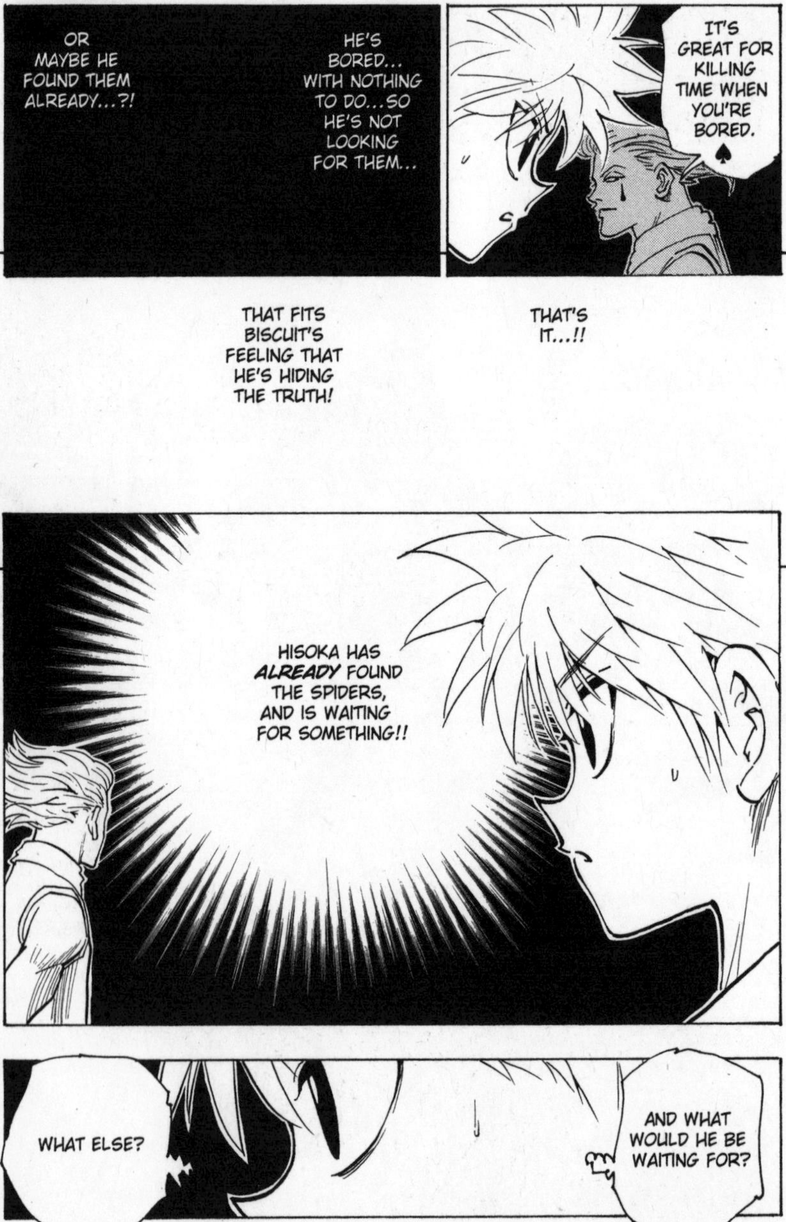
IT'S GREAT FOR KILLING TIME WHEN YOU'RE BORED. ♠
HE'S BORED... WITH NOTHING TO DO...SO HE'S NOT LOOKING FOR THEM...
OR MAYBE HE FOUND THEM ALREADY...?!
THAT'S IT...!!
THAT FITS BISCUIT'S FEELING THAT HE'S HIDING THE TRUTH!
HISOKA HAS ALREADY FOUND THE SPIDERS, AND IS WAITING FOR SOMETHING!!
AND WHAT WOULD HE BE WAITING FOR?
WHAT ELSE?

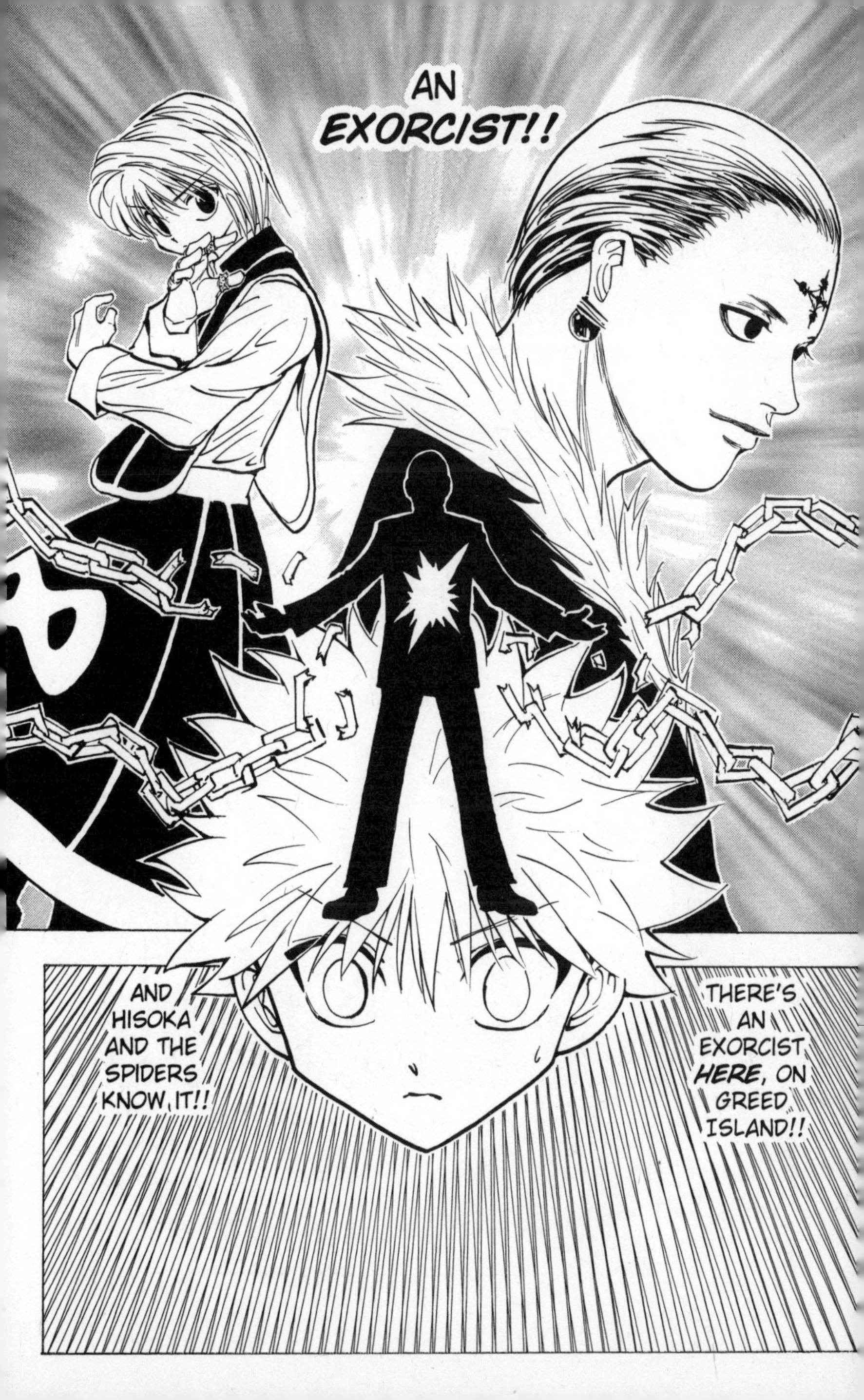
AN EXORCIST!!
THERE'S AN EXORCIST HERE, ON GREED ISLAND!!
AND HISOKA AND THE SPIDERS KNOW IT!!

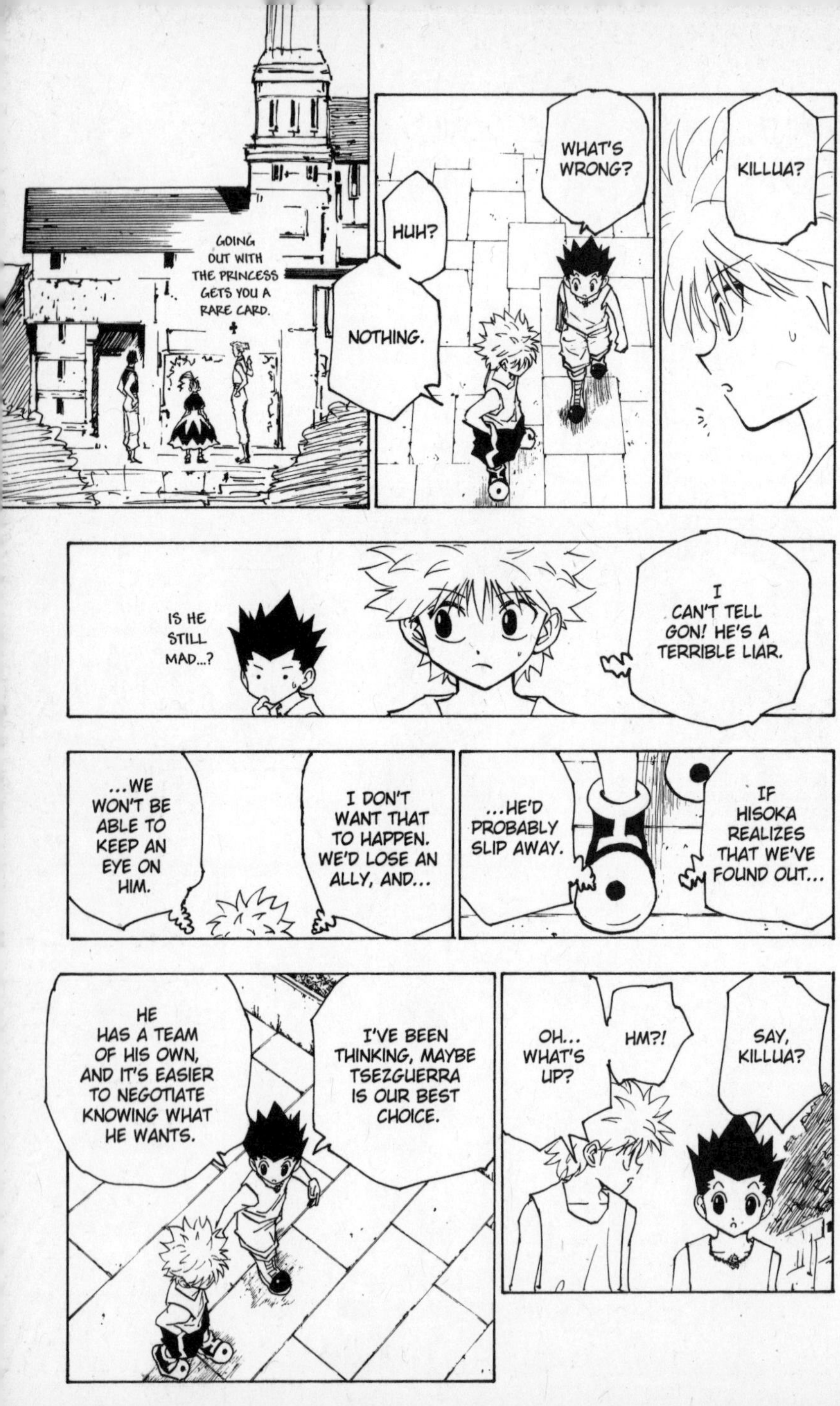
KILLUA?
WHAT'S WRONG?
HUH?
NOTHING.
GOING OUT WITH THE PRINCESS GETS YOU A RARE CARD. ♣
I CAN'T TELL GON! HE'S A TERRIBLE LIAR.
IS HE STILL MAD...?
IF HISOKA REALIZES THAT WE'VE FOUND OUT...
...HE'D PROBABLY SLIP AWAY.
I DON'T WANT THAT TO HAPPEN. WE'D LOSE AN ALLY, AND...
...WE WON'T BE ABLE TO KEEP AN EYE ON HIM.
SAY, KILLUA?
HM?!
OH... WHAT'S UP?
I'VE BEEN THINKING, MAYBE TSEZGUERRA IS OUR BEST CHOICE.
HE HAS A TEAM OF HIS OWN, AND IT'S EASIER TO NEGOTIATE KNOWING WHAT HE WANTS.

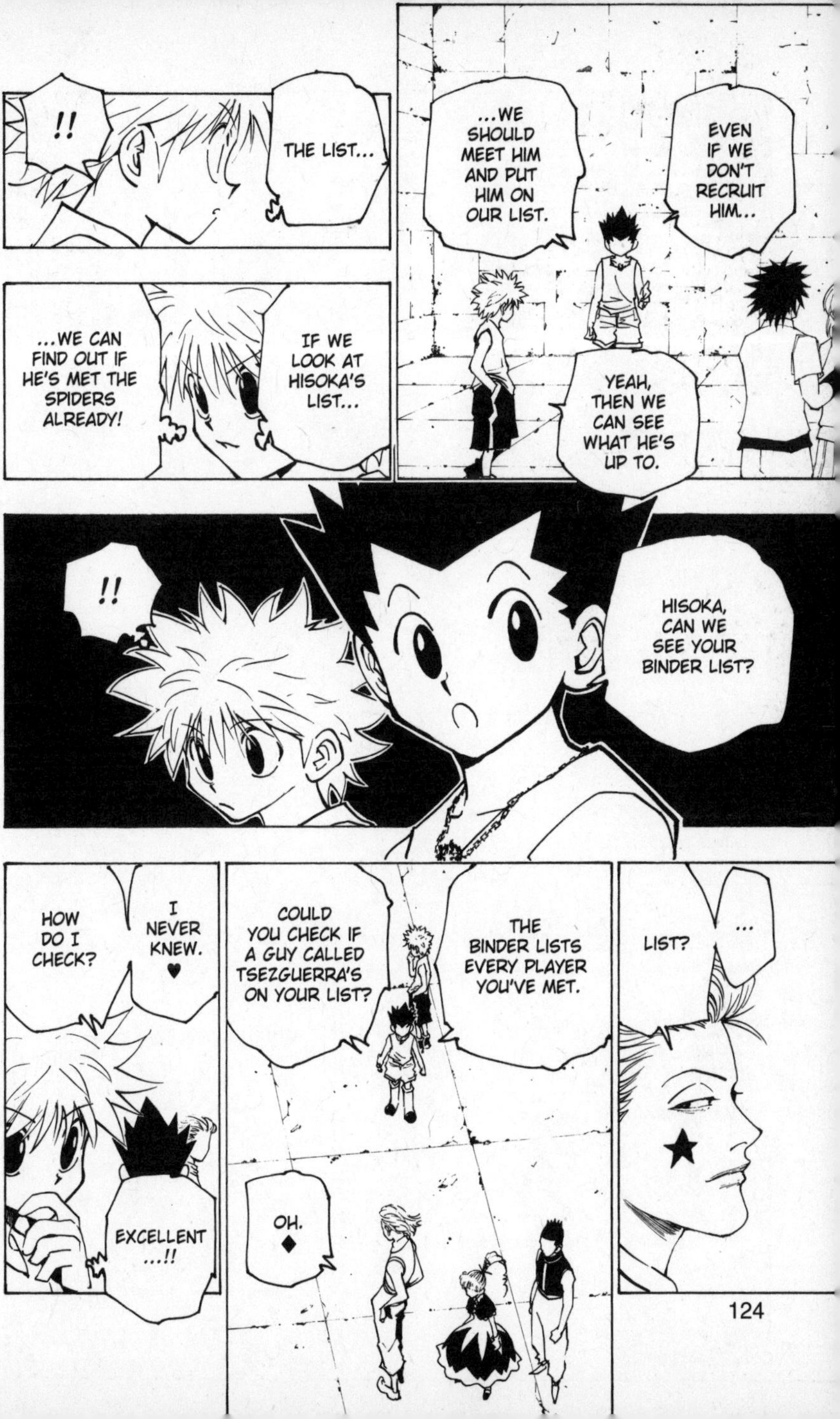
EVEN IF WE DON'T RECRUIT HIM...
...WE SHOULD MEET HIM AND PUT HIM ON OUR LIST.
YEAH, THEN WE CAN SEE WHAT HE'S UP TO.
THE LIST...
!!
IF WE LOOK AT HISOKA'S LIST...
...WE CAN FIND OUT IF HE'S MET THE SPIDERS ALREADY!
HISOKA, CAN WE SEE YOUR BINDER LIST?
!!
...
LIST?
THE BINDER LISTS EVERY PLAYER YOU'VE MET.
COULD YOU CHECK IF A GUY CALLED TSEZGUERRA'S ON YOUR LIST?
OH. ♦
I NEVER KNEW. ♥
HOW DO I CHECK?
EXCELLENT ...!!

READ THIS WAY

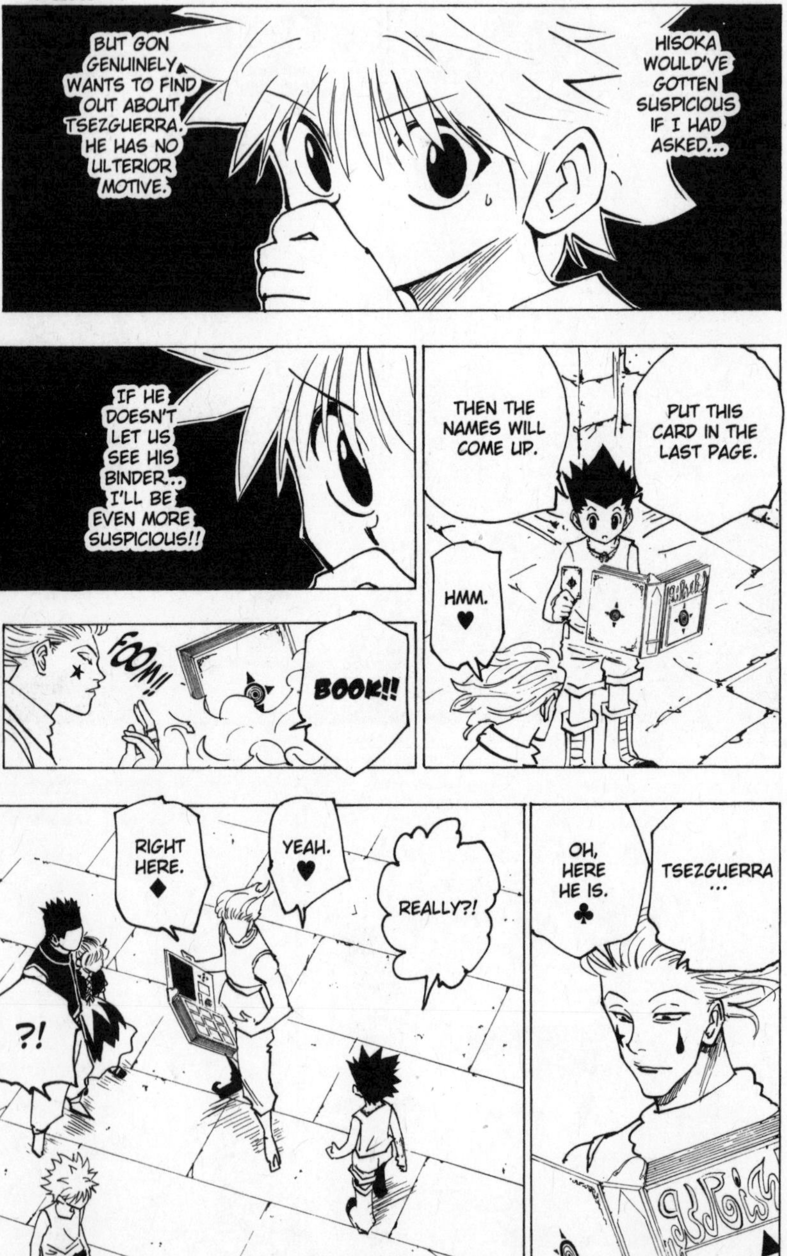

HISOKA WOULD'VE GOTTEN SUSPICIOUS IF I HAD ASKED...
BUT GON GENUINELY WANTS TO FIND OUT ABOUT TSEZGUERRA. HE HAS NO ULTERIOR MOTIVE.
PUT THIS CARD IN THE LAST PAGE.
THEN THE NAMES WILL COME UP.
HMM. ♥
IF HE DOESN'T LET US SEE HIS BINDER.. I'LL BE EVEN MORE SUSPICIOUS!!
BOOK!!
FOOM!!
TSEZGUERRA...
OH, HERE HE IS. ♣
REALLY?!
YEAH. ♥
RIGHT HERE. ♦
?!

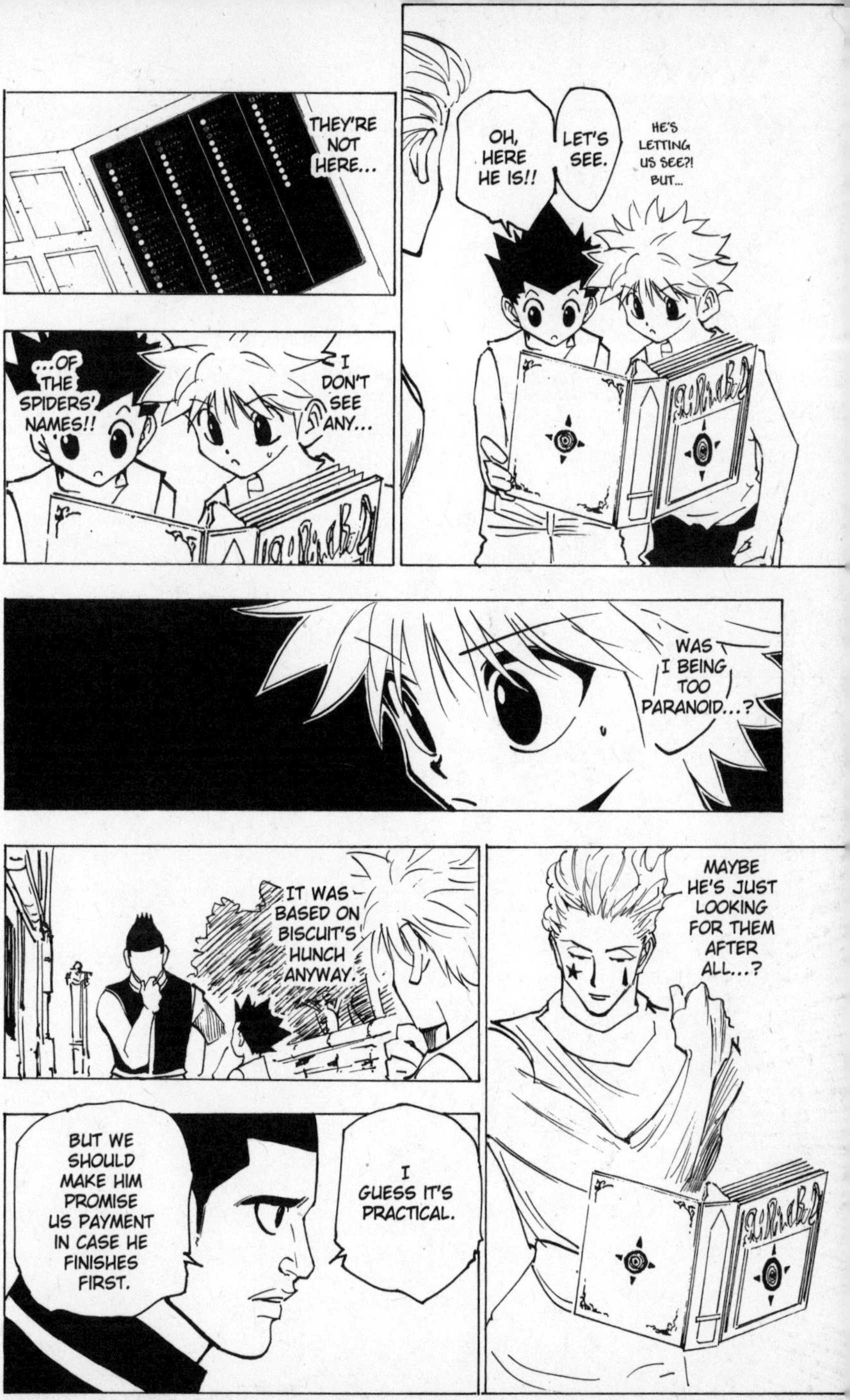
HE'S LETTING US SEE?! BUT...
LET'S SEE.
OH, HERE HE IS!!
THEY'RE NOT HERE...
I DON'T SEE ANY...
...OF THE SPIDERS' NAMES!!
WAS I BEING TOO PARANOID...?
MAYBE HE'S JUST LOOKING FOR THEM AFTER ALL...?
IT WAS BASED ON BISCUIT'S HUNCH ANYWAY.
I GUESS IT'S PRACTICAL.
BUT WE SHOULD MAKE HIM PROMISE US PAYMENT IN CASE HE FINISHES FIRST.

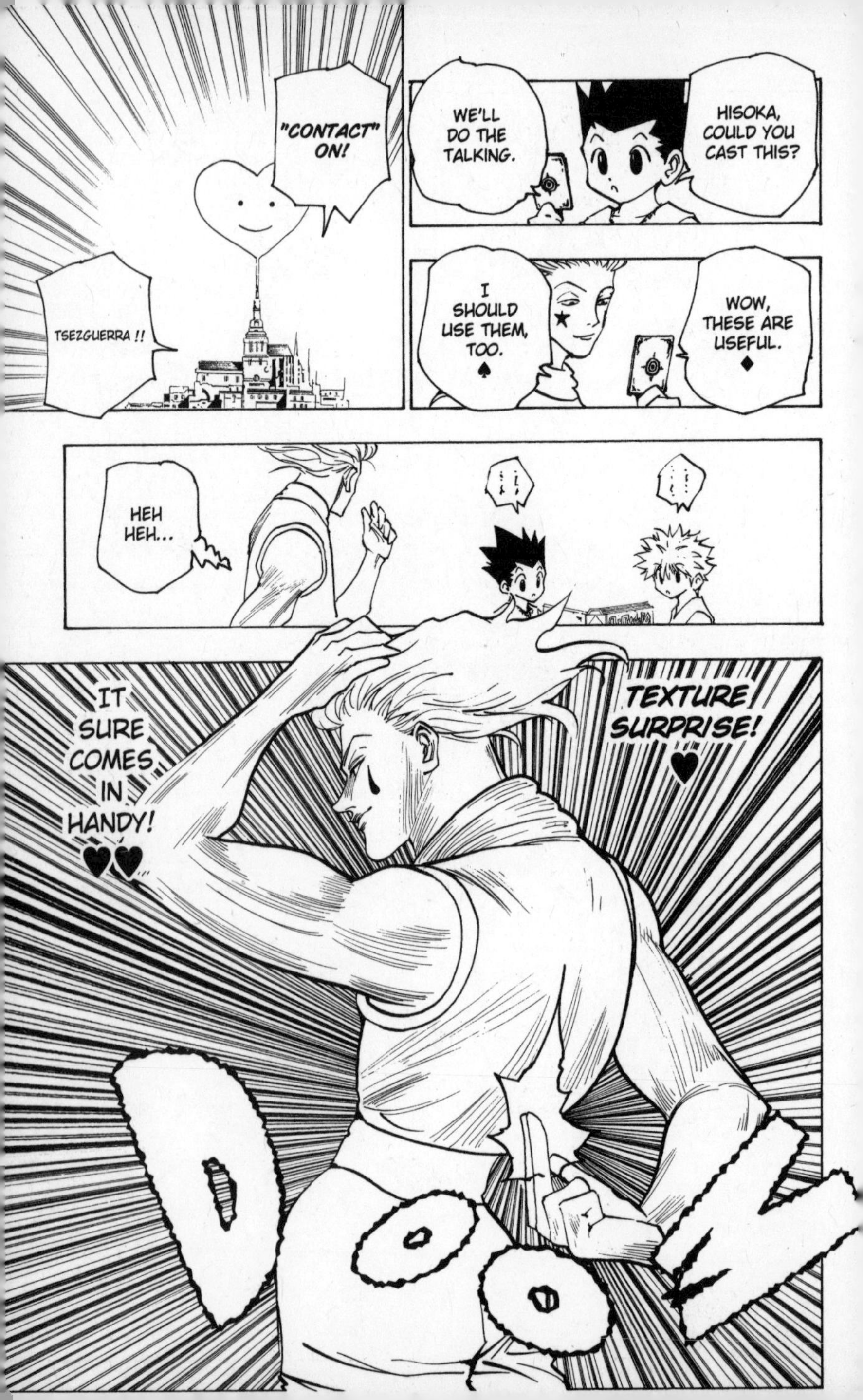
HISOKA, COULD YOU CAST THIS?
WE'LL DO THE TALKING.
WOW, THESE ARE USEFUL. ♦
I SHOULD USE THEM, TOO. ♠
"CONTACT" ON!
TSEZGUERRA !!
HEH HEH...
TEXTURE SURPRISE! ♥
IT SURE COMES IN HANDY! ♥♥
DOO

Draw Without Looking Part 5:
Rabid Dog

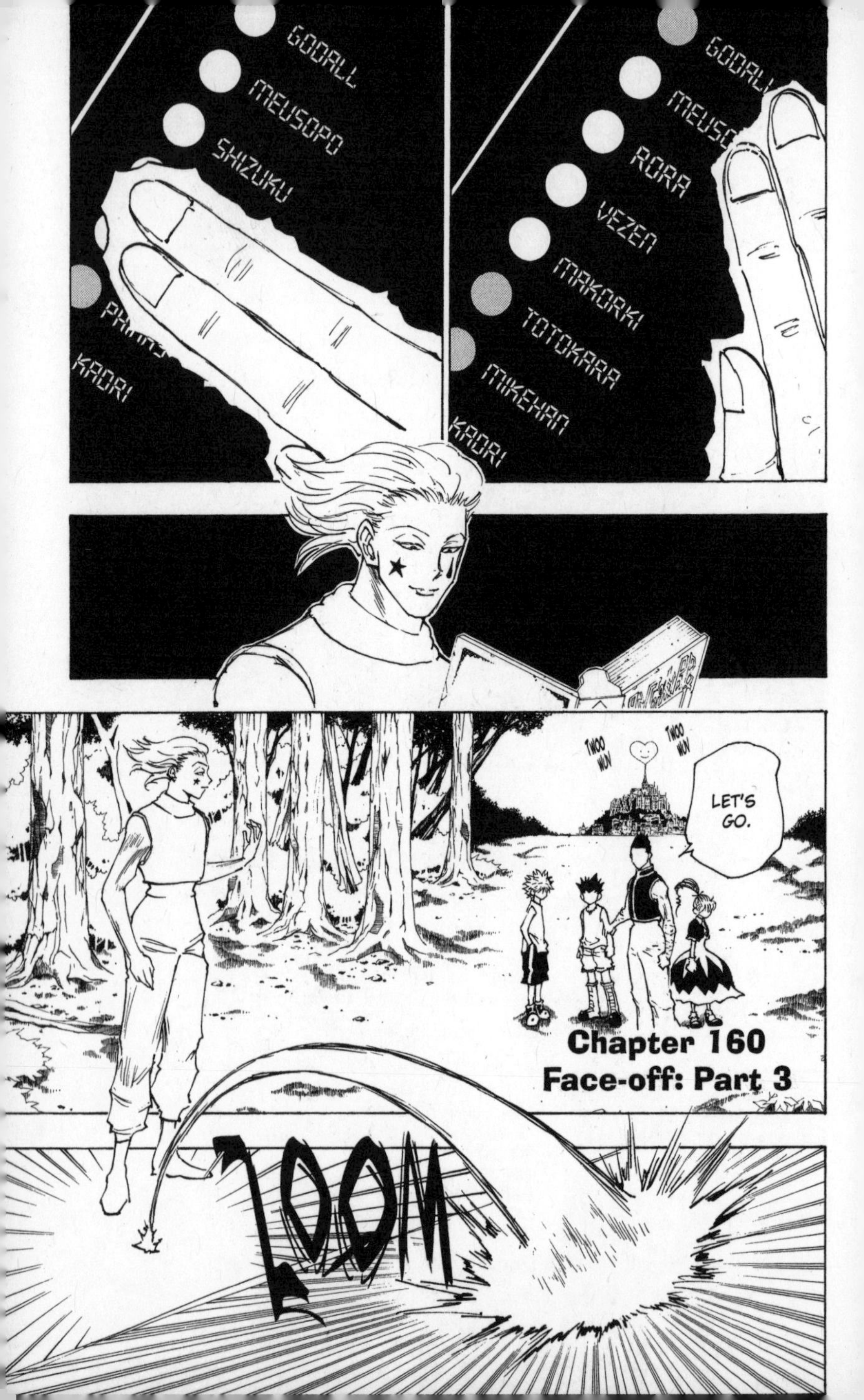
GOORAL
MEUSO
RORA
VEZEN
MAKORKI
TOTOKARA
MIKEHAN
KAORI
GOORALL
MEUSOPO
SHIZUKU
KAORI
TWOO WUV
TWOO WUV
LET'S GO.
DOOM

Chapter 160
Face-off: Part 3

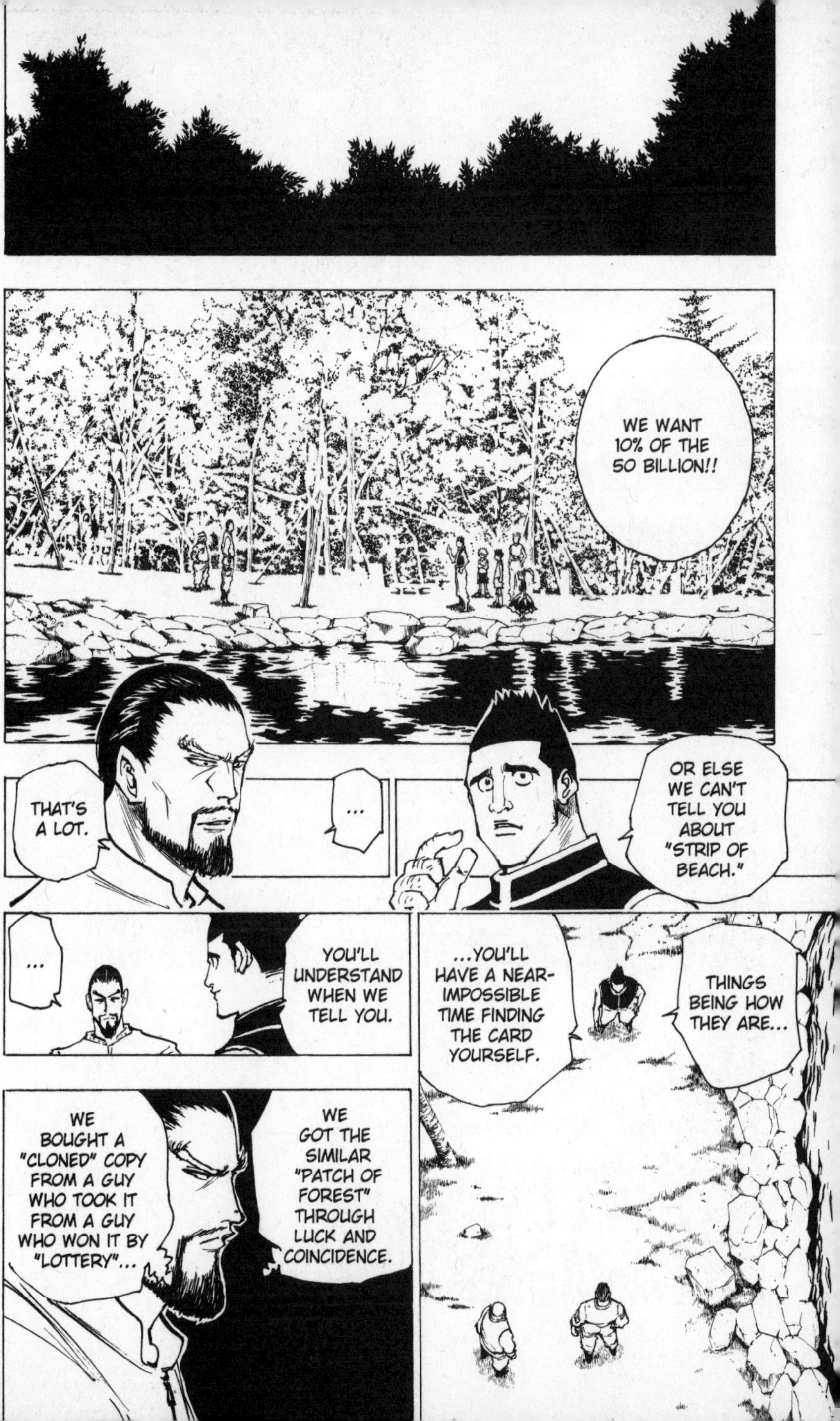
WE WANT 10% OF THE 50 BILLION!!
OR ELSE WE CAN'T TELL YOU ABOUT "STRIP OF BEACH."
...
THAT'S A LOT.
THINGS BEING HOW THEY ARE...
...YOU'LL HAVE A NEAR-IMPOSSIBLE TIME FINDING THE CARD YOURSELF.
YOU'LL UNDERSTAND WHEN WE TELL YOU.
...
WE GOT THE SIMILAR "PATCH OF FOREST" THROUGH LUCK AND COINCIDENCE.
WE BOUGHT A "CLONED" COPY FROM A GUY WHO TOOK IT FROM A GUY WHO WON IT BY "LOTTERY"...

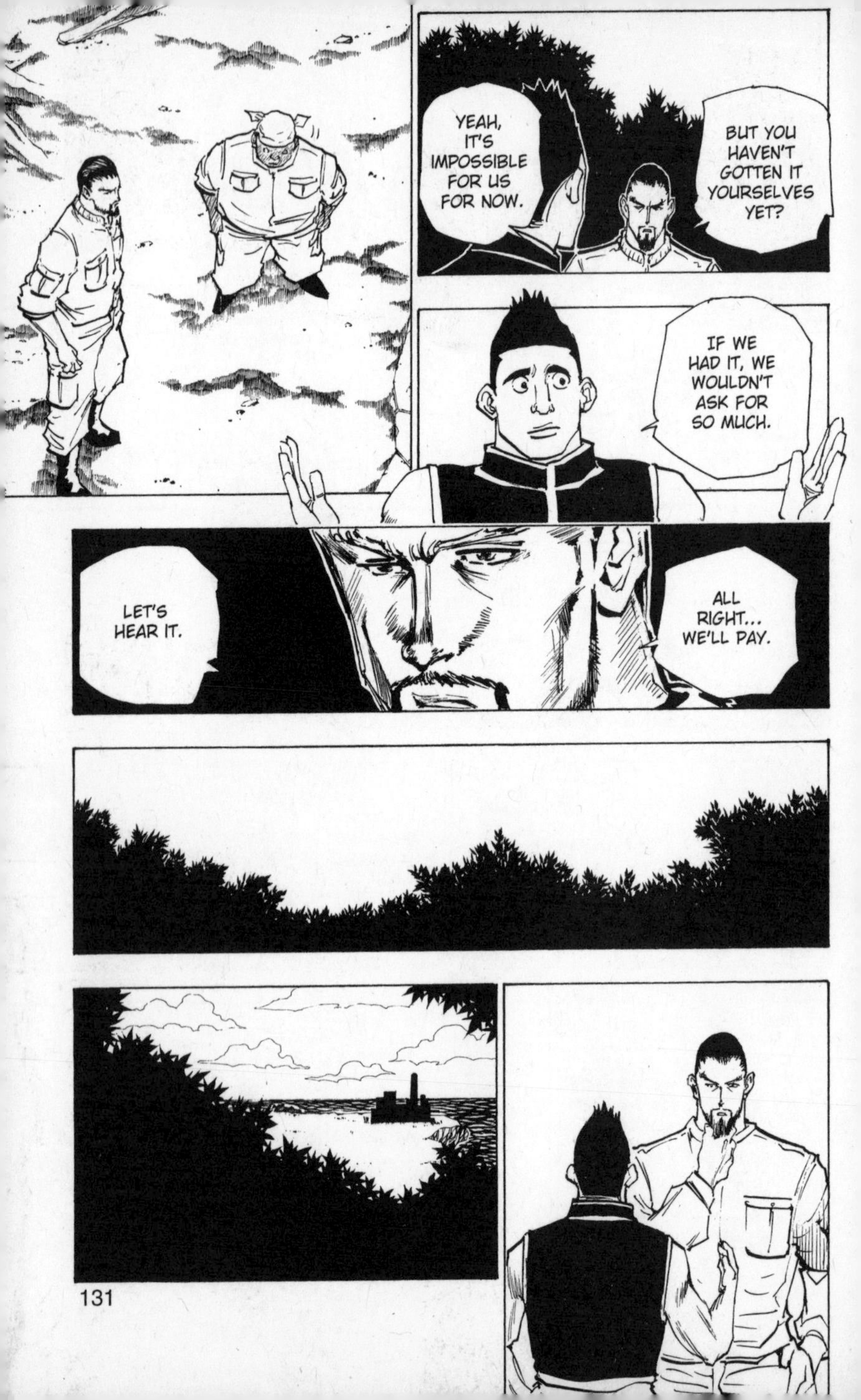
BUT YOU HAVEN'T GOTTEN IT YOURSELVES YET?
YEAH, IT'S IMPOSSIBLE FOR US FOR NOW.
IF WE HAD IT, WE WOULDN'T ASK FOR SO MUCH.
ALL RIGHT... WE'LL PAY.
LET'S HEAR IT.

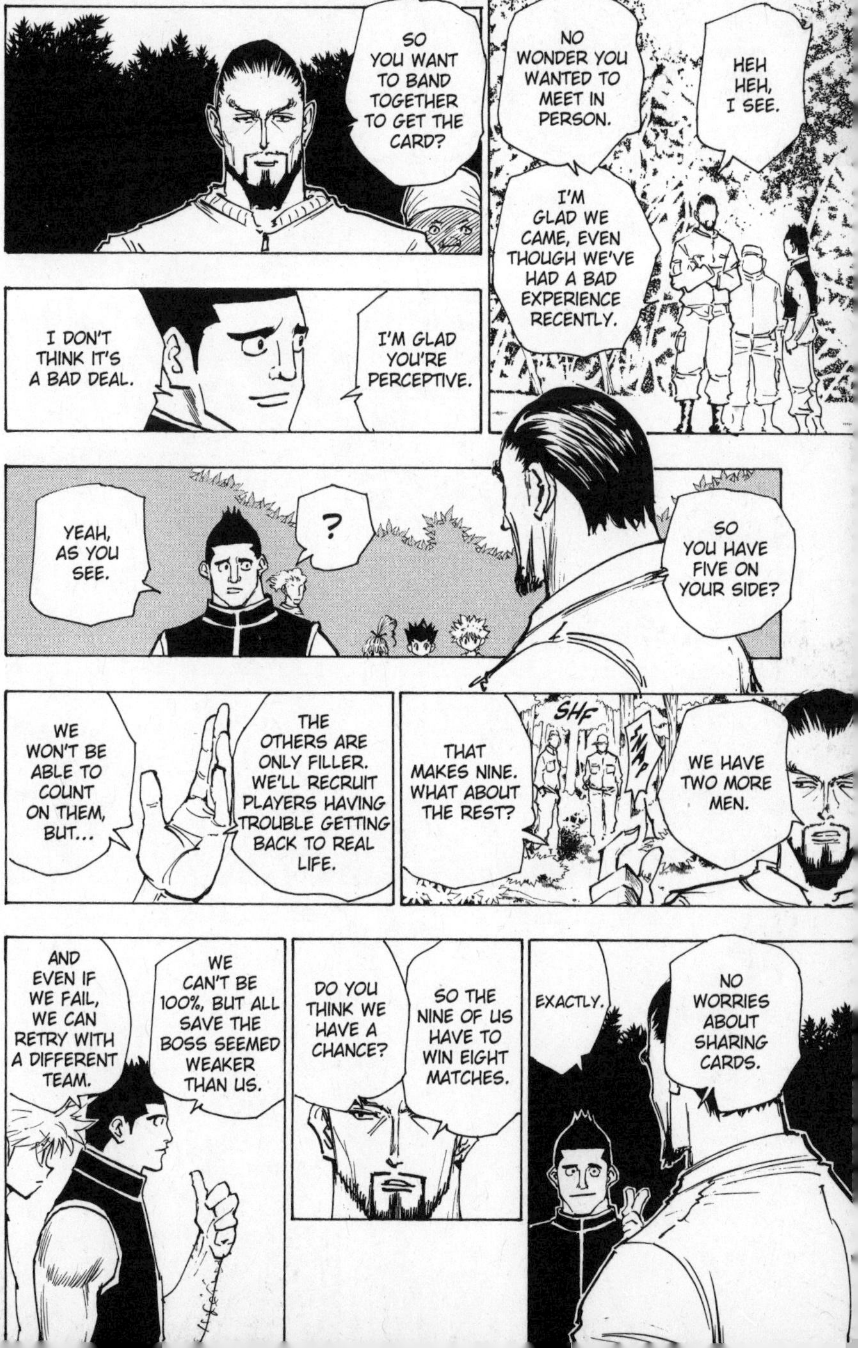
HEH HEH, I SEE.
NO WONDER YOU WANTED TO MEET IN PERSON.
I'M GLAD WE CAME, EVEN THOUGH WE'VE HAD A BAD EXPERIENCE RECENTLY.
SO YOU WANT TO BAND TOGETHER TO GET THE CARD?
I'M GLAD YOU'RE PERCEPTIVE.
I DON'T THINK IT'S A BAD DEAL.
SO YOU HAVE FIVE ON YOUR SIDE?
?
YEAH, AS YOU SEE.
WE HAVE TWO MORE MEN.
SHF
SNAP
THAT MAKES NINE. WHAT ABOUT THE REST?
THE OTHERS ARE ONLY FILLER. WE'LL RECRUIT PLAYERS HAVING TROUBLE GETTING BACK TO REAL LIFE.
WE WON'T BE ABLE TO COUNT ON THEM, BUT...
NO WORRIES ABOUT SHARING CARDS.
EXACTLY.
SO THE NINE OF US HAVE TO WIN EIGHT MATCHES.
DO YOU THINK WE HAVE A CHANCE?
WE CAN'T BE 100%, BUT ALL SAVE THE BOSS SEEMED WEAKER THAN US.
AND EVEN IF WE FAIL, WE CAN RETRY WITH A DIFFERENT TEAM.

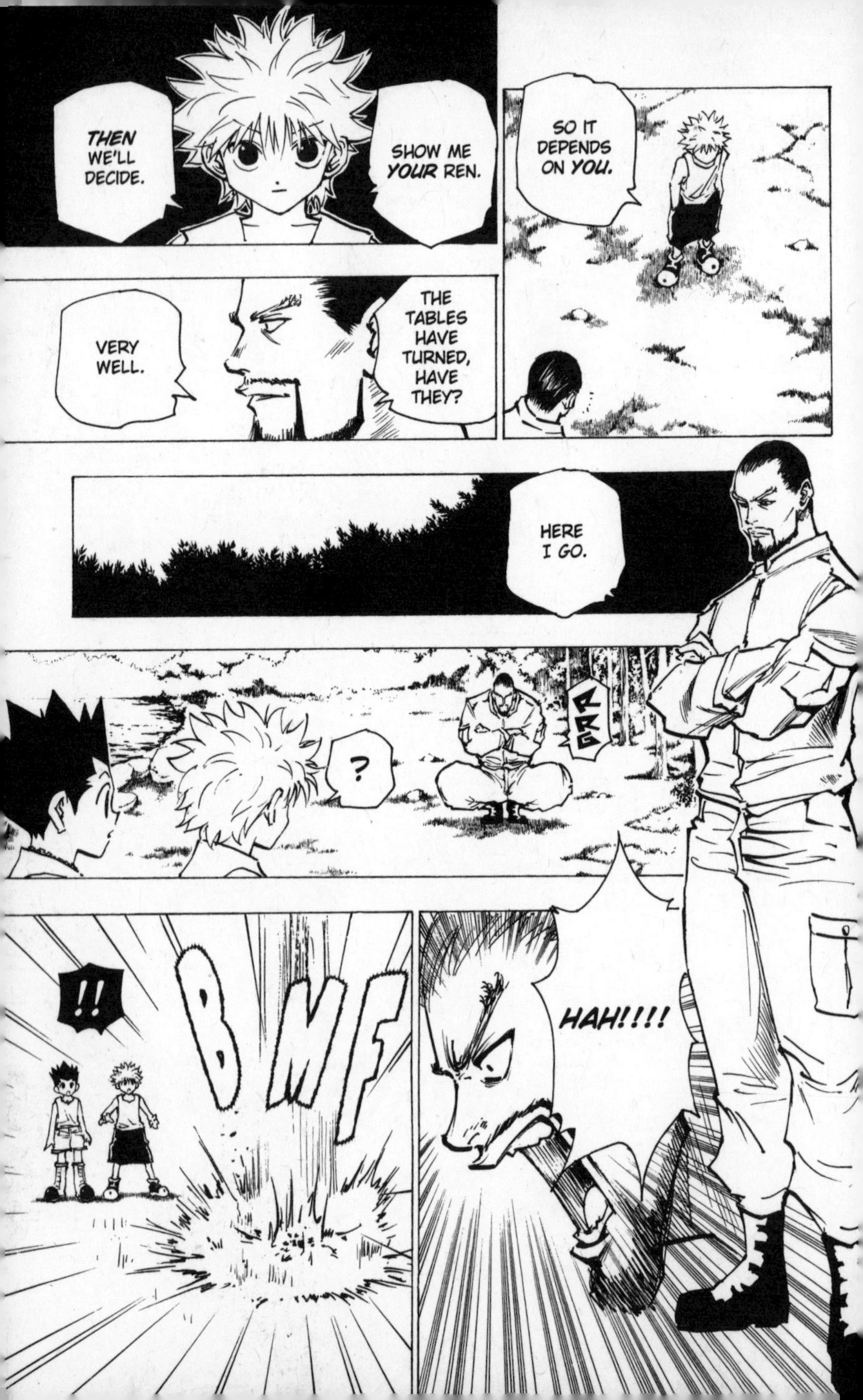
SO IT DEPENDS ON YOU.
SHOW ME YOUR REN.
THEN WE'LL DECIDE.
THE TABLES HAVE TURNED, HAVE THEY?
VERY WELL.
HERE I GO.
RRG
?
HAH!!!!
BMF
!!

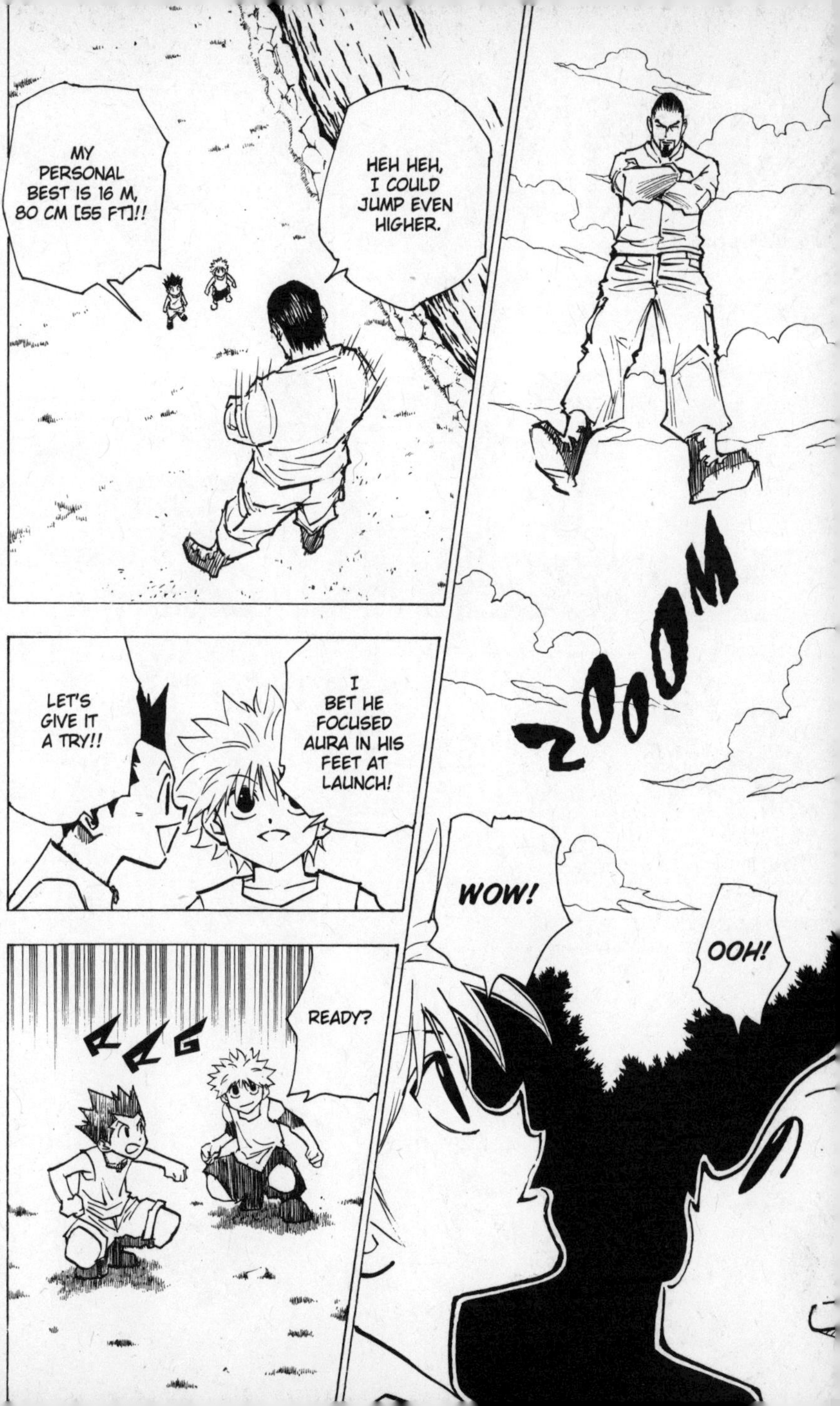
ZOOOM
OOH!
WOW!
HEH HEH, I COULD JUMP EVEN HIGHER.
MY PERSONAL BEST IS 16 M, 80 CM [55 FT]!!
I BET HE FOCUSED AURA IN HIS FEET AT LAUNCH!
LET'S GIVE IT A TRY!!
READY?
RRG

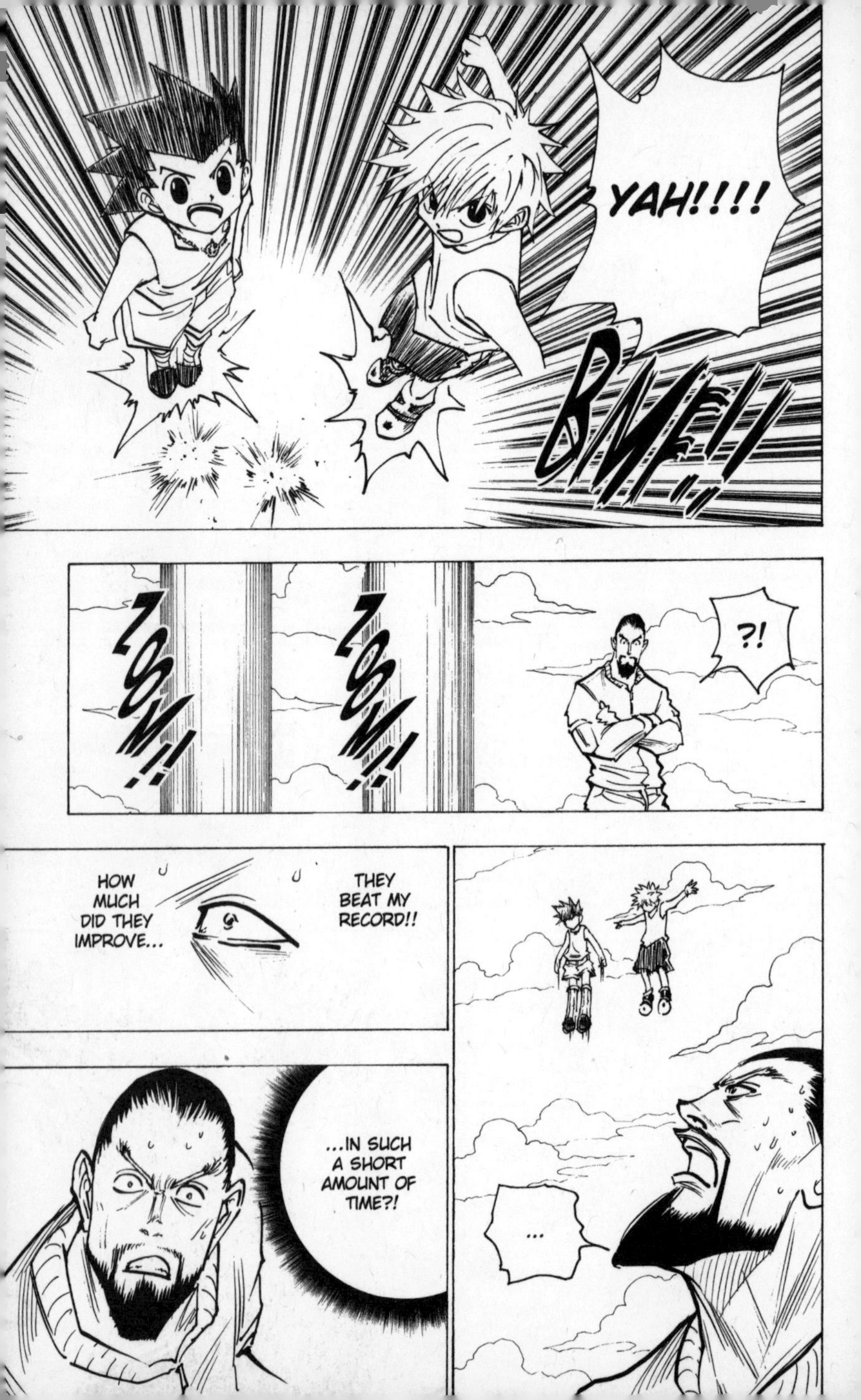
YAH!!!!
BWF!!
?!
ZOOM!!
ZOOM!!
...
THEY BEAT MY RECORD!!
HOW MUCH DID THEY IMPROVE...
...IN SUCH A SHORT AMOUNT OF TIME?!

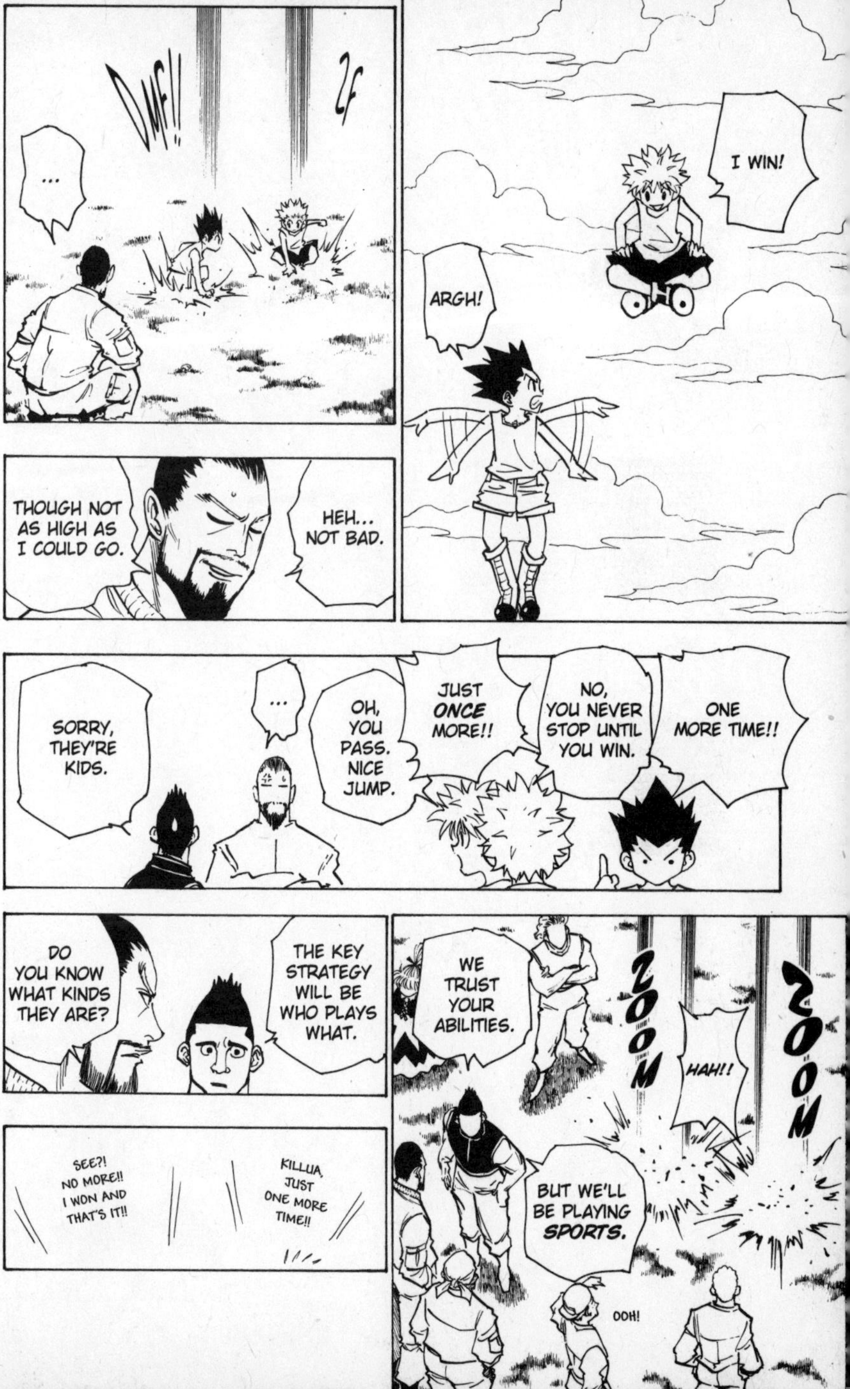
I WIN!
ARGH!
DMF!!
2F
...
HEH... NOT BAD.
THOUGH NOT AS HIGH AS I COULD GO.
ONE MORE TIME!!
NO, YOU NEVER STOP UNTIL YOU WIN.
JUST ONCE MORE!!
OH, YOU PASS. NICE JUMP.
...
SORRY, THEY'RE KIDS.
ZOOM
HAH!!
ZOOM
WE TRUST YOUR ABILITIES.
BUT WE'LL BE PLAYING SPORTS.
OOH!
THE KEY STRATEGY WILL BE WHO PLAYS WHAT.
DO YOU KNOW WHAT KINDS THEY ARE?
KILLUA, JUST ONE MORE TIME!!
SEE?! NO MORE!! I WON AND THAT'S IT!!

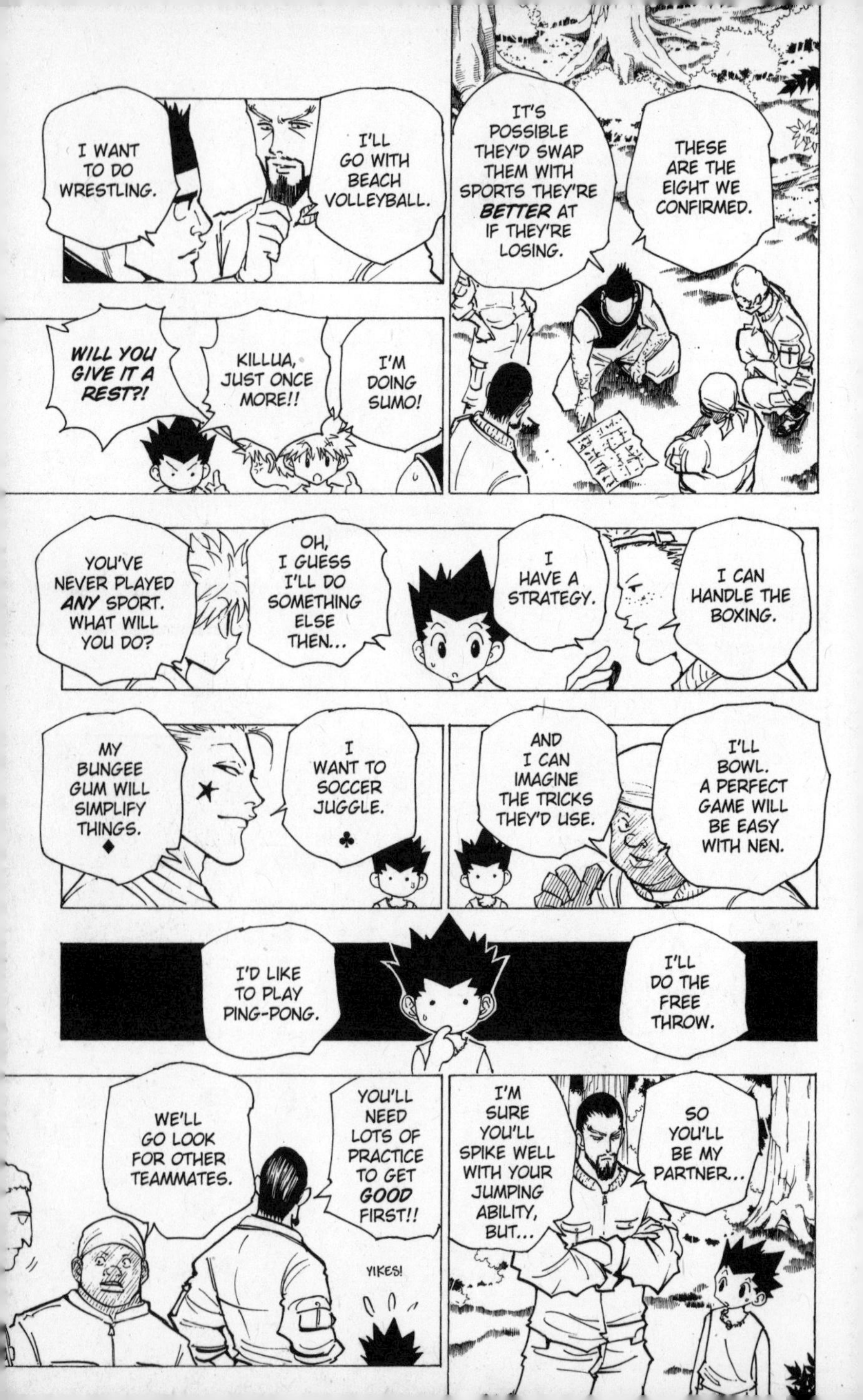
THESE ARE THE EIGHT WE CONFIRMED.
IT'S POSSIBLE THEY'D SWAP THEM WITH SPORTS THEY'RE **BETTER** AT IF THEY'RE LOSING.
I'LL GO WITH BEACH VOLLEYBALL.
I WANT TO DO WRESTLING.
I'M DOING SUMO!
KILLUA, JUST ONCE MORE!!
WILL YOU GIVE IT A REST?!
I CAN HANDLE THE BOXING.
I HAVE A STRATEGY.
OH, I GUESS I'LL DO SOMETHING ELSE THEN...
YOU'VE NEVER PLAYED **ANY** SPORT. WHAT WILL YOU DO?
I'LL BOWL. A PERFECT GAME WILL BE EASY WITH NEN.
AND I CAN IMAGINE THE TRICKS THEY'D USE.
I WANT TO SOCCER JUGGLE. ♣
MY BUNGEE GUM WILL SIMPLIFY THINGS. ♦
I'LL DO THE FREE THROW.
I'D LIKE TO PLAY PING-PONG.
SO YOU'LL BE MY PARTNER...
I'M SURE YOU'LL SPIKE WELL WITH YOUR JUMPING ABILITY, BUT...
YOU'LL NEED LOTS OF PRACTICE TO GET **GOOD** FIRST!!
WE'LL GO LOOK FOR OTHER TEAMMATES.
YIKES!

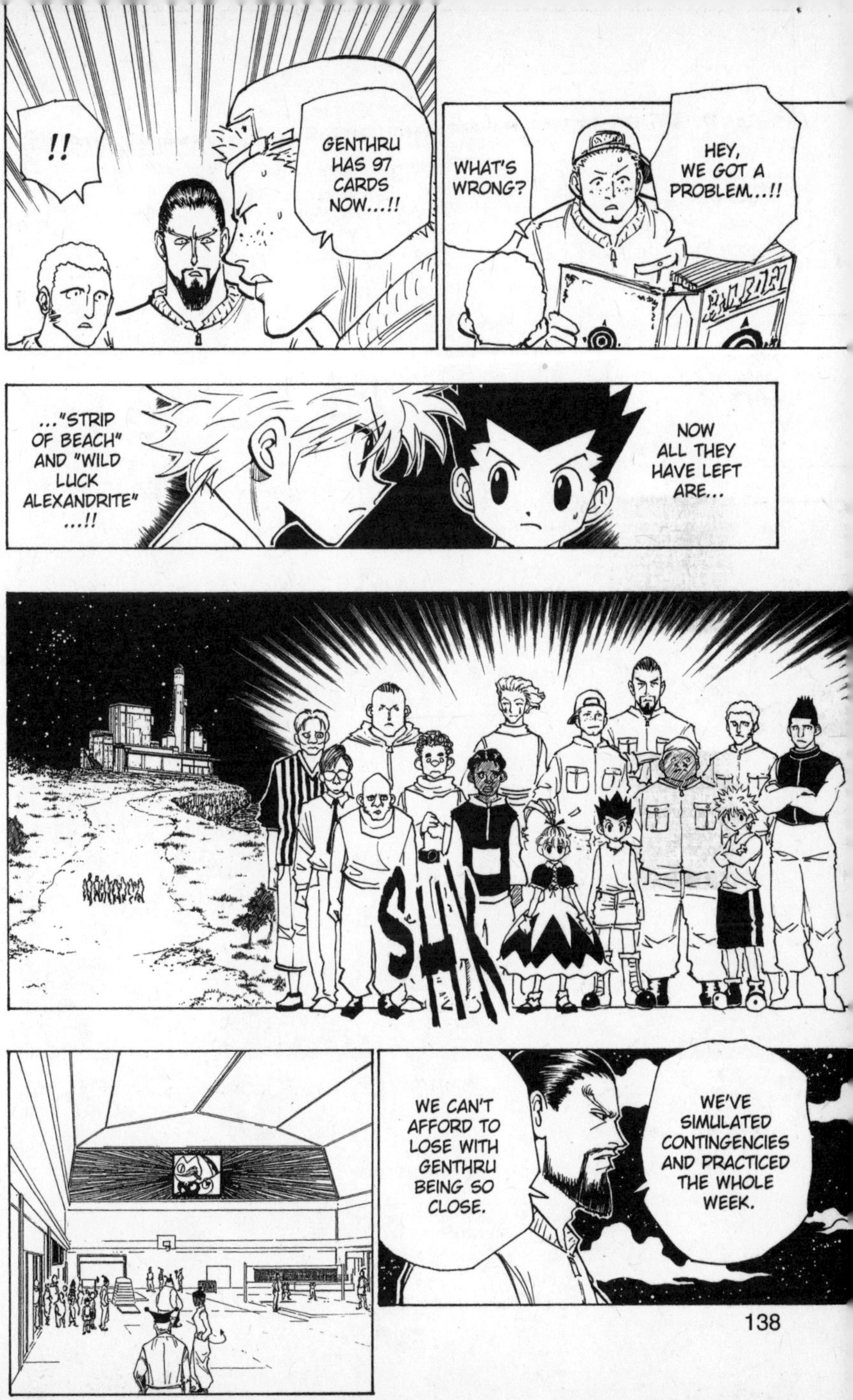
HEY, WE GOT A PROBLEM...!!
WHAT'S WRONG?
GENTHRU HAS 97 CARDS NOW...!!
!!
NOW ALL THEY HAVE LEFT ARE...
..."STRIP OF BEACH" AND "WILD LUCK ALEXANDRITE" ...!!
WE'VE SIMULATED CONTINGENCIES AND PRACTICED THE WHOLE WEEK.
WE CAN'T AFFORD TO LOSE WITH GENTHRU BEING SO CLOSE.

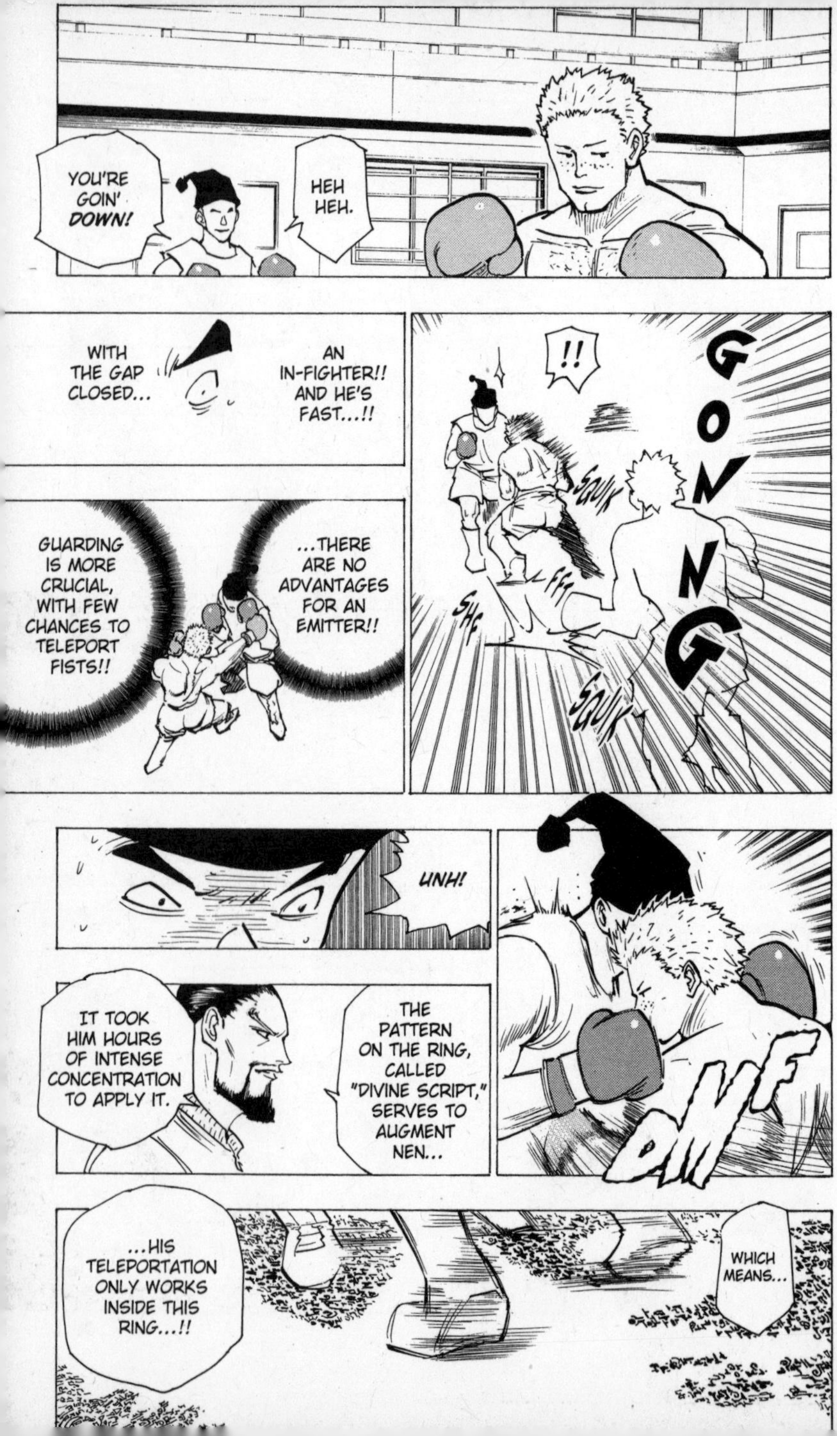
HEH HEH.
YOU'RE GOIN' DOWN!
GONG
!!
SQUK
FFF
SHF
SQUK
AN IN-FIGHTER!! AND HE'S FAST...!!
WITH THE GAP CLOSED...
...THERE ARE NO ADVANTAGES FOR AN EMITTER!!
GUARDING IS MORE CRUCIAL, WITH FEW CHANCES TO TELEPORT FISTS!!
DMF
UNH!
THE PATTERN ON THE RING, CALLED "DIVINE SCRIPT," SERVES TO AUGMENT NEN...
IT TOOK HIM HOURS OF INTENSE CONCENTRATION TO APPLY IT.
WHICH MEANS...
...HIS TELEPORTATION ONLY WORKS INSIDE THIS RING...!!

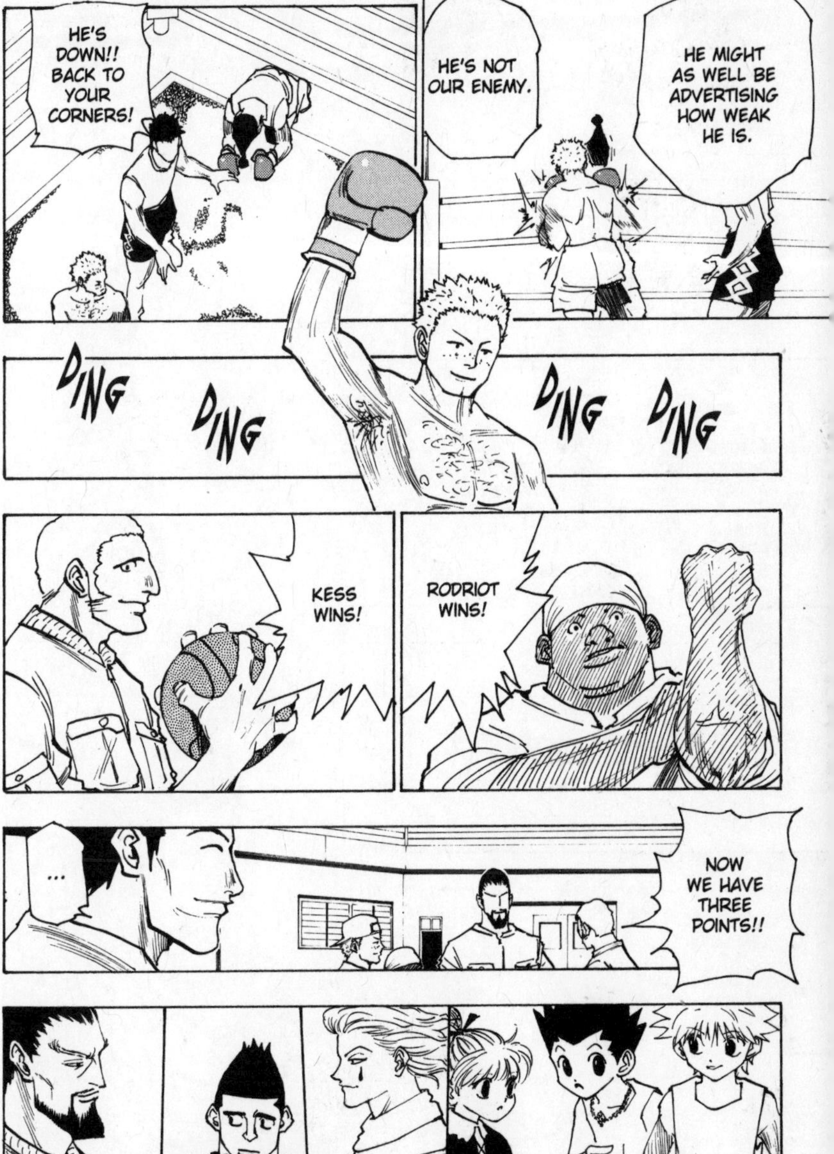
HE MIGHT AS WELL BE ADVERTISING HOW WEAK HE IS.
HE'S NOT OUR ENEMY.
HE'S DOWN!! BACK TO YOUR CORNERS!
DING
DING
DING
DING
RODRIOT WINS!
KESS WINS!
NOW WE HAVE THREE POINTS!!
...

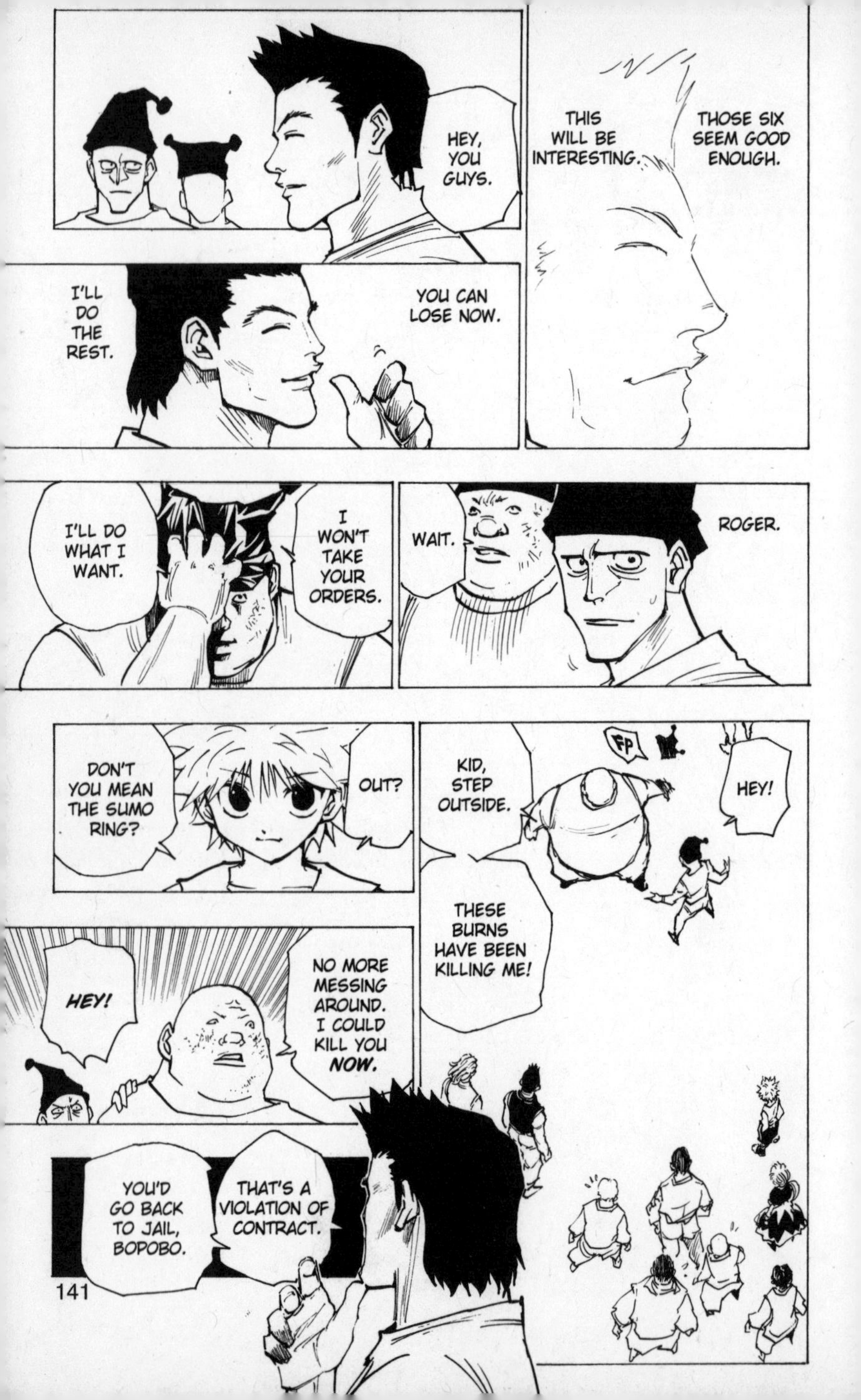
THOSE SIX SEEM GOOD ENOUGH.
THIS WILL BE INTERESTING.
HEY, YOU GUYS.
YOU CAN LOSE NOW.
I'LL DO THE REST.
ROGER.
WAIT.
I WON'T TAKE YOUR ORDERS.
I'LL DO WHAT I WANT.
HEY!
FP
KID, STEP OUTSIDE.
THESE BURNS HAVE BEEN KILLING ME!
OUT?
DON'T YOU MEAN THE SUMO RING?
NO MORE MESSING AROUND. I COULD KILL YOU *NOW.*
HEY!
THAT'S A VIOLATION OF CONTRACT.
YOU'D GO BACK TO JAIL, BOPOBO.

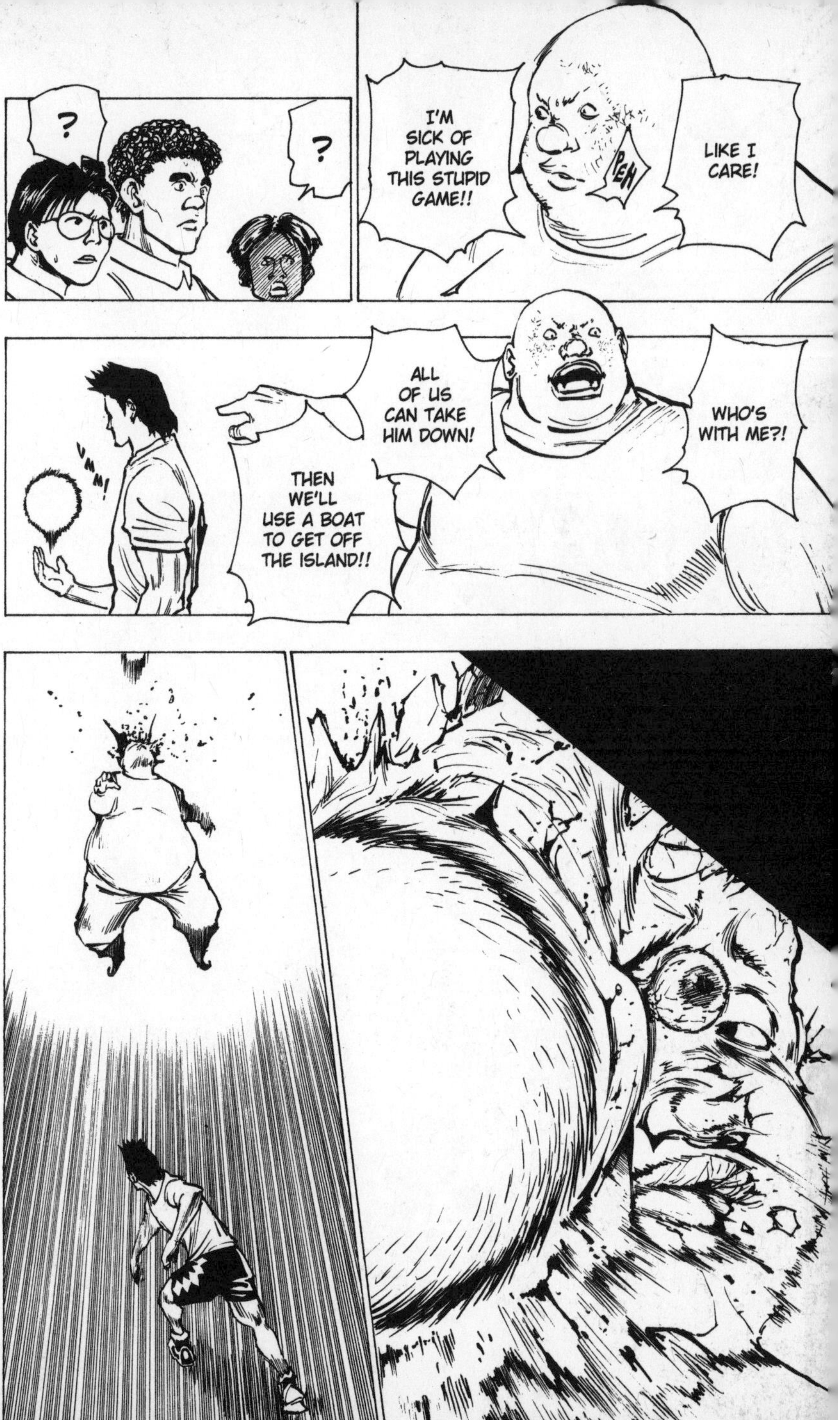
LIKE I CARE!
PEH
I'M SICK OF PLAYING THIS STUPID GAME!!
?
?
WHO'S WITH ME?!
ALL OF US CAN TAKE HIM DOWN!
THEN WE'LL USE A BOAT TO GET OFF THE ISLAND!!
VMM!

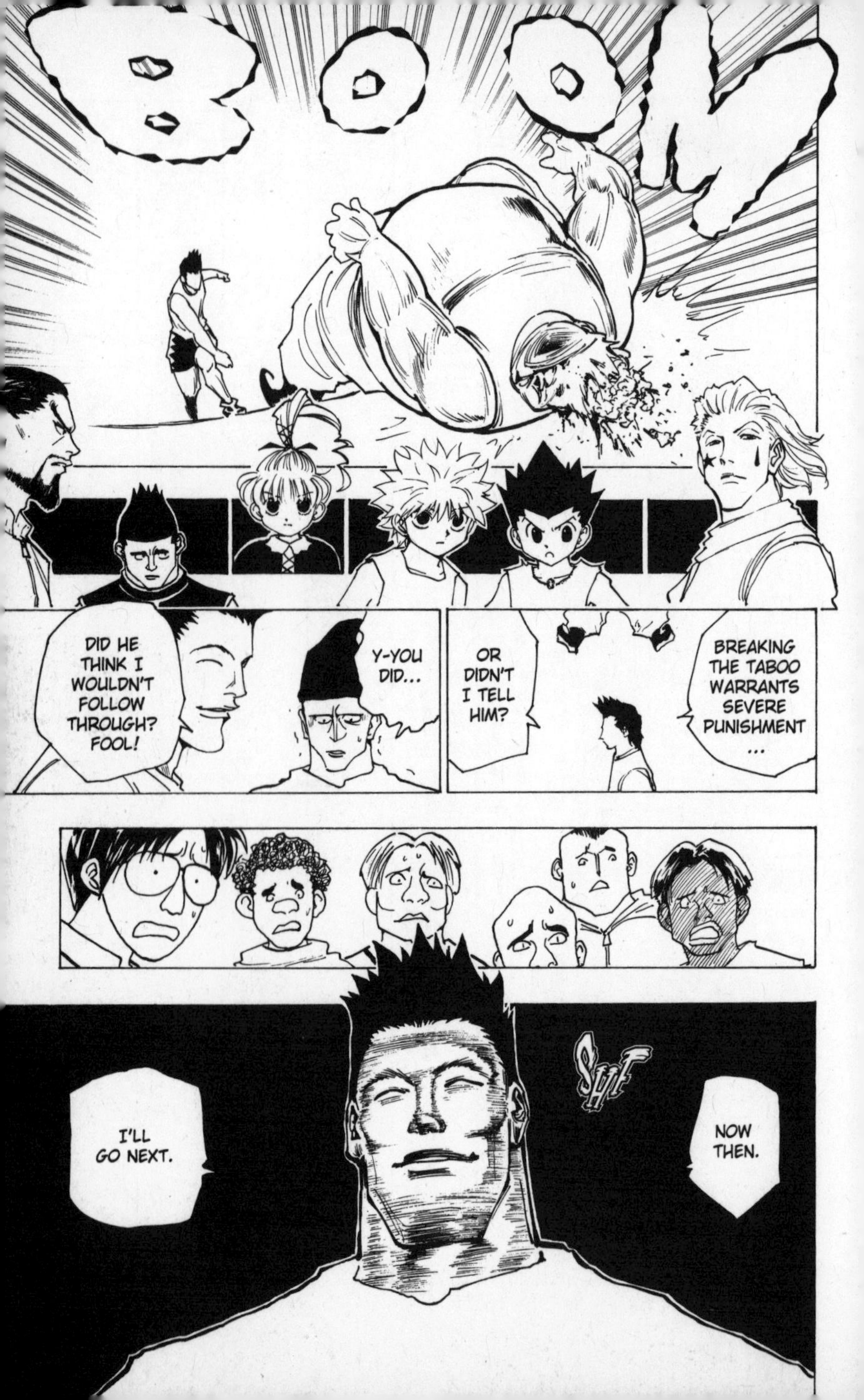
BOOM
BREAKING THE TABOO WARRANTS SEVERE PUNISHMENT ...
OR DIDN'T I TELL HIM?
Y-YOU DID...
DID HE THINK I WOULDN'T FOLLOW THROUGH? FOOL!
NOW THEN.
SHFF
I'LL GO NEXT.

1: PATCH OF FOREST (SS - 3)	THE ENTRANCE TO THE GIANT FOREST CALLED THE "MOUNTAIN GOD'S GARDEN" WHERE MANY UNIQUE ENDEMIC SPECIES LIVE. THEY ARE ALL TAME AND FRIENDLY.
2: STRIP OF BEACH (SS - 3)	THE ENTRANCE TO A CAVE CALLED "POSEIDON'S CAVERN." THE CAVE CHANGES ITS PATH AT EACH VISIT, CONFUSING INTRUDERS.
3: PITCHER OF ETERNAL WATER (A - 17)	A JAR FROM WHICH PURE, CLEAN WATER (1440 L PER DAY) CONTINUALLY FLOWS.
4: SKIN CARE HOT SPRINGS (A - 15)	A HOT SPRINGS THAT CURES YOU OF ANY SKIN CONDITION. BATHING IN IT FOR HALF AN HOUR A DAY GIVES YOU SKIN AS SOFT AND SMOOTH AS A BABY'S.
5: SPIRITED AWAY HOLLOW (S - 8)	ENTER AND THEN EXIT THIS HOLLOW AND YOU WILL BE TRANSPORTED TO A DESOLATE LOCATION WITHIN THE COUNTRY. CIRCUMSTANCES WILL ALLOW YOU TO RETURN TO WHERE YOU STARTED WITHOUT YOU HAVING TO SPEND ANY MONEY.
6: LIQUOR SPRING (A - 15)	DRAW SOME OF THIS SPRING'S WATER AND ONE HOUR LATER IT WILL BECOME A RANDOM ALCOHOLIC DRINK OF EXQUISITE TASTE AND EXTRAORDINARY QUALITY.
7: PREGNANCY STONES (S - 10)	CARRY A STONE (WEIGHING 7 LB. EACH) FOR ONE MONTH, AND YOU WILL GET PREGNANT, EVEN IF YOU'RE MALE. YOU MAY CHOOSE THE SEX OF THE BABY BY THE FEMALE OR THE MALE STONE.
8: MYSTERY POND (S - 10)	RELEASE ONE FISH INTO THIS POND, AND THERE WILL BE ONE MORE FISH OF THAT TYPE THE NEXT DAY. YOU CAN KEEP ANY COMBINATION OF FISH IN THIS POND, EVEN SALTWATER AND FRESHWATER FISH TOGETHER!
9: TREE OF PLENTY (S - 10)	A TREE THAT BEARS ALL SORTS OF FRUIT. NO MATTER HOW MUCH YOU HARVEST, IT WILL BE FULL AGAIN THE NEXT DAY. THE TYPE AND NUMBER OF FRUIT ARE RANDOM.

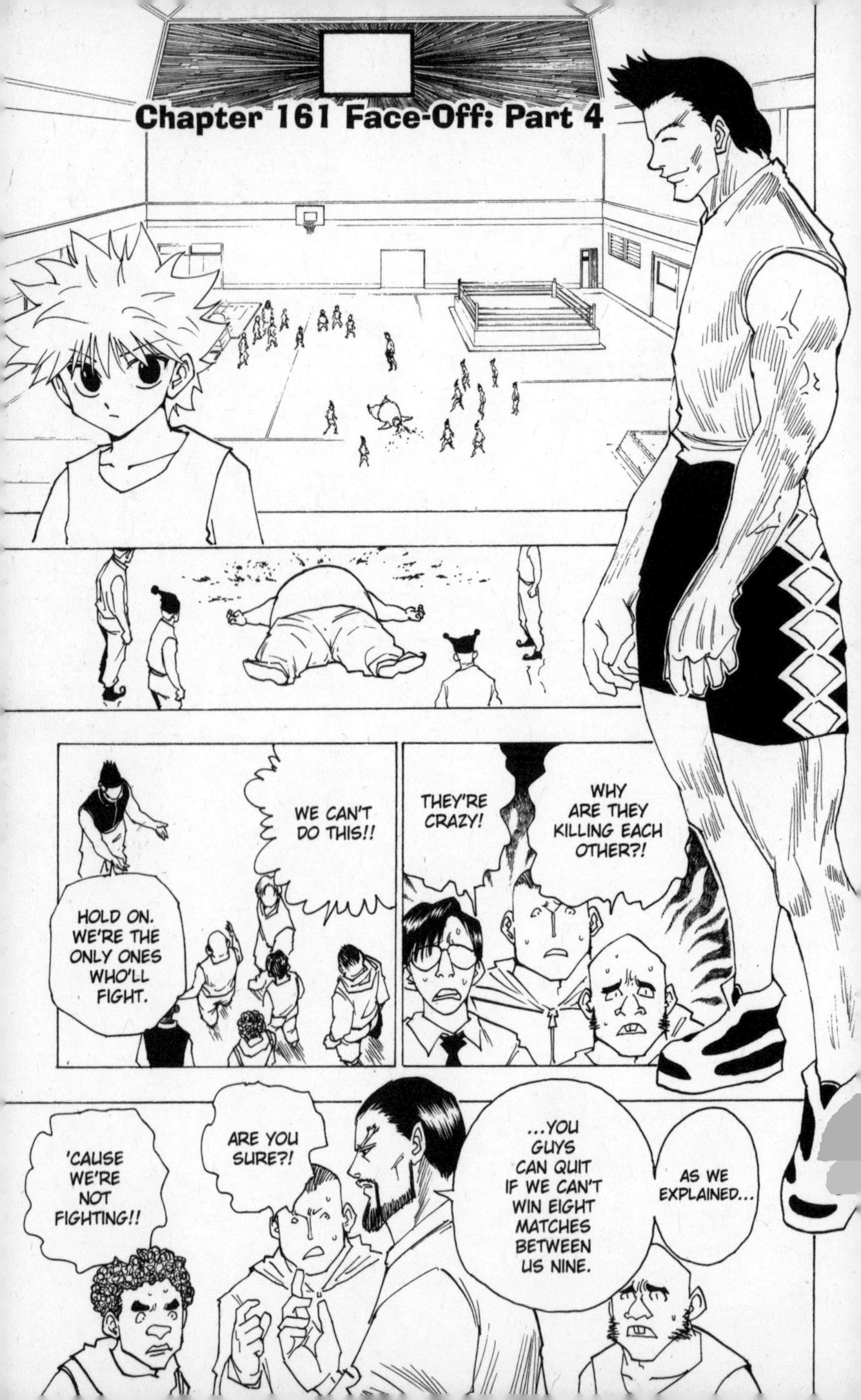
Chapter 161 Face-Off: Part 4
WHY ARE THEY KILLING EACH OTHER?!
THEY'RE CRAZY!
WE CAN'T DO THIS!!
HOLD ON. WE'RE THE ONLY ONES WHO'LL FIGHT.
AS WE EXPLAINED...
...YOU GUYS CAN QUIT IF WE CAN'T WIN EIGHT MATCHES BETWEEN US NINE.
ARE YOU SURE?!
'CAUSE WE'RE NOT FIGHTING!!

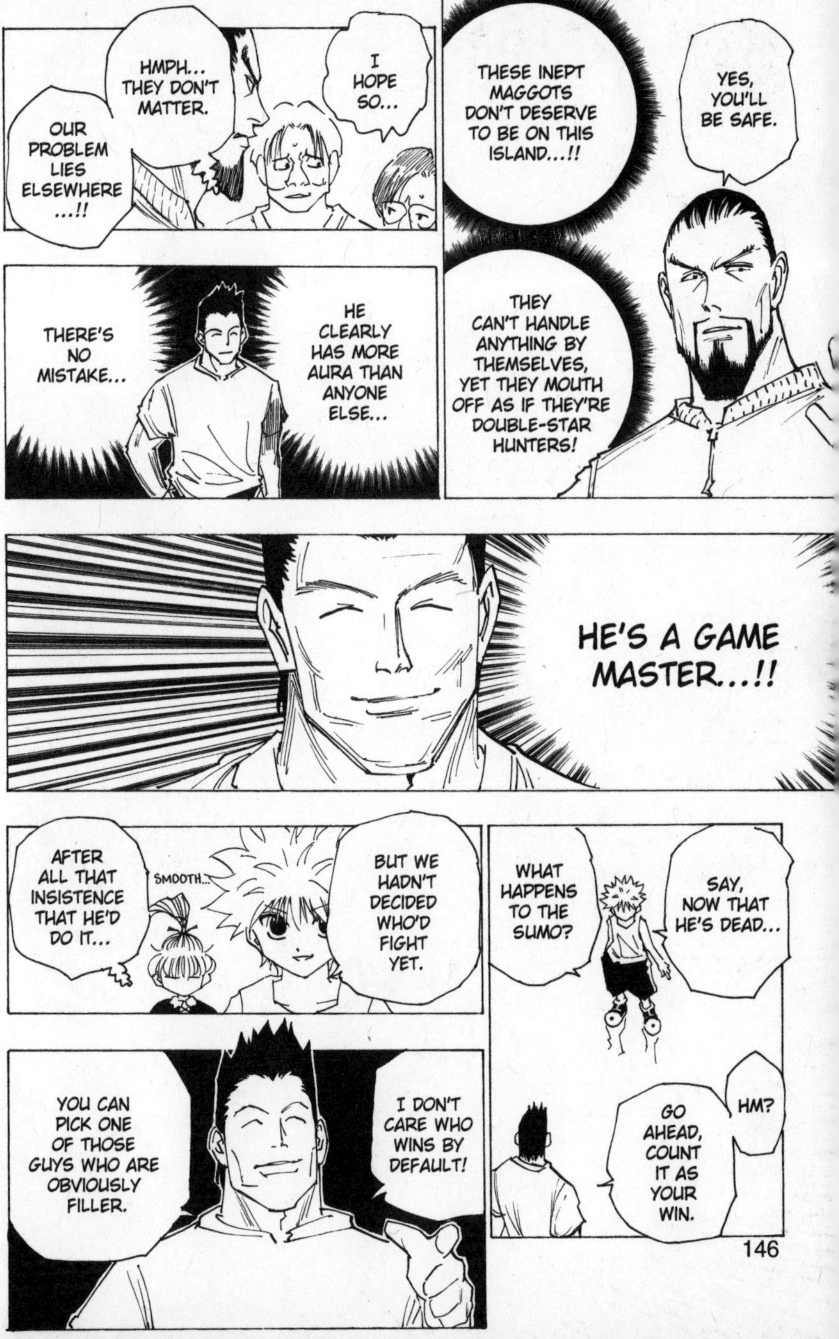
YES, YOU'LL BE SAFE.
THESE INEPT MAGGOTS DON'T DESERVE TO BE ON THIS ISLAND...!!
THEY CAN'T HANDLE ANYTHING BY THEMSELVES, YET THEY MOUTH OFF AS IF THEY'RE DOUBLE-STAR HUNTERS!
I HOPE SO...
HMPH... THEY DON'T MATTER.
OUR PROBLEM LIES ELSEWHERE ...!!
HE CLEARLY HAS MORE AURA THAN ANYONE ELSE...
THERE'S NO MISTAKE...
HE'S A GAME MASTER...!!
SAY, NOW THAT HE'S DEAD...
WHAT HAPPENS TO THE SUMO?
HM?
GO AHEAD, COUNT IT AS YOUR WIN.
BUT WE HADN'T DECIDED WHO'D FIGHT YET.
SMOOTH...
AFTER ALL THAT INSISTENCE THAT HE'D DO IT...
I DON'T CARE WHO WINS BY DEFAULT!
YOU CAN PICK ONE OF THOSE GUYS WHO ARE OBVIOUSLY FILLER.

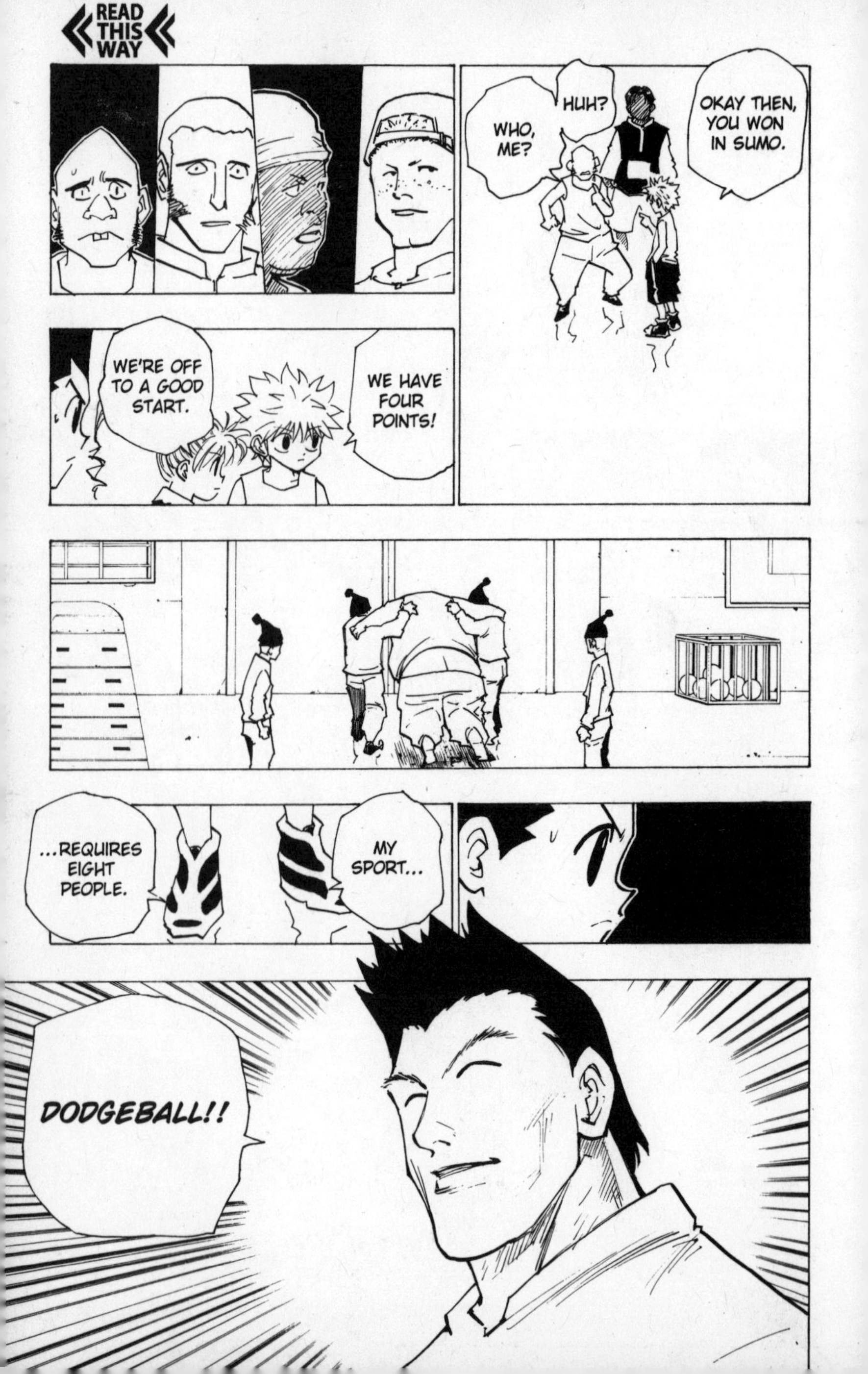
READ THIS WAY
OKAY THEN, YOU WON IN SUMO.
HUH?
WHO, ME?
WE HAVE FOUR POINTS!
WE'RE OFF TO A GOOD START.
MY SPORT...
...REQUIRES EIGHT PEOPLE.
DODGEBALL!!

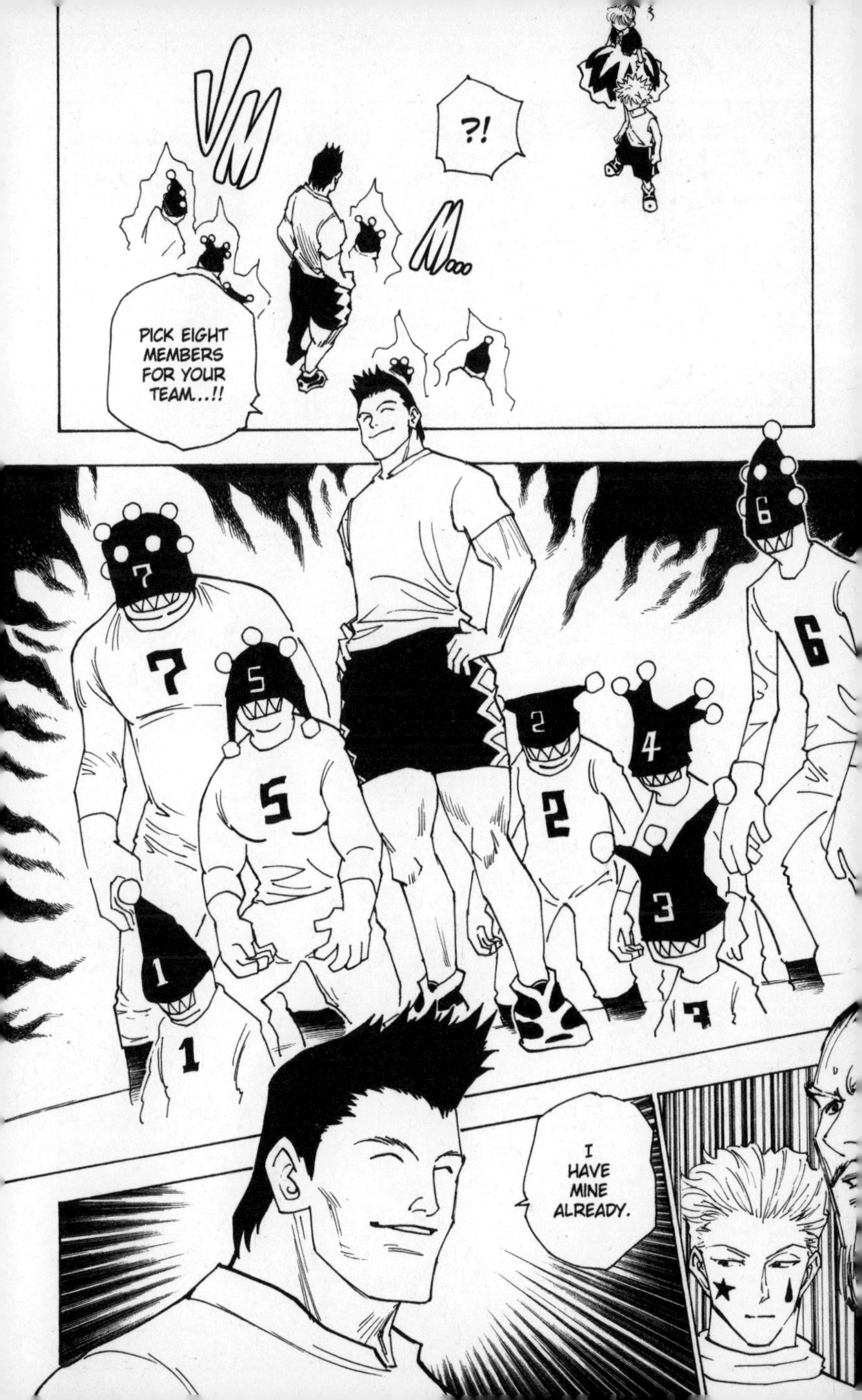
?!
PICK EIGHT MEMBERS FOR YOUR TEAM...!!
I HAVE MINE ALREADY.

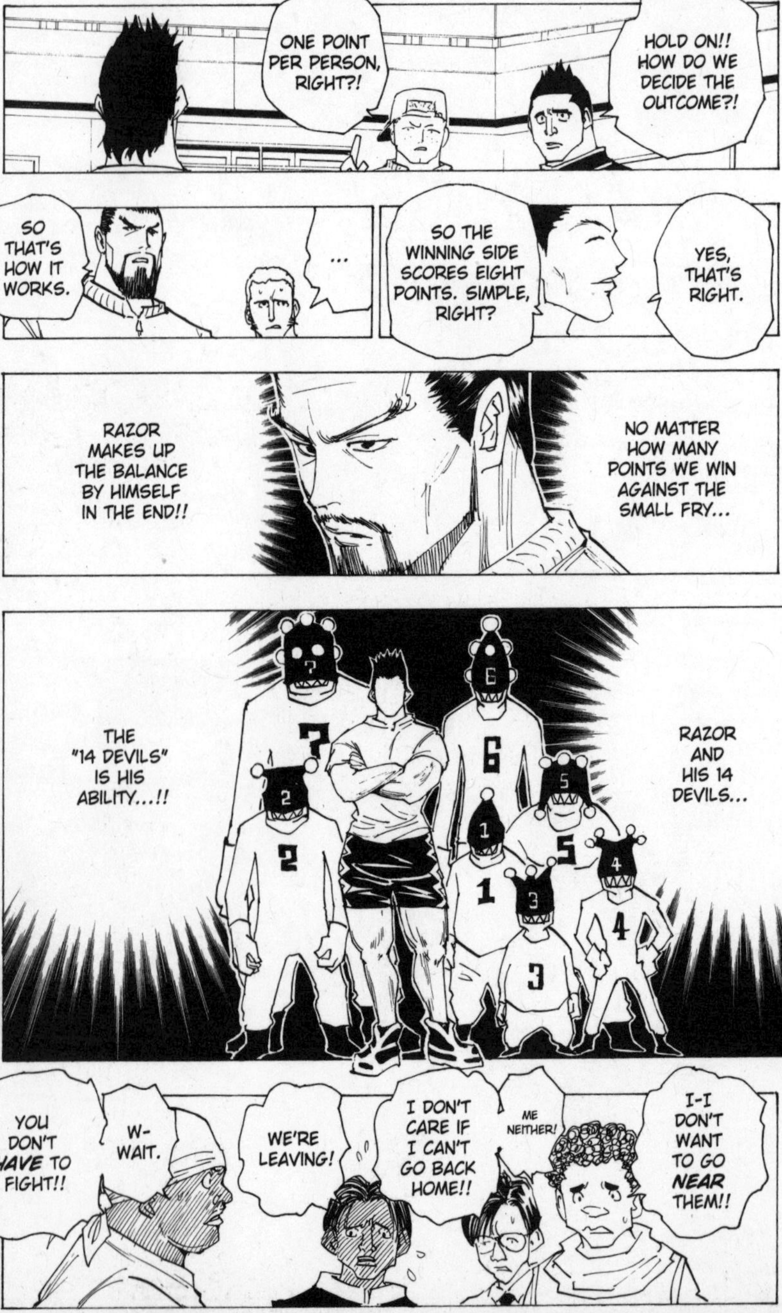
HOLD ON!! HOW DO WE DECIDE THE OUTCOME?!
ONE POINT PER PERSON, RIGHT?!
YES, THAT'S RIGHT.
SO THE WINNING SIDE SCORES EIGHT POINTS. SIMPLE, RIGHT?
...
SO THAT'S HOW IT WORKS.
NO MATTER HOW MANY POINTS WE WIN AGAINST THE SMALL FRY...
RAZOR MAKES UP THE BALANCE BY HIMSELF IN THE END!!
RAZOR AND HIS 14 DEVILS...
THE "14 DEVILS" IS HIS ABILITY...!!
I-I DON'T WANT TO GO *NEAR* THEM!!
ME NEITHER!
I DON'T CARE IF I CAN'T GO BACK HOME!!
WE'RE LEAVING!
W-WAIT.
YOU DON'T *HAVE* TO FIGHT!!

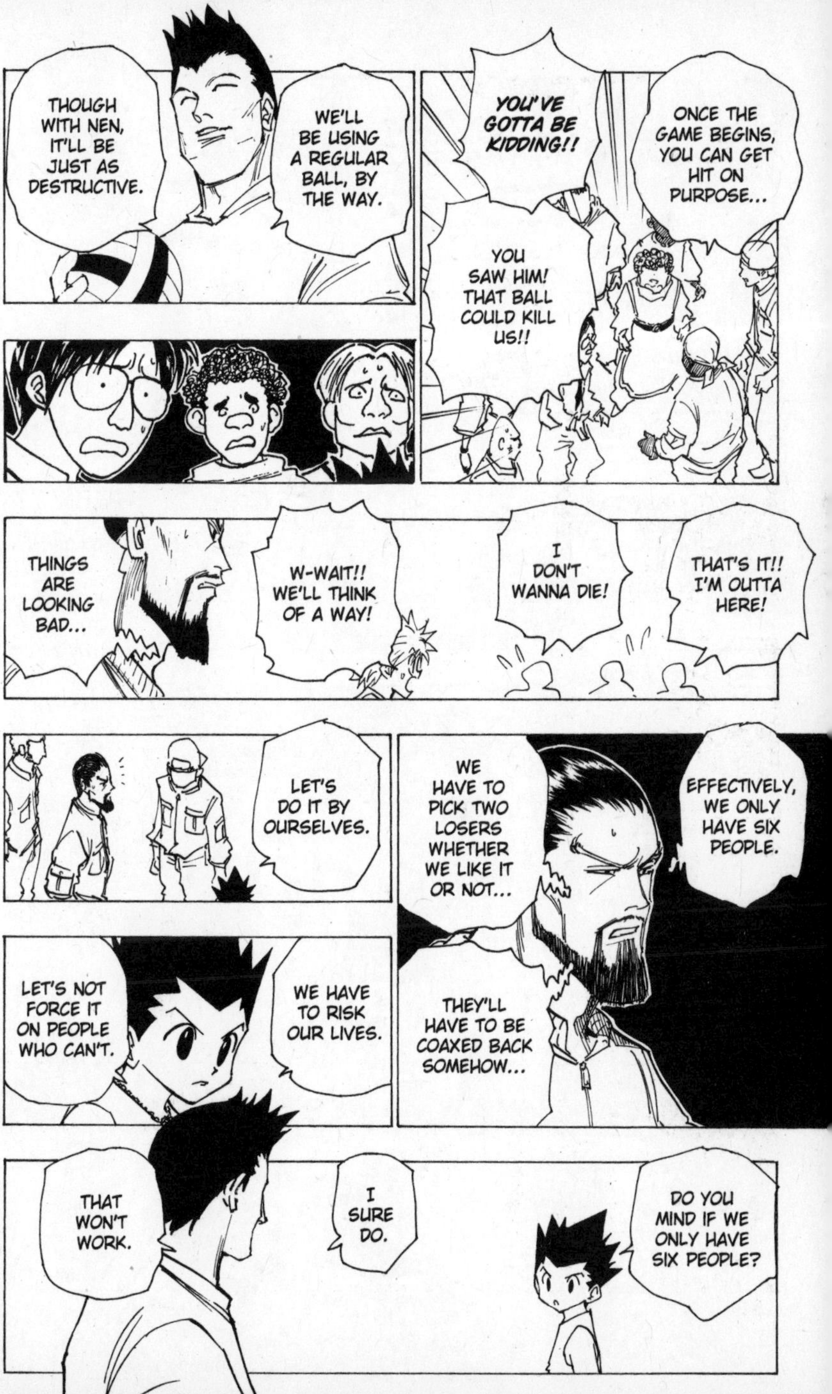
ONCE THE GAME BEGINS, YOU CAN GET HIT ON PURPOSE...
YOU'VE GOTTA BE KIDDING!!
YOU SAW HIM! THAT BALL COULD KILL US!!
WE'LL BE USING A REGULAR BALL, BY THE WAY.
THOUGH WITH NEN, IT'LL BE JUST AS DESTRUCTIVE.
THAT'S IT!! I'M OUTTA HERE!
I DON'T WANNA DIE!
W-WAIT!! WE'LL THINK OF A WAY!
THINGS ARE LOOKING BAD...
EFFECTIVELY, WE ONLY HAVE SIX PEOPLE.
WE HAVE TO PICK TWO LOSERS WHETHER WE LIKE IT OR NOT...
THEY'LL HAVE TO BE COAXED BACK SOMEHOW...
LET'S DO IT BY OURSELVES.
WE HAVE TO RISK OUR LIVES.
LET'S NOT FORCE IT ON PEOPLE WHO CAN'T.
DO YOU MIND IF WE ONLY HAVE SIX PEOPLE?
I SURE DO.
THAT WON'T WORK.

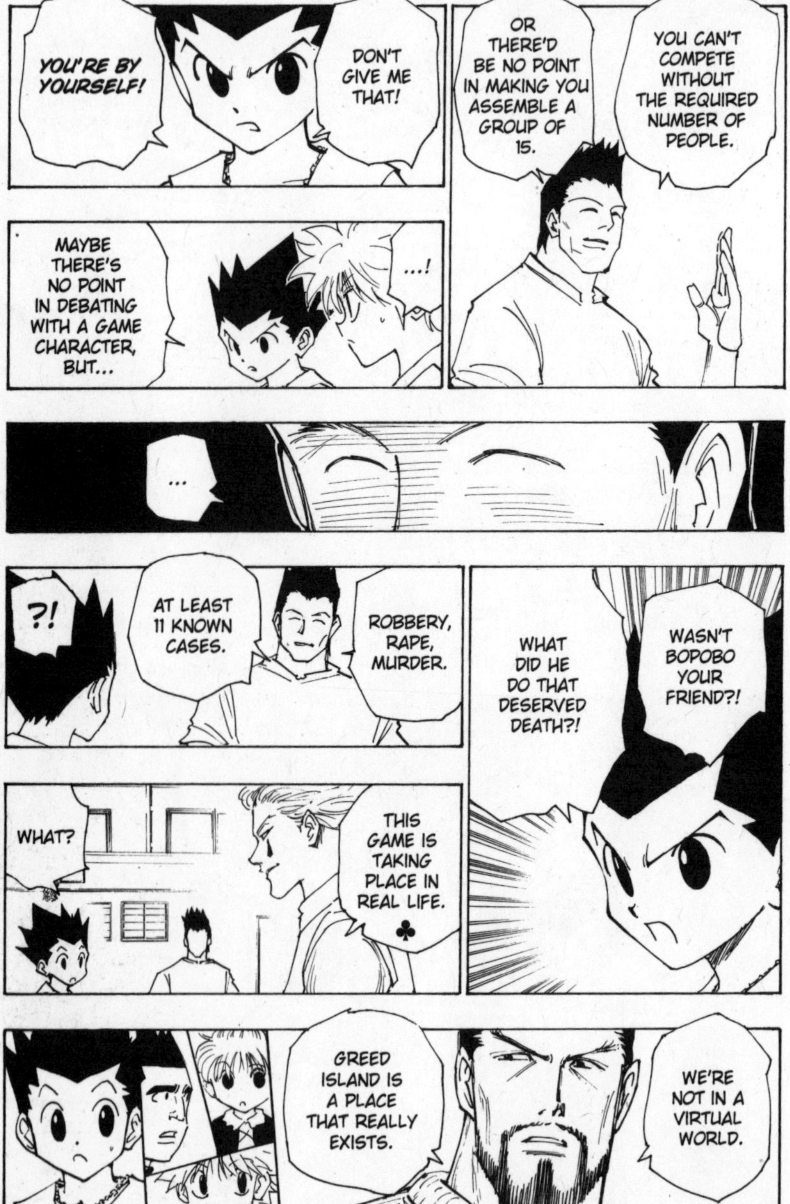
YOU CAN'T COMPETE WITHOUT THE REQUIRED NUMBER OF PEOPLE.
OR THERE'D BE NO POINT IN MAKING YOU ASSEMBLE A GROUP OF 15.
DON'T GIVE ME THAT!
YOU'RE BY YOURSELF!
...!
MAYBE THERE'S NO POINT IN DEBATING WITH A GAME CHARACTER, BUT...
...
WASN'T BOPOBO YOUR FRIEND?!
WHAT DID HE DO THAT DESERVED DEATH?!
ROBBERY, RAPE, MURDER.
AT LEAST 11 KNOWN CASES.
?!
THIS GAME IS TAKING PLACE IN REAL LIFE. ♣
WHAT?
WE'RE NOT IN A VIRTUAL WORLD.
GREED ISLAND IS A PLACE THAT REALLY EXISTS.

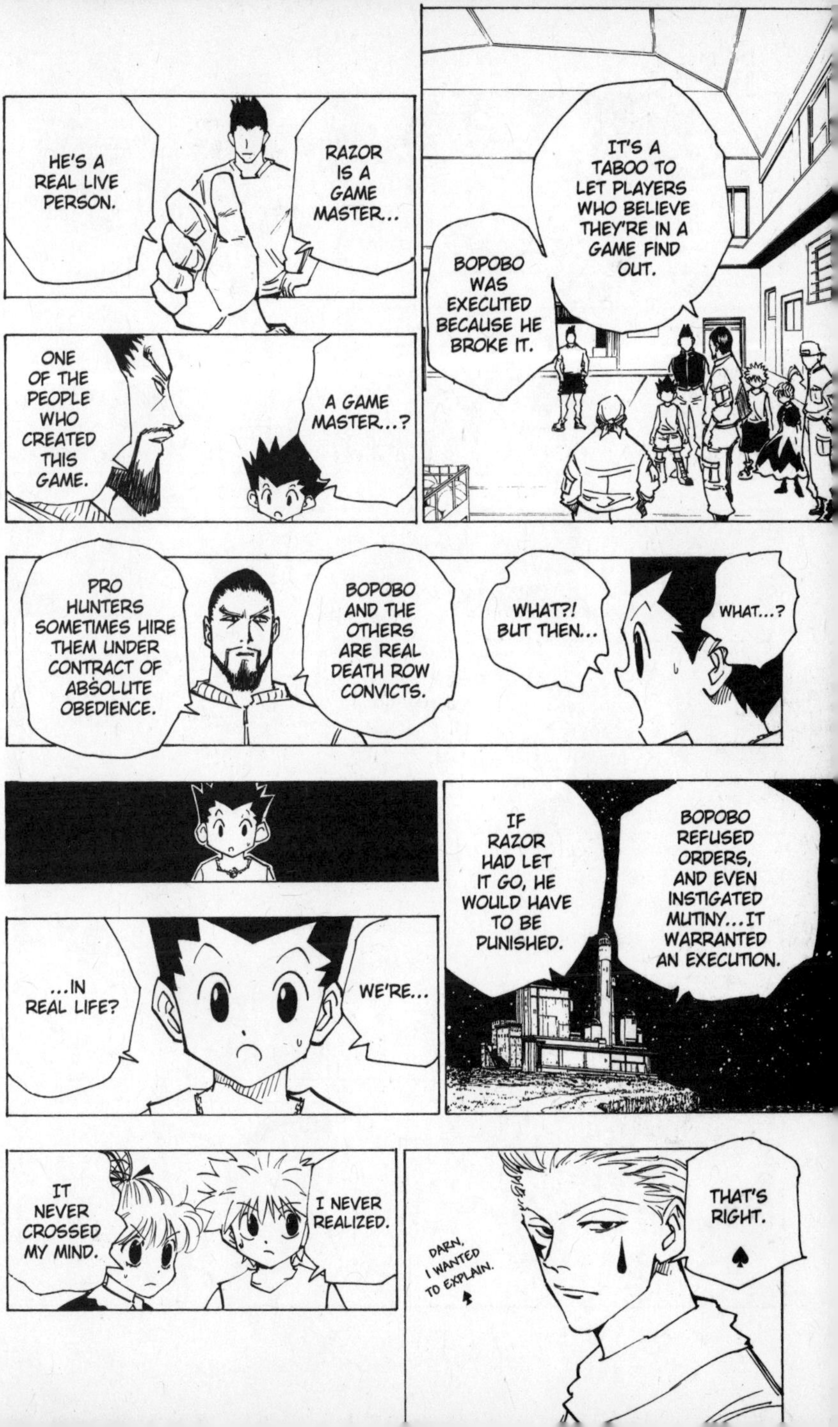
IT'S A TABOO TO LET PLAYERS WHO BELIEVE THEY'RE IN A GAME FIND OUT.
BOPOBO WAS EXECUTED BECAUSE HE BROKE IT.
RAZOR IS A GAME MASTER...
HE'S A REAL LIVE PERSON.
A GAME MASTER...?
ONE OF THE PEOPLE WHO CREATED THIS GAME.
WHAT...?
WHAT?! BUT THEN...
BOPOBO AND THE OTHERS ARE REAL DEATH ROW CONVICTS.
PRO HUNTERS SOMETIMES HIRE THEM UNDER CONTRACT OF ABSOLUTE OBEDIENCE.
BOPOBO REFUSED ORDERS, AND EVEN INSTIGATED MUTINY...IT WARRANTED AN EXECUTION.
IF RAZOR HAD LET IT GO, HE WOULD HAVE TO BE PUNISHED.
WE'RE...
...IN REAL LIFE?
THAT'S RIGHT.
DARN, I WANTED TO EXPLAIN.
I NEVER REALIZED.
IT NEVER CROSSED MY MIND.

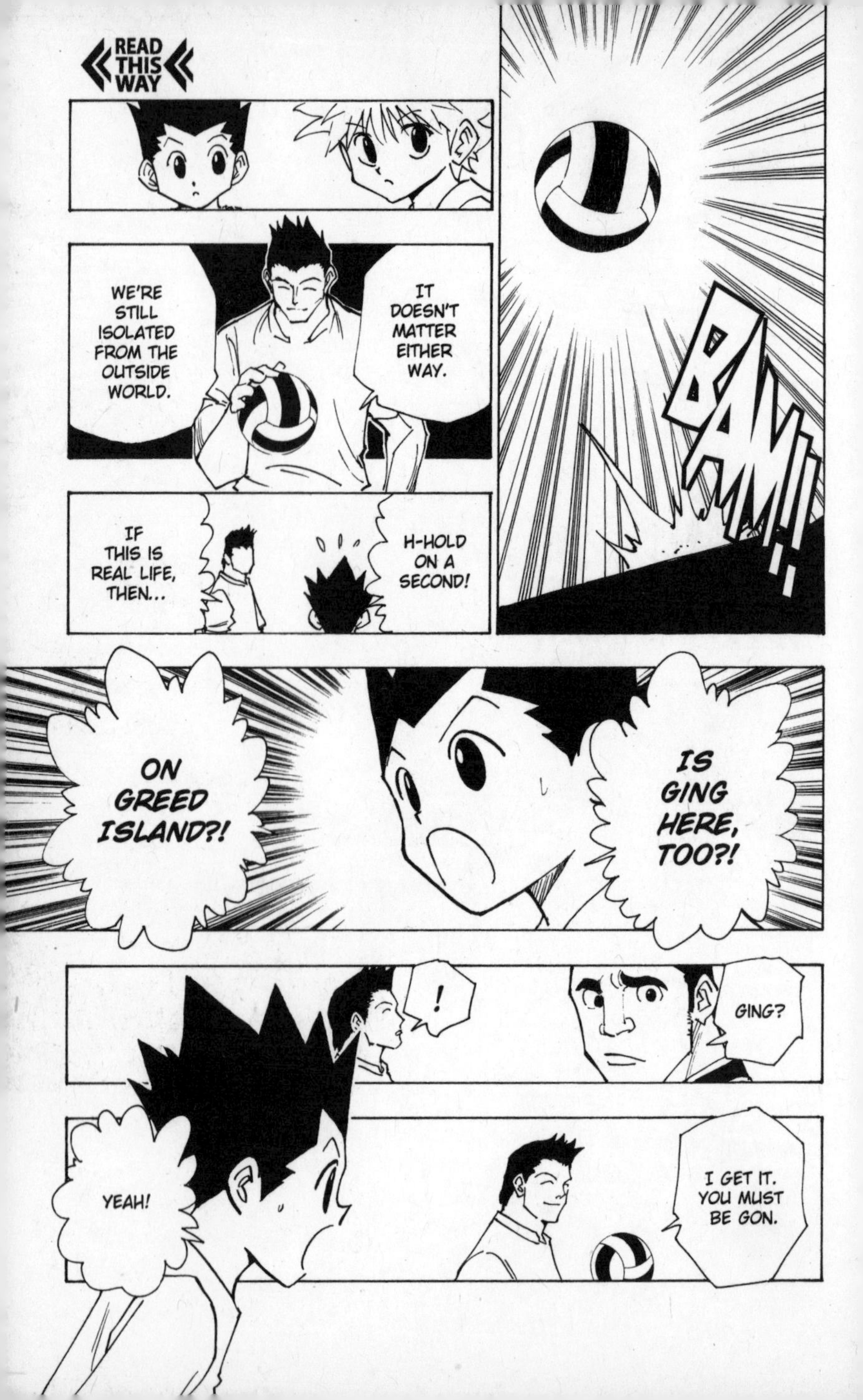
READ THIS WAY
BAM!!
IT DOESN'T MATTER EITHER WAY.
WE'RE STILL ISOLATED FROM THE OUTSIDE WORLD.
H-HOLD ON A SECOND!
IF THIS IS REAL LIFE, THEN...
IS GING HERE, TOO?!
ON GREED ISLAND?!
GING?
!
I GET IT. YOU MUST BE GON.
YEAH!

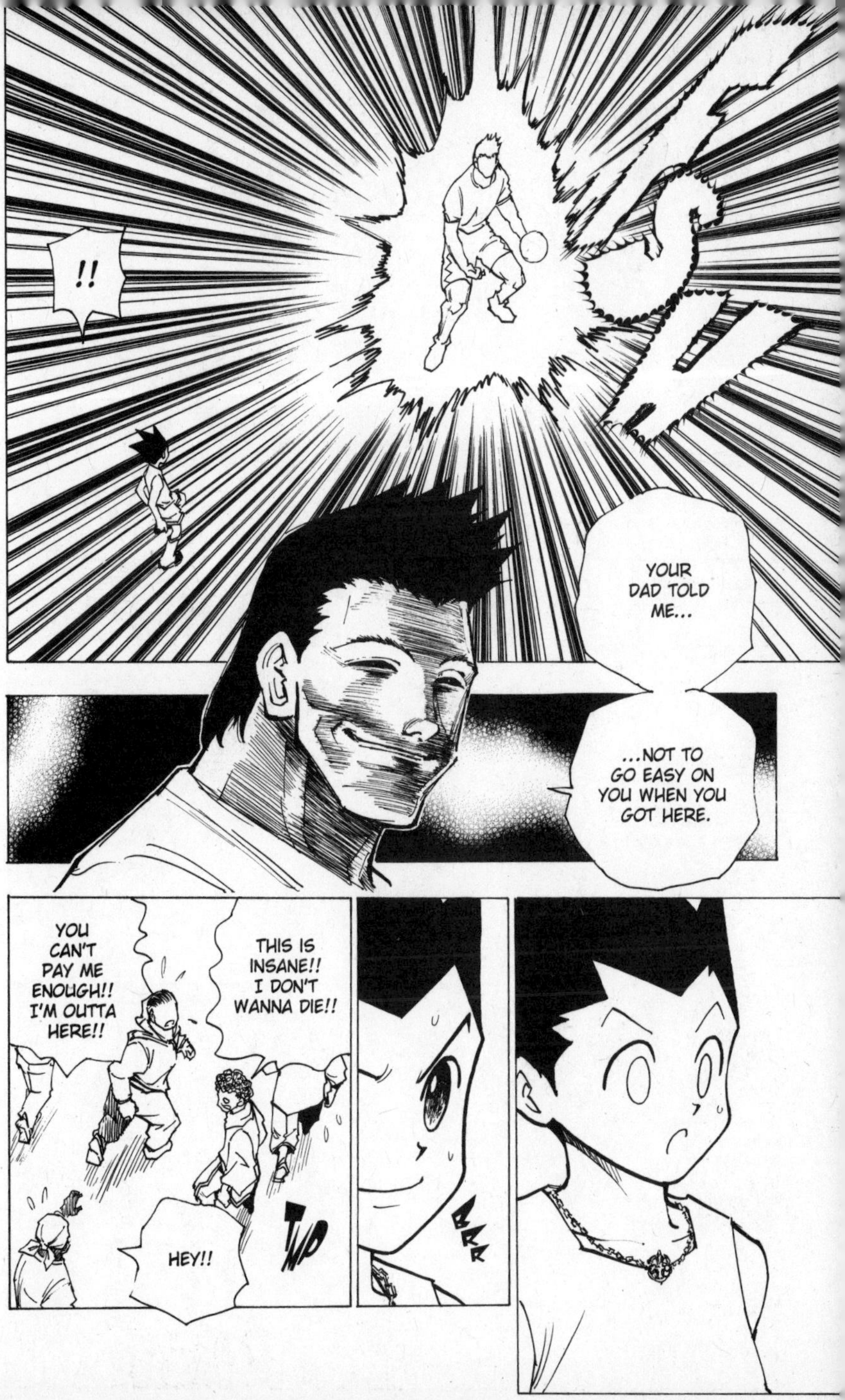
!!
YOUR DAD TOLD ME...
...NOT TO GO EASY ON YOU WHEN YOU GOT HERE.
BRR
THIS IS INSANE!! I DON'T WANNA DIE!!
YOU CAN'T PAY ME ENOUGH!! I'M OUTTA HERE!!
TMP
HEY!!

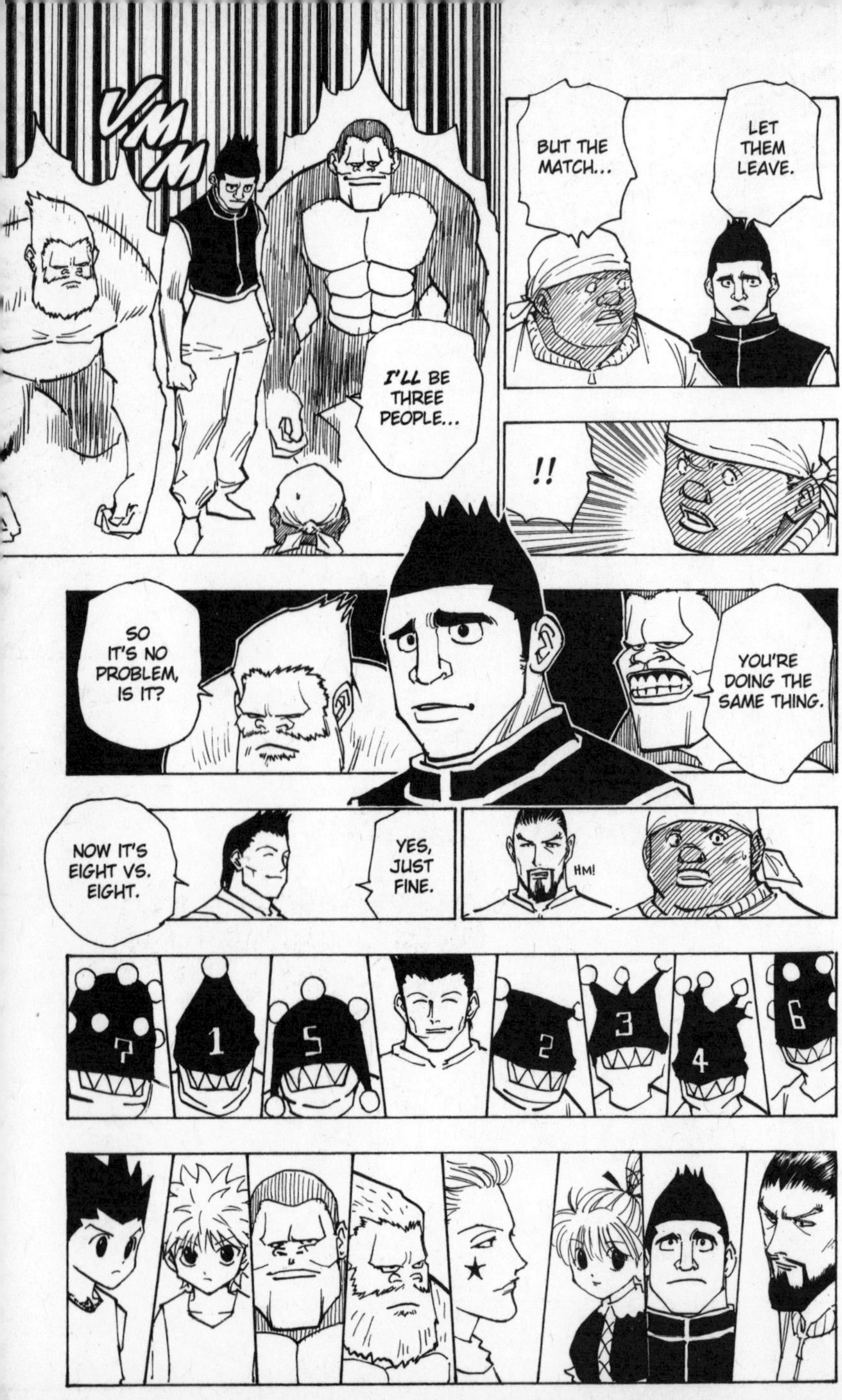

LET THEM LEAVE.
BUT THE MATCH...
UMM
I'LL BE THREE PEOPLE...
!!
YOU'RE DOING THE SAME THING.
SO IT'S NO PROBLEM, IS IT?
HM!
YES, JUST FINE.
NOW IT'S EIGHT VS. EIGHT.
6
4
3
2
5
1
7

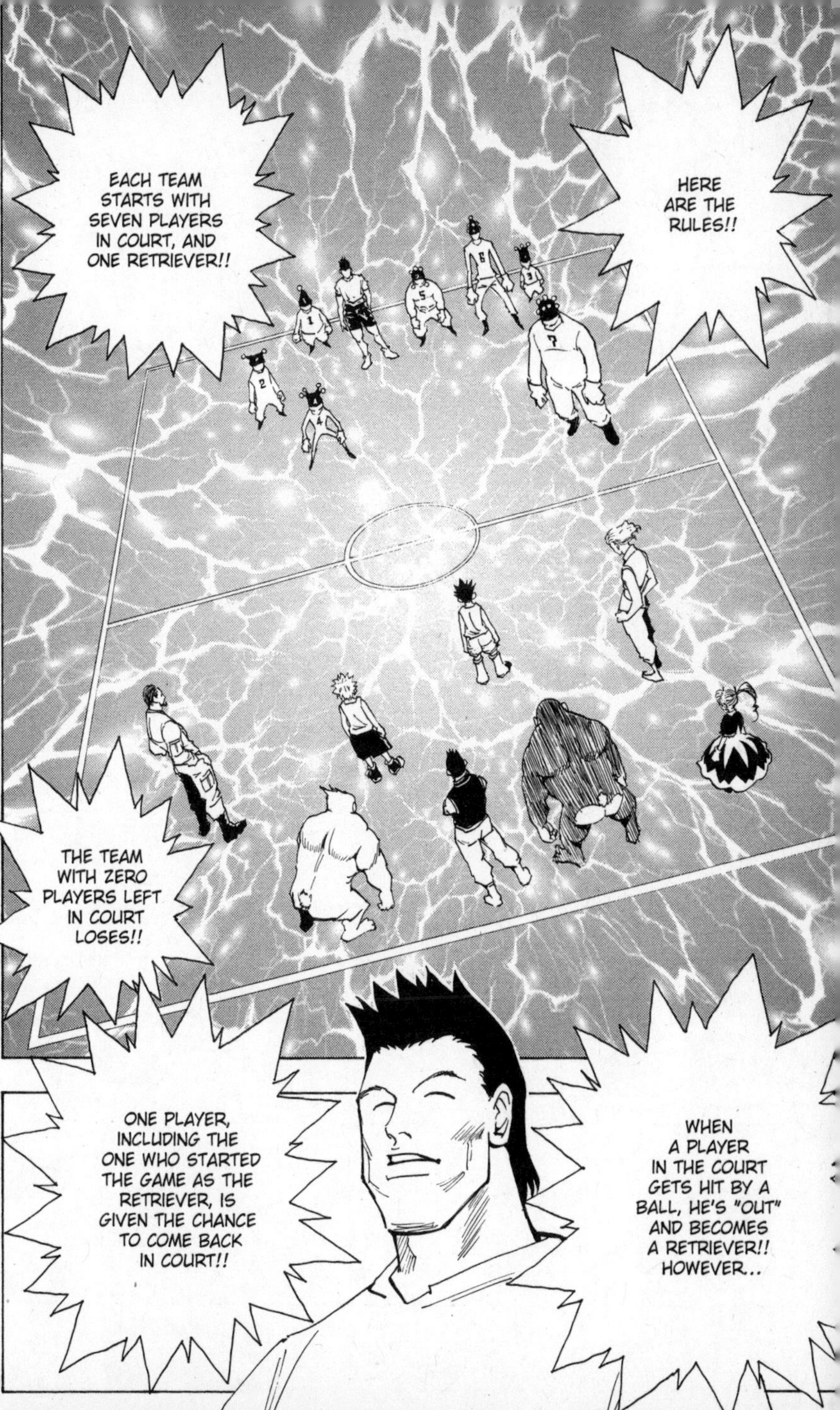
HERE ARE THE RULES!!
EACH TEAM STARTS WITH SEVEN PLAYERS IN COURT, AND ONE RETRIEVER!!
THE TEAM WITH ZERO PLAYERS LEFT IN COURT LOSES!!
WHEN A PLAYER IN THE COURT GETS HIT BY A BALL, HE'S "OUT" AND BECOMES A RETRIEVER!! HOWEVER...
ONE PLAYER, INCLUDING THE ONE WHO STARTED THE GAME AS THE RETRIEVER, IS GIVEN THE CHANCE TO COME BACK IN COURT!!

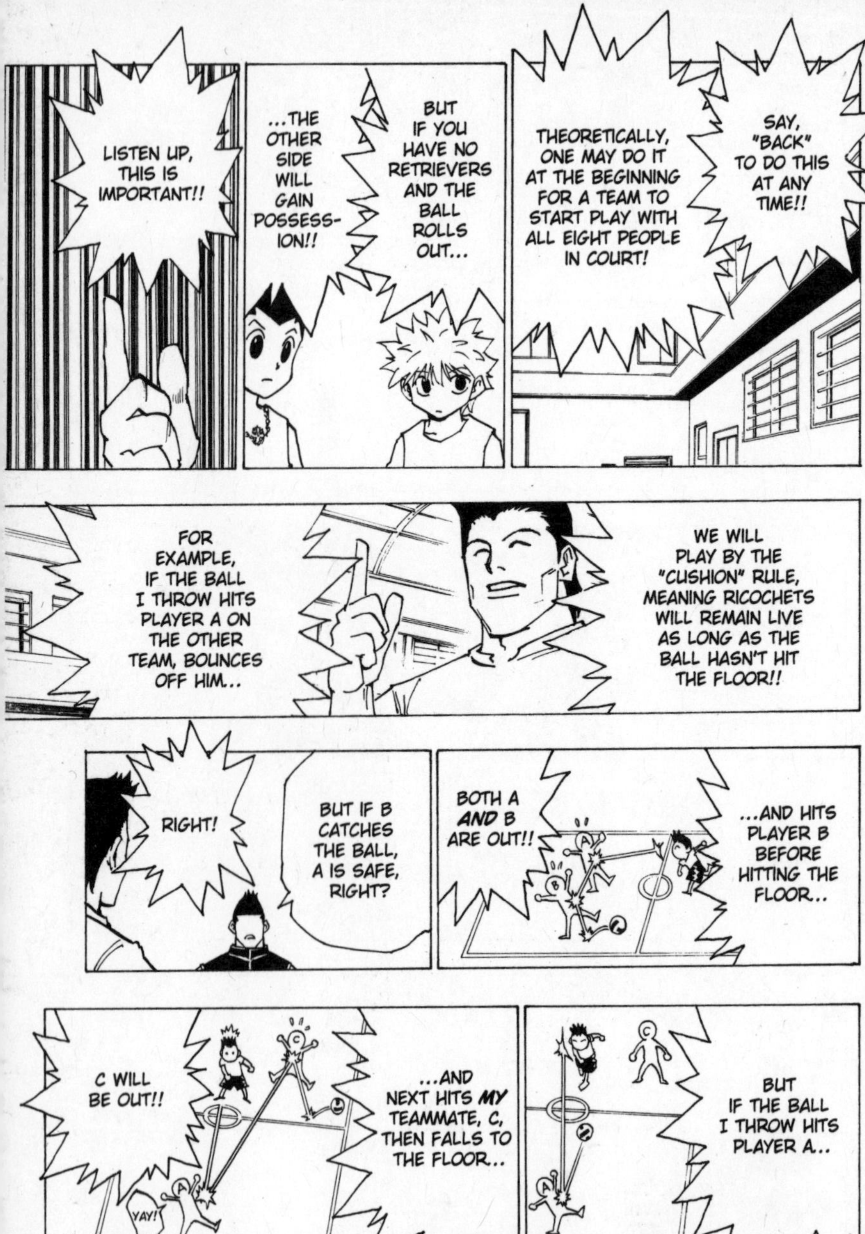
SAY, "BACK" TO DO THIS AT ANY TIME!!
THEORETICALLY, ONE MAY DO IT AT THE BEGINNING FOR A TEAM TO START PLAY WITH ALL EIGHT PEOPLE IN COURT!
BUT IF YOU HAVE NO RETRIEVERS AND THE BALL ROLLS OUT...
...THE OTHER SIDE WILL GAIN POSSESSION!!
LISTEN UP, THIS IS IMPORTANT!!
WE WILL PLAY BY THE "CUSHION" RULE, MEANING RICOCHETS WILL REMAIN LIVE AS LONG AS THE BALL HASN'T HIT THE FLOOR!!
FOR EXAMPLE, IF THE BALL I THROW HITS PLAYER A ON THE OTHER TEAM, BOUNCES OFF HIM...
...AND HITS PLAYER B BEFORE HITTING THE FLOOR...
BOTH A *AND* B ARE OUT!!
BUT IF B CATCHES THE BALL, A IS SAFE, RIGHT?
RIGHT!
BUT IF THE BALL I THROW HITS PLAYER A...
...AND NEXT HITS *MY* TEAMMATE, C, THEN FALLS TO THE FLOOR...
C WILL BE OUT!!
YAY!

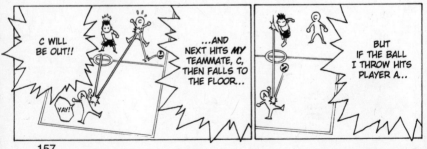

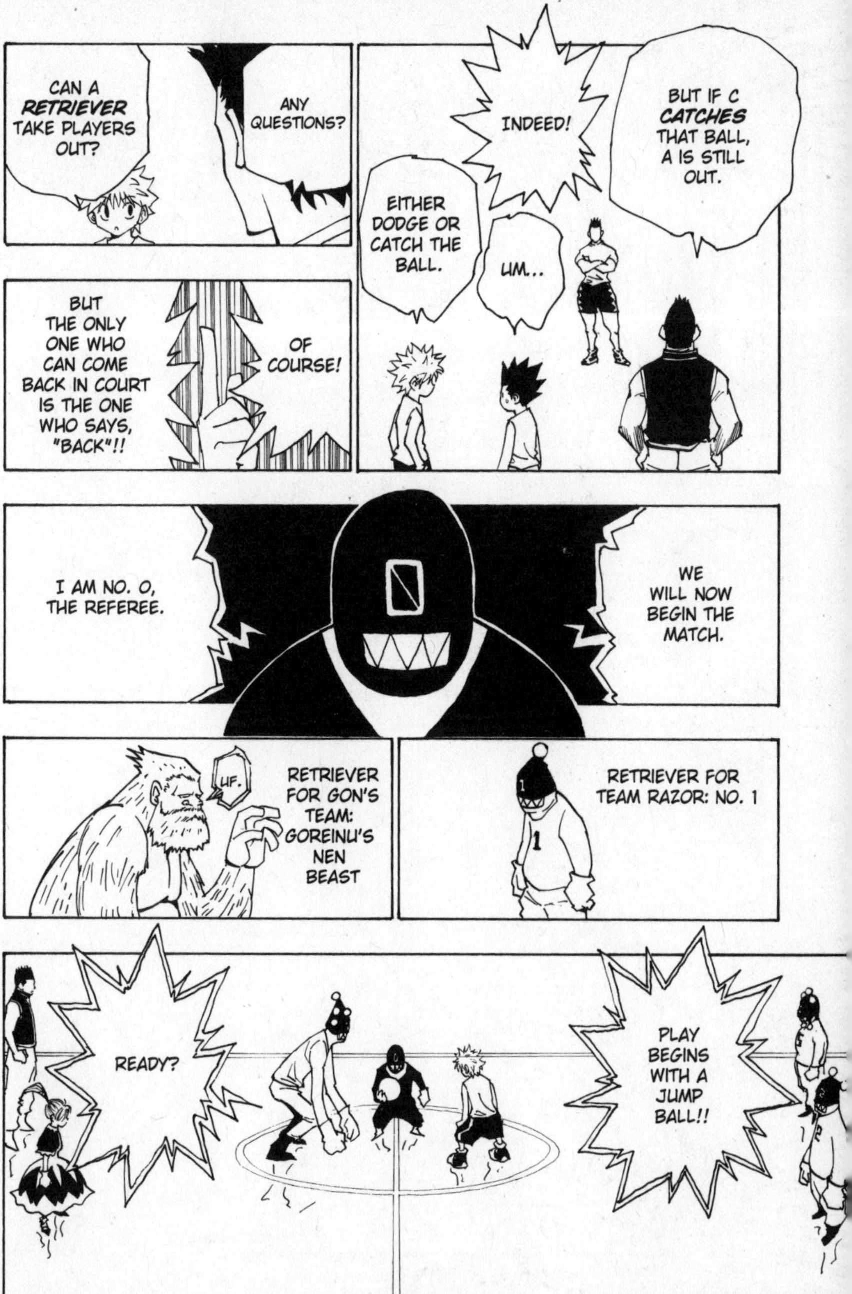
BUT IF C *CATCHES* THAT BALL, A IS STILL OUT.
INDEED!
EITHER DODGE OR CATCH THE BALL.
UM..
ANY QUESTIONS?
CAN A *RETRIEVER* TAKE PLAYERS OUT?
OF COURSE!
BUT THE ONLY ONE WHO CAN COME BACK IN COURT IS THE ONE WHO SAYS, "BACK"!!
I AM NO. 0, THE REFEREE.
WE WILL NOW BEGIN THE MATCH.
RETRIEVER FOR TEAM RAZOR: NO. 1
RETRIEVER FOR GON'S TEAM: GOREINU'S NEN BEAST
UF.
PLAY BEGINS WITH A JUMP BALL!!
READY?

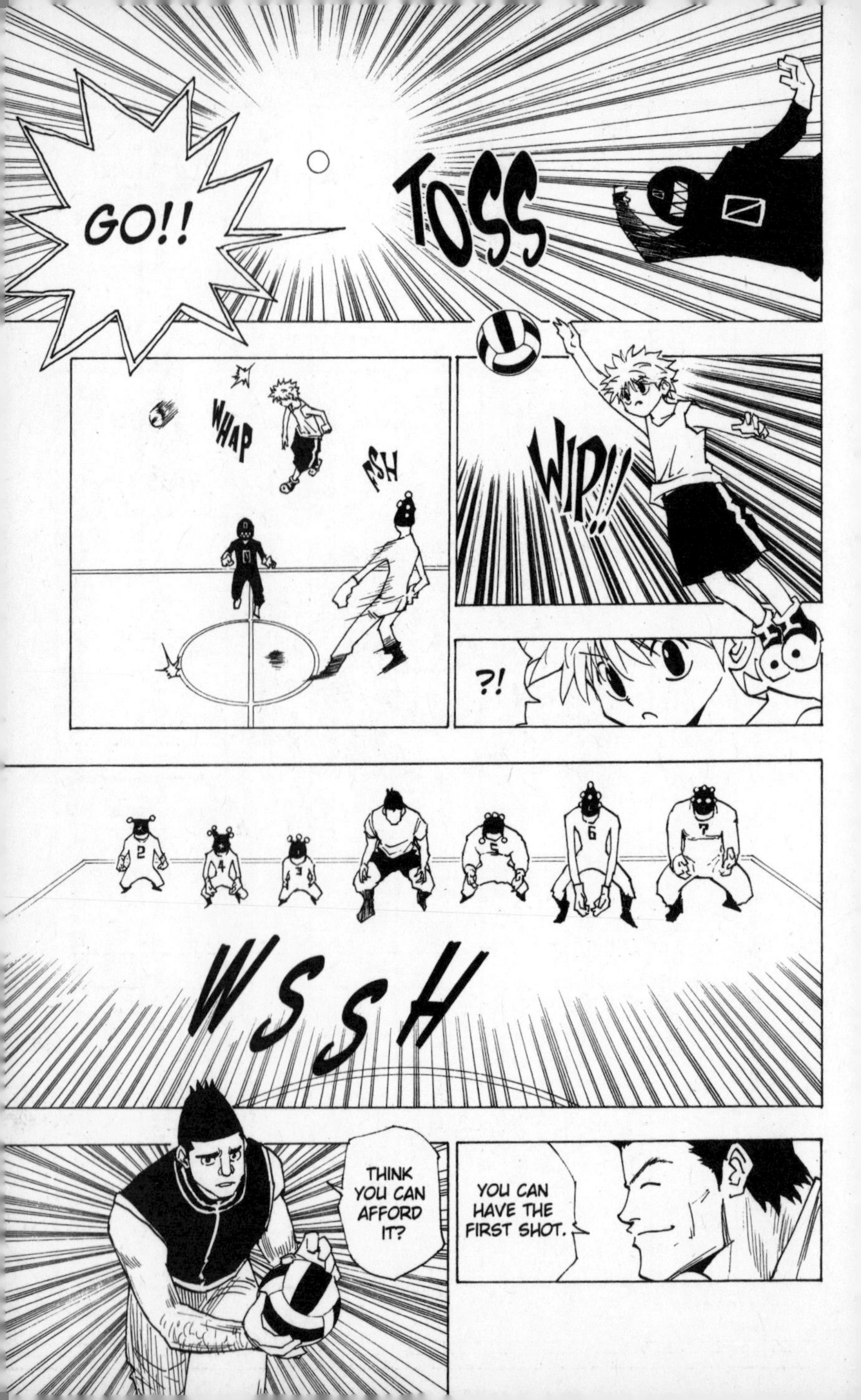
TOSS
GO!!
WIP!!
?!
WHAP
FSH
WSSH
YOU CAN HAVE THE FIRST SHOT.
THINK YOU CAN AFFORD IT?

10: GOLDEN GUIDEBOOK (4-20)	A TRAVEL GUIDE THAT LISTS WHERE AND WHEN YOU CAN MEET PEOPLE OF THE OPPOSITE SEX WHO ARE YOUR TYPE.
11: GOLDEN SCALES (B - 30)	WHEN FACED WITH A TWO-OPTION CHOICE, THESE SCALES WILL TELL YOU WHICH IS BETTER FOR YOUR FUTURE.
12: GOLDEN DICTIONARY (5 - 10)	EACH DAY YOU WILL FIND A WORD GLOWING GOLD. YOU SHOULD LEARN THOSE WORDS BECAUSE THEY WILL COME IN HANDY THE NEXT DAY.
13: LUCK BANKBOOK (4 - 20)	REFRAIN FROM USING THE LITTLE THINGS OF GOOD LUCK IN YOUR DAILY LIFE, AND YOU CAN ACCUMULATE AND CONVERT THEM INTO CASH.
14: CONNECTION SEVERING SCISSORS (B - 22)	CUT A PICTURE OF SOMEONE YOU DON'T WANT TO SEE WITH THESE SCISSORS, AND YOU WILL NEVER SEE THEM AGAIN. CAUTION: IT WILL TAKE EFFECT ON EVERYONE IN THE PICTURE (EXCEPT YOURSELF).
15: PICKLE GENIE (5 - 10)	THIS GENIE WILL GRANT YOU THREE WISHES, BUT YOU NEED TO SUGGEST 1000 POTENTIAL, SIGNIFICANTLY DIFFERENT WISHES AND HE WILL CHOOSE THREE FROM AMONG THEM. (NO CHEATING BY ASKING FOR DIFFERENT INCREMENTS OF MONEY.)
16: FAIRY KING'S ADVICE (5 -6)	THE FAIRY KING OFFERS YOU GENTLE, APT ADVICE ON WHAT YOU LACK OR WHAT YOU SHOULD FIX. THE ANNOYING THING IS HE APPEARS WHEN HE WANTS TO.
17: ANGEL'S BREATH (55 - 3)	SHE CURES ONE PERSON OF ALL WOUNDS AND ILLS, RESTORING THEM TO PERFECT HEALTH. SHE WILL ONLY APPEAR ONCE.
18: IMP'S WINK (4 - 18)	YOU WILL EXPERIENCE THE MOST AMAZING ECSTASY WHEN SHE WINKS AT YOU. SHE CAN APPEAR MULTIPLE TIMES. BE WARNED, IT CAN GET ADDICTIVE.

Chapter 162 Face-Off: Part 5

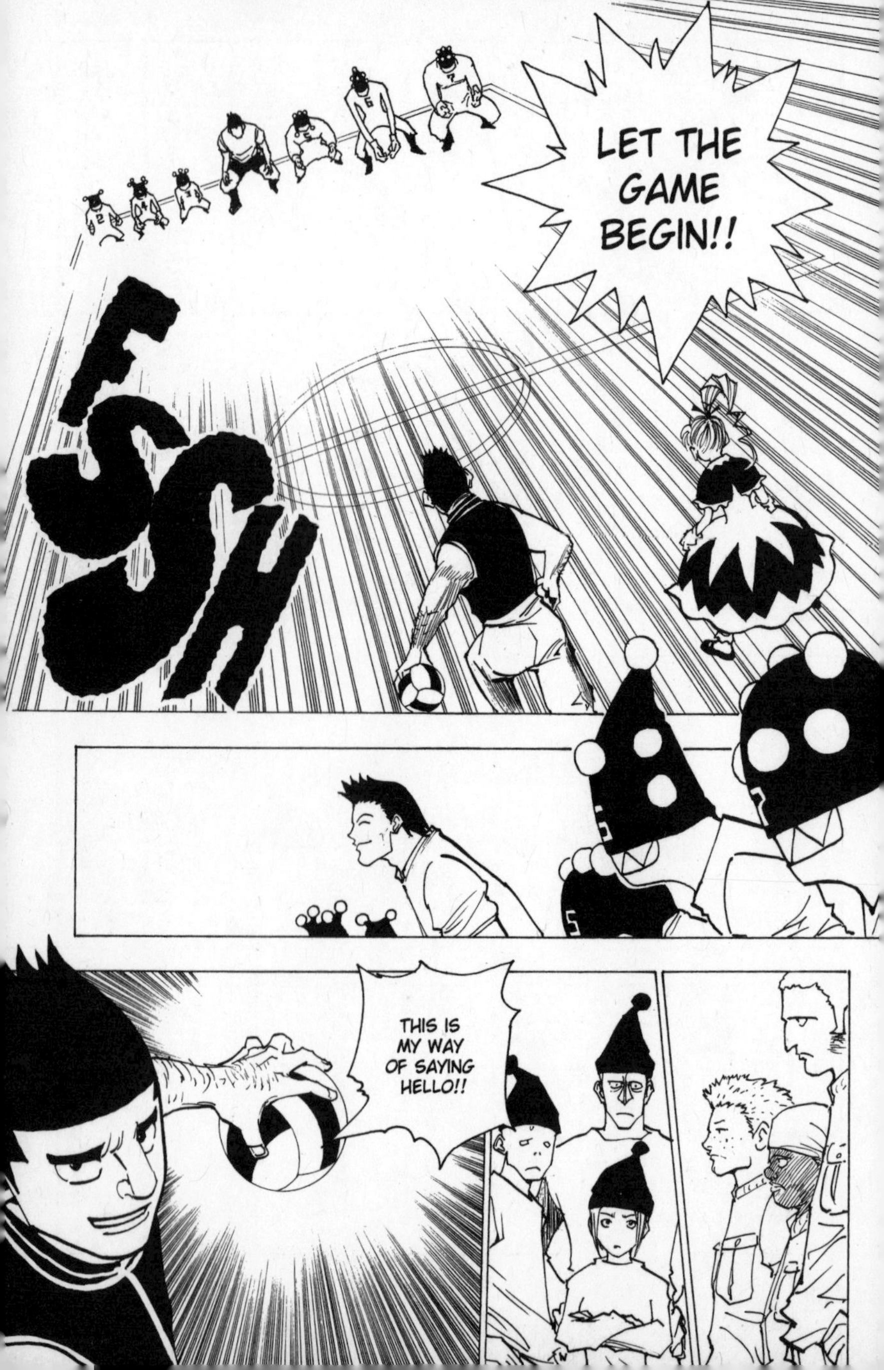
LET THE GAME BEGIN!!
FSH
THIS IS MY WAY OF SAYING HELLO!!

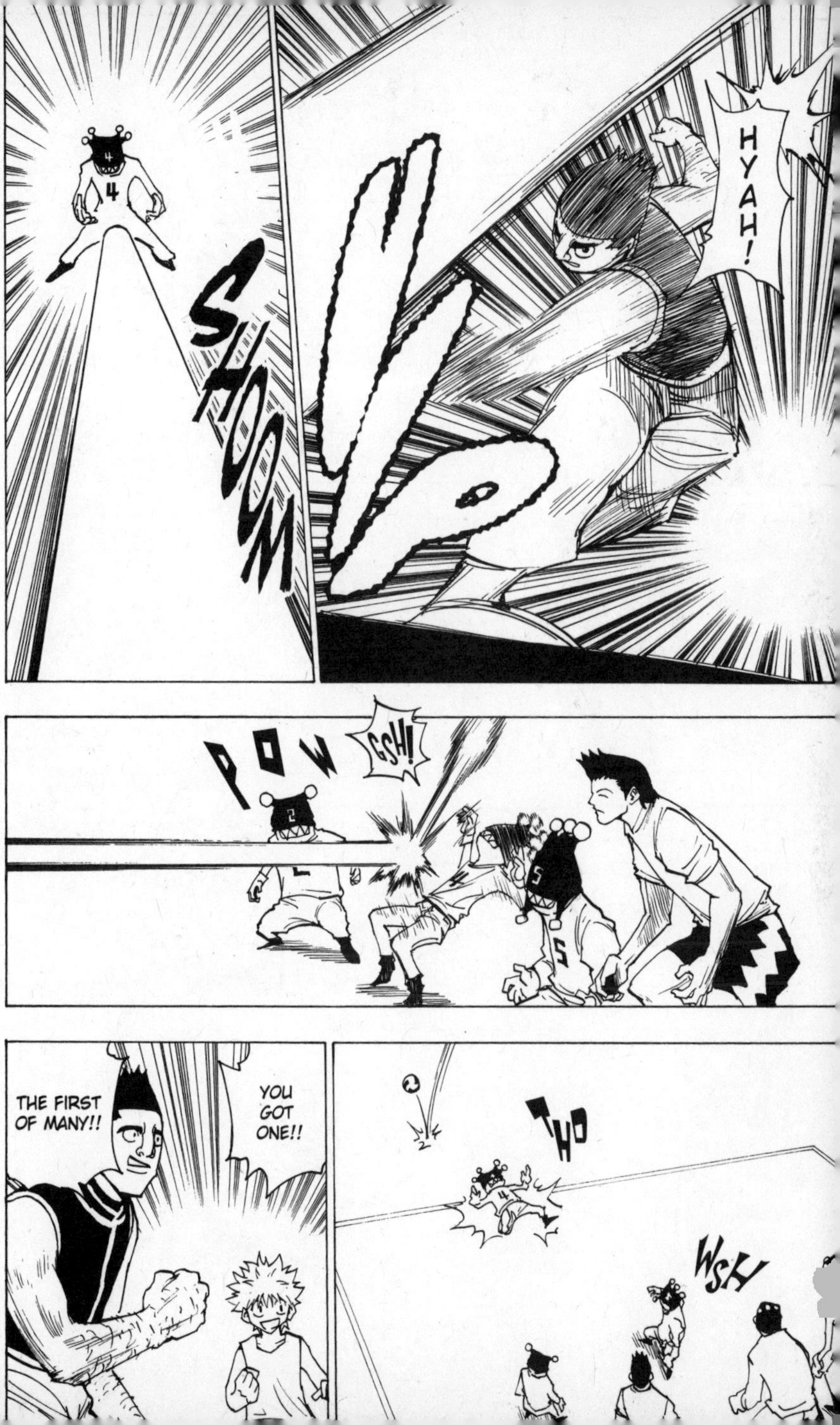
HYAH!
SHOOM
POW
GSH!
YOU GOT ONE!!
THE FIRST OF MANY!!
THO
WSH

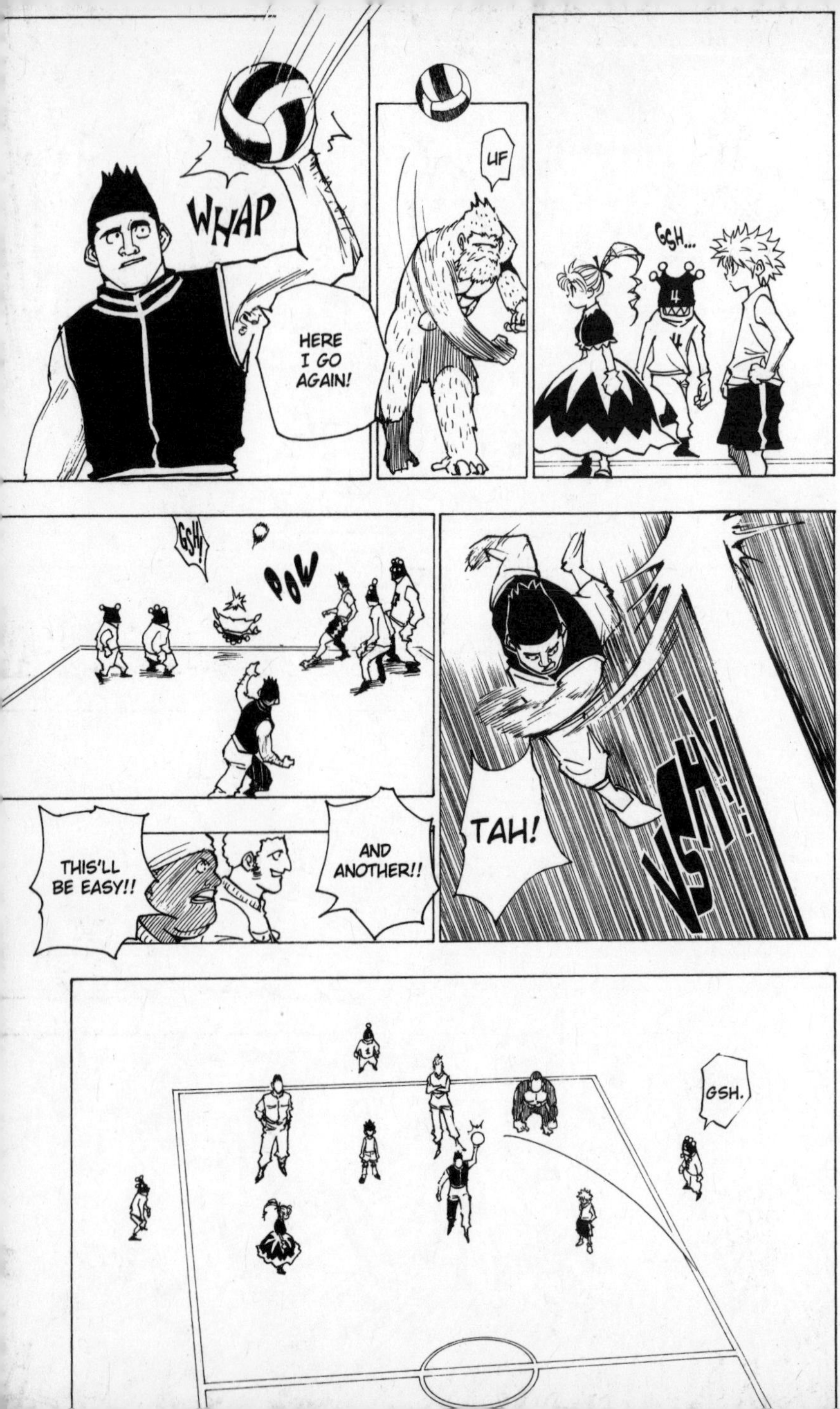
GSH...
UF
HERE I GO AGAIN!
WHAP
TAH!
VSH!!
GSH!
POW
AND ANOTHER!!
THIS'LL BE EASY!!
GSH.

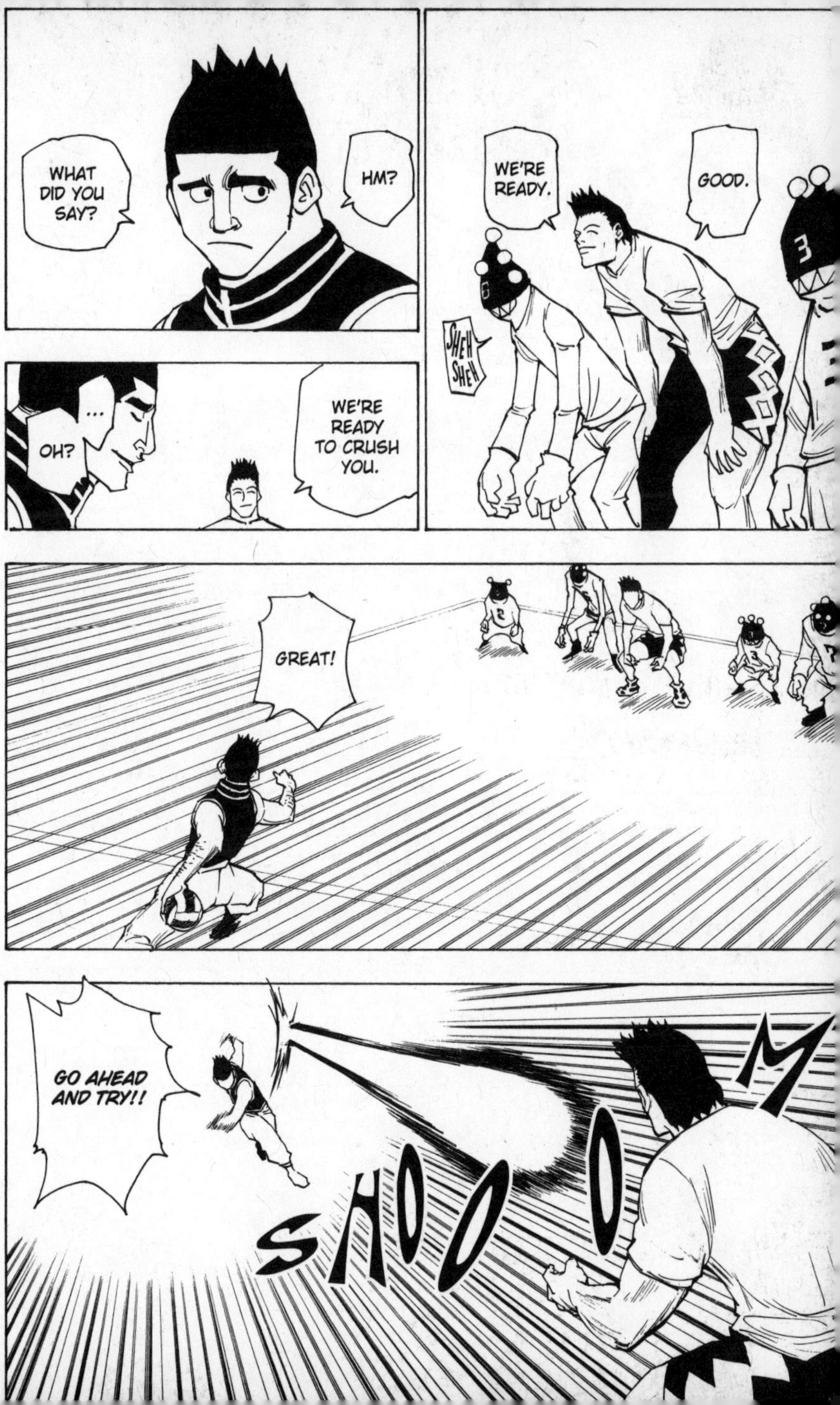
GOOD.
WE'RE READY.
SHEH SHEH
HM?
WHAT DID YOU SAY?
WE'RE READY TO CRUSH YOU.
...
OH?
GREAT!
GO AHEAD AND TRY!!
SHOOOOM

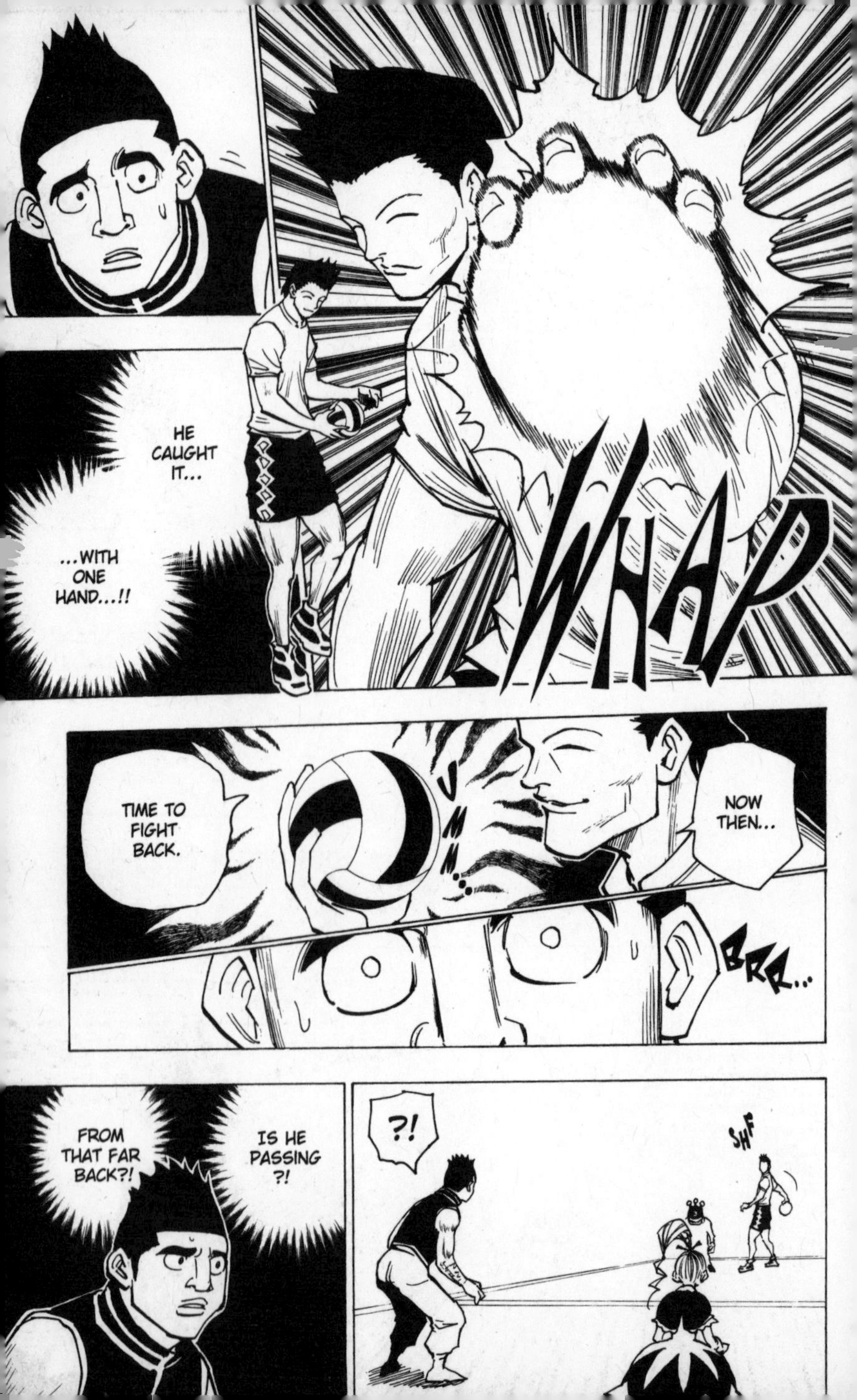
WHAP
HE CAUGHT IT...
...WITH ONE HAND...!!
NOW THEN...
TIME TO FIGHT BACK.
VMM...
BRR...
SHF
?!
IS HE PASSING ?!
FROM THAT FAR BACK?!

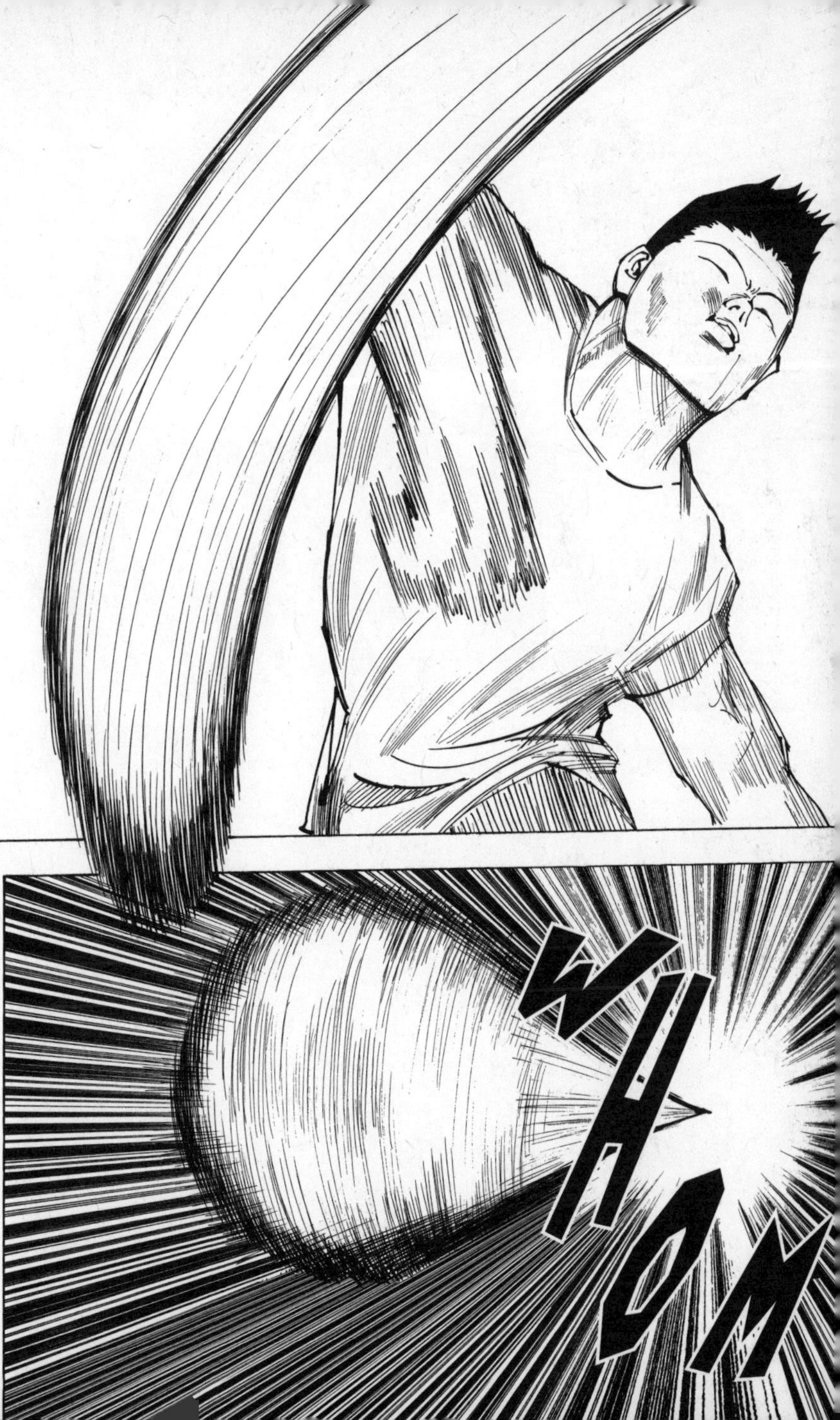
WHOM

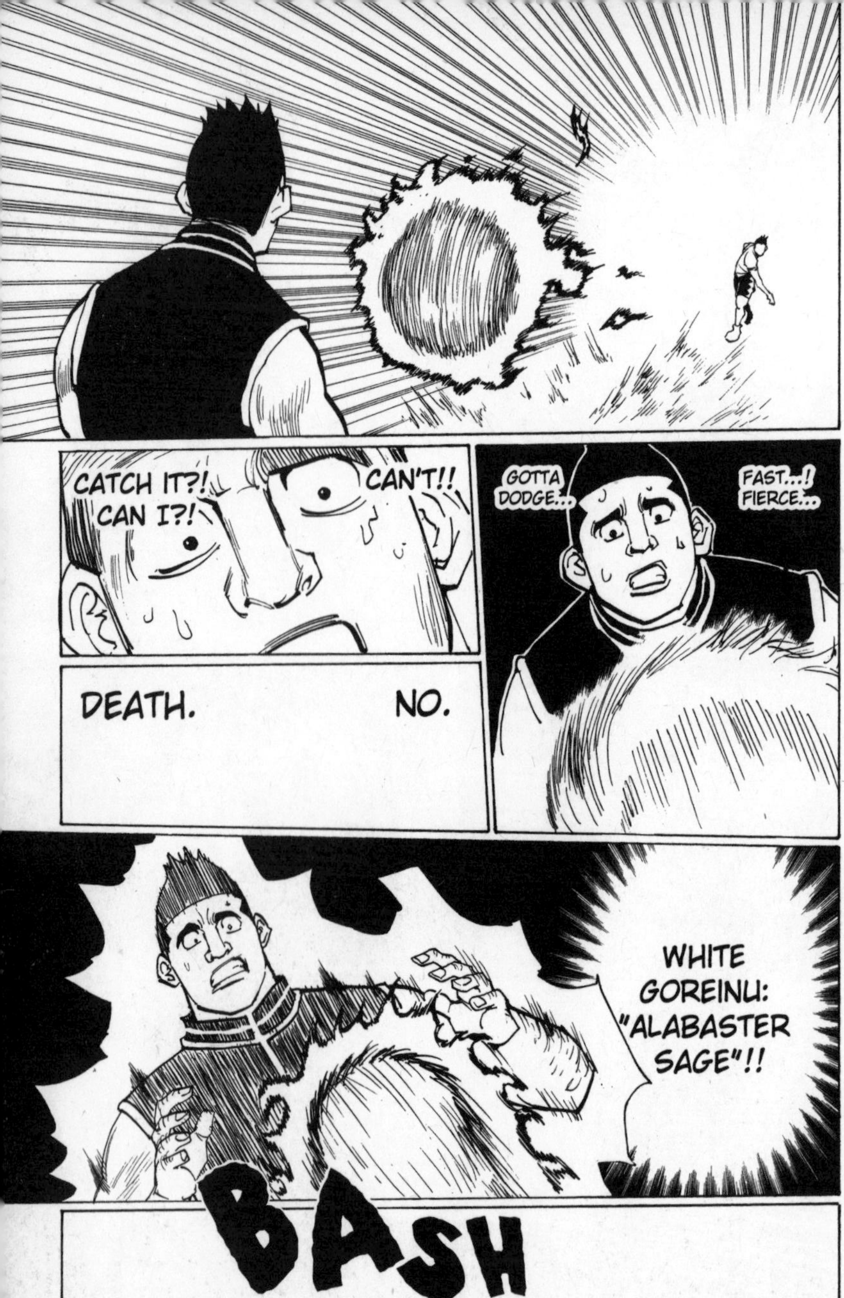
FAST...! FIERCE...
GOTTA DODGE...
CAN'T!!
CATCH IT?! CAN I?!
NO.
DEATH.
WHITE GOREINU: "ALABASTER SAGE"!!
BASH

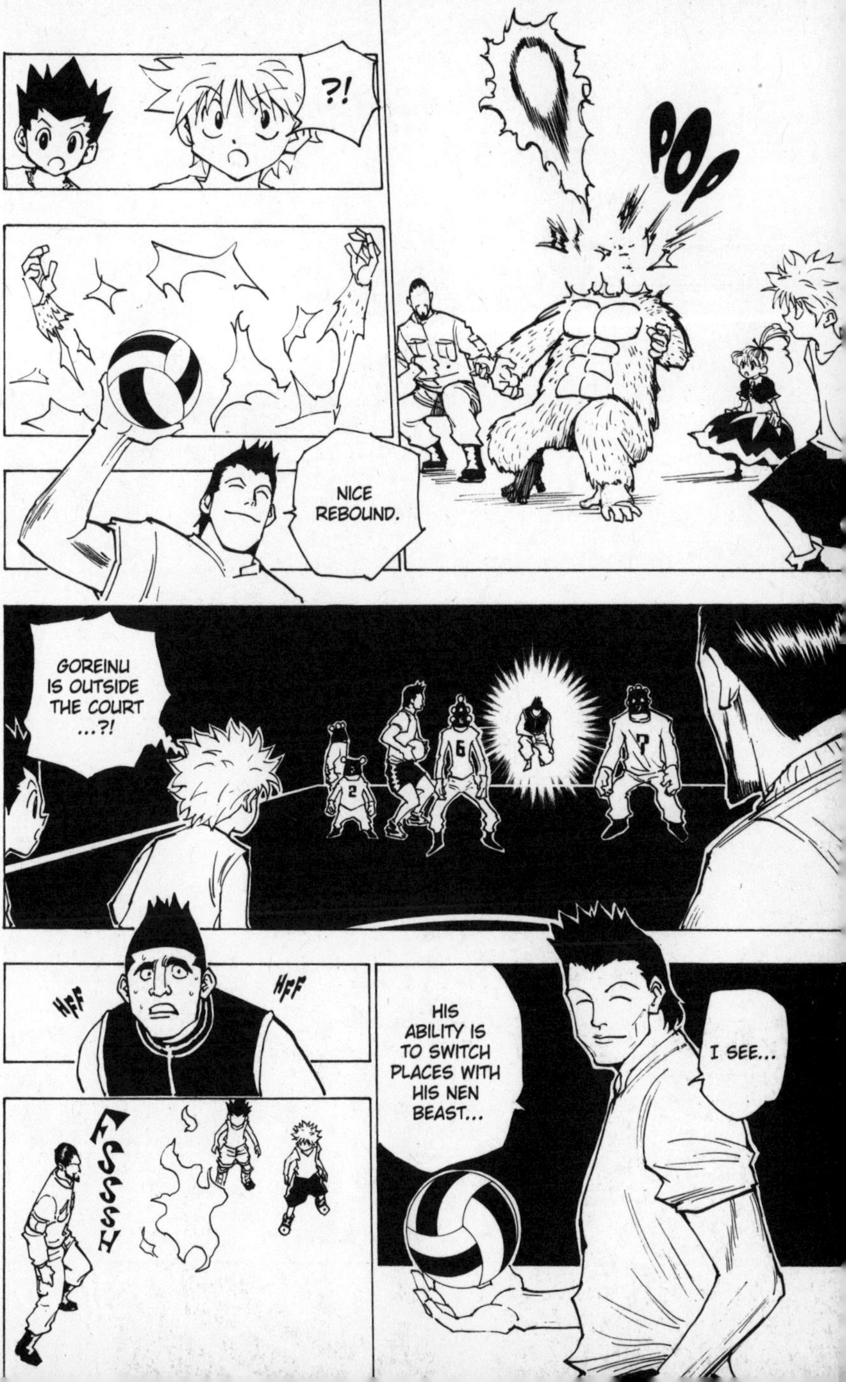
POP
?!
NICE REBOUND.
GOREINU IS OUTSIDE THE COURT ...?!
I SEE...
HIS ABILITY IS TO SWITCH PLACES WITH HIS NEN BEAST...
HFF
HFF
FSSSH

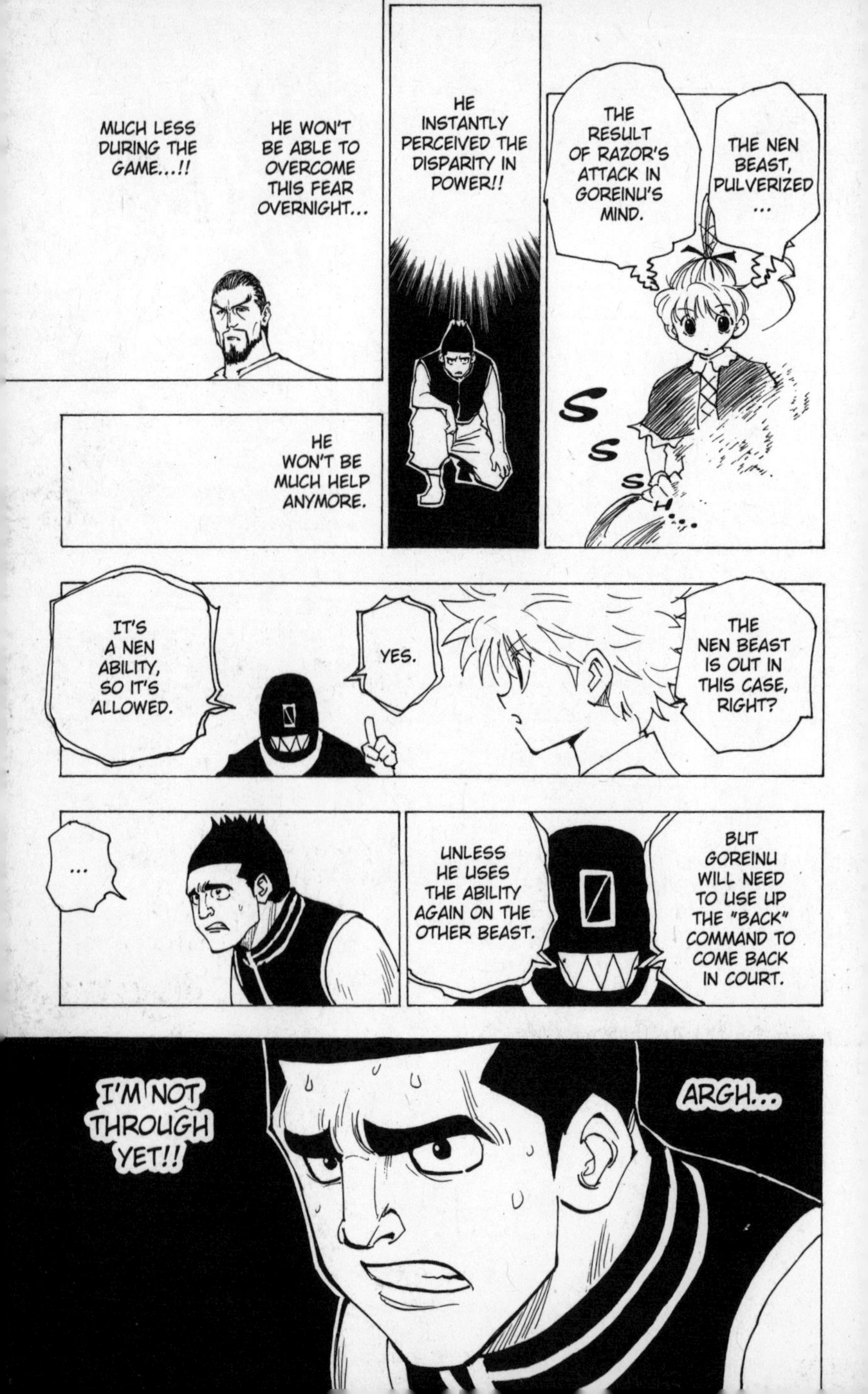
THE NEN BEAST, PULVERIZED...
THE RESULT OF RAZOR'S ATTACK IN GOREINU'S MIND.
SSSH...
HE INSTANTLY PERCEIVED THE DISPARITY IN POWER!!
HE WON'T BE ABLE TO OVERCOME THIS FEAR OVERNIGHT...
MUCH LESS DURING THE GAME...!!
HE WON'T BE MUCH HELP ANYMORE.
THE NEN BEAST IS OUT IN THIS CASE, RIGHT?
YES.
IT'S A NEN ABILITY, SO IT'S ALLOWED.
BUT GOREINU WILL NEED TO USE UP THE "BACK" COMMAND TO COME BACK IN COURT.
UNLESS HE USES THE ABILITY AGAIN ON THE OTHER BEAST.
...
ARGH...
I'M NOT THROUGH YET!!

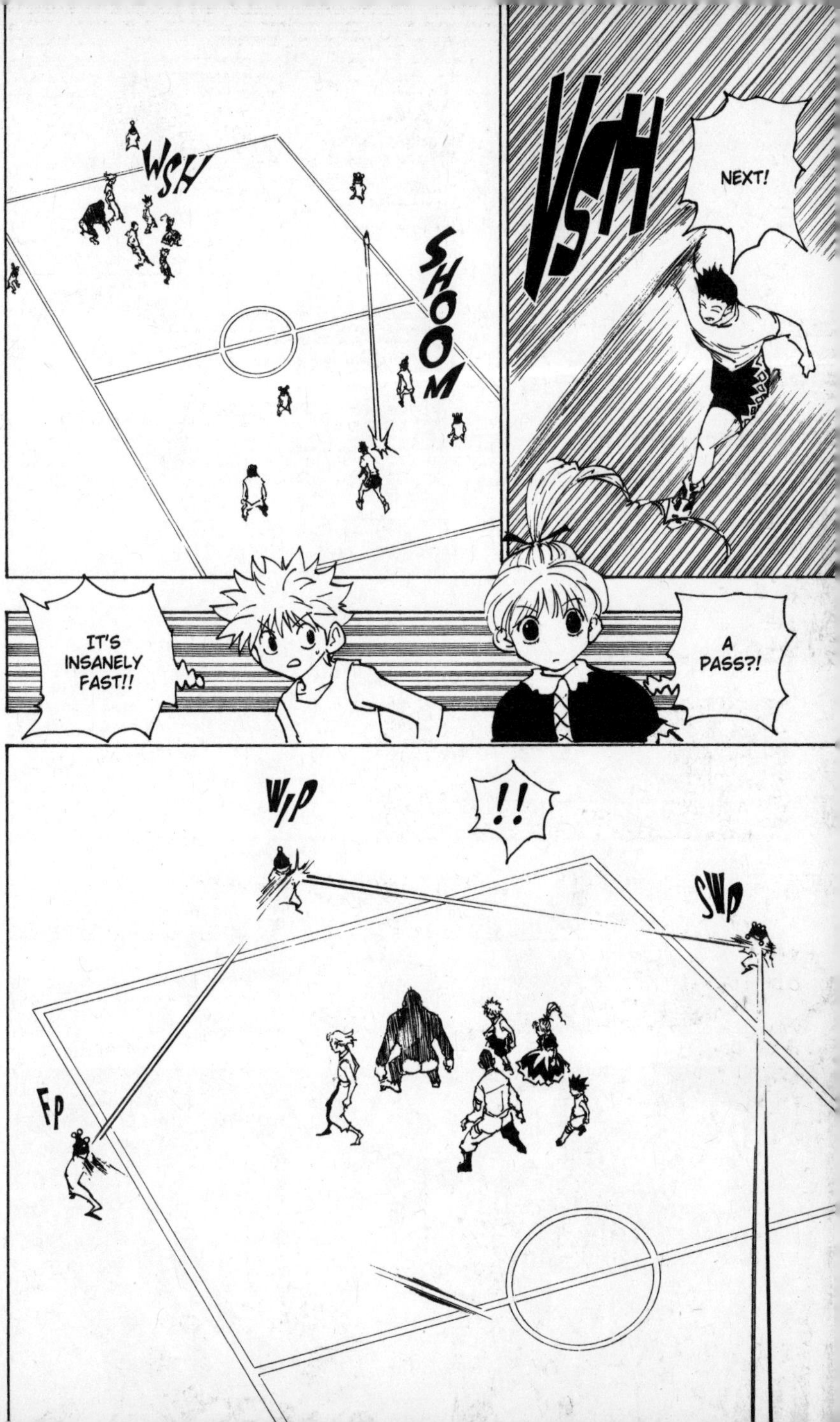
VSH
NEXT!
WSH
SHOOM
A PASS?!
IT'S INSANELY FAST!!
SWP
!!
WIP
FP

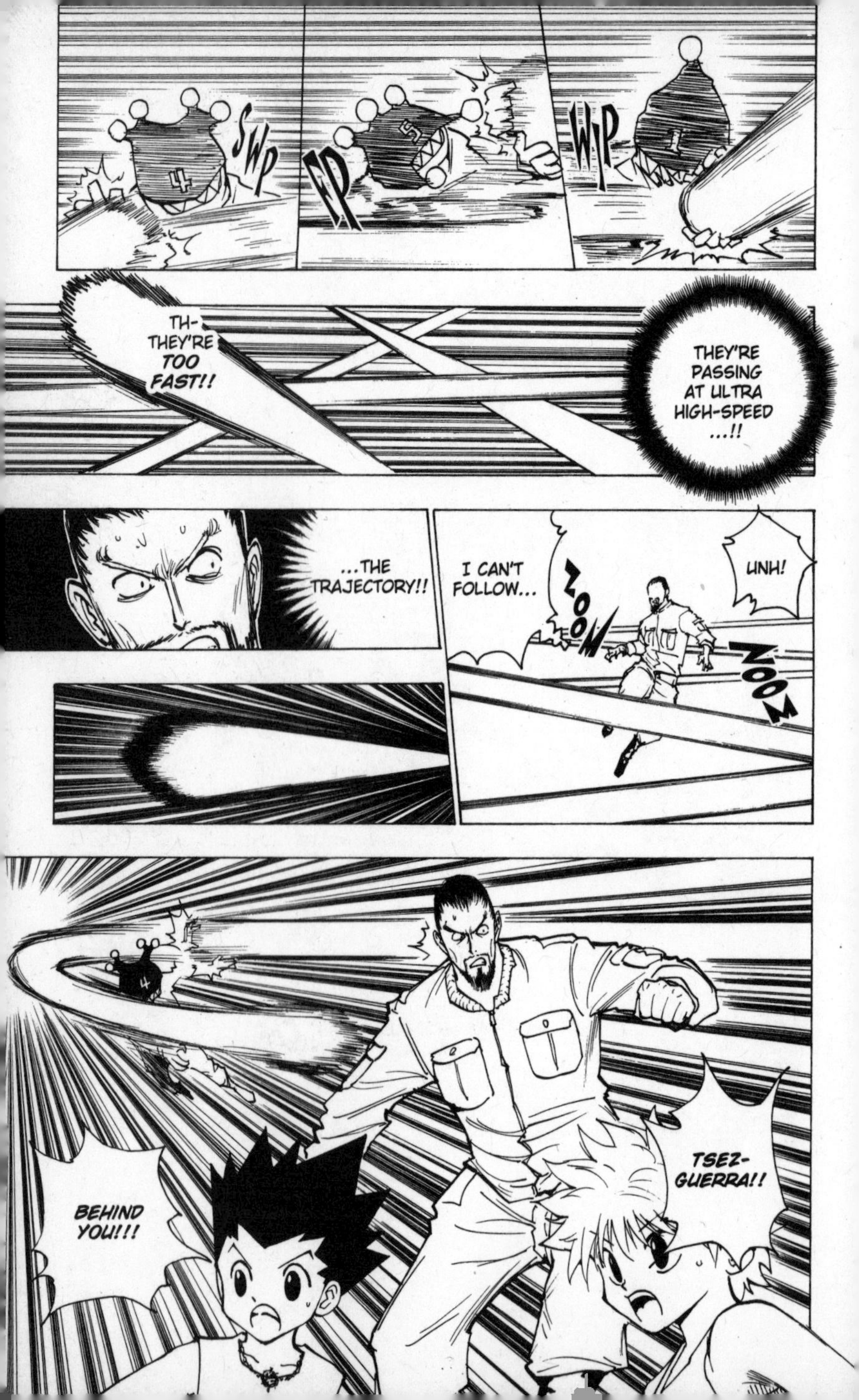
WIP
FP
SWP
THEY'RE PASSING AT ULTRA HIGH-SPEED ...!!
TH- THEY'RE TOO FAST!!
UNH!
ZOOM
I CAN'T FOLLOW...
ZOOM
...THE TRAJECTORY!!
TSEZ-GUERRA!!
BEHIND YOU!!!

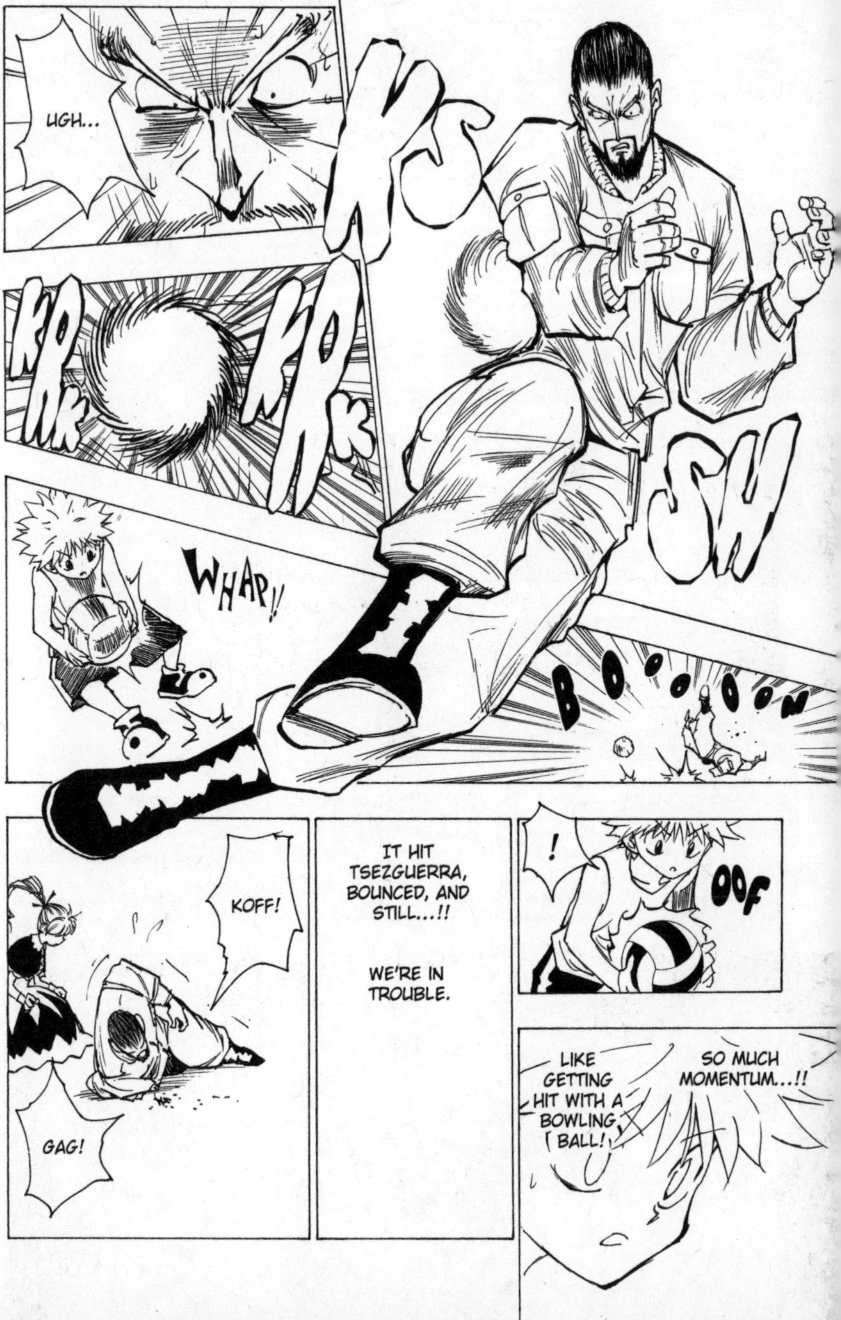
UGH...
WHAP!!
BOOOOOOM
!
OOF
SO MUCH MOMENTUM...!!
LIKE GETTING HIT WITH A BOWLING BALL!
IT HIT TSEZGUERRA, BOUNCED, AND STILL...!!
WE'RE IN TROUBLE.
KOFF!
GAG!

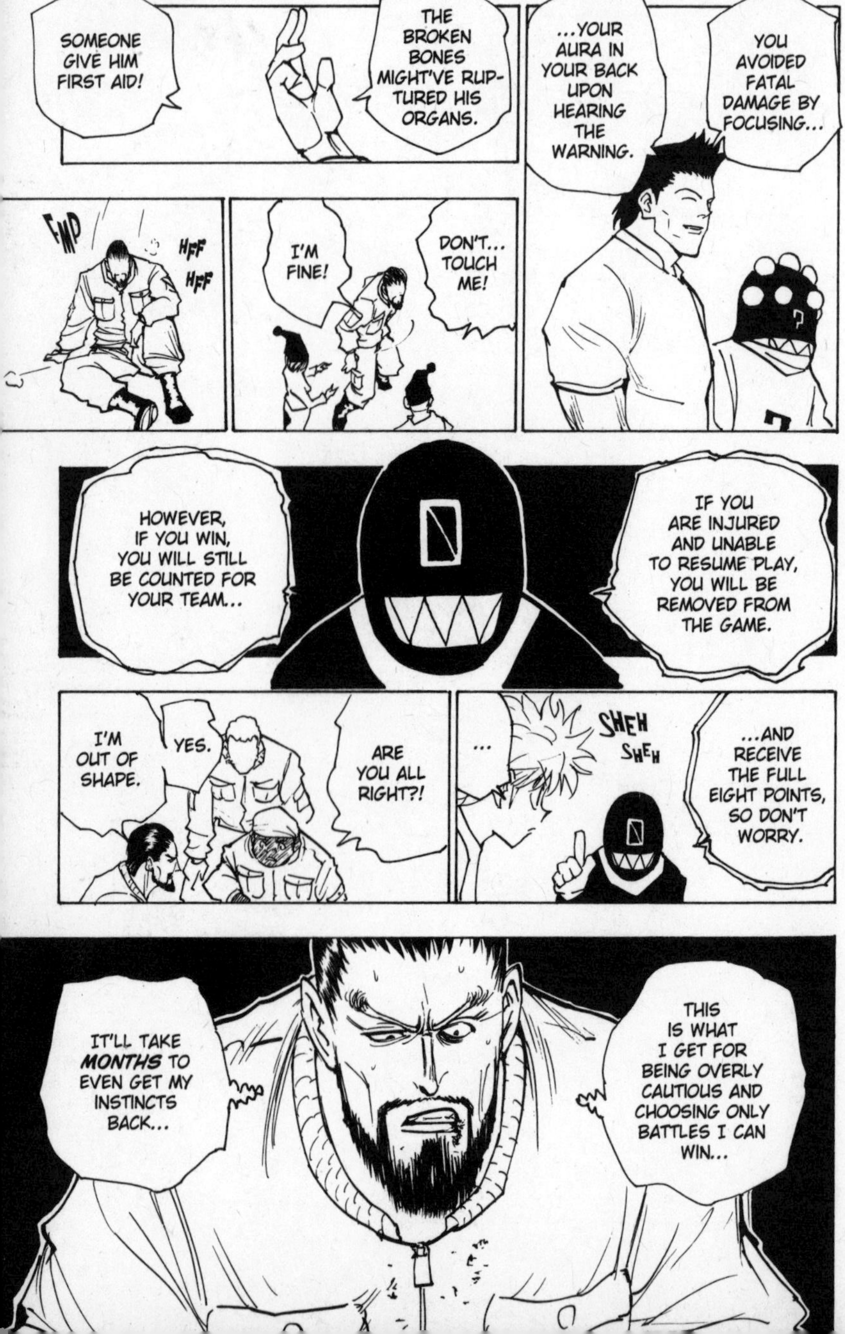
YOU AVOIDED FATAL DAMAGE BY FOCUSING...
...YOUR AURA IN YOUR BACK UPON HEARING THE WARNING.
THE BROKEN BONES MIGHT'VE RUPTURED HIS ORGANS.
SOMEONE GIVE HIM FIRST AID!
DON'T... TOUCH ME!
I'M FINE!
FMP
HFF
HFF
IF YOU ARE INJURED AND UNABLE TO RESUME PLAY, YOU WILL BE REMOVED FROM THE GAME.
HOWEVER, IF YOU WIN, YOU WILL STILL BE COUNTED FOR YOUR TEAM...
...AND RECEIVE THE FULL EIGHT POINTS, SO DON'T WORRY.
SHEH
SHEH
...
ARE YOU ALL RIGHT?!
YES.
I'M OUT OF SHAPE.
THIS IS WHAT I GET FOR BEING OVERLY CAUTIOUS AND CHOOSING ONLY BATTLES I CAN WIN...
IT'LL TAKE *MONTHS* TO EVEN GET MY INSTINCTS BACK...

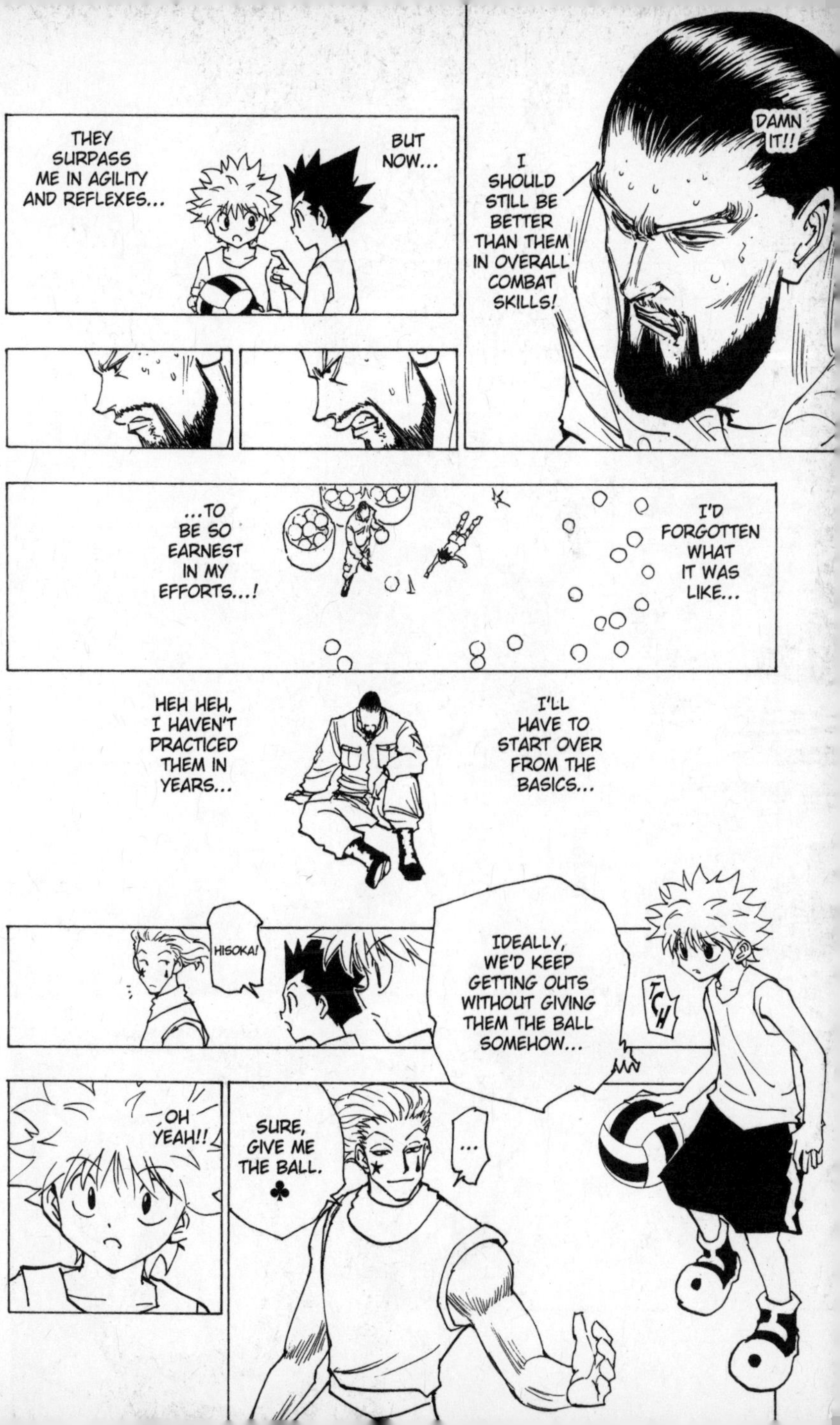
DAMN IT!!
I SHOULD STILL BE BETTER THAN THEM IN OVERALL COMBAT SKILLS!
BUT NOW...
THEY SURPASS ME IN AGILITY AND REFLEXES...
I'D FORGOTTEN WHAT IT WAS LIKE...
...TO BE SO EARNEST IN MY EFFORTS...!
I'LL HAVE TO START OVER FROM THE BASICS...
HEH HEH, I HAVEN'T PRACTICED THEM IN YEARS...
IDEALLY, WE'D KEEP GETTING OUTS WITHOUT GIVING THEM THE BALL SOMEHOW...
TCH
HISOKA!
...
SURE, GIVE ME THE BALL. ♣
OH YEAH!!

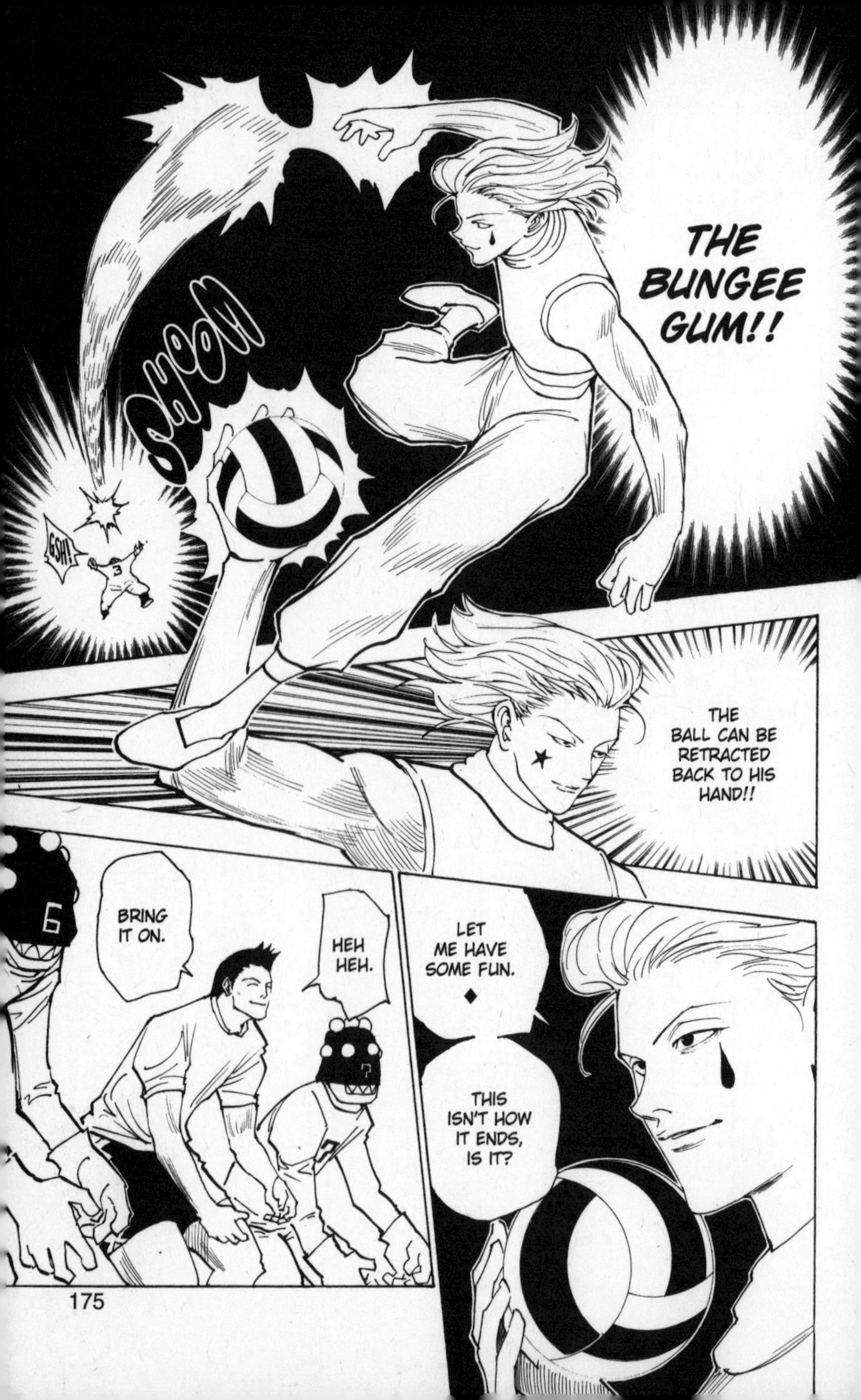
THE BUNGEE GUM!!
SHOOO
GSH!
THE BALL CAN BE RETRACTED BACK TO HIS HAND!!
LET ME HAVE SOME FUN. ◆
THIS ISN'T HOW IT ENDS, IS IT?
HEH HEH.
BRING IT ON.

Item	Description
19: POLTERGEIST PILLOW (A - 13)	SLEEP ON THIS PILLOW AND YOUR ASTRAL FORM WILL BE ABLE TO WANDER AT WILL. BUT YOU WILL TURN INTO A REAL GHOST IF YOU DO NOT RETURN TO YOUR BODY WITHIN 24 HOURS.
20: MOOD CLOCK (B - 30)	THIS CLOCK SETS YOUR CURRENT STATE OF MIND. TURN IT TO NOON AND YOU WILL MAINTAIN PERFECT SERENITY. THUS YOU CAN ADJUST YOUR EMOTIONS ACCORDING TO THE SITUATION.
21: X-RAY GOGGLES (B - 27)	YOU CAN SEE THROUGH THINGS. AN ADJUSTMENT DIAL ALLOWS YOU TO SET THE X-RAY DEPTH. THE ONLY THING IT CANNOT SEE THROUGH IS A PACK OF SPELL CARDS FROM MASADORA.
22: TORAEMON (A - 22)	A BEAST ON THE VERGE OF EXTINCTION, IT HAS A HABIT OF STUFFING THINGS IN ITS 4-D POCKET. YOU NEVER KNOW WHAT KIND OF TREASURES IT COULD HAVE PICKED UP.
23: TOME OF A THOUSAND TALES (B - 30)	A BOOK THAT SHOWS YOU A DIFFERENT STORY EACH TIME YOU OPEN IT. IF YOU WANT TO STAY ON THE SAME STORY WHEN YOU PUT IT DOWN, USE THE SPECIAL INCLUDED BOOKMARK.
24: HYPOTHETICAL T.V. (A - 20)	INPUT A HYPOTHETICAL SITUATION WITH THE INCLUDED REMOTE, AND THIS TV WILL SHOW YOU A 30-HOUR DOCUMENTARY OF THE POSSIBILITIES. YOU ARE ALSO ABLE TO RECORD.
25: RISKY DICE (B - 30)	A TWENTY-SIDED DIE WITH ONE SKULL FACE AND 19 STAR FACES. GREAT THINGS HAPPEN WHEN YOU ROLL A STAR, BUT ROLLING THE SKULL WILL BE BAD ENOUGH TO CANCEL OUT ALL THE PREVIOUS GREAT EVENTS.
26: NIGHT SHIFT DWARVES (A - 20)	THEY CAN DO ANY WORK YOU COULD DO, AND THEY WILL WORK AS LONG AS YOU ARE ASLEEP. THEY CANNOT DO ANYTHING BEYOND YOUR ABILITIES.
27: BOOK OF V.I.P. PASSES (B - 25)	YOU CAN GO ANYWHERE WITH THESE PASSES. BOOK OF 1000.

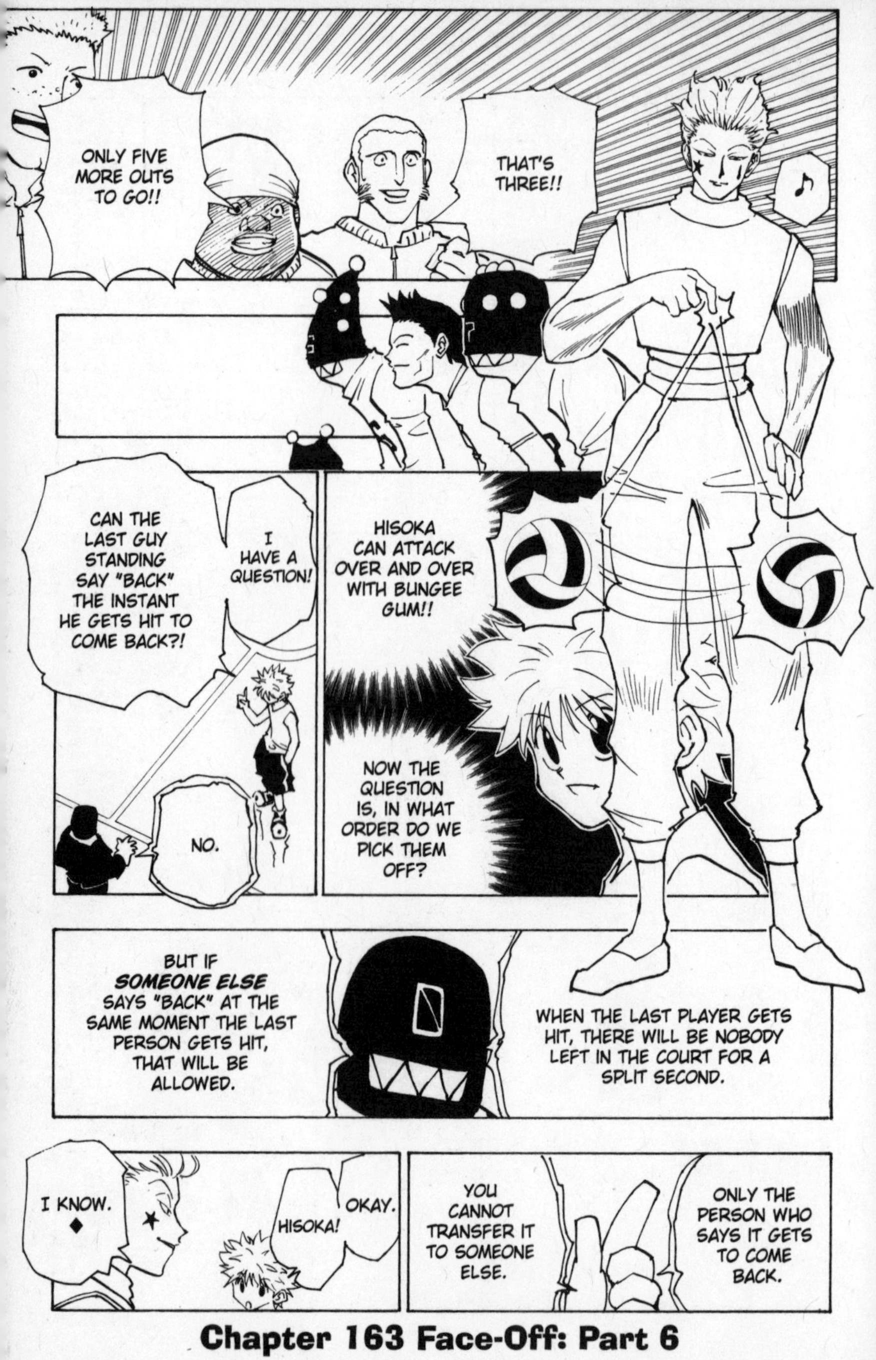
♪
THAT'S THREE!!
ONLY FIVE MORE OUTS TO GO!!
HISOKA CAN ATTACK OVER AND OVER WITH BUNGEE GUM!!
NOW THE QUESTION IS, IN WHAT ORDER DO WE PICK THEM OFF?
I HAVE A QUESTION!
CAN THE LAST GUY STANDING SAY "BACK" THE INSTANT HE GETS HIT TO COME BACK?!
NO.
WHEN THE LAST PLAYER GETS HIT, THERE WILL BE NOBODY LEFT IN THE COURT FOR A SPLIT SECOND.
BUT IF *SOMEONE ELSE* SAYS "BACK" AT THE SAME MOMENT THE LAST PERSON GETS HIT, THAT WILL BE ALLOWED.
ONLY THE PERSON WHO SAYS IT GETS TO COME BACK.
YOU CANNOT TRANSFER IT TO SOMEONE ELSE.
OKAY.
HISOKA!
I KNOW. ♦

Chapter 163 Face-Off: Part 6

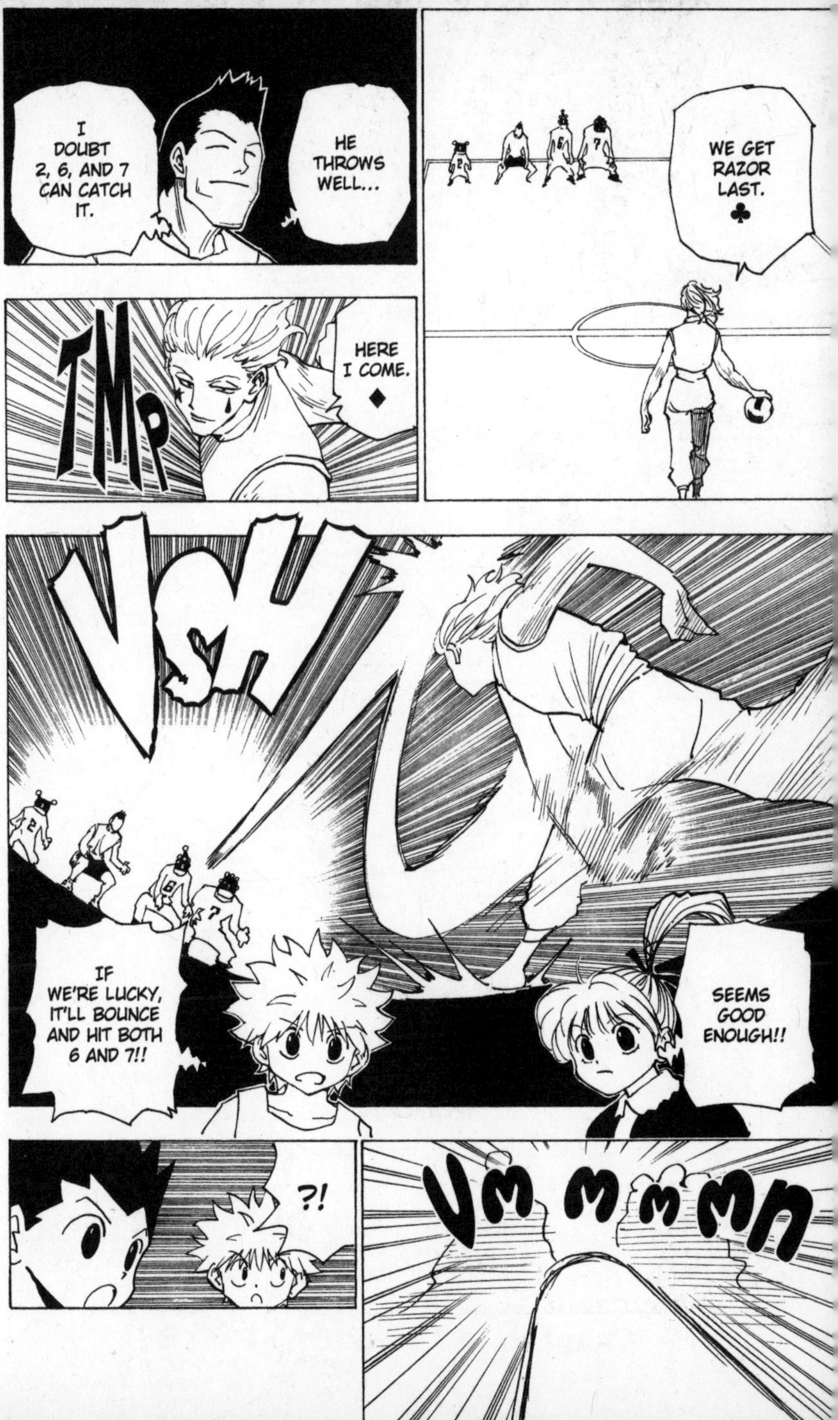
WE GET RAZOR LAST. ♣
HE THROWS WELL...
I DOUBT 2, 6, AND 7 CAN CATCH IT.
HERE I COME. ◆
TMP
VSH
SEEMS GOOD ENOUGH!!
IF WE'RE LUCKY, IT'LL BOUNCE AND HIT BOTH 6 AND 7!!
VMMMMN
?!

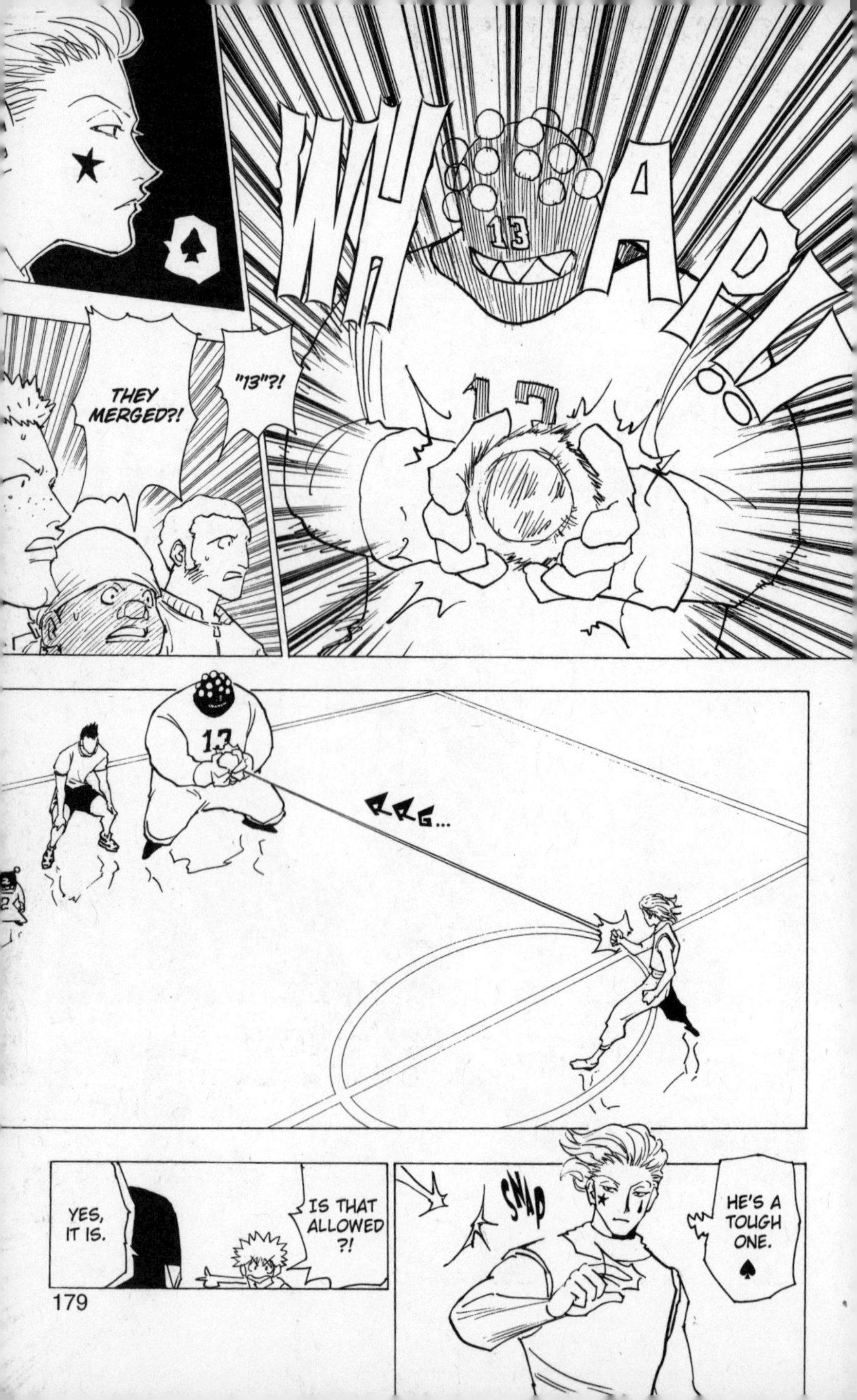
WHAP
"13"?!
THEY MERGED?!
RRG...
SNAP
HE'S A TOUGH ONE. ♠
IS THAT ALLOWED ?!
YES, IT IS.

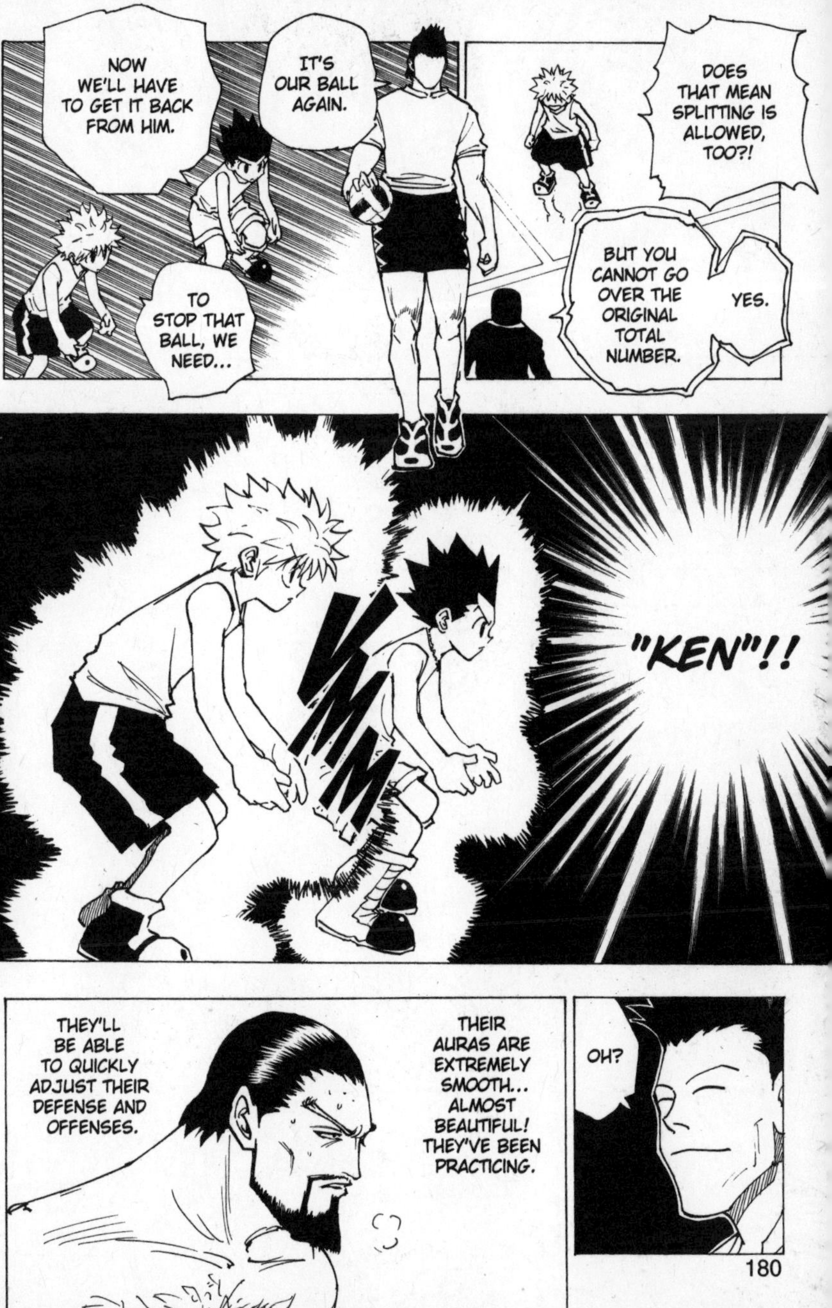
DOES THAT MEAN SPLITTING IS ALLOWED, TOO?!
YES.
BUT YOU CANNOT GO OVER THE ORIGINAL TOTAL NUMBER.
IT'S OUR BALL AGAIN.
NOW WE'LL HAVE TO GET IT BACK FROM HIM.
TO STOP THAT BALL, WE NEED...
"KEN"!!
VMMM
OH?
THEIR AURAS ARE EXTREMELY SMOOTH... ALMOST BEAUTIFUL! THEY'VE BEEN PRACTICING.
THEY'LL BE ABLE TO QUICKLY ADJUST THEIR DEFENSE AND OFFENSES.

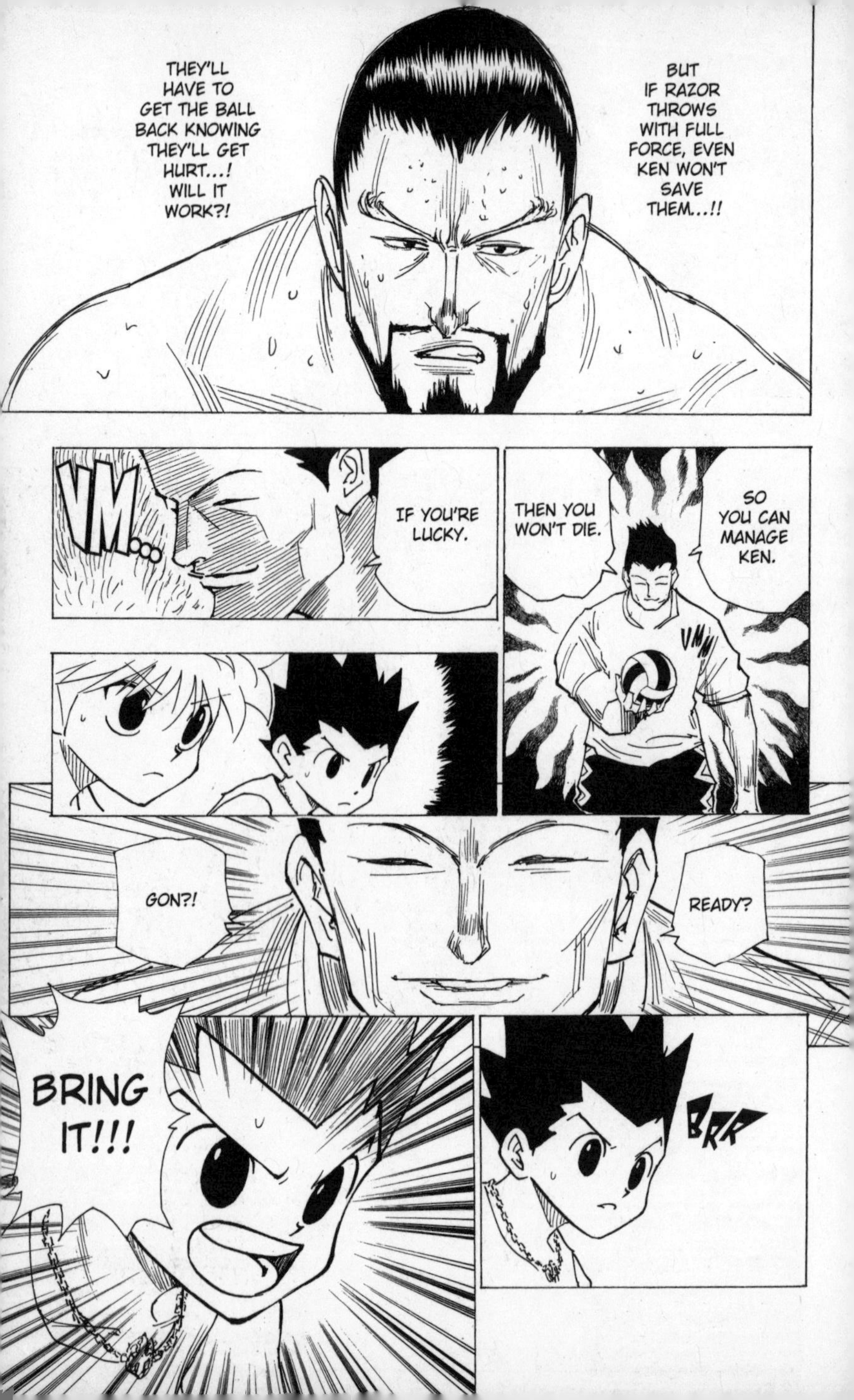
BUT IF RAZOR THROWS WITH FULL FORCE, EVEN KEN WON'T SAVE THEM...!!
THEY'LL HAVE TO GET THE BALL BACK KNOWING THEY'LL GET HURT...! WILL IT WORK?!
SO YOU CAN MANAGE KEN.
THEN YOU WON'T DIE.
VMM
IF YOU'RE LUCKY.
VM...
READY?
GON?!
BRR
BRING IT!!!

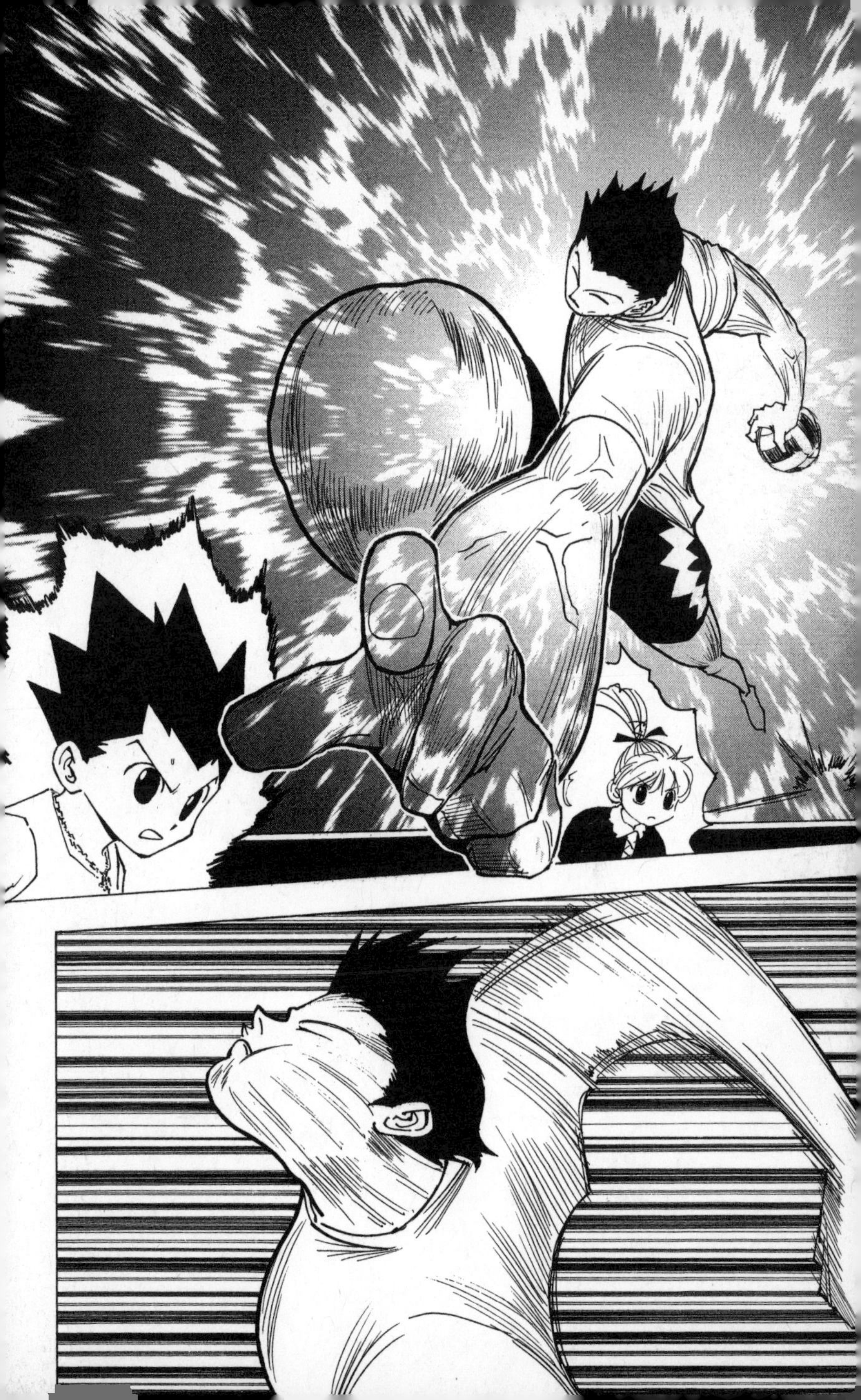

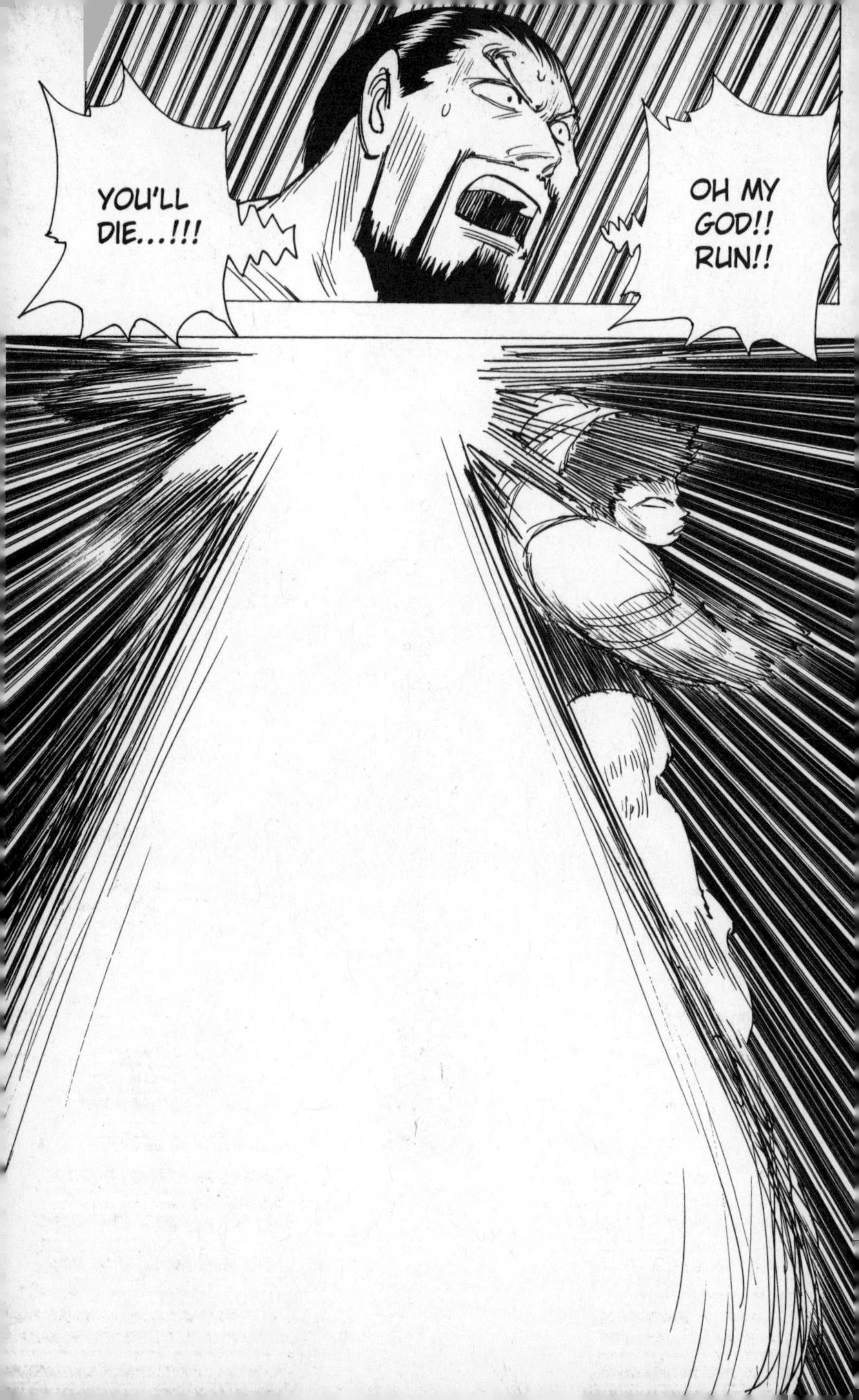
OH MY GOD!! RUN!!
YOU'LL DIE...!!!

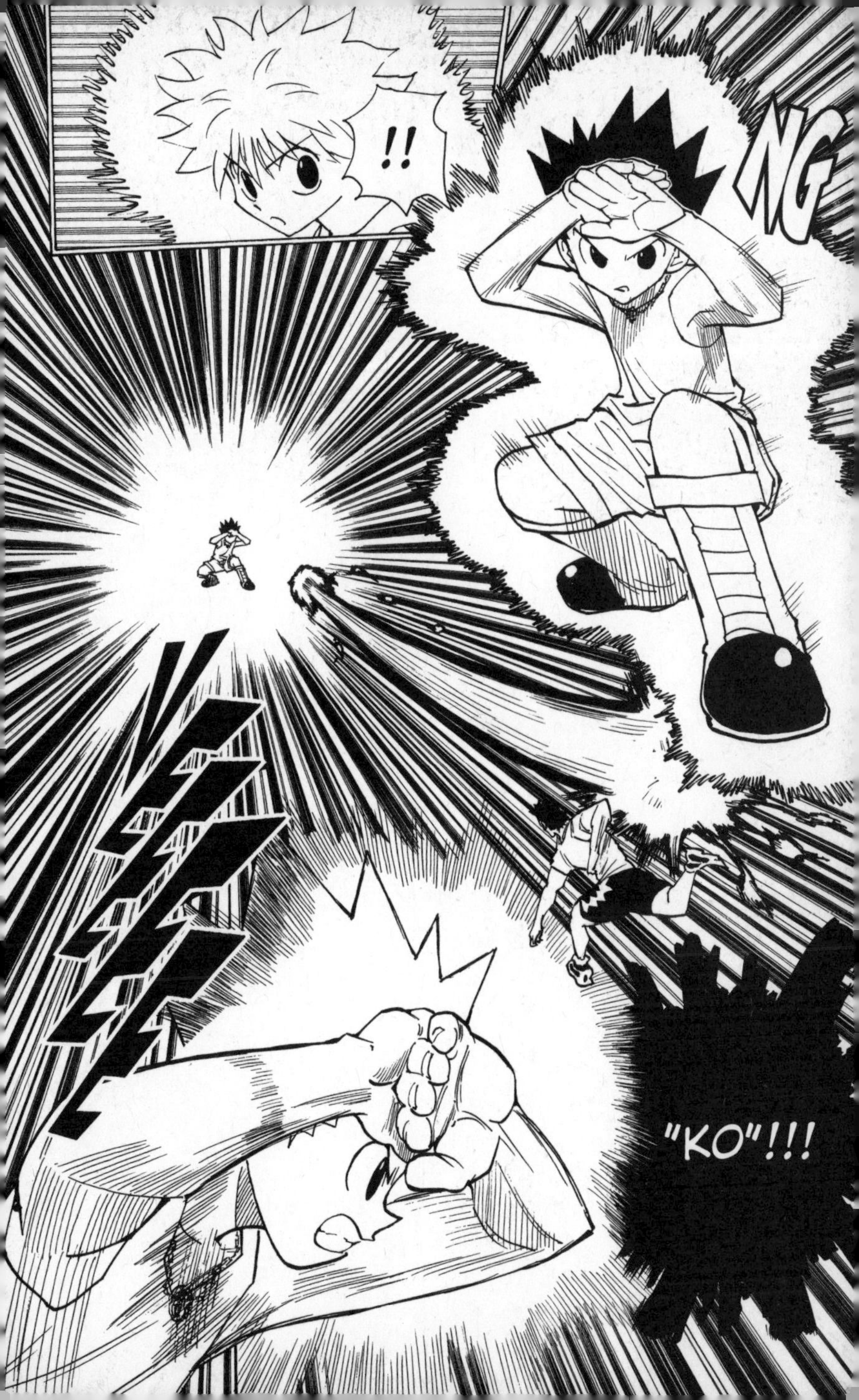

NG
!!
"KO"!!!

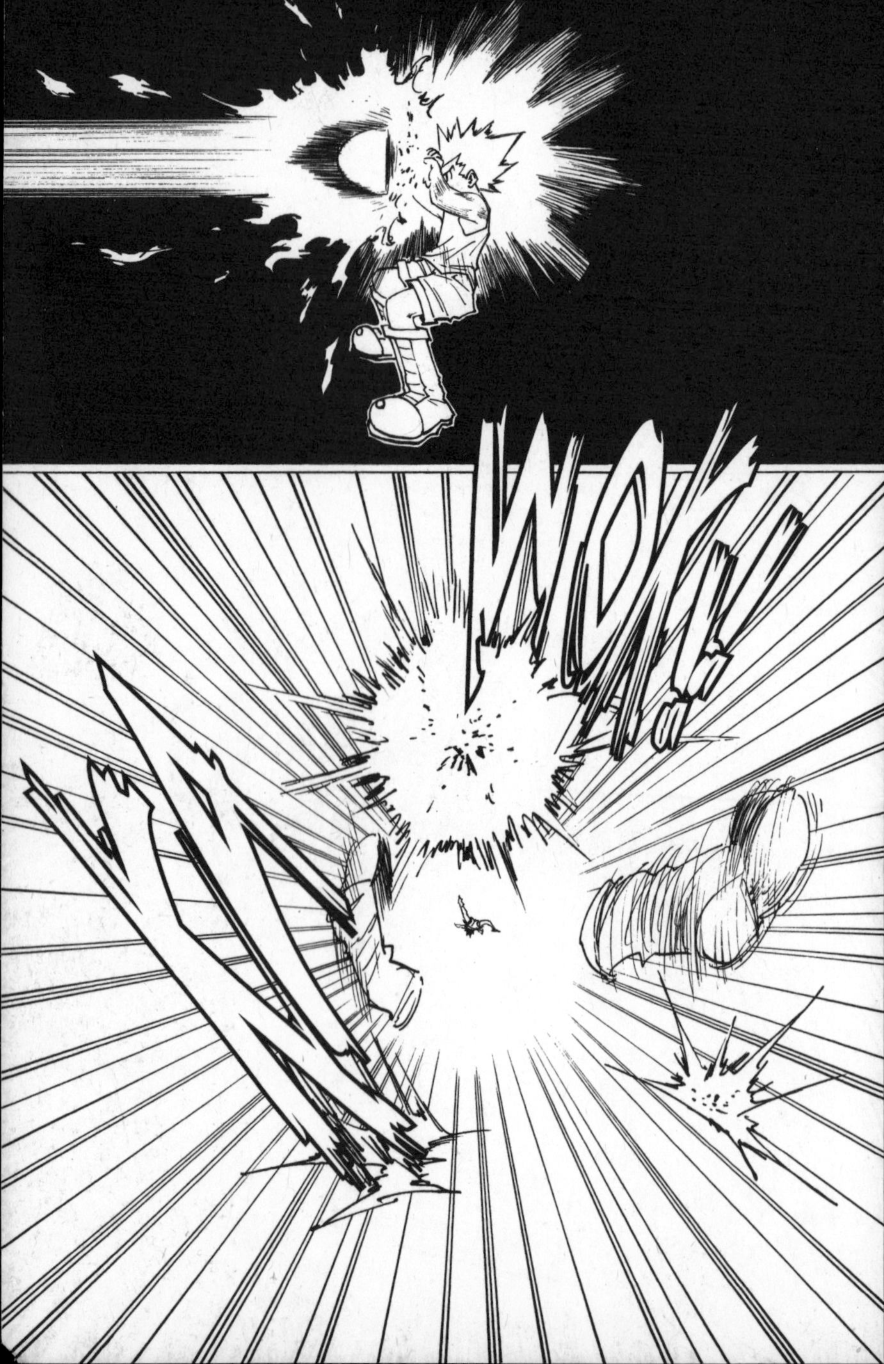
WOK!

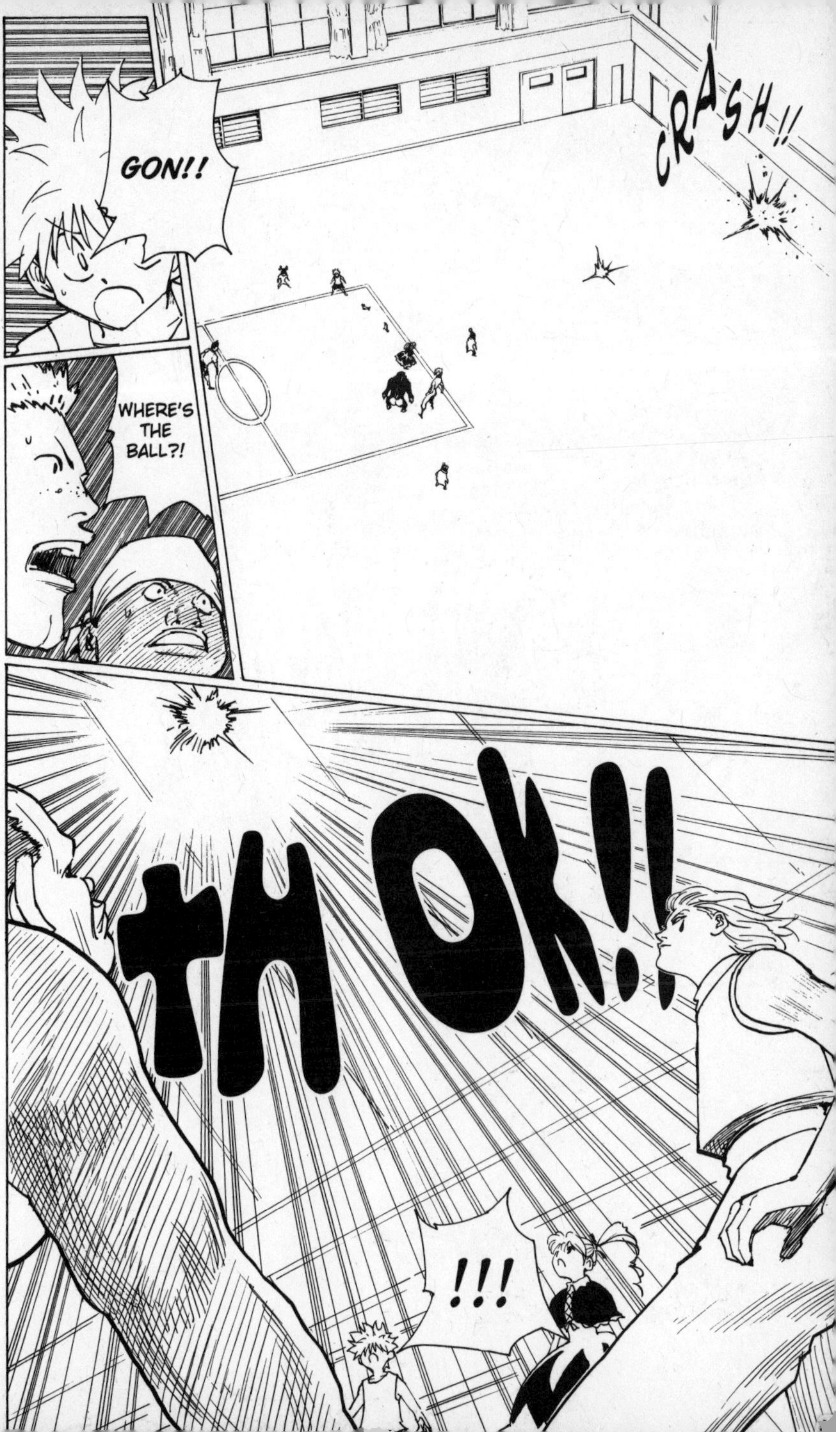
CRASH!!
GON!!
WHERE'S THE BALL?!
THOK!!
!!!

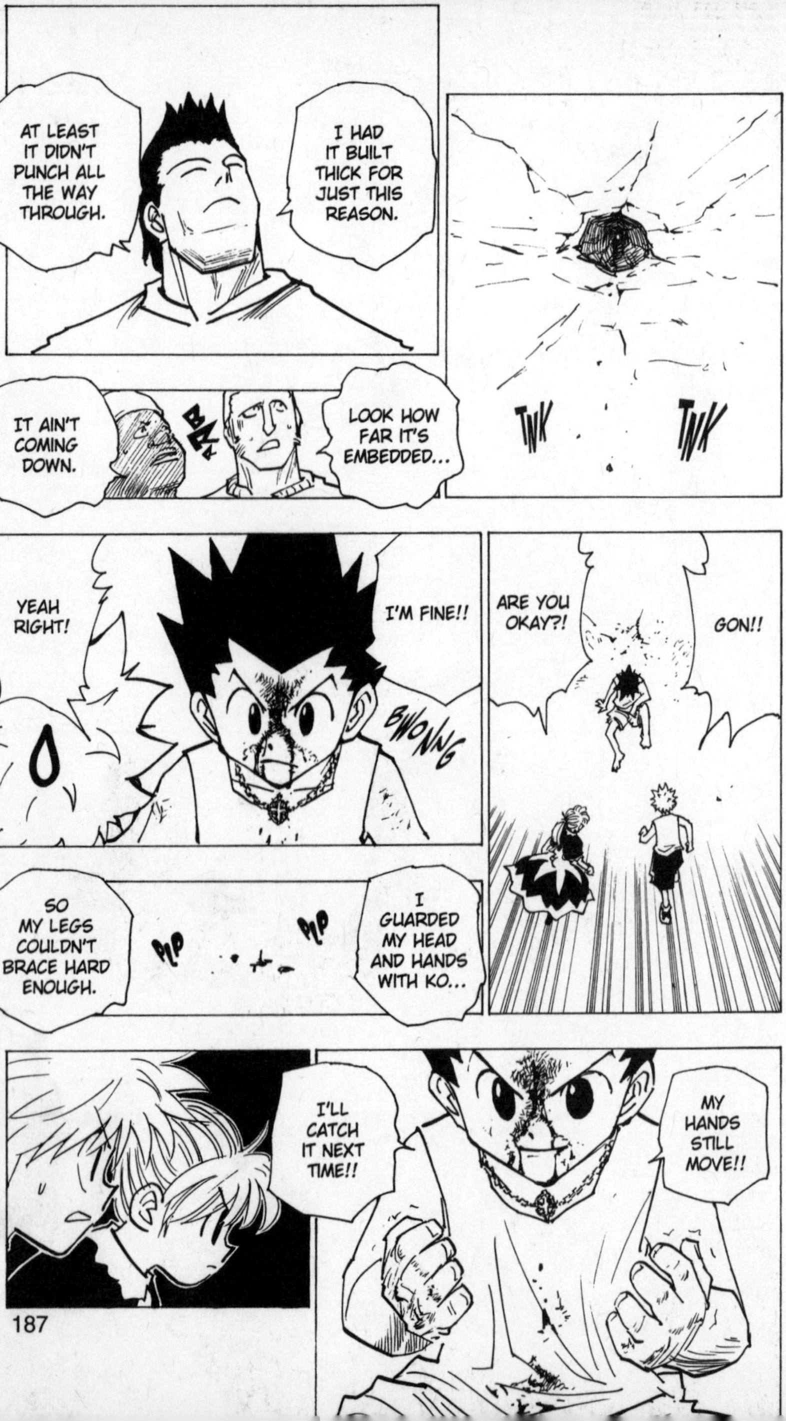
TNK
TNK
I HAD IT BUILT THICK FOR JUST THIS REASON.
AT LEAST IT DIDN'T PUNCH ALL THE WAY THROUGH.
LOOK HOW FAR IT'S EMBEDDED...
BRR
IT AIN'T COMING DOWN.
GON!!
ARE YOU OKAY?!
I'M FINE!!
BWONNG
YEAH RIGHT!
I GUARDED MY HEAD AND HANDS WITH KO...
PLIP
PLIP
SO MY LEGS COULDN'T BRACE HARD ENOUGH.
MY HANDS STILL MOVE!!
I'LL CATCH IT NEXT TIME!!

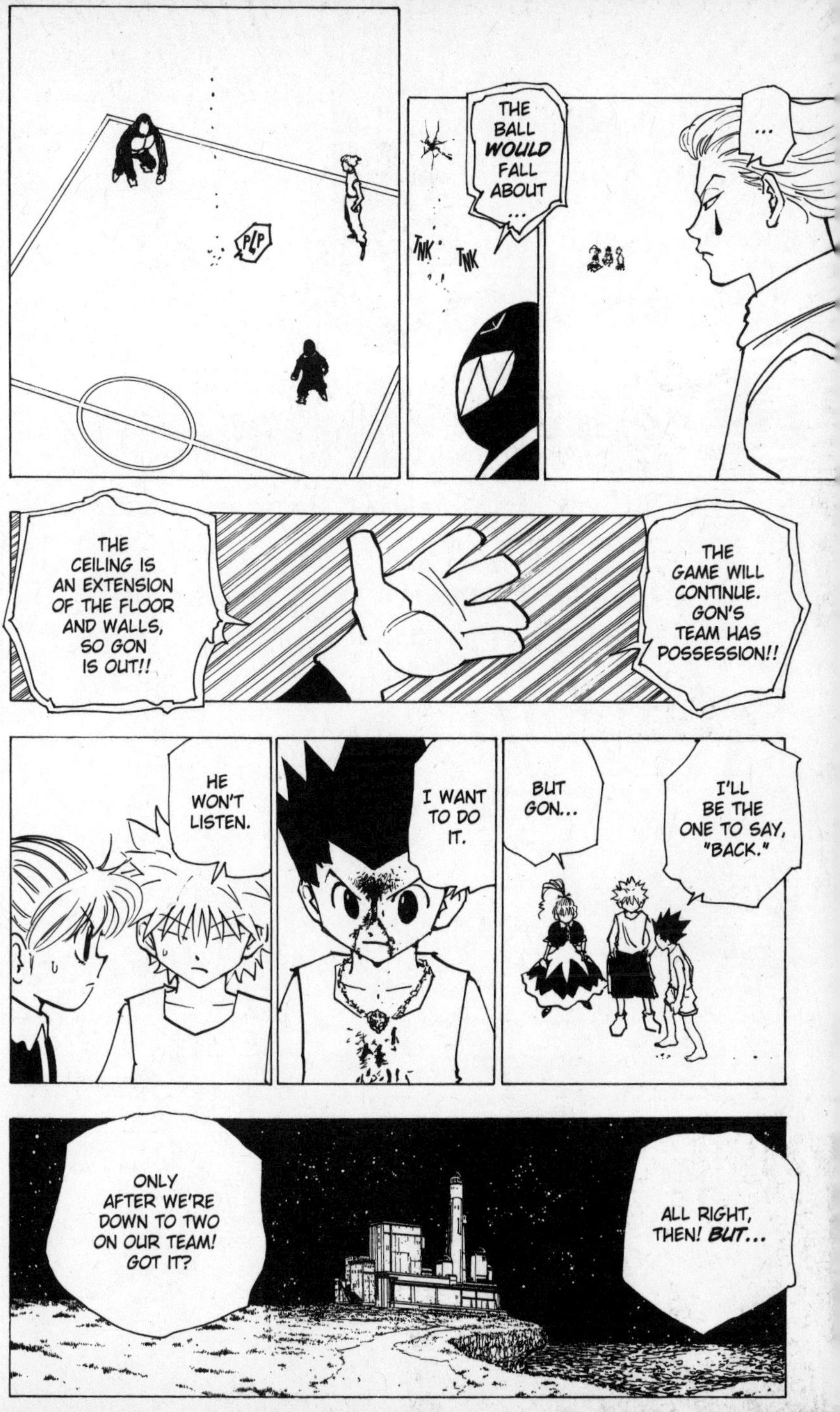
...
THE BALL WOULD FALL ABOUT ...
TNK
TNK
PLP
THE GAME WILL CONTINUE. GON'S TEAM HAS POSSESSION!!
THE CEILING IS AN EXTENSION OF THE FLOOR AND WALLS, SO GON IS OUT!!
I'LL BE THE ONE TO SAY, "BACK."
BUT GON...
I WANT TO DO IT.
HE WON'T LISTEN.
ALL RIGHT, THEN! BUT...
ONLY AFTER WE'RE DOWN TO TWO ON OUR TEAM! GOT IT?

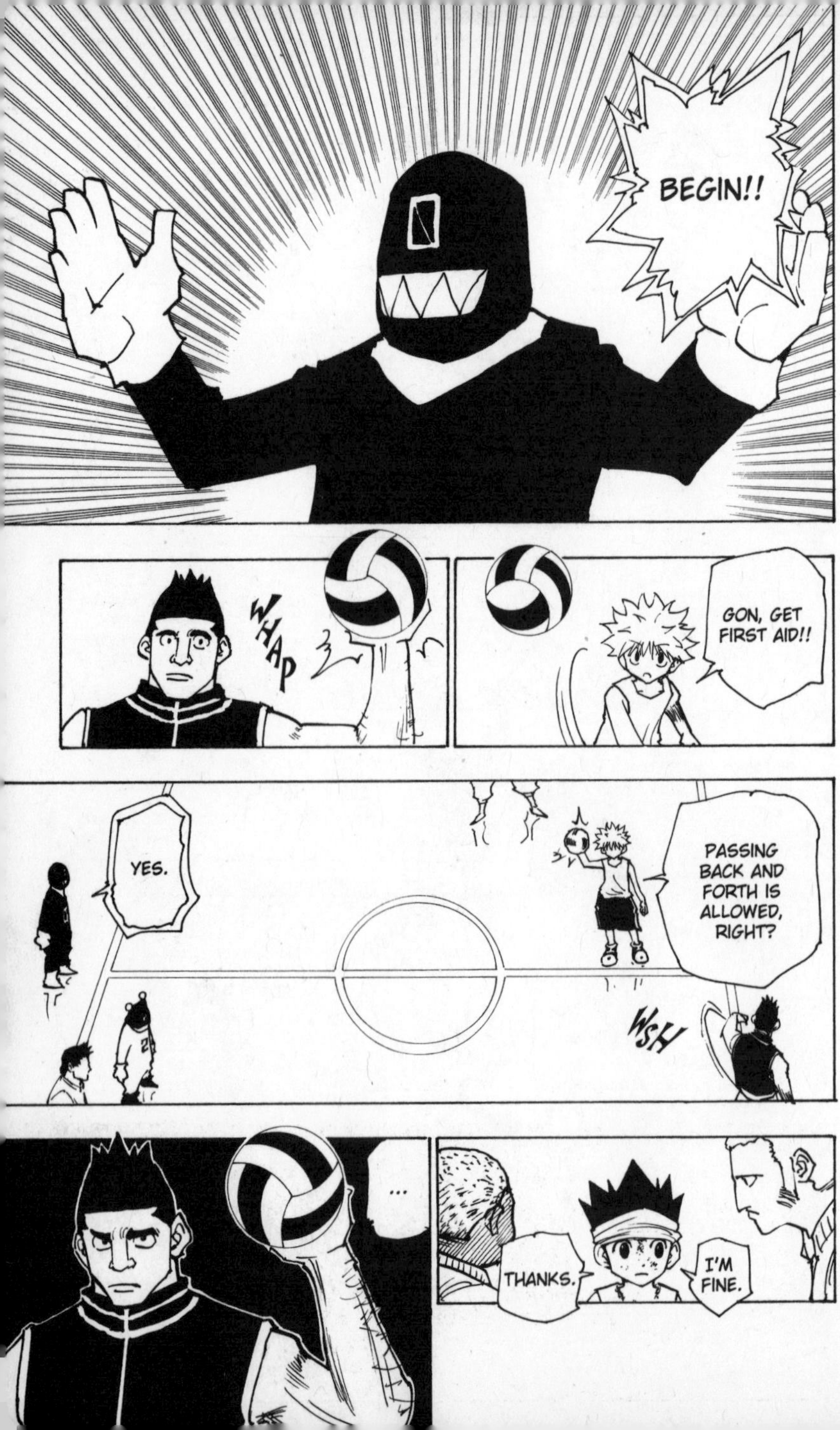
BEGIN!!
GON, GET FIRST AID!!
WHAP
PASSING BACK AND FORTH IS ALLOWED, RIGHT?
YES.
WSH
I'M FINE.
THANKS.
...

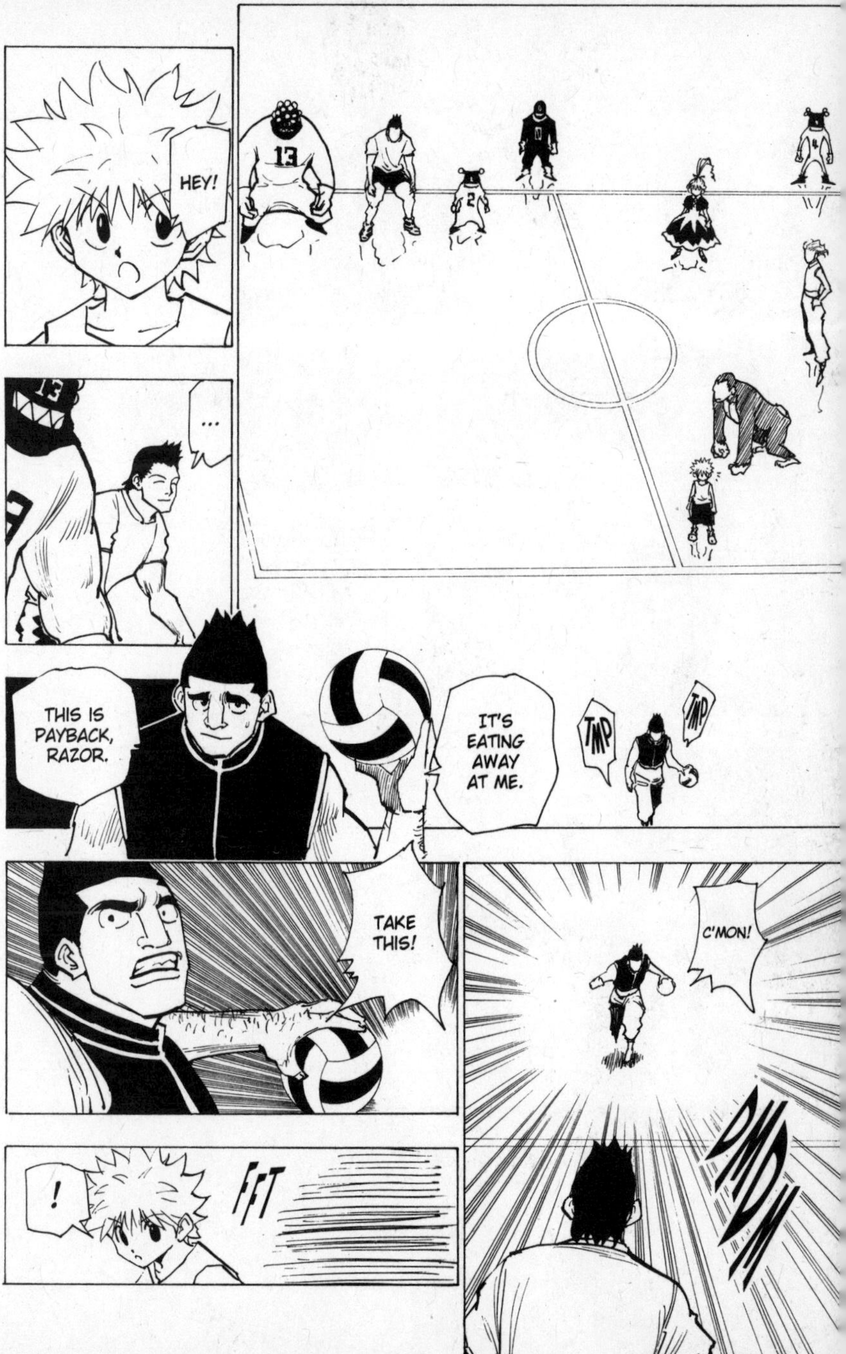
HEY!
...
TMP
TMP
IT'S EATING AWAY AT ME.
THIS IS PAYBACK, RAZOR.
C'MON!
DMMM
TAKE THIS!
!
FFT

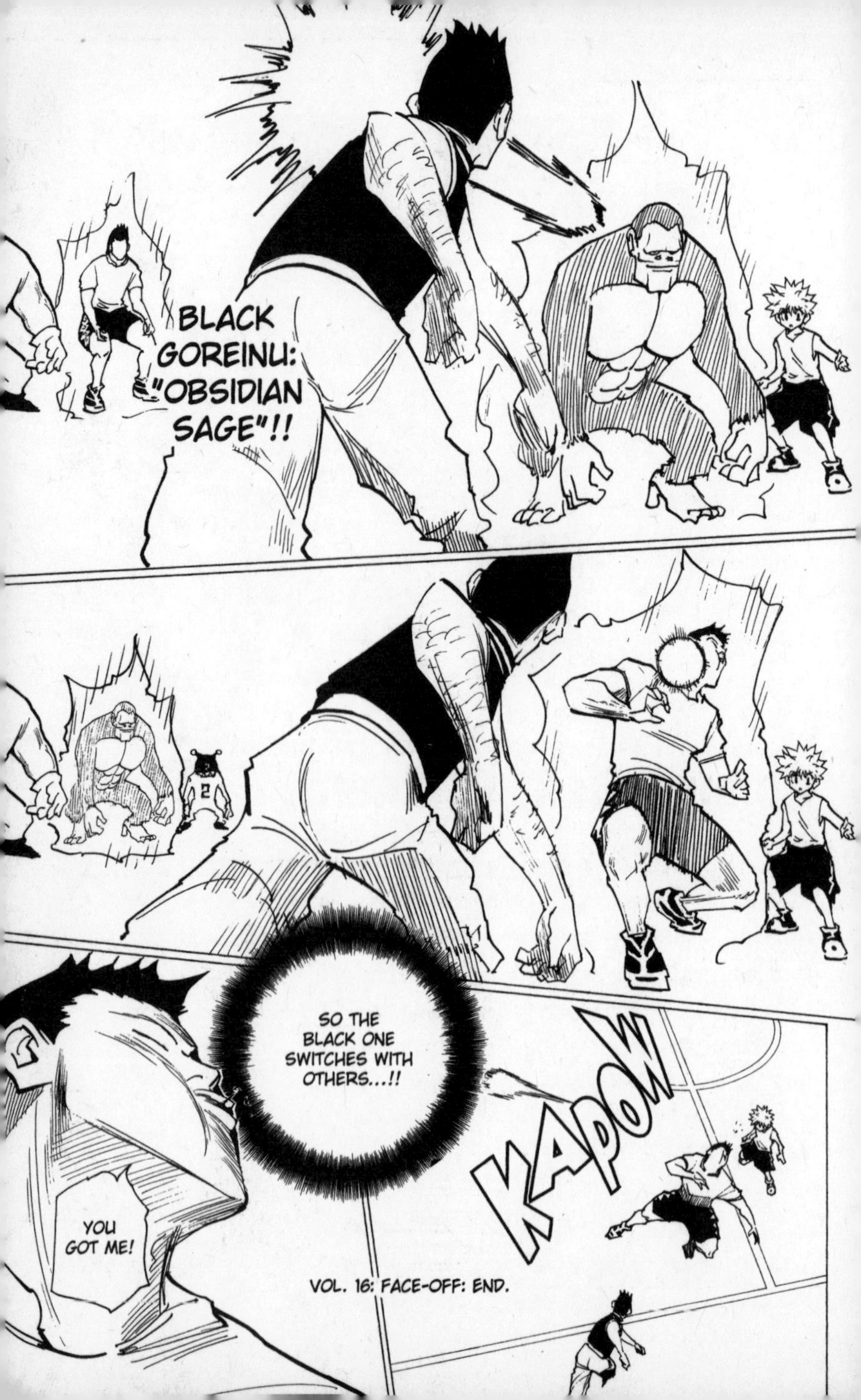
BLACK GOREINU: "OBSIDIAN SAGE"!!
SO THE BLACK ONE SWITCHES WITH OTHERS...!!
KAPOW
YOU GOT ME!
VOL. 16: FACE-OFF: END.

Coming Next Volume...

The conclusion to the greatest dodgeball game ever! With the match over, Hisoka heads back to the Spiders to keep searching for an exorcist. Meanwhile, Tsezguerra's quest for the cards heats up when the Bombers decide he's their only real competition and go after him, killing everyone in their way! While this is happening, Gon and Biscuit are doing even more training. As the game goes on and cards are lost and gained, who will survive Greed Island?!

Available now!

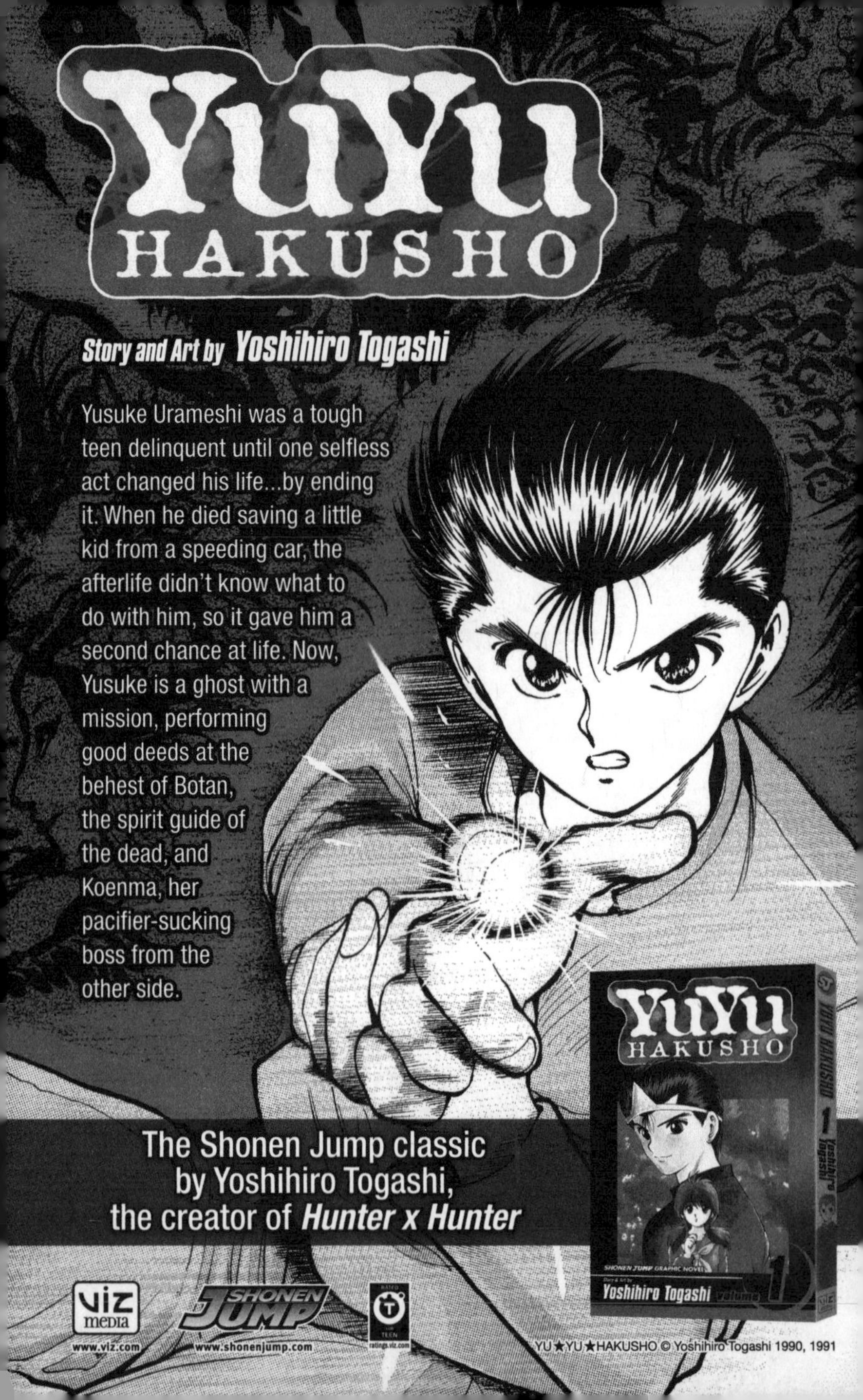
YuYu
HAKUSHO
Story and Art by Yoshihiro Togashi
Yusuke Urameshi was a tough teen delinquent until one selfless act changed his life...by ending it. When he died saving a little kid from a speeding car, the afterlife didn't know what to do with him, so it gave him a second chance at life. Now, Yusuke is a ghost with a mission, performing good deeds at the behest of Botan, the spirit guide of the dead, and Koenma, her pacifier-sucking boss from the other side.
YuYu
HAKUSHO
Yoshihiro Togashi
The Shonen Jump classic
by Yoshihiro Togashi,
the creator of *Hunter x Hunter*
VIZ media
www.viz.com
SHONEN JUMP
www.shonenjump.com
ratings.viz.com
YU★YU★HAKUSHO © Yoshihiro Togashi 1990, 1991

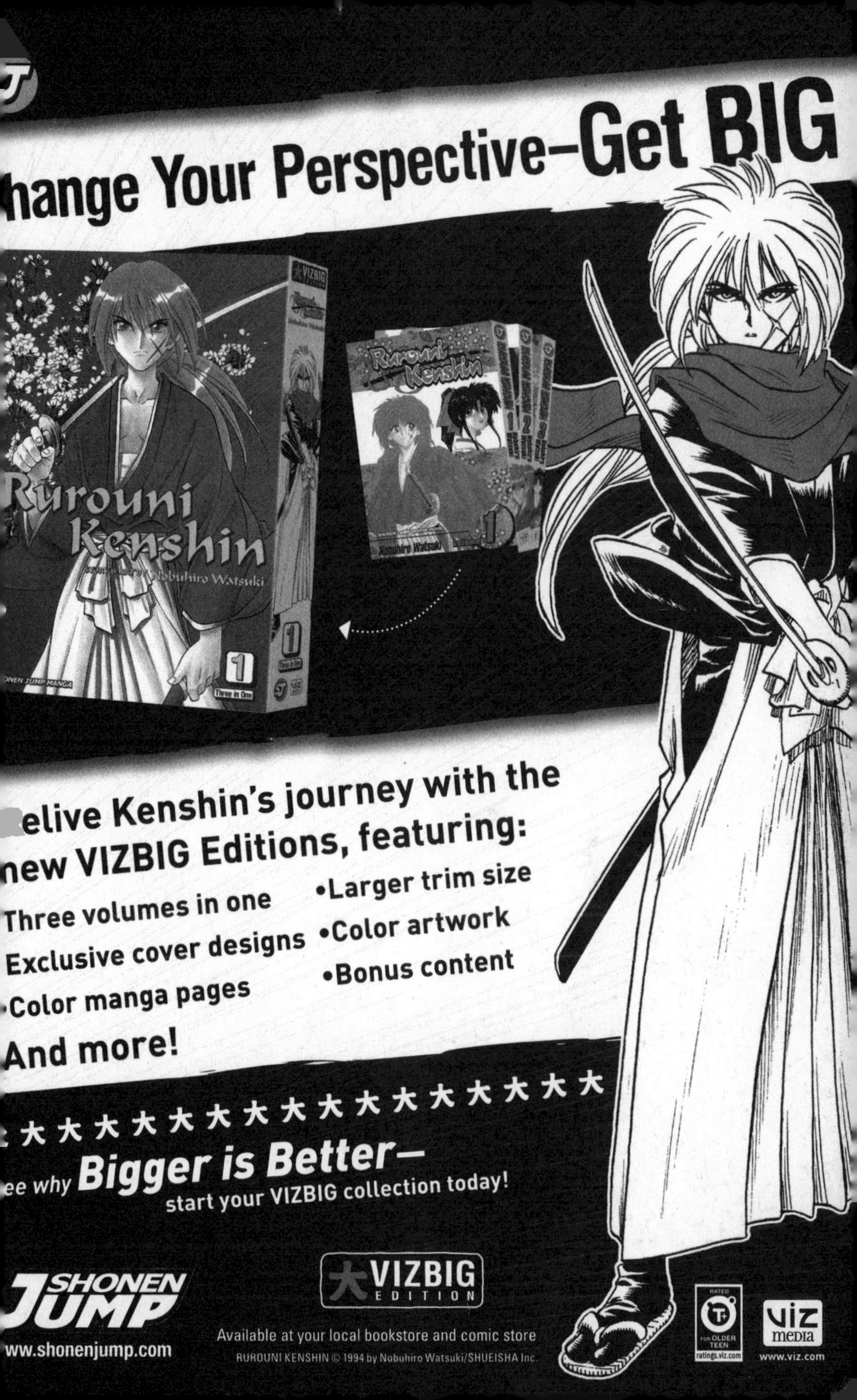
hange Your Perspective–Get BIG
Rurouni Kenshin
Nobuhiro Watsuki
elive Kenshin's journey with the
new VIZBIG Editions, featuring:
Three volumes in one
•Larger trim size
Exclusive cover designs
•Color artwork
•Color manga pages
•Bonus content
And more!
ee why Bigger is Better—
start your VIZBIG collection today!
SHONEN JUMP
www.shonenjump.com
VIZBIG EDITION
Available at your local bookstore and comic store
RUROUNI KENSHIN © 1994 by Nobuhiro Watsuki/SHUEISHA Inc.
RATED T+ FOR OLDER TEEN
ratings.viz.com
VIZ media
www.viz.com

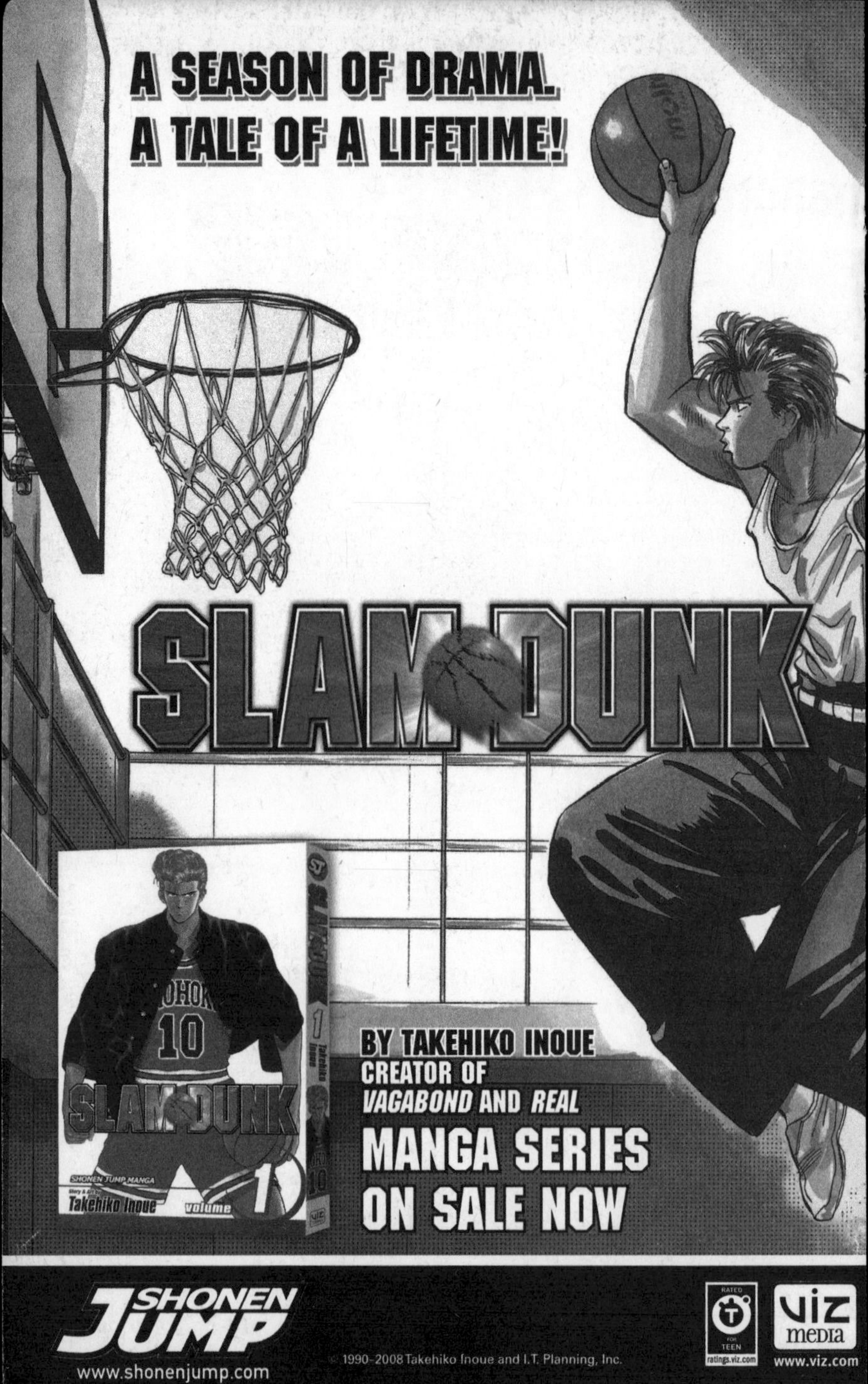
A SEASON OF DRAMA.
A TALE OF A LIFETIME!
SLAM DUNK
SLAM DUNK
SHONEN JUMP MANGA
Takehiko Inoue
volume 1
BY TAKEHIKO INOUE
CREATOR OF
VAGABOND AND *REAL*
MANGA SERIES
ON SALE NOW
SHONEN JUMP
www.shonenjump.com
© 1990-2008 Takehiko Inoue and I.T. Planning, Inc.
RATED T FOR TEEN
ratings.viz.com
VIZ media
www.viz.com

THE ACTION-PACKED SUPERHERO COMEDY ABOUT ONE MAN'S AMBITION TO BE A HERO FOR FUN!

ONE-PUNCH MAN

STORY BY
ONE | ART BY
YUSUKE MURATA

Nothing about Saitama passes the eyeball test when it comes to superheroes, from his lifeless expression to his bald head to his unimpressive physique. However, this average-looking guy has a not-so-average problem—he just can't seem to find an opponent strong enough to take on!

Can he finally find an opponent who can go toe-to-toe with him and give his life some meaning? Or is he doomed to a life of superpowered boredom?

RATED
TEEN
ratings.viz.com

SHONEN JUMP

VIZ media
www.viz.com

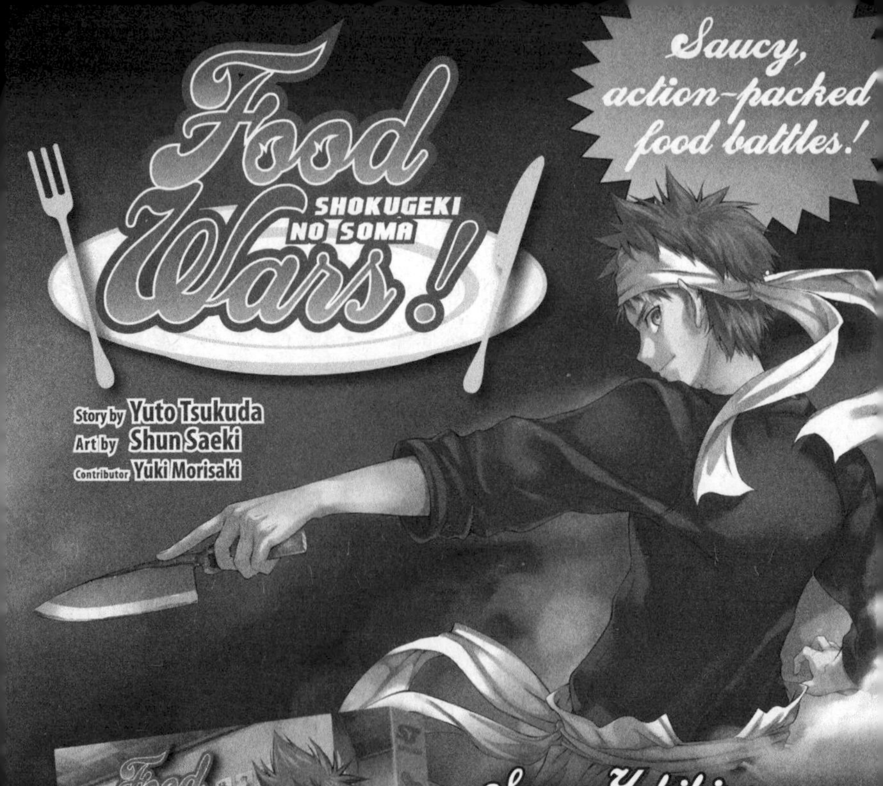
Food Wars!
SHOKUGEKI NO SOMA
Saucy, action-packed food battles!
Story by Yuto Tsukuda
Art by Shun Saeki
Contributor Yuki Morisaki

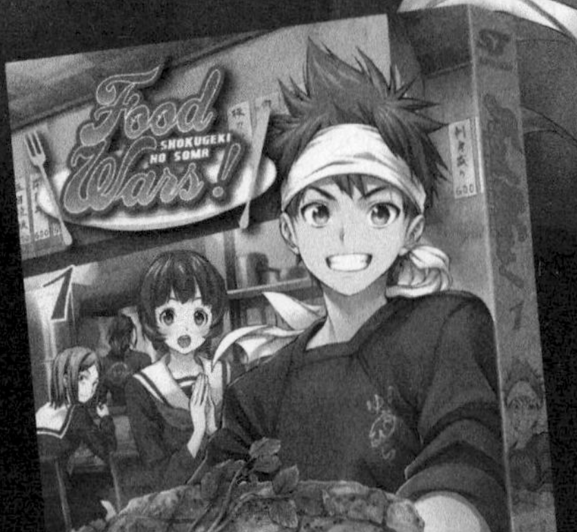
Food Wars!
SHOKUGEKI NO SOMA
1
Story by Yuto Tsukuda
Art by Shun Saeki
Contributor Yuki Morisaki

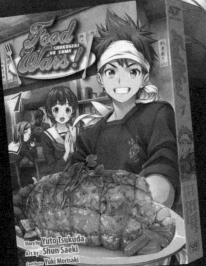

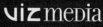

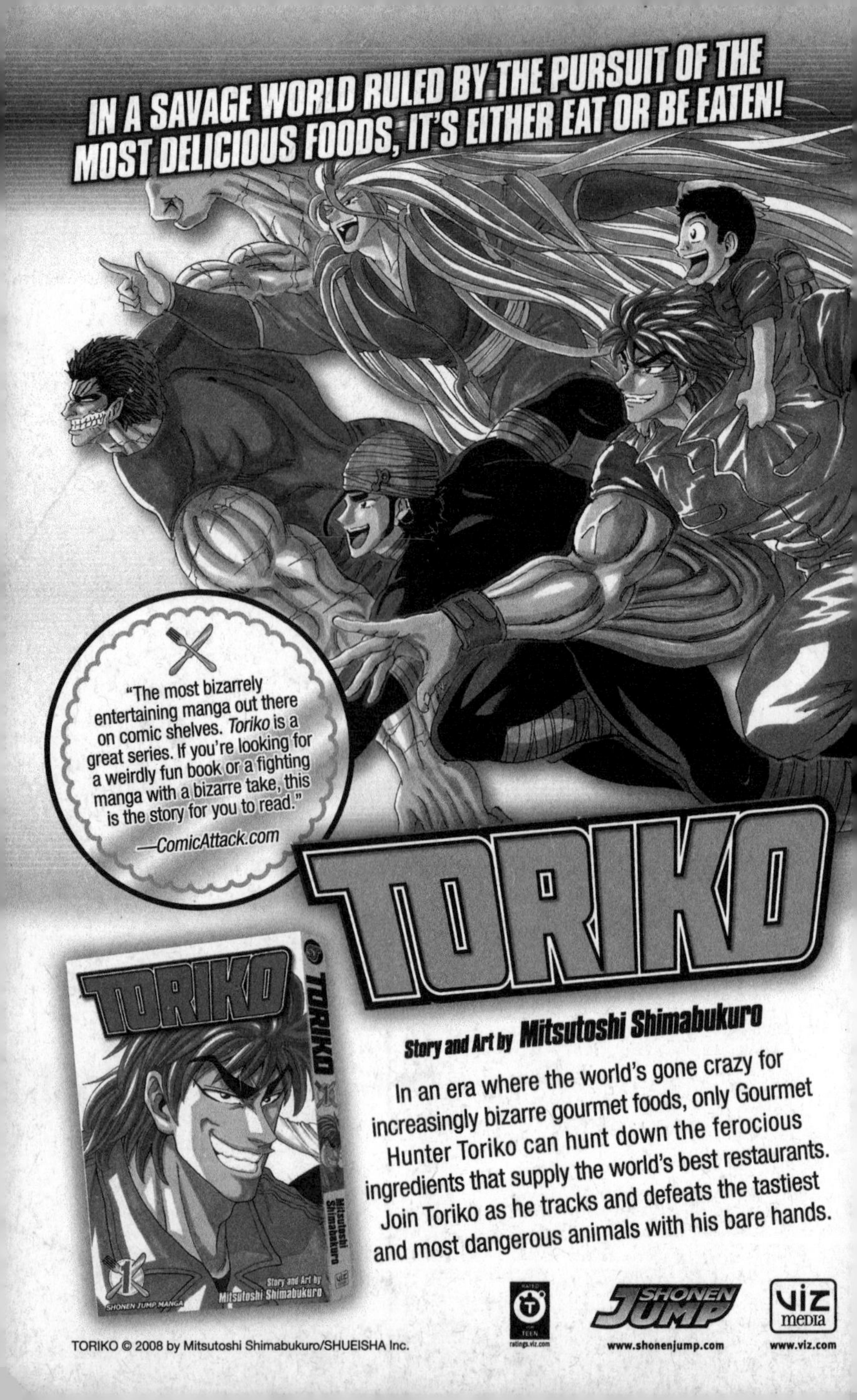

IN A SAVAGE WORLD RULED BY THE PURSUIT OF THE MOST DELICIOUS FOODS, IT'S EITHER EAT OR BE EATEN!
"The most bizarrely entertaining manga out there on comic shelves. *Toriko* is a great series. If you're looking for a weirdly fun book or a fighting manga with a bizarre take, this is the story for you to read."
—ComicAttack.com
TORIKO
TORIKO
TORIKO
1
SHONEN JUMP MANGA
Mitsutoshi Shimabukuro
Story and Art by Mitsutoshi Shimabukuro
Story and Art by Mitsutoshi Shimabukuro
In an era where the world's gone crazy for increasingly bizarre gourmet foods, only Gourmet Hunter Toriko can hunt down the ferocious ingredients that supply the world's best restaurants. Join Toriko as he tracks and defeats the tastiest and most dangerous animals with his bare hands.
RATED T TEEN
ratings.viz.com
SHONEN JUMP
www.shonenjump.com
viz media
www.viz.com
TORIKO © 2008 by Mitsutoshi Shimabukuro/SHUEISHA Inc.

You're Reading the Wrong Direction!!

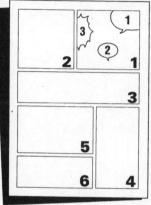

Whoops! Guess what? You're starting at the wrong end of the comic!

…It's true! In keeping with the original Japanese format, **Hunter x Hunter** is meant to be read from right to left, starting in the upper-right corner.

Unlike English, which is read from left to right, Japanese is read from right to left, meaning that action, sound effects and word-balloon order are completely reversed… something which can make readers unfamiliar with Japanese feel pretty backwards themselves. For this reason, manga or Japanese comics published in the U.S. in English have sometimes been published "flopped"—that is, printed in exact reverse order, as though seen from the other side of a mirror.

By flopping pages, U.S. publishers can avoid confusing readers, but the compromise is not without its downside. For one thing, a character in a flopped manga series who once wore in the original Japanese version a T-shirt emblazoned with "M A Y" (as in "the merry month of") now wears one which reads "Y A M"! Additionally, many manga creators in Japan are themselves unhappy with the process, as some feel the mirror-imaging of their art skews their original intentions.

We are proud to bring you Yoshihiro Togashi's **Hunter x Hunter** in the original unflopped format. For now, though, turn to the other side of the book and let the adventure begin…!

—Editor